Corpora and Intercultural Studies

Volume 5

This book series publishes original monographs and edited volumes in the investigations of different types of corpora (including text, speech and video) with a particular focus on intercultural studies. The differences in language use expressed in comparable corpora can be analyzed from an intercultural perspective. The emphasis is on excellence and originality in scholarship as well as synergetic interdisciplinary approaches and multicultural perspectives. Books exploring the role of the intercultural studies in the research fields of translation, linguistics, and culture, with a corpus-based approach will be especially welcome. The series publishes books that deal with emerging issues as well as those that offer an in-depth examination of underlying issues.

The target audiences of this series include both scholars and professionals who are interested in issues related to intercultural communication across different cultures and social groups, which are reflected by the investigation in comparable corpora.

Corpora and Intercultural Studies book series is published in conjunction with Springer under the auspices of School of Foreign Languages (SFL), Shanghai Jiao Tong University (SJTU). The first series editor is the Dean of SFL at SJTU, and the book series editorial board consists of leading scholars in the research field of corpora and intercultural studies in the world.

More information about this series at http://www.springer.com/series/15588

(Kathy) Ling Lin

Perspectives on the Introductory Phase of Empirical Research Articles

A Study of Rhetorical Structure and Citation Use

Springer

(Kathy) Ling Lin
School of Foreign Languages
Shanghai Jiao Tong University
Shanghai, China

ISSN 2510-4802 ISSN 2510-4810 (electronic)
Corpora and Intercultural Studies
ISBN 978-981-32-9203-1 ISBN 978-981-32-9204-8 (eBook)
https://doi.org/10.1007/978-981-32-9204-8

This Springer imprint is published by the registered company Springer Nature Singapore Pte Ltd.
The registered company address is: 152 Beach Road, #21-01/04 Gateway East, Singapore 189721, Singapore

This book is dedicated to the memory of Shenghua Chen, my wonderful mom who gave me life and endless love, and Prof. Stephen Evans, my superb doctoral supervisor who introduced me to the wonderland of EAP, genre and corpus research and thus opened up a new world to me. They instilled in me the belief to live in the present and always to be grateful for what makes your life worthwhile.

Acknowledgements

I am greatly indebted to my late supervisor Prof. Stephen Evans for his unflagging support, invaluable guidance and inspiration in carrying out the research for this book. I am also deeply grateful to Prof. Winnie Cheng, Prof. Foongha Yap, Dr. Paul Thompson, Prof. An Cheng and Dr. Becky Kwan for their insightful comments and sage advice. Likewise, my appreciation goes to all the interviewees at Birmingham University, Hong Kong Polytechnic University, Hong Kong University and Chinese University of Hong Kong, for providing crucial support for my research. Very warm thanks also to Susie Sui, Peter Leung, Isaac Mwinlaaru, Jim Chan, Jenny Wan and Maggie Leung for their support and encouragement for my research over the years.

Last but not least, I am thankful to my loving husband Jianfeng Wen and my father Shuiping Lin, without whose constant encouragement, support and understanding this book might never have been written.

Some of the work described in this book is substantially supported by Shanghai Planning Office of Philosophy and Social Sciences Research Fund (Project No.: 2017EYY007) and a grant from Shanghai Municipal Education Commission and Shanghai Education Development Foundation (Project No.: 15CG10).

Contents

Abbreviations

AL	Applied linguistics
APF	Announcing principal research findings
C	Conclusion
CAL	Corpus of applied linguistics
CALI	The sub-corpus for the Introduction section of empirical research articles from applied linguistics
CALL	The sub-corpus for the Literature Review section of empirical research articles from applied linguistics
CARS	The create-a-research-space model posited by Swales (1990)
CCE	Corpus of civil engineering
CCEI	The sub-corpus for the Introduction section of empirical research articles from civil engineering
CCEL	The sub-corpus for the Literature Review section of empirical research articles from civil engineering
CE	Civil engineering
CRA	Corpus of research articles
D	Discussion
EAP	English for academic purposes
ERAs	Empirical research articles
ESP	English for specific purposes
IMRD	The traditional framework for the macro-structure of the empirical research article which comprises the four sections (viz. Introduction, Method, Results and Discussion)
I	Introduction
IBC	The Introduction–Body–Conclusion model for structuring research articles
L1	Speaking English as the first language
L2	Speaking English as the second language
LR	Literature Review
M	Method

NR	New rhetoric
NS	Native speakers of English
NNS	Non-native speakers of English
PS	The practical problem-solving introductions written by experts in civil engineering
R	Results
RAs	Research articles
R-CARS	The revised create-a-research-space model proposed in Swales (2004)
[RD]	The blended Results and Discussion section
RT CARS	The research-oriented traditional creating a research space introductions
RTE	*Research in the teaching of English*
RVs	Reporting verbs
SFL	Systemic functional linguistics
TR	Theoretical review

Chapter 1
Introduction

1.1 Background to the Study

Driven by economic, political, and social forces, the continuing global spread of English has exerted far-reaching influences upon the developments in all social domains (e.g., marketing, tourism, and education) (Ammon, 2006; Doiz, Lasagabaster, & Sierra, 2013; Jenkins, 2013). In particular, in academic and educational contexts, English has become the preferred language for the world-wide exchange of ideas and the growth and dissemination of knowledge (Ferguson, 2007). A dramatic expansion of English-medium instruction has also taken place in many institutes of higher education in countries where English is not the native language, including those in the "expanding" and "outer" circles (Kachru, 1985, 1992), in recent decades. Closely associated with this development are the great concerns of many senior administrators with the international rankings of their institutions.

As an important part of the rankings, the participation of the staff and the research students in the international academic forums has been greatly encouraged and has gained increasing momentum. In particular, the academic staff, who are subject to the "publish-or-perish" culture of the academy, strive to publish their research in English-language international journals, particularly those that are incorporated into the Institute for Scientific Information (ISI) databases. This will not only add considerable citation rates to their works and make them more visible on the world stage, but may also help them to gain recognition and promotion in their institutions (Feak & Swales, 2009). In some research fields, especially those in sciences and engineering, the use of English is so dominant that, a scholar is very likely to be excluded from the web of global scholarship, if he or she does not read and write in English. As Hyland (2006: 26) points out, generally speaking, English-language periodicals constitute over 95% of all publications in the *Science Citation Index*.

Furthermore, the importance of English as an academic lingua franca is manifested in the fact that whether using English or not could possibly affect the overall evaluation of the texts composed (Ammon, 2003). For instance, as long as two decades ago, Vandenbroucke (1989) and Nylenna, Riis, and Karlsson (1994) respectively reported

(Kathy). L. Lin, *Perspectives on the Introductory Phase of Empirical Research Articles*, Corpora and Intercultural Studies 5, https://doi.org/10.1007/978-981-32-9204-8_1

how a thesis in English and a manuscript in English were valued more highly (regarding their content) than when they were written in other national languages by the referees.

While there is a greater demand for writing for publication in English and writing degree theses in English, novice scholars, especially those using English as an additional language, often encounter considerable challenges in their strategic deployment of English language resources to construct effective texts in English. This has inevitably resulted in the request for English for academic purposes (EAP) provision from both the teaching and research circles. As facilitating novice writers' research writing becomes a major concern in EAP research and teaching, published research articles (RAs) from all disciplines have been frequently analyzed for generating useful pedagogical insights.

Previous research on RAs has deepened our understanding of this genre and yielded many significant findings that can be directly applied to EAP pedagogy. In studies of RAs, two traditional research strands are the rhetorical structural analysis and the relevant linguistic analysis (Del Saz-Rubio, 2011; Kanoksilapatham, 2005). In terms of the structural aspects of the RAs, the bulk of the existing research has been on the move- and step-structure of their principal sections. The Introduction section has been the subject of considerable scholarly attention since Swales's pioneering and seminal discovery of the four-move schema (Swales, 1981) and his later conception of the classic "Create-a-Research-Space" (CARS) model (Swales, 1990). Swales's move-based approach to genre analysis has also provided the theoretical foundation for research into the three other sections in the "conventional" Introduction-Method-Results-Discussion (IMRD) macro-structure of empirical research articles (ERAs), namely, Method (M) (e.g., Bruce, 2008; Kanoksilapatham, 2005), Results (R) (e.g., Bruce, 2009; Lim, 2010), and Discussion (D) (e.g., Holmes, 1997; Peacock, 2002). In contrast, the sections that are not represented in the IMRD framework, e.g., the Literature Review (LR) section, have been rarely studied. This is perhaps a consequence of the long-term preoccupation with the "canonical" IMRD framework and the apparent dearth of empirical research into the macro-structure of the ERA.

In the EAP literature, the classic IMRD model has long been used as the starting point for both the move-based analyses of the "four" major sections and the micro-level studies of linguistic features. As regards the sections not fully accounted for in the IMRD framework, such as the LR and Conclusion (C) sections, they have been frequently analyzed as a part of their neighboring conventional sections with perhaps partly similar elements and communicative functions as theirs. For example, a functionally distinct LR section may be considered as a part of the Introduction section and an independent C section as a variant of the D section (Hsieh, Tsai, Lin, Liou, & Kuo, 2006). Consequently, we do not have a clear understanding of the status and the internal structure of and language use in these sections that are not represented in the conventional IMRD model and have been largely overlooked by EAP researchers.

In the introductory phase of the ERA, which refers to the section(s) used before the Method section with the role of orienting the reader to the about-to-be-presented research, the Introduction has been conventionally considered as the only section.

Since Swales proposed the classic CARS model in 1990, studies of introductions have concentrated on the variability of this model in different contexts and the variations in rhetorical structure of this sub-genre across cultures, languages, disciplines and sub-disciplines. However, a large number of these studies have been conducted on schematic structures of the RA Introduction across different languages and cultures (e.g., Duszak, 1994; Hirano, 2009; Lee, 2001; Loi & Evans, 2010; Taylor & Chen, 1991) with fewer ones on cross- and within-disciplinary variations (e.g., Crookes, 1986; Ozturk, 2007; Samraj, 2002). Hardly any systematic studies have been undertaken on the rhetorical comparison of and generic interrelationship between the Introduction and its related part-genres apart from Samraj (2005), who compared the rhetorical organization of a genre set (viz., the Introduction and the abstract accompanying the RA) and explored the variations in their relationship across disciplinary boundaries. Based upon 12 RAs in two related disciplines (viz., conservation biology and wildlife behavior), Samraj observed that conservation biology introductions are structurally more similar to abstracts than are wildlife behavior introductions to abstracts, and the relationship between the two part-genres varies across disciplines. As such, disciplinary variation in research writing is not only exhibited in rhetorical structure, but in generic interrelatedness. Overall, while the Introduction section remains a part-genre of intense interest to genre analysts, more studies need to be undertaken on discipline- and sub-discipline-specific features of its structures, and the relationship between it and its related part-genres. Research into such relatively under-explored aspects may generate considerable pedagogical insights and add to our understanding of introductions and their related sub-genres in general.

As noted above, the LR section is a possible related part-genre of the Introduction section in the opening phase of the ERA, because of their partly overlapping content elements and communicative functions. Most notably, there is an obligatory step "reviewing items of previous research" posited for article introductions in the widely-cited CARS model (Swales, 1990), which overlaps with the main traditional task of the independent LR section suggested by its nomenclature "reviewing previous literature". However, the importance of the LR section has not received sufficient scholarly attention and its status in the whole ERA has not yet been convincingly verified (e.g., by a large-scale, systematic macro-structural study of contemporary ERAs across different disciplines).

In contrast, the Introduction section has attracted considerable research attention since the inception of ESP genre research in the 1980s, and has hence become a widely-acknowledged key part-genre. Inevitably, it "overshadows" the other three major sections represented in the IMRD framework (i.e., the M, R and D sections) (Kwan, 2005: 17) as well as others that are not fully accounted for in it such as the LR section. Although a handful of researchers (e.g., Braine, 1995; Swales, 2004; Yang & Allison, 2004) have alluded to the presence of LRs in (some of) the RAs they examined, a prevalent belief they hold is that literature reviewing is a rather discursive practice, and different research writers, novice or seasoned, may have their own distinct individual preferences for constructing an LR section. The LR thus seems to be a special part-genre that is not as susceptible to the traditional genre analysis as others such as the Introduction, M and D sections. This is perhaps another important reason for the paucity of research into the rhetorical structure of the LR section in ERAs.

While the LR section in the ERA is perhaps an intuitively familiar yet rarely explored part-genre, the only two studies that have touched on its rhetorical structure are Kwan, Chan, and Lam (2012) and Tessuto (2015). Kwan et al.'s valuable study has generated many useful findings. For example, it has discovered that the LRs of 80 RAs in Information Systems are rhetorically structured around the three moves of the CARS model (Swales, 1990), specified each move-specific strategy,[1] and made an effective statistical comparison of the frequency counts of the strategies used. Nevertheless, its particular focus is on evaluation strategies associated with Move 2 and is therefore different from the traditional genre-based analyses that aim for a comprehensive view of the rhetorical structure of the genre or part-genre under investigation. Hence, it does not present a complete picture of the micro-structure of this section. Details about some important aspects of its structure have not been provided, e.g., the move and strategy combination patterns and the internal arrangement of the rhetorical strategies and moves. It therefore does not provide us with a comprehensive analysis of the rhetorical structure of this part-genre in ERAs of Information Systems, not to mention that of LRs in ERAs from other disciplines.

Tessuto (2015) analyzed the generic structure of 90 empirical law RAs chosen from three top-ranking journals. He identified the LR section (or the "Background Review" section in his words) as an ERA component unit not represented in the IMRD model. Given that, in his view, the Background Review section and the Introduction have similar communicative purposes, he applied the three-move CARS model (Swales, 1990) to the structural analysis of the Background Review section. However, similar to Kwan et al. (2012), this study only presents quantitative findings on the use of each move and step; no information on the move and step configurations and the sequences and arrangement of these elements has been provided. Even for the only new element identified in this section, i.e., Step 12A "Defining and Developing Methods, Theories, Concepts, Issues, Phenomena" in Move 3, no detailed explanations have been given. Another crucial point is that, while both this study and Kwan et al. have confirmed that LRs in ERAs from Information Systems and the legal area are rhetorically structured around the three moves of the CARS model (Swales, 1990), the generalizability of this conclusion merits further exploration.

The literature reviewed to this point has suggested that there is currently only a very limited understanding of the rhetorical structure of the LR section in ERAs. Little EAP provision is also available on how to structure this section. Student writers in the EAP classroom may thus feel perplexed, when they repeatedly encounter this section in recent ERAs from their own disciplines. Some possible questions they may have in their mind are: How many different formats there are for the introductory phase of the ERA, e.g., a single CARS-style Introduction section (cf. Swales, 1990) or an Introduction section followed by a separate LR section; whether the widely-reported

[1] The term "strategy" rather than "step" was adopted in Kwan et al. (2012) since many of the move constituents were found not to be obligatory and arranged in fixed sequences (see also Kwan, 2005, 2006). See more explanations of the two terms "strategy" and "step" in Sect. 2.1.3.3.

and long-established IMRD framework reflects current writing practices; why some published writers include an independent LR section in their writing after they have referred to the literature in the Introduction section; what the similarities and differences are between the Introduction section with a subsequent LR and that without such a following section in terms of their structures, functions and language use; and what the difference is between the possible element of reviewing previous literature in the Introduction section and the separate LR section and how they play their individual and distinct roles in the ERA. Thereby, it seems necessary to verify the status of the LR section in the ERA and extend the research scope from a single "Introduction" section of the ERA, which has traditionally been the sole focus of much previous research, to the entire introductory phase following the format of "I+LR" (i.e., containing both sections).

Another significant research strand in ESP studies is the linguistic analysis of genres or part-genres. In view of the focus of this study on both the Introduction and LR sections of the ERA, one of the most representative language features traditionally shared by them—citation use—is closely examined. In the existing body of literature on citation use in academic writing, there are some identified limitations as follows. First, the novice research writers' (particularly L2 student writers') difficulties with and problems in citation use (e.g., Borg, 2000; Campbell, 1990; Sun, 2008; Yeh, 2010) have been intensively studied, but pertinent cross-generic and cross-disciplinary variations (e.g., Hyland, 1999, 2000, 2002; Thompson & Tribble, 2001) have received less attention. No comparative research into citation use in the Introduction and LR sections of the ERA across disciplines has yet been undertaken. Second, the frequency distribution of citations across rhetorical sections of the ERA or the thesis is far more frequently focused on whereas the variations in the use of many multi-layered citation features in both formal and functional terms across these part-genres have been largely overlooked. Third, previous citation studies in the field of applied linguistics have mostly been text-based. An integrated use of the text-based analysis with other supplemental ethnographic methods such as the interview study may provide a more thorough and in-depth understanding of disciplinary citation practices.

To overcome these inadequacies, the present study examines the use of a set of citation features (viz., citation density, citation forms, reporting verbs (RVs) and citation functions) in both Introduction and LR sections of the ERA across two contrasting disciplines, namely, civil engineering (CE) and applied linguistics (AL), with foci on cross-generic and cross-disciplinary variations. In addition to the textual analysis, a semi-structured interview study of expert writers' perceptions of their own as well as the entire disciplinary structural and citation practices in the introductory part is conducted. This emic view is essential to our contextual understandings of all these research issues.

On a final note, there remains no study surveying published advice on the organization of ERAs and only a few (Harwood, 2004; Thompson, 2001; Thompson & Tribble, 2001) on that about citation practices in academic writing. Consequently, an updated survey of published recommendations on citation use and the structure of the introductory phase of the ERA (and the entire ERA) is conducted, the comparison of which with actual expert practices is integrated into our discussion of textual findings (see Chaps. 4–7). This may help to inform EAP pedagogy and materials development.

1.2 The Scope and Objective of the Study

To bridge the above-mentioned research gaps and inform EAP pedagogy, this project, as mentioned before, for the first time innovatively extends the research scope from a single "I" section of the ERA, which has frequently been the sole focus of many previous studies, to the entire introductory phase following the pattern of "I+LR". As indicated in Fig. 1.1, the project comprises three related studies: two lead-in studies respectively from the cross-sectional and diachronic perspectives on the major structural format of the introductory phase and the status of the separate LR section in the whole ERA in particular; and a third study on the rhetorical structure of and citation use in the new type of the introductory phase structured in "I+LR" with a multi-perspective approach (viz., the cross-disciplinary, cross-generic, emic, and published advice vs. actual expert practices perspectives). The two lead-in studies provide the essential rationale for the subsequent focused analysis of the "I+LR" introductory part of ERAs in two representative disciplines (viz., CE and AL) in terms of its rhetorical structure, citation use, and the possible link between them.

Correspondingly, the objectives of this project are specified as follows:

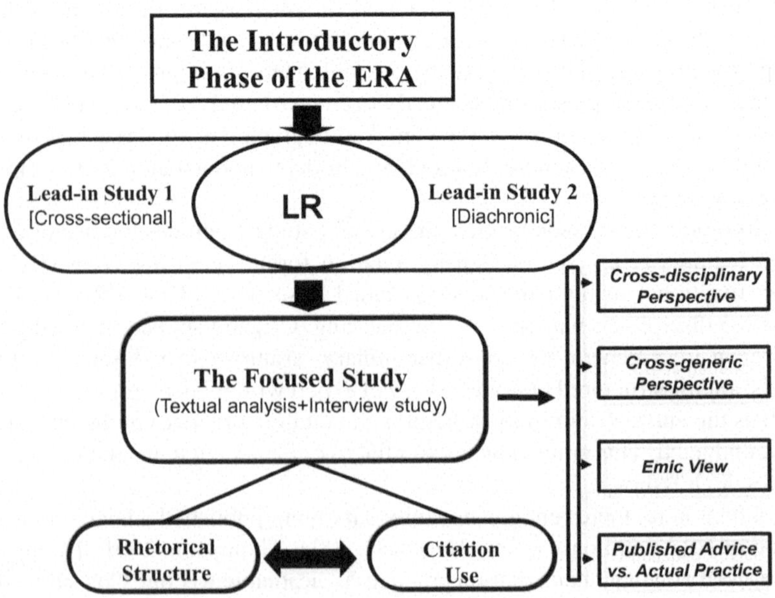

Fig. 1.1 Research design of the study

- To examine the macro-structure of ERAs in a wide range of disciplines in order to identify their major sections and to ascertain the status of the independent LR section in the whole ERA;
- To document the macro-structural development of ERAs in two representative yet contrasting disciplines (viz., AL and CE) during the period of 1980–2010 with special foci on the changing structural forms of the introductory phase of ERAs and the status of the separate LR section;
- To study the rhetorical structure of and citation use in the introductory phase structured in "I+LR" in the fields of AL and CE;
- To understand disciplinary expert views and perceptions of structuring the introductory phase of the ERA and of using citations in it in AL and CE.

The first two objectives are fulfilled by the two lead-in studies and the other two by the focused analysis of the introductory phase structured in "I+LR" from AL and CE. These research objectives necessitate the combined use of a set of methods such as genre analysis, corpus linguistic study and the interview study, which are detailed in Chap. 3. The findings generated from this project have profound implications for EAP research, theory and pedagogy. It not only enriches our understanding of the macro-structure of the contemporary ERA and its structural evolution in the recent three decades, but also provides possible structures for the LR section and the preceding Introduction. In the comparative study of the use of multi-layered citation features in these two sections, a new category of RVs termed "Stative RVs" has been identified and a new classification of citation functions into the rhetorically complex citation functions and the rhetorically simpler citation functions has been proposed. Interesting similarities and differences in the patterned use of citations and citation elements in these two sections with the partly overlapping element and function (viz., "reviewing previous literature) provide useful pointers for the related EAP research writing teaching and learning. Many valuable insights contributed by experienced disciplinary writers intervewed help to inform EAP pedagogy as well, such as their adherence of the principle "article content, form and function matching together" in organizing ERAs and their different concerns in deciding whether to use a single Introduction section or both the Introduction and the LR sections before the Method section. In all, the project yields considerable significant pedagogical insights, produces some useful points of reference for future studies, and opens up many possibilities for further research.

1.3 Organization of This Book

Following this opening chapter is Chap. 2, where a comprehensive literature review is presented. This review covers the following areas: the definition of and the three main approaches to genre; the connotations of some important notions associated with genre (viz., communicative purpose, discourse community, and moves, steps, and strategies); the different types of RAs as a particular genre; the previous research into the macro-structure of the ERA, the rhetorical structure of the introductory part of the ERA (in particular the Introduction and LR sections), and citation use in academic discourse.

Chapter 3 describes the research design of the study in detail and presents the specific research questions and methods. Chapter 4 reports on a large-scale cross-sectional study of the macro-structure of ERAs across 39 disciplines, the core findings of which offer key justifications for the whole research project. Chapter 5 presents a diachronic study of the macro-structural evolution of ERAs in two particular disciplines (viz., AL and CE), further highlighting the need for more systematic research into the rhetorical structure of and language use in the traditionally overlooked ERA sections such as the LR section, which is a focus of the present study. In Chap. 6, the rhetorical structure of the Introduction section and the LR section is investigated using ESP genre-based approach (Swales, 1990, 2004), with their inter-relationship discussed. In Chap. 7, in-depth analyses of multi-layered citation features in both functional and formal terms in the two adjoining sections (viz., the Introduction and LR sections) are presented. In the main findings chapters (i.e., Chaps. 4–7), the published advice on structuring and using citations in the ERA and the 12 interviewees' accounts of their own and disciplinary structural and citation practices are incorporated into the discussion of the textual findings. Chapter 8 summarizes the main findings and considers their pedagogical and research implications, and draws the monograph to a conclusion with an overall evaluation of the study's significance and limitations and a set of recommendations for future research.

References

Ammon, U. (2003). Global English and the non-native speaker: Overcoming disadvantage. In H. Tonkin & T. G. Reagan (Eds.), *Language in the twenty-first century: Selected papers of the millennial conferences of the center for research and documentation on world language problems, held at the University of Hartford and Yale University*. Amsterdam; Philadelphia: J. Benjamins Pub. Co (pp. 23–34).

Ammon, U. (2006). Language planning for international scientific communication: An overview of questions and possible solutions. *Current Issues in Language Planning, 7*(1), 1–30.

Borg, E. (2000). Citation practices in academic writing. In P. Thompson (Ed.), *Patterns ad perspectives: Insights for EAP writing practice* (pp. 26–44). Reading, UK: CALS, The University of Reading.

Braine, G. (1995). Writing in the natural sciences and engineering. In D. Belcher & G. Braine (Eds.), *Academic writing in a second language: Essays on research and pedagogy* (pp. 113–134). Norwood, NJ: Ablex.

Bruce, I. (2008). Cognitive genre structures in methods sections of research articles: A corpus study. *Journal of English for Academic Purposes, 7*(1), 38–54.

Bruce, I. (2009). Results sections in sociology and organic chemistry articles: A genre analysis. *English for Specific Purposes, 28*(2), 105–124.

Campbell, C. (1990). Writing with others' words: Using background reading text in academic compositions. In B. Kroll (Ed.), *Second language writing: Research insights for the classroom* (pp. 211–230). Cambridge: Cambridge University Press.

Crookes, G. (1986). Towards a validated analysis of scientific text structure. *Applied Linguistics, 7,* 57–70.

Del Saz-Rubio, M. M. (2011). A pragmatic approach to the macro-structure and metadiscoursal features of research article introductions in the field of agricultural sciences. *English for Specific Purposes, 30*(4), 258–271.

Doiz, A., Lasagabaster, D., & Sierra, J. M. S. (Eds.). (2013). *English-medium instruction at universities: Global challenges*. Bristol: Multilingual Matters.

Duszak, A. (1994). Academic discourse and intellectual styles. *Journal of Pragmatics, 21*(3), 291–313.

Feak, C. B., & Swales, J. M. (2009). *Telling a research story: Writing a literature review*. Ann Arbor: The University of Michigan Press.

Ferguson, G. (2007). The global spread of English, scientific communication and ESP: Questions of equity, access and domain loss. *Ibérica, 13,* 7–38.

Harwood, N. (2004). Citation analysis: A multidisciplinary perspective on academic literacy. In M. Baynham, A. Deignan, & G. White (Eds.), *Applied linguistics at the interface* (pp. 79–89). London: Equinox.

Hirano, E. (2009). Research article introductions in English for specific purposes: A comparison between Brazilian Portuguese and English. *English for Specific Purposes, 28*(4), 240–250.

Holmes, R. (1997). Genre analysis and the social sciences: An investigation of the structure of research article discussion sections in three disciplines. *English for Specific Purposes, 16*(4), 321–337.

Hsieh, W. M., Tsai, T. C., Lin, M. C., Liou, H. C. U, & Kuo, C. H. (2006). Exploring genre sets: Research article sections in illustrative humanities and science disciplines. In *The 23PrdP International Conference on English Teaching and Learning in the ROC, Taipei* (pp. 249–262).

Hyland, K. (1999). Academic attribution: Citation and the construction of disciplinary knowledge. *Applied Linguistics, 20*(3), 341–367.

Hyland, K. (2000). *Disciplinary discourses: Social interaction in academic writing*. London: Longman Pearson Education.

Hyland, K. (2002). Activity and evaluation: Reporting practices in academic writing. In J. Flowerdew (Ed.), *Academic discourse* (pp. 115–130). Harlow: Pearson Education Limited.

Hyland, K. (2006). *English for academic purposes: An advanced resource book*. London: Routledge.

Jenkins, J. (2013). *English as a lingua franca in the international university: The politics of academic English language policy*. Abingdon, GB: Routledge.

Kachru, B. B. (1985). Standards, codification and sociolinguistic realism: The English language in the outer circle. In R. Quirk & H. G. Widdowson (Eds.), *English in the world: Teaching and learning the language and literatures* (pp. 11–30). Cambridge: Cambridge University Press.

Kachru, B. B. (1992). *The other tongue: English across cultures* (2nd ed.). Urbana: University of Illinois Press.

Kanoksilapatham, B. (2005). Rhetorical structure of biochemistry research articles. *English for Specific Purposes, 24*(3), 269–292.

Kwan, B. S. C. (2005). *A genre analysis of literature reviews in doctoral theses*. Unpublished doctoral dissertation, City University of Hong Kong.

Kwan, B. S. C. (2006). The schematic structure of literature reviews in doctoral theses of applied linguistics. *English for Specific Purposes, 25,* 30–55.

Kwan, B. S. C., Chan, H., & Lam, C. (2012). Evaluating prior scholarship in literature reviews of research articles: A comparative study of practices in two research paradigms. *English for Specific Purposes, 31,* 188–201.

Lee, S. (2001). *A contrastive rhetoric study of Korean and English research paper introductions*. Unpublished doctoral dissertation, University of Hawaii.

Lim, J. M. (2010). Commenting on research results in applied linguistics and education: A comparative genre-based investigation. *Journal of English for Academic Purposes, 9*(4), 280–294.

Loi, C. K., & Evans, S. M. (2010). Cultural differences in the organization of research article introductions from the field of educational psychology: English and Chinese. *Journal of Pragmatics, 42*(10), 2814–2825.
Nylenna, M., Riis, P., & Karlsson, Y. (1994). Multiple blinded reviews of the same two manuscripts: Effects of referee characteristics and publication language. *The Journal of American Medical Association, 272*(2), 149–151.
Ozturk, I. (2007). The textual organization of research article introductions in applied linguistics: Variability within a single discipline. *English for Specific Purposes, 26*(1), 25–38.
Peacock, M. (2002). Communicative moves in the discussion section of research articles. *System, 30*(4), 479–497.
Samraj, B. (2002). Introductions in research articles: Variations across disciplines. *English for Specific Purposes, 21*(1), 1–17.
Samraj, B. (2005). An exploration of a genre set: Research article abstracts and introductions in two disciplines. *English for Specific Purposes, 24*(2), 141–156.
Sun, Y. H. (2008). Citation problems of Chinese MA theses and pedagogical implications. *The Journal of Asia TEFL, 5*(1), 1–27.
Swales, J. M. (1981). *Aspects of article introductions*. Birmingham, U.K.: The University of Aston, Language Studies Unit.
Swales, J. M. (1990). *Genre analysis: English in academic and research settings*. Cambridge; New York: Cambridge University Press.
Swales, J. M. (2004). *Research genres: Explorations and applications*. Cambridge; New York: Cambridge University Press.
Taylor, G., & Chen, T. (1991). Linguistic, cultural, and sub-cultural issues in contrastive discourse analysis: Anglo-American and Chinese scientific texts. *Applied Linguistics, 12*(3), 319–336.
Tessuto, G. (2015). Generic structure and rhetorical moves in English-language empirical law research articles: Sites of interdisciplinary and interdiscursive cross-over. *English for Specific Purposes, 37*(1), 13–26.
Thompson, P. (2001). *A pedagogically-motivated corpus-based examination of PhD theses: Macrostructure, citation practices and uses of modal verbs*. Unpublished doctoral dissertation, The University of Reading.
Thompson, P., & Tribble, C. (2001). Looking at citations: Using corpora in English for academic purposes. *Language Learning and Technology, 5*(3), 91–105.
Vandenbroucke, J. P. (1989). On not being born a native speaker of English. *British Medical Journal, 298*, 1461–1462.
Yang, R. Y., & Allison, D. (2004). Research articles in applied linguistics: Structures from a functional perspective. *English for Specific Purposes, 23*(3), 264–279.
Yeh, C. (2010). Citation practices in TESL research articles: A comparative study. *Asian ESP Journal, 6*(2), 40–64.

Chapter 2
Genre Structure and Citation

This chapter reviews the pertinent literature for this study. As the study is mainly concerned with move structure and citation features of the introductory phase of the ERA, the chapter is organized into two parts: genre analysis of RAs as a particular research genre and citation study. The first four sections (Sects. 2.1–2.4) comprise the first part: Sect. 2.1 outlines the conceptualizations of *genre* and related terminology such as *communicative purposes, discourse community, moves, steps* and *rhetorical strategies*, and reviews the three main approaches to genre analysis, viz., the New Rhetoric (NR) approach, the Systemic Functional Linguistics (SFL) approach, and the English for Specific Purposes (ESP) approach; Sect. 2.2 addresses the different types of RAs, the macro-structure and the major sections of RAs; Sects. 2.3 and 2.4 focus on the rhetorical structure of the Introduction section and other introductory parts respectively. Following these, in Sect. 2.5, a comprehensive review of literature on citation is presented, which constitutes the second important part of this chapter. The final section summarizes the preceding sections and concludes the chapter.

2.1 Genre

Knowing, understanding, using and producing relevant genres is essential in academic and professional communication. However, as Allison (1999: 144) points out, "genre is easier to exemplify than to define". In Sect. 2.1.1, diverse conceptualizations of this elusive term will be presented and discussed in order to offer theoretical underpinnings for this study. Widely-recognized in the genre-based research literature, there are three major traditions (Hyon, 1996)—the ESP, the SFL and the NR—that have shaped our current understandings of the construct of *genre*. Despite the extensively-discussed diverging focuses in their theoretical positions, pedagogical applications and methodological techniques, they cross-fertilize and inform each other, and tend to converge at some points (Sect. 2.1.2). Mainly adopting the ESP approach, the present study clarifies some important concepts that frame *genre* in this tradition such as *communicative purpose* (Sect. 2.1.3.1) and *disciplinary community*

(Kathy). L. Lin, *Perspectives on the Introductory Phase of Empirical Research Articles*, Corpora and Intercultural Studies 5, https://doi.org/10.1007/978-981-32-9204-8_2

(Sect. 2.1.3.2), and some essential methodological units commonly used in genre analysis such as *moves, steps* and *rhetorical strategies* (Sect. 2.1.3.3).

2.1.1 Definitions of Genre

With classical thoughts of Aristotle and other philosophers arguably premised as the origin of *genre*, this term was initially used in the fields of rhetoric, literature and media. It was then extended to linguistics over three decades ago and has undergone significant changes throughout its history.

Deriving from the French (and originally Latin) word for "kind" or "class" (Rosmarin, 1985: 23), *genre* has been predominantly used for the function of grouping things for around 2000 years (Allen, 1989). However, in the modern genre theory, *genre* as a complex and dynamic mechanism has been conceptualized from vastly different perspectives, most notably by the three major schools (viz., the ESP, SFL and NR) in linguistic and rhetoric traditions.

In the ESP tradition, a much-cited definition of "genre" is that given by Swales:

> Genre is a class of communicative events, the members of which share some set of communicative purposes. These purposes are recognized by the expert members of the parent discourse community, and thereby constitute the rationale of the genre. This rationale shapes the schematic structure of the discourse and influences and constrains choices of content and style. Communicative purpose is both a privileged criterion and one that operates to keep the scope of a genre as here conceived narrowly focused on comparable rhetorical action. In addition to purpose, exemplars of a genre exhibit various patterns of similarity in terms of structure, style, content and intended audience. If all high probability expectations are realized, the exemplar will be viewed as prototypical by the parent discourse community. The genre names inherited and produced by discourse communities and imported by others constitute valuable ethnographic communication, but typically need further validation. (Swales, 1990: 58)

In this definition, *communicative purpose, discourse community* and *genre* seem to be interconnected with each other (see more detailed elaborations on *communicative purpose, discourse community* in Sect. 2.1.3); a genre is typically characterized by its communicative goal(s), shared by all its members and readily recognized by established members of the discourse community. It is also established members who place constraints on what can be accepted generally in terms of textual content, register features and forms for a particular genre (Paltridge, 2001); however, these practitioners are also apt to exploit these constraints to "achieve private intentions within the framework of socially recognized purpose(s)" (Bhatia, 1993: 12).

In line with Swales's above-mentioned definition, Bhatia (1993: 12) also regards *genre* as "a recognizable communicative event characterized by a set of communicative purpose(s) identified and mutually understood by the members of the professional or academic community in which it regularly occurs". Nevertheless, his observation of the skillful use of generic resources by some community members to accomplish their private intentions, as mentioned above, points to the flexible and dynamic nature of genre; as he himself realizes, this also "brings in the psychological, particularly cognitive, level of genre construction" in addition to Swales's "good fusion of linguistic and sociological factors" (Bhatia, 1993: 16) in defining genre.

SFL theorization of genre as firmly grounded in Hallidayan systemic-functional linguistics (Halliday, 1994), stresses the close links among the underlying typified "generic" or "schematic" structure, linguistic forms and context [see *context of situation* and *context of culture* originally from Malinowski (1946/1923, 1935) referred to in Eggins (1994)]. As the SFL genre theory is developed and enriched by students and followers of Halliday (e.g., Martin, 1984, 1985, 1992; Martin & Rose, 2007, 2008) at the University of Sydney, it is also frequently referred to as the Sydney School (Hyon, 1996). *Genre*, in this school, is defined as "a staged, goal-oriented, purposeful activity in which speakers engage as members of our culture" (Martin, 1984: 25): *goal-oriented* and *purposeful* because genres are used to get things done (Martin, 1985); *staged* because it normally takes us a few steps to fulfill the particular goal (Martin & Rose, 2007); the situated engagement of members of the institutional culture underlines the crucial roles of the social, cultural and contextual factors in the construction, interpretation and reproduction of genres. Representative examples of *genre* identified in this school are the "Key Genres" such as *recount, information report, explanation, exposition, narrative, discussion, procedure* and *news story* (Macken-Horarik, 2002: 21–22).

The NR genre research, also called Rhetorical Genre Studies (Bawarshi & Reiff, 2010), views *genre* as "typified rhetorical actions based in recurrent situations" (Miller, 1984: 159). In other words, *genre* is interpreted as "typical ways of engaging rhetorically with recurring situations" (Freedman & Medway, 1994: 2). Different from the ESP and the SFL researchers' product view of *genre* with the prime focus on textual features, the NR scholars hold the process-oriented view of *genre*, centering more on the dynamic and fluid relations between text and context. As Medway (2002: 123) contended, "[i]dentifying patterns of text format, syntactical and lexical choice, and discursive ordering, (…) is no longer considered sufficient for pinning down the genre"; rather, its identification "should arise from a particular socially recognizable motivation". The New Rhetoricians, with greater emphases on social purposes and situational contexts, favor "contextual" methods and can be somewhat dismissive of any analysis of the language of texts. Based on this feature, Flowerdew (2002, 2011) reclassifies the three traditions into *non-linguistic* or *contextual* (the NR) versus *linguistic* approaches (the ESP and the SFL). However, such a categorization was criticized by Coe (2002: 197), who maintained that "a genre is neither a text type nor a situation, but rather the functional relationship between a type of text and a type of situation" from an NR perspective. Though Flowerdew's dichotomy appears a little simplistic and unsatisfactory in fully disclosing different theoretical connotations of *genre* in the three schools, a combined use of the linguistically focused ESP or SFL approaches and the more ethnographic NR approach as proposed by him may be a valid and powerful way of analyzing a genre (Flowerdew & Wan, 2006, 2010; Kwan, 2005).

While the three schools theorize *genre* from different perspectives with contrasting foci, they all highlight the sophisticated, evolving and dynamic nature of *genre* and take account of both text-internal and text-external factors (though with disparate weighing). Both the textual (product) view and the process view of *genre* are desirable as they are complementary rather than exclusive to each other. They are all potentially valuable starting points for research and the adoption of them is determined by specific research needs and perspectives taken towards the genre.

2.1.2 Approaches to Genre

The aforementioned three major approaches to *genre* identified by Hyon (1996) have gained wide recognition and currency in genre research within the field of applied linguistics (AL). Commonalities and distinctions among them in various aspects ranging from theoretical implications to instructional practices have been teased out and delineated by a host of genre investigators (Bawarshi & Reiff, 2010; Flowerdew, 2011; Johns, 2002; Paltridge, 1995, 2007).

As indicated in Sect. 2.1.1, the different theoretical orientations of the three schools in genre analysis, and their distinct principal analytical methods and pedagogical foci are derived from their respective theoretical bases, the groups of learners and corresponding contexts they mainly address, and the disparate goals underlying their views of genre (Paltridge, 2007). Drawing on a variety of linguistic theories, corpus-based analytical techniques and discourse models, ESP genre research examines the "move" structure as well as linguistic properties of a genre in relation to its communicative purpose and propositional content in order to provide useful inputs for the non-native speaker of English (NNS) graduate-level students' academic writing instruction. Initially focusing on academic genres, the ESP approach was then extended to the analysis of professional genres such as legal and business genres (Bhatia, 1993, 2004). To understand the complex realities of language use in the world of professions and to realize the manifold goals of genre-based analysis of professional discourse, Bhatia (2004) developed a multi-dimensional and multi-perspective model as an integrated genre analytical tool. While this multi-dimensional and multi-perspective methodological framework is instrumental in an interdiscursive and critical genre analysis of professional practice (Bhatia, 2012), the present study is situated in the EAP context that focuses on the application of genre analysis to develop pedagogical solutions. Therefore, this study is predominantly a rhetorical structural and linguistic analysis of the ERA as genre and its part-genres (viz., Introductions and LRs), drawing on Swales's ESP genre analysis approach and linguistic frameworks for analyzing citation signals and formal and functional features. Insiders' perspectives, experience and views on how to structure and use citation languages in Introductions and LRs are only supplemental, but nevertheless provide an insightful perspective of the structural and language use under study.

SFL genre research, underpinned by Hallidayan systemic-functional linguistics, chiefly analyzes school genres to fulfill the literacy needs of primary and secondary schools in Australia and elsewhere, with some exceptional cases in ESP contexts. Similar to the ESP, the SFL genre analysis aims to derive prototypical or conventionalized organizational patterns of a genre particularly appropriate for certain contexts. However, "exemplars or instances of genres vary in their prototypicality" (Swales, 1990: 49), meaning that some texts might be less prototypical in terms of language use and schematic structures, while some others might resemble the "prototype" to a larger degree. Notably, the SFL approach employs a fairly complicated set of functional terms rather than the more straightforward linguistic/grammatical terms (used in the ESP tradition) in textual analysis and descriptions, in addition to the intricate, specialized and not easily understood linguistic models (Hyland, 2003). For this reason, practitioners following this approach normally need special training, and thus its application in pedagogy is not as wide as that of the ESP approach. Nevertheless, in SFL genre-based instruction, a salutary systematic teaching/learning cycle has been developed and extensively used in classroom genre-learning (Martin, 2009).

Strongly influenced by anthropology, sociology, rhetoric and poststructuralism, the NR approach focuses primarily on writing contexts and evolving processes of the genre (Johns, 2011). Originally developed from concerns with North American first language composition, rhetoric, and professional writing, the NR school studies *genre* "as the motivated, functional relationship between text type and rhetorical situation" (Coe, 2002: 195). As genres are responses of the actors to the dynamic social milieu, they are not immutable, as demonstrated in a series of diachronic studies (Bazerman, 1984, 1988; Dudley-Evans & Henderson, 1990), and the context-driven approach is dominant in this tradition.

While the new rhetoricians are less concerned with and "somewhat circumspect" about pedagogical applications of the NR perspective (Flowerdew, 2011: 119), the context-driven pedagogy associated with it for promoting learners' "genre awareness" rather than "genre acquisition/learning" (Johns, 2011: 61) does not enjoy similarly wide popularity among practitioners as the text-driven pedagogy recommended by the other two schools. As Johns's survey of literacy instructors' views towards the notion of genre and their teaching of/about genre conducted in the 2009s Language Writing Symposium revealed, the ESP and SFL approaches are overwhelmingly taken up by them as they are more accessible, less abstract, and particularly helpful for novice writers. However, the NR also contributes some enlightening pedagogical advice, as Johns (2003: 210–211) remarks, "certainly ESL/EFL composition instructors should acquaint themselves with the literature in the New Rhetoric, if for no other reason than to provide cautions against reductionist pedagogies that portray text descriptions as fixed templates instead of opportunities for studying evolving, negotiated, situated discourses."

Indeed, in the past three decades, many genre scholars have been preoccupied with differences among three major research traditions in their theoretical bases, nature and applications. They mostly explicate and promote distinct tenets and stances of the schools they belong to. However, a noticeable new trend in genre research and genre-based teaching today is to reconcile, negotiate and integrate these different traditions by drawing the best from them, to adopt multiple approaches to varied genres with more contextualized analysis in order to achieve a fuller understanding of the genre under investigation (Bhatia, 1993, 2004; Flowerdew, 2011; Sayfouri, 2010; Tardy, 2011).

While on the one hand genre analysts need to go beyond the text and incorporate ethonographic and informed "insiders' views" into their genre-based descriptions (Bhatia, 1993, 2004; Kwan, 2005; Tickoo, 1994), on the other hand, the value of the traditional linguistic and structural analysis for revealing genre-specific textual conventions should not be overlooked, as Yunick states:

> Quantitative, correlational work serves two functions alongside ethnographic work to identify not only phenomena general to many genres, but also significant patterns of meaning making that might not emerge from ethnography alone. (Yunick, 1997: 326)

Therefore, in the focused study of the introductory phase of the ERA presented in this project, a combined method is employed: both a text-based analysis of its rhetorical structure and citation use with "insiders" from the two disciplines consulted and an interview study of the perceptions and views of expert members of the two disciplinary discourse communities towards their structural and citational practices are conducted.

2.1.3 *Relevant Terminology*

In view of the research object and purpose of this study, I am mainly concerned with genre in an EAP context, and therefore base my analysis more closely on the perspective of the ESP school. To inform the methodological framework of this study, the important notions associated with genre such as *communicative purpose* (Sect. 2.1.3.1) and *discourse community* (Sect. 2.1.3.2) as well as the basic functional elements in move analysis like *moves, steps* and *strategies* (Sect. 2.1.3.3) are outlined as follows.

2.1.3.1 Communicative Purpose

In the ESP approach to genre analysis, *communicative purpose* is a key determinant of genre membership (Bhatia, 1993, 2001; Swales, 1990). However, unlike the formal features of genre exponents, communicative purposes embedded in them are not overt and thus difficult to be specified and operationalized.

A genre consists of "a class of communicative events, the members of which share some set of communicative purposes" (Swales, 1990: 58). Whilst regulating propositional contents, schematic patterning and lexico-grammatical use of the genre, communicative purposes can normally be recognized by expert members of the discourse community. Take thank-you letters as an instance, they form a genre since they have the same purpose of expressing gratitude, notwithstanding their possibly varied length, subject content and language expressions.

In genre analysis, it is rather difficult to establish the set of communicative purpose(s) for a genre, since, on the one hand, the world of discourse is dynamic, complex and unpredictable, and on the other, this entails expertise in both "text-internal" and "text-external" aspects (Bhatia, 2001, 2004). Genre analysts usually encounter few problems in interpreting text-internal aspects of language use, but need to consult the specialist informant in dealing with text-external factors such as institutional contexts, community culture and private intentions of some established members of the discourse community. This explains the necessity and importance of having the specialist informant in genre analysis, a practice adopted in the present study.

Askerhave and Swales (2001), however, challenged *communicative purpose* as the prioritized criterion in determining genre membership by arguing that it might be multiple, layered, intricate, and sometimes can even be misinterpreted by "insiders". They proposed that it could be temporarily ascribed in the initial stage of analyzing a genre. After subsequent detailed work on "extensive text-in-context enquiry" and some contextual analyses, genre analysts can reevaluate and calibrate the originally proposed purpose of the genre (Askerhave & Swales, 2001: 209). This indicates that rather than as a quick, immediate and one-off method to categorize texts, *communicative purpose* should be treated as a "long-term outcome" of a repeated analysis and validation (Askerhave & Swales, 2001: 207).

2.1.3.2 Discourse Community

Another concept closely related to genre is *discourse community*, which is defined as "socio-rhetorical networks that form in order to work towards sets of common goals" (Swales, 1990: 9). This notion highlights the social nature of *genre*, and indicates "intercommunity diversity and intra-community homogeneity" in the use of generic structures and language resources on account of their distinct socially recognized shared goals (Hyland, 2003: 23). Not surprisingly, it has gained currency in accounting for and predicting sorts of variations in generic forms across disciplines particularly in the EAP literature.

According to Swales (1990: 24–27), there are six defining features of discourse communities. A discourse community:

1. has a broadly agreed set of common public goals;
2. has mechanisms of intercommunication among its members;
3. uses its participatory mechanisms primarily to provide information and feedback;
4. utilizes and hence possesses one or more genres in the communicative furtherance of its aims;
5. has acquired some specialist lexis in addition to owning genres;
6. has a threshold level of members with a suitable degree of relevant content and discoursal expertise.

In his 1990 monograph, Swales also illustrated a hobby group named "The Hong Kong Study Circle" as a perfect example of "discourse community". However, in effect, it is still not easy to operationalize this rather abstract concept in a consistent manner. There are still many uncertainties surrounding this notion, e.g., how wide is the scope of discourse community? Is it mainly physical or virtual? Does it only promote commonalities among members in their practices or allow a certain degree of heterogeneity? To what extent does it allow for that difference, if any?

While remaining a problematic concept, discourse community was redefined by Swales (1993) as something that only makes sense in people's engagement in community conventions. This insightful view refutes previous criticisms of its static, structuralist and unchanging nature. However, it was not until his 1998 volume that Swales further specified clearly two types of discourse community: Place Discourse Community (PDC) and Focus Discourse Community (FDC). As he explained, PDC represents "a group of people who regularly work together, have developed a set of genres for regulation of the roles that each has to play within the community, and has a set of traditions and a sense of its own history" (Swales, 1998: 22); FDC denotes a grouping of people that connect each other and gain membership by virtue of their common interests. This conceptualization of discourse community is adopted in the current study, i.e., it can be either interpreted as a physical PDC (e.g., most of the expert writers interviewed come from two large departments in a UK university, representing established members of their respective disciplinary communities) or as an FDC with less physical presence and yet shared cultural values and interests (e.g., the journal editors and reviewers, and the readers of the ERAs from the two disciplines collected for structural and language analyses in this study). In the detailed examination of expert citation and structural use in the introductory phase of the ERA, *discourse community* is a useful tool for enhancing our understanding of disciplinary as well as individualized practices.

What follows are explanatory accounts of the three methodological units considered in the schematic analysis of the introductory part in this study: *moves*, *steps* and *strategies*.

2.1.3.3 Moves, Steps and Strategies

As a functional discourse unit characterizing the genre, a move appears regularly and "performs a coherent communicative function in a written or spoken discourse" (Swales, 2004: 228). Within a genre, moves are interconnected and contribute collectively to the overall communicative purpose of the genre. In this study, I adopt Lewin, Fine, and Young's (2001: 36) practice that moves are considered for "characterize[ing] a genre as prototypical rather than obligatory". In other words, all moves do not have to be present in every genre instance, and whether there can be regular (not obligatory) rhetorical moves identified for a genre determines whether it has a prototypical structure.

However, in the previous literature, there seems to be inconsistent and varied criteria for move identification, ranging from relying on lexico-grammatical signals (e.g., Dudley-Evans, 1986, 1994) to semantic properties (Samraj, 1989) and to rhetorical functions (Swales, 1990). As such, there are widely different realization forms for a move, being from one or several paragraphs to a single clause (Swales, 2004). Since "move" is a functional concept, in this study, a "functional-semantic" approach (Kwan, 2005, 2006; Kwan & Chan, 2014) is employed for identifying them (Sect. 3.4.1.4). The main criterion for determining a move and its boundaries is the distinct communicative intent of each corresponding text segment, with possible related linguistic signals (already identified in previous studies) resorted to as a supplemental means. A similar method is applied to the identification of move elements ("steps" or "strategies", see their definitions as below) as well.

"Steps", also called "sub-moves" or "stages" (Bhatia, 2001: 86), are obligatory constituent elements of a move that occur in a fixed sequence. For instance, in Swales's (1990) Create-a-Research-Space (CARS) model for introductions to RAs, the two elements of Move 3 (i.e., "Announcing principal findings" and "Indicating RA structure") can be qualified as steps only if they have a 100% occurrence rate in all texts examined and co-occur in this fixed order.

In addition to "steps", a move can also be realized in "rhetorical strategies" (Bhatia, 1993, 2001; Kwan, 2006), which however are optional and do not appear in a fixed order. Despite this and similar to "steps", "strategies" have local purposes, which contribute to the communicative intention of the move where they occur. Intuitively speaking, "strategies" tend to appear more often in a complex and flexibly structured genre because of their nature and status, as in the case of Kwan's theme-bound CARS model (Sect. 2.4.1.3).

Considering the research need of this study, "sub-moves" is used in a somewhat different sense from what has been accounted for in Bhatia (2001: 86). As aforementioned, Bhatia considered "steps" and "sub-moves" as two equivalent concepts. However, in this study, "sub-moves" simply refers to move constituents, disregarding whether they are obligatory or optional and whether they appear in a fixed sequence or not. Therefore, it denotes move elements of an all-encompassing nature. In another words, both "steps" and "strategies" can be considered as "sub-moves". In the present study, "sub-moves" has been used to describe the rhetorical structure of introductions (Sect. 6.2) and their subsequent LR sections (Sect. 6.3) in AL and CE ERAs.

2.2 Research Articles (RAs) as a Genre

The immense disciplinary development and the unprecedented enthusiasm of academics to share and exchange their research ideas and outputs have greatly contributed to the emergence and increasing use of diverse research genres, such as book reviews, conference presentations, conference proceedings articles and research notes. Among them, the RA has been the subject of most scholarly attention (Yang & Allison, 2003). In the following subsections, a general account of different categories of the traditional RA (Sect. 2.2.1) and a critical review of the previous research into its macro-structure with the main sections identified (Sect. 2.2.2) are presented.

2.2.1 Categories of RAs

According to Swales (2004), RAs can be classified into three main types, i.e., empirical (experimental) or data-based RAs (with the acronym "ERAs" mentioned before), theoretical RAs, and review RAs. ERAs report research findings derived from direct observation or various kinds of experimental studies (Weissberg & Buker, 1990), including the controlled scientific experiment, correlational research, questionnaire survey, case study, and studies that use computer-generated models to explain or predict phenomena observed in the laboratory or in nature. Such articles are based on evidence as opposed to theory or conjecture, and can usually be replicated in follow-up studies. In practice, RAs containing the heading Method (or variations on this theme, such as "Experimental", "Empirical design", "The study" and "Data and research design") could normally be identified as empirical. However, due to the intrinsic nature of some disciplines, experiments are never or rarely undertaken in them [such as astrophysics, theoretical physics, as noted by Tarone, Dwyer, Gillette, and Icke (1981) and Swales (2004)] and thus other types of RAs like theoretical and review pieces may predominate.

The theoretical RA, according to Lester and Lester (2006), traces the development of a theory, compares theories or discusses controversies surrounding a theory and makes analytical deductions from the issues discussed with a view to resolving problems. It should be noted that some articles in the fields of biostatistics and engineering that simply report the findings, which are usually simplified equations generated from the computer modelling or graphical simulation, belong to the category of logical argumentative theoretical RAs.

Reviews can be either a review of the literature on a topic (e.g., a "state-of-the-art" article) or a review of a literary work. The former is an analysis and discussion of secondary sources such as journal articles and monographs, and thus does not entail the presentation of primary data; the latter refers to writing about literature, which may be regarded as a "critique" or an "evaluation".

As it is believed that (the part-genres of) different sorts of RAs possess distinct structural and stylistic characteristics of their own (Crookes, 1986), the present study confines its analyses to ERAs. Another important note is that, traditionally, the "canonical" IMRD pattern is only applied to the ERA. Consequently, in both the first lead-in study, which examines its applicability to current research writing practices, and the second lead-in study, which investigates the status of the IMRD model in empirical research writing over the past 30 years, the collected RAs were categorized first before further detailed structural analyses. This is to ensure that only empirical studies are subject to scrutiny.

2.2.2 *Textual Overview of Empirical Research Articles (ERAs)*

The present study focuses on the ERA, I will therefore give a detailed review of previous research into the overall structure of the ERA (Sect. 2.2.2.1) with some comments on its major sections (Sect. 2.2.2.2).

2.2.2.1 The Macro-structure of ERAs

Research articles (RAs), the key contemporary genre for the communication and dissemination of new academic knowledge, have undergone profound textual changes over their entire 350-year history. Evolving from the standard epistolary form representing "genteel culture" (Valle, 1997), the first English RAs emerged with the founding of the Royal Society of London and its affiliated journal (*the Philosophical Transactions of the Royal Society of London*) in the 1660s. For the first two centuries, the RA was mostly a purely descriptive or narrative report of randomly observed events or phenomena (Atkinson, 1992, 1999). The report of "experiments" (also termed the "data-based" or, in this study, the ERA) was in the minority, but has rapidly increased in proportions over subsequent centuries and has now developed into a conventional article type. This seems inevitable, due to significant scientific advances and researchers' relationships with nature shifting from a view that natural laws could be discerned through direct or manipulated observation to a view that intentional explorations are needed for studying the nature of things (Swales, 1990).

The modern ERA is a highly conventualized genre. Concerning its macro-structure, the classic "Introduction-Method-Results-Discussion" ("IMRD") model is widely regarded as the "norm" (e.g., Lester and Lester, 2006). Such articles comprise four major sections, namely Introduction (I), Methods (M), Results (R) and Discussion (D). Previous diachronic studies characterizing textual changes during various historical periods in different disciplines have painted a general picture of ERA structural evolution from the un-sectionalized unelaborated sequential narrative in the 17th century gradually towards the near uniformity of the IMRD-structured issue-oriented report in the twentieth century (e.g., Atkinson, 1992, 1999; Bazerman, 1984, 1988; Biber & Conrad, 2009b; Dudley-Evans & Henderson, 1990; Valle, 1997). Their findings about its development at the pre-IMRD stage could be summarized as follows. Generally, for the first 200 years, experimental reports were rare, variously structured and narrative in nature. During the nineteenth century, explicit top-level discourse structures such as "theory → experiment → discussion" (Atkinson, 1999) and "theory → specific hypothesis → experimental trial-as-final proof" (Bazerman, 1988) appeared with theoretical aspects of the RAs gaining noticeable importance. The nineteenth century also witnessed continuing expansions of method descriptions and comprehensive reviews of previous literature. In sharp contrast, in the twentieth century, accounts of methodological information were downplayed, theoretical discussions fore-grounded and reviews of the literature became selective and focused (Atkinson, 1999; Bazerman, 1984).

The twentieth century also witnessed growing conventionalization within specific rhetorical sections [e.g., introductions following Swales's (1990) classic CARS model] (Atkinson, 1999; Dudley-Evans & Henderson, 1990) and the rapid development of the IMRD structure (Day & Gastel, 2006). For example, Atkinson (1992) found that medical reports started to be organized in a format approximating the current IMRD model in the mid-1940s. By the mid-1980s, the IMRD approach had become firmly established and was the default pattern for presenting the findings of empirical investigations. Examining the changing features of spectroscopic ERAs, Bazerman (1984) observed that the highly-conventionalized IMRD format was commonly used in the 1950s. Sollaci and Pereira (2004) is the only study that has examined the specific rate at which the use of the IMRD increased. They analyzed the structure of RAs in internal medicine from 1935 to 1985 and found that the pace of IMRD increments was slow for the first two decades (1935–1955) and yet for the subsequent 20 years (1955–1975), the frequency of the IMRD-structured articles more than quadrupled. The IMRD structure thus took the lead (80%) in the 1970s and was the only pattern used in RAs in the 1980s. Although the specific time point at which the "standard" IMRD pattern became prevalent in research writing may vary slightly in different disciplines, there is a clear overall trend towards the IMRD-standardization during the twentieth century.

This "standardization" process is an intriguing and complex one and took place in response to the changing needs of disciplinary discourse communities, the continuing development of the disciplines, and the ever-evolving wider social, historical and cultural contexts (Bazerman, 1988). It appears to have been spurred by strong recommendations of journal editors and various research associations such as the American National Standards Institute after World War II, and the possible influence of traditional disciplines such as physics (Sollaci & Pereira, 2004).

The research reviewed to this point indicates that the textual development of ERAs at the pre-IMRD stage and its trend towards the uniform IMRD-standardization in the 20th century have been well described. In other words, a number of historical studies focused on its macro-structural evolution in the early periods, e.g., Bazerman (1988) on that during 1665–1800, and Valle (1997) on that during 1711–1870. Many other studies also examined its macro-structural development in the 20th century, which is however usually before or up to the 1980s, e.g., Atkinson (1992) on RA structural development during the period of 1735–1985, Atkinson (1999) on that during 1675–1975, Bazerman (1984) on that during 1893–1980, and Dudley-Evans and Henderson (1990, 1993) on that during 1891–1980. However, the continuing development of ERAs from the 1980s onwards seems not have been covered in the diachronic literature.

Although the widely-reported IMRD framework is perhaps the most influential one and has become the 'normative' organizational format for structuring the entire ERA, as Swales (1990) noted, there is a lack of empirical evidence for its validity and applicability across the disciplinary spectrum. Indeed, the overall generic structure of ERAs has itself been the subject of surprisingly little empirical research in

ESP (Swales, 2004). This means that the long-established IMRD framework (Kinneavy, 1971; Stanley, 1984) has provided the starting-point for Swalesian analyses of the "four" major sections (viz., the Introduction, Method, Results, and Discussion sections) as well as micro-level studies of linguistic features, such as reporting verbs and clauses (Hewings, Lillis, & Vladimirou, 2010), hedges (Hyland, 2000) and metadiscourse markers (Ädel & Mauranen, 2010). Therefore, sections that are not represented in this framework, such as the LR section, the merged (as opposed to separate) Results and Discussion section, which is represented here as [RD],[1] and the Conclusion section (C), are largely overlooked. The move and step structure of these part-genres has rarely been investigated in ESP research.

A second consequence of ESP scholars' (conscious or subconscious) adoption of the "canonical" IMRD model is that it has limited the scope of some of their analyses. A case in point is Nwogu's (1997) valuable study of a corpus of medical RAs. In compiling his corpus, Nwogu (1997: 122) evidently excluded papers that did not follow the standard macro-structure: "to qualify for selection, all papers had to have the traditional IMRD sections of the research article." While it is possible that medical RAs conformed rigidly to the IMRD pattern at that particular juncture in the discipline's evolution, the omission of "unconventional" papers may have prevented the author from identifying emerging trends in RA organization in the medical field. If indeed IMRD was not the "standard" structure in medical research at this time, he may have overlooked an important variation on the theme of IMRD or possibly another organizational pattern altogether such as Introduction-Body-Conclusion (IBC). As we shall see (Sects. 4.3.1 and 5.2), IMRD is not an especially prevalent pattern in contemporary RA writing, so strict adherence to such a structure when conducting move-based or linguistic analyses is likely to result in incomplete or unrepresentative findings.

Another problem that flows from the adoption of IMRD is that sections not fully accounted for in this structure, such as LR, [RD] and C, are subsumed under one of the four conventional sectional headings. In other words, the IMRD framework is imposed on RAs that may diverge subtly or significantly from what is held to be the standard pattern. In practice, this might entail incorporating a separate, functionally distinct literature review or background section in a CARS-inspired analysis of introductions or, as in Hsieh, Tsai, Lin, Liou, and Kuo (2006), treating the conclusion as a variant of the discussion section, thereby possibly overlooking the precise communicative purposes of LR or C in prominent patterns such as ILM[RD]C and IM[RD]C (Sect. 4.3.1).

As noted above, the body of research into the generic structures of ERAs is at present somewhat limited. Among the few studies in this area, those of Posteguillo (1999), Yang and Allison (2004), and Stoller and Robinson (2013) are perhaps the most illuminating. Posteguillo's (1999) study was based on an analysis of 40 RAs from three core journals in computer science. On the basis of his analysis, Posteguillo (1999) concluded that the traditional IMRD framework was not applicable and that,

[1]Merging is represented in this study with square brackets. For example, [MRD] = the blended Method, Results and Discussion section; [MR] = the coalesced Method and Results section.

in fact, no systematic structural model could be identified to account for the majority of the papers in his corpus. Posteguillo (1999) attributed his findings to the fact that computer science was not a well-established discipline at the time and thus a standard schematic structure had yet to emerge. Another explanation is that most of the RAs he examined were evidently of a theoretical nature as they were found to be organized in either a problem-algorithm pattern or a model-implementation pattern. As Swales (2004) notes, the IMRD framework is not applicable to theoretical (and review) RAs. This illustrates the importance of categorizing RAs before embarking on a detailed analysis, a process that was conducted in the first lead-in study to ensure that only empirical papers were subject to scrutiny (Sect. 4.2.2.1).

Yang and Allison (2004) analyzed the macro-structure of primary and secondary RAs in AL. Although they did not report the specific patterns for structuring the 20 "primary" RAs, that is, papers which report the findings of an original investigation (also termed "experimental" RAs or ERAs in the present study), they found some sections not accounted for in the classic IMRD framework such as separate sections for literature review, theoretical basis and research questions between I and M, [RD] and the frequently-used independent "Pedagogic Implications". More details will be reviewed in Sect. 2.2.2.2. In a recent structural study of 60 chemistry journal articles, Stoller and Robinson (2013) found two predominant structural patterns specific to the field, i.e., IMR[DC] and IM[R(DC)], with the Conclusion section typically included in the Discussion section.

At present, therefore, our knowledge of RA macro-structures is far from complete. Such studies that have been conducted in this area are limited in scope and scale in that they have generally been based on relatively small datasets in single disciplines in the fields of science and engineering. Yang and Allison's (2004) analysis of RAs in AL is one of the few studies conducted in the social sciences/humanities. Another limitation of this small body of research is that many of the papers selected for analysis dated from the 1980s and 1990s and thus may not reflect current writing practices in the ever-evolving world of academic research and publishing (Atkinson, 1999; Bazerman, 1988; Dudley-Evans & Henderson, 1990; Ferguson, 1997). Indeed, it is possible that the continued preoccupation with IMRD in RA-related research, textbooks and reference materials (e.g., Körner, 2008; Pyrczak & Bruce, 2007) betrays the influence of the pioneering work on genre analysis in the 1980s and early 1990s, when the papers chosen for analysis presumably reflected RA writing practices during these and earlier periods.

Therefore, the first lead-in study (Chap. 4) seeks to address some of the limitations of scope, scale and timeframe outlined above by reporting the findings of a cross-disciplinary study of the structural patterns of ERAs in 39 disciplines in the fields of engineering, applied sciences, social sciences and the humanities, including hitherto overlooked or under-researched disciplines such as anthropology, social work and nursing. Meanwhile, major sections (in particular those not represented in the IMRD model in the opening and closing phases of the RA) have been identified and highlighted, which provides important justifications for the focused study of this project and enriches our genre knowledge substantially.

In addition, since several recent cross-sectional studies such as Yang and Allison (2004) and Stoller and Robinson (2013) have identified the sections not accounted for in the IMRD framework or predominant structural patterns apart from it as aforementioned, it seems that some movement away from IMRD has been in progress since the 1980s or even earlier and a stark contrast seemingly appears between the extensive use of the IMRD format in/before the 1980s and the macro-structural diversity revealed in recent ERAs. Nevertheless, these are only our assumptions and little diachronic evidence is available to confirm them. Further, in the first lead-in study, sections such as the LR have been identified as major ERA sections but have not been accounted for in the conventional IMRD model; however, whether they are new developments in contemporary ERAs is still unknown. To address this question and bridge the above research gaps, the second lead-in study examines the macro-structural changes of ERAs in AL and Civil Engineering (CE) in the past 30 years (1980–2010), with a particular focus on the changing structural patterns of the introductory phase (Chap. 5). The reasons for focusing on AL and CE are specified in Sect. 3.3.

2.2.2.2 Sections in ERAs

In the EAP literature, far fewer studies have been devoted to the overall structure of ERAs than those to the rhetorical structure of their individual sections (Kuteeva & McGrath, in press). This, together with the long-standing preoccupation with the IMRD norm, means that the status of the sections not fully accounted for in the IMRD model such as C, [RD] and LR (Chaps. 4 and 5) have tended to be underestimated by researchers, EAP practitioners and apprentice writers.

Generally speaking, the existing EAP genre research mainly focuses on the four "conventional" RA sections set out in the traditional IMRD framework (i.e., I, M, R and D). Among them, the Introduction has been a particular focus of attention since Swales (1981, 1990) developed his groundbreaking framework for analyzing this part-genre: the CARS model. Swales's move-based approach to genre analysis has not only stimulated a range of discipline-specific and cross-disciplinary studies of RA introductions (e.g., Samraj, 2002; Ozturk, 2007), but has also provided the theoretical foundation for research into the other three "conventional" sections, namely, Method (e.g., Bruce, 2008; Kanoksilapatham, 2005), Results (e.g., Brett, 1994; Bruce, 2009; Lim, 2010; Thompson, 1993; Williams, 1999) and Discussion (e.g., Holmes, 1997; Hopkins & Dudley-Evans, 1988; Peacock, 2002). In contrast, little research has been conducted into sections that are not represented in the IMRD framework, but which nevertheless (as the two lead-in studies in Chaps. 4 and 5 reveal) often appear in RAs across the disciplinary spectrum, namely, the LR, [RD], and C sections.

Regarding the opening phase of the ERA, which is a particular focus of this study, several researchers (e.g., Braine, 1995; Kwan, Chan, & Lam, 2012; Yang & Allison, 2004) have noted the use of additional sections between the traditional independent I and M. For instance, Braine (1995) reported the use of an innovative "theory" section in three of the six empirical reports from botany and engineering fields; Yang and Allison (2004) found that the stand-alone LR section was used for literature reviews, theoretical basis or research questions by published writers in four of the six primary RAs in *TESOL Quarterly* and three of the five RAs in *Applied Linguistics*. They attributed such use of the separate LR section to journal interests and requirements, the nature or orientation of the research, and whether there are some important theoretical concepts that should be defined or some controversial theoretical ground that needs to be explicated; Holmes (1997) observed the frequent employment of an LR after I by academics in political science and sociology (but not history) and thus inferred that LR might be a representative component of ERAs in the social sciences. In Kwan et al. (2012), the LR section, defined as the section(s) between the introduction and the methodology sections where previous literature is reviewed, is found to be a quasi-obligatory RA part-genre in the field of Information Systems (i.e. being used in over 80% of the RAs in its four source journals).

Although these few studies have noticed the repeated presence of the LR as an independent section between I and M in some RAs, a common belief is that literature reviewing is a complex, flexible, strategic scholarly discursive practice and different writers may have their own individual preferences in structuring the LR (Swales & Lindeman, 2002). For instance, they can recount previous studies in a chronological order, or "from general to specific", or according to their results, methods or importance. This apparent diversity and complexity involved in structuring the LR has led to their common assumption about the "insusceptibility" of this part-genre to the traditional genre analysis that has so far been successfully applied to the schematic study of other part-genres such as I, D and M. Nonetheless, Kwan's (2005, 2006) meticulous schematic structural analysis of the LR in theses is one of the few convincing instances refuting this general assumption. Furthermore, within the body of research into the rhetorical structure of part-genres of RAs and theses, the Introduction has received overwhelming scholarly attention and the CARS-related studies (CARS-validation studies) have become a major strand of research since Swales's introduction of his seminal work in the 1980s. Other part-genres, including LRs, have therefore been "overshadowed" by the Introduction, in Kwan's (2005: 17) words, "a 'star' part-genre".

As Kwan (2005: 17) eloquently argued, "the fact that introductions and literature reviews are often invoked interchangeably perpetuates the tendency to take the two as the same part-genre and reduces the value of research into the latter". All these factors, among others, help to explain genre analysts' past prevailing structuralist thinking about the organizational format of the introductory phase (i.e., regarding it as an important RA part mainly containing a single Introduction section with "rare" exceptional cases including an LR as well). In this case, they would be very likely to disregard the importance of LRs and overlook the function and status of this special part-genre.

In addition to the LR, the frequent use of other "unconventional" sections such as [RD] and C not fully accounted for in the IMRD framework have been noted in several previous works (Swales, 1990; Yang & Allison, 2003, 2004). For example, Swales (1990: 170) mentions that Results and Discussion could be blended into a single section and "additional or substituted sections labeled Conclusion, Implications or Applications and so on" are sometimes used in the concluding part of the ERA. However, he did not explain the importance of these "unconventional" sections and the relationship between them and the traditional four sections. In terms of the status of these sections, some scholars (e.g., Hsieh et al., 2006; Kwan & Chan, 2014) regarded them as parts of the related traditional section. For instance, as aforementioned, Hsieh et al. (2006) treated the Conclusion as a variant of the Discussion section. Kwan and Chan (2014) considered multiple post-Results sections (e.g., "Implications", "Limitations" and "Conclusion") collectively as a Discussion section. Similar practices have also been followed in many academic writing manuals (e.g., Swales & Feak, 2004; Weissberg & Buker, 1990).

In contrast, in Yang and Allison's (2004) study of 20 "primary" RAs, the "Pedagogic Implications" section has been assigned an independent status with its own communicative purpose. This could be justified by its frequent occurrence in their corpus (6 instances out of 20 primary RAs), reflecting pedagogical issues as a major concern in the field of applied linguistics. More importantly, this practice could also be justified by its distinct and prominent communicative focus—"Drawing pedagogic implications", an important step whose average occurrence was as high as 2.83 in this section, contrasting with 0.75 and 1.1 respectively in the Discussion and Conclusion. However, their practice of treating the merged Results and Discussion section [RD] as a variant of the Results section is questionable. The rationale behind this practice, they claimed, was that all five instances of [RD] in their data displayed no apparent difference from other RA sections that deal with findings (including the Results section), and instead contained two overlapping elements with them (i.e., "the presentation and discussion of research results"). Nonetheless, I argue that the Results, Discussion and the merged Results and Discussion section may all contain such elements, yet their overall functional weightings, communicative emphases, internal discourse structures and even the sequence or arrangement of some overlapping moves and steps might be essentially different, which entails further detailed moves- and steps-based examination of them. As Cargill and O'Connor (2009) commented, the conflated result and discussion [RD] section should be different in nature from the separate Result and Discussion sections. Therefore, Yang and Allison's (2004) treatment of [RD] as a variant of the separate R section has perhaps underestimated the significance of the blended results and discussion as a communicatively distinct section. This has indeed become the standard means of presenting research findings in many disciplines (Sect. 4.3.2), such as building services engineering, land surveying and civil and structural engineering.

Despite the non-uniform sectioning of the concluding part in previous studies (Kwan & Chan, 2014), in this study, an independent status would be assigned to those "unconventional" sections that have their own unique communicative functions or functional foci (in cases where they have multiple communicative purposes). This was conducted in my two lead-in studies (see Chap. 3) to ensure that the precise communicative purposes of such sections (e.g., LR or C) would not be overlooked in prominent patterns such as ILM[RD]C and IM[RD]C (Sect. 4.3.1).

2.3 Introductions in RAs

The introduction section is considered to be one of the most difficult parts to write in the whole RA (Swales, 1981, 1984). A considerable number of the writers, as Swales (1990) points out, tend to feel perplexed from the very initial stage of writing this part as they are faced with a good many difficult choices in terms of language use and information arrangement, e.g., how to express negative elements in the most appropriate manner, which optional moves should be included, how to maintain coherence when making transitions between levels of information, and how to conform to the linear progression of sentences, hierarchical discourse structures and the general-to-specific flow of the introduction. Consequently, delaying writing this part till the rest of the whole article is completed has not only been a preferred practice among some (even experienced) writers (Swales, 1990, 2004), but also a piece of advice frequently given by EAP instructors or writing manuals to student writers (e.g., Cacavas & Kaplan, 1994). Presumably they share the viewpoint that this practice can ensure that the introduction accurately reflects the major content of the text even if some changes occur in the composing process of the body part and writers may know better what kind of openings they should construct after completing the main part of the text.

It is these actual difficulties posed to early-career academics and research students in composing the introductions that have become the primary motive force for theoretical and empirical research into the discourse structure of the RA Introduction (Sect. 2.3.3). Before reviewing the voluminous literature on this part-genre, this section critically discusses "introductions" as an umbrella term (Sect. 2.3.1), followed by an account of its intriguing dual-nature and multi-functions (Sect. 2.3.2), which have been regarded as a primary source of novice writers' difficulties in writing this part.

2.3.1 Definitions of Introductions

"Introductions", as a cover term, can refer to "introductory texts whose characteristics may vary according to the different contexts in which they are situated" (Kwan, 1996: 10). As such, the rhetorical structure of any sub-genre of introductions, e.g., the RA introduction (Swales, 1990, 2004), the thesis introduction (Soler-Monreal, Carbonell-Olivares, & Gil-Salom, 2011), the academic book introduction (Bhatia, 1997), and even the theoretical RA introduction (Arvay & Tanko, 2004; Futász, 2006), and the experimental RA introduction (Ozturk, 2007), is essentially "a response to the genre of the parent text type" (Kwan, 1996: 7). For this reason, the object of the present research is specified as the ERA introduction.

An "introduction", as pointed out by Bhatia (1997: 183), "has a single dominant fairly general function of introducing a written or spoken academic event". In the same vein, the ERA Introduction in this study has a main socially recognized common communicative purpose of introducing the article. However, with the unprecedented competition in the academic context and the widespread use of electronic technology and multimedia resources (often with an embedded advertising value) (Bhatia, 2004), the ERA Introduction may have been endowed with an increasingly visible private promotional purpose. This has resulted in the likely mixing of both communicative functions within this particular genre.

2.3.2 Functions of Introductions

The above-mentioned difficulties involved in writing the introductory portion of the RA are mainly derived from its multiple functions and dual nature, the two interrelated and intertwined aspects. Based on the extant literature, the Introduction section of the RA has at least the following functions: (1) to introduce some basic knowledge of the research field and/or the background information to readers so that they may better understand the core of the RA; (2) to delimit the research scope; (3) to introduce the present study; (4) to attract and maintain the interest of a "busy readership" (Swales, 1981: 7); (5) to promote the current research by briefly addressing its main research findings and contributions, and/or sometimes offering some additional positive evaluative comments. The former three functions reflect the "objective" ("informative") nature of the RA Introduction while the latter two social functions reveal its "persuasive" nature with a special emphasis on writers' personal intentions. The dual nature of the Introduction has been highlighted by genre analysts such as Bhatia (1997, 2004) and Swales (1981, 1990, 2004), and especially its "persuasive" nature and writers' self-promotional purposes and strategies have aroused a great deal of scholarly interest in recent years. As Swales emphasized in his early work, the RA Introduction is prima facie "a problem-solution discourse type governed by objectivity and reason", while in essence it is "a plea for acceptance and designed accordingly" (Swales, 1984: 82) and "the appropriate macro-speech-act label for journal-introductions would be 'persuasion' as well" (Swales, 1981: 11) in addition to "description".

2.3.3 Genre Analysis of Introductions

In the literature on the rhetorical structure of RA Introductions, various theoretical models have been proposed by a host of genre analysts, most notably Swales's influential series of models, different versions of the problem-solution pattern and the secondary-storying model (Sect. 2.3.3.1). To empirically validate the effectiveness of relevant models and obtain useful findings to inform EAP pedagogy and materials writing, previous researchers have investigated the structure of the Introduction from multiple perspectives (e.g., the cross-disciplinary, cross-cultural and cross-generic perspectives) (Sect. 2.3.3.2).

2.3.3.1 Swales's Models and Other Alternative Models

All inquiries into the schematic structure of the Introduction section, whatever approach or combination of approaches they have adopted, aim to generate the theoretical framework nearest to its prototype, which is believed to potentially benefit novice research writers and academic writing teaching practice as a whole. This section explicates the series of theoretical frameworks for the rhetorical structure of the Introduction section proposed and continually revised by Swales (1981, 1990, 2004) as well as other alternative theoretical models.

1. Swales's models

Previous studies (e.g., Hirano, 2009; Kanoksilapatham, 2011; Samraj, 2002) have reiterated that Swales' CARS model (1990) is a milestone in ESP genre analysis of the RA Introduction; but few of them have offered an integrated, close and critical account of the development of the whole series of his theoretical models for the rhetorical structure of the RA Introduction in the past three decades. The following review of Swales's continuous efforts to model the discourse structure of the Introduction section—from his (1981) initial four-move schema to the classic three-move CARS model (1990) and the later revised CARS model (2004)—may give us a first glimpse of the development in ESP genre analysis of RA introductions.

Swales's four-move schema for the structure of the RA Introduction (1981)
According to Swales (1981), available style guides and reference materials on English research writing could hardly meet the needs of EAP classroom teaching before the 1980s, as most of them were of low-quality and rarely informed by findings derived from analyses of real RAs. An important reason is that there existed only a very limited number of previous studies on the rhetorical organization of RAs and RA sections at and before that time. Instead, materials writers tended to rely on their intuitions, and their own prior composing and teaching experience (Swales, 1981, 1984). In addition, among all RA sections, the more conventionalized Method and Results sections with generally less varied structures, had drawn far more attention from both EAP materials writers and teachers than the more communicatively complex sections such as the Introduction and the Discussion, which however pose greater difficulties to apprentice research writers.

All these concerns motivated Swales's (1981) pioneering study on aspects of article introductions. Originally his research attempted to examine how research writers report previous studies. Yet, after he realized that this element tended to be lodged in the Introduction section, he shifted his research focus to this particular part-genre. Based on his groundbreaking analysis of 48 RA introductions from three main areas (viz., the hard sciences such as physics and chemical engineering, the biology/medical field, and the social sciences such as educational psychology and language), Swales posited a four-move schema for the rhetorical organization of the RA Introduction (Fig. 2.1). According to this schema, four obligatory moves supposedly occur in sequence with no cyclicity considered: Move1 Establishing the Field (through claiming centrality, making generalizations about the state-of-the-art and

THE FOUR MOVES

Move 1	**Establishing the Field** A) Showing Centrality B) Stating Current knowledge C) Ascribing Key Characteristics
Move 2	**Summarizing Previous Research**
Move 3	**Preparing for Present Research** A) Indicating a Gap B) Question-Raising C) Extending a Finding
Move 4	**Introducing Present Research** A) Giving the Purpose B) Describing present research

Fig. 2.1 Swales's (1981) four-move schema for the rhetorical structure of article introductions

ascribing key features to the research area); Move 2 Summarizing Previous Research; Move 3 Preparing for Present Research (by means of gap-indication, question-raising or research-extension); Move 4 Introducing Present Research (by stating the research aim or describing the general research content).

Although Swales's (1981) four-part schema served as a useful starting point for the follow-up empirical structural analyses of this part-genre, it embodied a number of evident weaknesses. First of all, Move 1 (Establishing the Field) and Move 2 (Summarizing Previous Research) are hard to separate (Bley-Vroman & Selinker, 1984; Crookes, 1986). In other words, "reviewing previous research" was postulated as a separate move (Move 2), contradicting with other researchers' observations (Jacoby, 1986, 1987; Samraj, 2002) that references to previous studies are in fact distributed throughout the Introduction and indeed even the entire RA.

Secondly, the selection of short RA introductions (of usually between 100 and 500 words) with at least one reference to previous research in Swales's (1981) study resulted in limited revelations from his analysis and the restricted explanatory power of his four-move schema, e.g., neither cyclical patterns nor all possible steps (especially in the final two moves) could be identified. The preset criteria for selecting texts in Swales's (1981) analysis might have precluded a panoramic view of the rhetorical structure of the RA Introduction to a significant degree. This implies the paramount importance of the main principles for selecting texts for analysis. As Bley-Vroman and Selinker (1984: 3) eloquently commented, the random selection of "highly-valued texts" for structural analysis ("highly-valued" in terms of either their content or forms) could better ensure more valid and convincing findings that may effectively facilitate research writing pedagogy.

Moreover, as his four-move framework was generated based on only 48 RA introductions from three broad areas, some particular structural features characterizing RA introductions in other disciplines could not be well accounted for. Additionally, Swales indicated the optional nature of some moves and yet did not specify under which context these moves could be omitted. The last limitation seems to be inevitable as it concerns the nature of ESP genre analysis, i.e., the somewhat subjective and intuition-based nature of the analysis with apparent difficulties in creating clearly-defined labels for moves and steps and the lack of "explicitly stated and consistent analytical principles" (Kwan, 1996: 11). Swales (1981) himself also recognized this problem:

> I hope that the remarks I have so far made in this section indicate my hope that we can discover at least a few of the things that are really 'going on' in the composition of journal-introductions; that we are looking for insights rather than frequent tables or straightforward descriptions of syntactic structures. We are therefore faced with severe problems in establishing terminology. The major problem in this type of discourse analysis is the inter-related one of subjectivity and circularity….In effect, the discourse analyst labels something as x and then begins to see x occurring all over the place. One way out—and the one adopted by Pettinari among others—is to employ a specialist informant to provide a commentary on the texts. As this has not been done in this case, I am open to the charge that my unsubstantiated and ill-defined terminological labels that are supposed to capture what is really happening on the page are typically little more than a reflection of my own perceptual predispositions. (Swales, 1981: 14)

Swales's three-move CARS (Creating a Research Space) model (1990)
In view of the above-mentioned deficiencies in his (1981) initial four-move schema, Swales (1990) developed the more influential CARS model to account for the rhetorical organization of the RA Introduction. Compared with its predecessor, it manifests the following new features: (1) noticeably, the labels for the three rhetorical moves of the CARS model (see Fig. 2.2) bear strong metaphorical coloring. The ecological analogy incorporated into this newly-envisioned model not only "adequately captures a number of characteristics of RA introductions: the need to re-establish in the eyes of the discourse community the significance of the research field itself; the need to 'situate' the actual research in terms of that significance; and the need to show how this niche in the wider ecosystem will be occupied and defended" (Swales, 1990: 142), but makes it fairly attractive, interesting, unique and easier to be accepted and applied especially by the new entrants into academic discourse communities; (2) the reduction into three major moves in the CARS model with the status of the literature review part lowering from an independent move (Move 2 "Summarizing Previous Research" in his 1981 four-move schema) to the current subsidiary step of Move 1 (Step 3 "Reviewing Items of Previous Research") helps to make a far stronger logical connection among the moves. More importantly, in this way, all associated steps within Move 1 generally proceed from the report of the general information to the more specific one; (3) the adding of "and/or" between steps to a certain extent indicates the obligatory/optional nature of some particular steps while at the same time providing room for flexibility of the schematic structure upon need, e.g., the iteration of some step-cycles or the omission of some steps; (4) in an attempt to incorporate more steps newly observed by other genre analysts or himself of real

Move 1	**Establishing a territory**	
Step1-1	Claiming centrality	
	and/or	
Step1-2	Making topic generalization(s)	
	and/or	
Step1-3	Reviewing items of previous research	
Move 2	**Establishing a niche**	*Declining rhetorical effort*
Step2-1A	Counter-claiming	
	or	
Step2-1B	Indicating a gap	
	or	
Step2-1C	Question-raising	
	or	
Step2-1D	Continuing a tradition	
Move 3	**Occupying the niche**	*Weakening knowledge claims*
Step3-1A	Outlining purposes	
	or	
Step3-1B	Announcing present research	
Step3-2	Announcing principle findings	
Step3-3	Indicating RA structure	*Increasing explicitness*

Fig. 2.2 Swales's CARS model for RA introductions (Swales, 1990: 141)

texts, Swales added one step (Step 1A Counter-claiming) to Move 2 and two steps (Step 2 Announcing Principal Findings and Step 3 Indicating RA Structure) to Move 3.

Since its introduction in 1990, Swales's CARS model has attracted a great deal of scholarly attention. Various kinds of data have been used to test its applicability across different disciplines, languages and cultures. These analyses, however, revealed some problems with this model, and while discussing relevant critique points, a complete account of the definitions of each move and step in this widely-reported framework seems to be necessary.

According to the CARS model, the introduction can be partitioned into three parts: Move 1 Establishing a Territory, Move 2 Establishing a Niche, and Move 3 Occupying a Niche. Move 1 functions to establish the broad setting and situate the research in this setting by delineating the research scope, emphasizing its central status and describing the "state-of-the-art". There are three possible realizations for this move (see Fig. 2.2). The first step "Centrality-claiming", as explained by Swales (1990: 144), refers to "appeals to the discourse community whereby members are asked to accept that the research about to be reported is part of a lively, significant or well-established research area". It is frequently placed at the beginning of the Introduction, yet sometimes it could be reversed with Step 2 (see instances presented in Swales, 1990: 145). In the two corpora that Swales has examined in detail (Swales, 1981;

Swales & Najjar, 1987), this step occurred in around half of the 158 introductions, indicating that it was a relatively common option for writers. The second step (Step 1-2), which is a general summary of the current state-of-the-art on the research issue, can mainly be classified into two broad categories of knowledge or practice, or phenomena, and appears to be of a more neutral nature than its preceding step (Swales, 1990). Although Swales (1990) has listed typical linguistic exponents for the former two steps of the CARS model as subsidiary means for step identification, some genre analysts (e.g., Anthony, 1999; Lee, 2001) still found it difficult to determine whether some opening sentences are any of these two steps. In Lee's (2001) study, the raters even reported their disagreement in discerning Step 1-1 versus Step 1-2 in a certain number of cases.

As a far more frequently-used step, "Reviewing Items of Previous Research" (Step 1-3) has indeed been reported by Swales (1990) and others (e.g., Anthony, 1999) as an obligatory one. This final step is one of the main locations where the writers would usually include numerous citations. Probably for this reason, citation has been specially highlighted by Swales with respect to its role, forms and usage in his description of this step. As it is believed to be a most representative language feature commonly shared by the LR section and the Introduction section (the obligatory step "Reviewing Items of Previous Research" in the CARS model), the comparative study of it in these two part-genres and of the connection between the use of it and the rhetorical movement of them in the present project would be significant.

Move 2 seems to be a single-step move with four alternatives: "counter-claiming certain facets of the research topic (Step 2-1A)", "identifying the gaps in existing research (Step 2-1B)", "raising doubts and questions about some aspects of the research area (Step 2-1C)" and "extending particular research traditions (Step 2-1D)". In comparison with the other two moves, Move 2 is perhaps least fixed in terms of its content and could even be omitted in some RA introductions due to a lack of substantial literature in relatively new disciplines (e.g., Crookes, 1986; Swales, 1981), or a different social or cultural tradition with less need to compete for research space (e.g., Fredrickson & Swales, 1994).

It seems reasonable and necessary to add the "and" condition between steps in Move 2, as recommended by Anthony (1999), for the use of multiple steps at this point could also be common and natural. However, this has been overlooked by Swales (1990). With regard to the occurrence of each single step within Move 2, previous research shows that the gap-indication step (Step 2-1B) is the most commonly-used one while the use of the last two optional steps (Step 2-1C and Step 2-1D) appears to be quite rare (Lee, 2001; Swales, 2004). Swales also summarized various linguistic exponents of this move in his 1990 volume, e.g., the adversative sentence-connectors that signal the opening of the negative comment on the established territory (*however, nevertheless, yet, unfortunately and but*), the verbs (*suffer, is limited to*), the adjective phrases (*time consuming, expensive, not sufficiently accurate*), the negative or quasi-negative quantifiers (*no, little, none of, few/very few*) and the nouns (*failure, limitation*) for niche-establishment.

Although the feature of possible "cyclicity" is not clearly represented in the CARS model (Fig. 2.2), Swales (1990: 158) did comment upon it as opposed to "the composite configuration" in terms of the arrangement of Move 1/Step 3 ("Reviewing Items of Previous Research") and Move 2 ("Establishing a Niche"). He pointed out that there were at least three essential variables that could affect the writer's choice of a cyclic structure: the length of the RA Introduction, the nature of the discipline and the tradition of the chosen research area. As he observed, the cycle of Move 1/Step 3 and Move 2 is more likely to recur in longer RA Introductions where the writer has adequate space to establish the niche after reviewing each item of previous research. Moreover, this cyclic structure is generally frequently employed by research writers from the social sciences rather than those from the natural and life sciences and engineering. In particular, when the focused field has a research tradition that seems to be of a "branching" rather than of a "linear and accumulative" nature (Swales, 1990: 158), the cyclical organization is apparently more favorable.

Move 3 is the main location where the writer would indicate to what extent and in which ways the present research bridges the gap created in Move 2 or adds to the state-of-the-art. Thus, there seems to be a logical linking between the use of Move 2 and that of the ensuing Move 3.

Actually, Move 3 is not always placed towards the end of the Introduction. Swales (1990) reported the adoption of the fronted-Move 3 subtype in one out of four RAs published in *Research in the Teaching of English* (RTE) in 1988 and in two out of 16 RAs also from RTE in 1987. It is assumed that the use of the fronted-Move 3 subtype has the possible double-edged sword effects, i.e., it would on the one hand reject a wider readership (Swales, 1990), but on the other hand offer a shortcut to enable interested readers to reach key points of the whole text. Yet, this entails more future empirical studies to validate.

Among the three steps of Move 3, Step 3-1 is the only obligatory one (Swales, 1990), which contains either a purposive or a descriptive statement on the to-be-announced research. Step 2 "Announcing Principal Research Findings" (APF) is an interesting element, where the writer can briefly yet forcefully stress the selling points of his or her research, particularly, its special contributions to the knowledge field. The use of this step is traditionally more favored by academics in science and engineering than their colleagues in the social sciences and humanities. This is borne out in Swales and Najjar's (1987) examination of the use of APF in 110 introductions, where they found that 45% of the RA introductions in physics employed the Step 2 option, contrasting with only 6.8% of those in educational psychology.

Swales's (1990: 161) definition of Move 3-Step 3 as an option "to indicate in varying degrees of detail the structure and occasionally the content of the remainder of the RA" could actually pose difficulties to genre analysts in identifying this step. As incisively commented by Anthony (1999), to indicate the content of the RA is very likely to involve some details of the research findings (Step 3-2) and of the research per se (Step 3-1B). This ambiguity in its operational definition, however, might on the other hand suggest that the occurrence of each step-option within Move 3 would not be as clear-cut as we assumed before. Furthermore, the final step is indeed not favored by research writers in most of the disciplines, despite Cooper's

(1985) report that nearly 67% of the IEEE introductions he examined employed a Step 3. Swales (1990: 161) tactfully attributed this high incidence in Cooper's study to "the absence of an established schema for research reporting in a new and rapidly evolving field".

Swales's revised CARS model (2004)
After critically revisiting his original CARS model and integrating pertinent insightful findings derived from other empirical research (e.g., Anthony, 1999; Kwan, 1996; Samraj, 2002) into the move-and-step structure of the RA Introduction from a variety of disciplinary fields, Swales (2004) formulated a revised CARS (R-CARS) model. In the R-CARS model, there are still three obligatory rhetorical moves with the former two unchanged and the final move relabeled as "Presenting the Present Work", which is in essence a plain equivalent of the original Move 3 "Occupying the Niche" in his 1990 CARS schema. The major amendments are made to some specific steps encapsulated under these three moves in terms of their categories and labels, or rather, the reduction into a single rhetorical step in Move 1, the condensing of the three realizations in Move 2 of the 1990 CARS schema into an all-embracing "Gap-indication" step (Move 2-Step 1), the inclusion of a new optional step "Presenting Positive Justification" (Move 2-Step 2) to Move 2 and that of three optional steps (Steps 2-4, see Fig. 2.3) and one PISF step "Stating the Value of the Present Research" to Move 3.

Swales's R-CARS model undoubtedly possesses a larger degree of flexibility and is of a more all-encompassing nature than the previous version (Sheldon, 2011). It acknowledges Samraj's (2002: 3) criticism of the distribution of literature review (the step "needs not just appear in the first move but can also be embedded within other steps, such as indicating a gap") by indicating the possible cycling of Moves 1 and 2. Considering this as well as difficulties involved in distinguishing the two opening steps of Move 1 (viz., "Claiming Centrality" and "Making Topic Generalizations") (Bley-Vroman & Selinker, 1984; Crookes, 1986), Swales (2004) compressed all step options in Move 1 into an exclusive broad category "Topic Generalization of Increasing Specificity". However, this single unitary step seems to be somewhat overgeneralized (Del Saz-Rubio, 2011; Sheldon, 2011), and hence we may probably "miss interesting strategies employed by the authors" (Adnan, 2008: 48). To overcome this weakness, genre analysts either incorporated the previous three specific steps of Move 1 in the 1990 CARS model into the amended 2004 framework (e.g., Del Saz-Rubio, 2011) or devised a series of subcategories for this step themselves (e.g., Sheldon, 2011).

Moreover, as mentioned before, one of the inherent limitations of the Swalesian tradition of analysis is the perceived vagueness in the operational definitions of some specific moves and steps as well as "the personal interpretation of lexis yielding subjective findings" (Kwan, 1996: 11), causing difficulties in clearly distinguishing the neighboring moves or steps. In the process of differentiating the two optional steps (Step 2-1A "Counter-claiming" and Step 2-1B "Indicating a Gap") of Move 2 in the original CARS model, Kwan astutely observed that lexical items such as *suffer from, is confined to, is limited to,* and *time consuming* could be interpreted

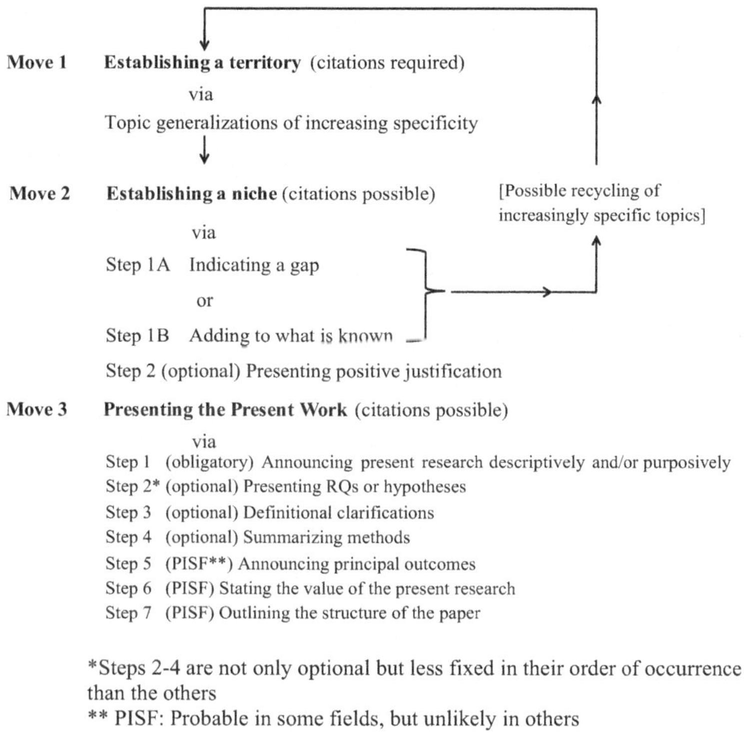

Fig. 2.3 Swales's revised CARS model for RA introductions (Swales, 2004: 230, 232)

as indicators of both steps. In addition, the first three optional steps in Move 2 are fairly similar in their communicative purposes, i.e., to point out and create the gaps in previous literature. In consequence, Swales (2004) generalized them into a single optional step for Move 2 in his R-CARS model (viz., Step 1A Indicating a Gap). As Step 2-1D "Continuing a Tradition" seems to Swales a rather vague and odd term, he rephrased it as "Adding to What is Known", a much more explicit step. Lastly, an optional step "Presenting Positive Evaluation", which was newly identified in Samraj's (2002) study of the schematic structure of the RA Introduction in two related fields (viz., wildlife behavior and conservation biology), has been considered incorporating into the current R-CARS framework.

In Move 3, there is only one obligatory step "Announcing Present Research Descriptively and/or Purposively", which is a conceptual blending of the two variations for Step 3-1 in the 1990 CARS model. In addition to the two optional steps "Definitional Clarifications" (Step 3) and "Stating the Value of the Present Research" (Step 6) proposed by Anthony (1999) in his examination of the rhetorical organization of 12 introductions in the field of software engineering, the other two steps (Steps 2 and 4) have also been taken on board due to other considerations, such as the evolution of research writing practice, changing beliefs and academic conventions of disciplinary discourse communities and other contextual variables.

Despite Swales's endeavors in making his 2004 R-CARS framework more readily accommodate the discourse practices of academic writers with different language and cultural backgrounds (Sheldon, 2011), its application is not as wide as expected, and some genre analysts (e.g., Ozturk, 2007) still chose his original 1990 CARS model as the theoretical underpinnings in their studies of the move-and-step structure of the introductions (see Tables 2.2 and 2.3 in Sect. 2.3.3.2). The main reason may lie in the dramatic condensing of steps in Move 1 and Move 2 (Del Saz-Rubio, 2011). To partly compensate for this, Sheldon even posited eight sub-steps for the only step of Move 1 ("Topic Generalizations of Increasing Specificity") to substantiate Swales's R-CARS framework for her comparative structural analysis of the RA Introduction across different language groups. At times, the "generalizability" of a model seems to be enhanced at the expense of its exact "specificity". The degree of a formulated model's "explicitness" and its explanatory power is therefore largely dependent upon (inter alia) the balance between these two seemingly contradictory aspects (viz., its "generalizability" and "specificity").

Summary of Swales's (1981, 1990, 2004) **models**

As relatively robust and viable frameworks for the discourse structure of the RA Introduction, Swales's series of models have taken into account both communicative functions and forms of this part-genre (Ahmad, 1997) which actually consists of a series of moves and their associated steps arranged in certain sequences with the possible cyclicity involved. This important merit of Swales's models–focusing on both the form and function of the introductions and the relationship between them–ensures their pedagogical as well as theoretical value (Jogthong, 2001).

As Paltridge (2001: 18) commented, "Swales's work in the area of genre analysis has always had a strong pedagogical focus". To extract "pedagogically-employable generalizations" (Swales, 1981: 10) from real textual analyses could be understood as one of the major motivations for his continuous efforts in improving his theoretical frameworks for the rhetorical organization of the Introduction. Just as Swales himself stated, the models should be evaluated in terms of their pedagogical value rather than their truth-value.

2. Two alternative models

Apart from Swales's move-analysis frameworks, there exist alternative models with potential referencing value accounting for the rhetorical structure of the RA Introduction. The most representative ones are various versions of the problem-solution model and the second-storying model.

Problem-solution model

From the early 1970s onward, an array of different versions of the problem-solution model for the rhetorical organization of the RA Introduction were proposed by discourse analysts (Hoey, 1979; Najjar, 1990; Toulmin, 1972; Zappen, 1983). Borrowing the Darwinian notion "an ecological niche", Toulmin (1972: 296) advocated that "a new specialization needs its own niche" and innovative scientists tend to establish their status and fame by staking out their own knowledge claims. The overarching task for researchers is thus to identify and occupy "the niche" (or specifically "the problem"), which is regarded as the motive force behind an intellectual discipline and defined as the gap between the discipline's explanatory ideals and current knowledge. This is well-illustrated in his own formula: Scientific Problems = Explanatory Ideals-Current Capacities (Toulmin, 1972: 152). Based on Toulmin's work, Zappen (1983: 131) put forward a five-step problem-solution schema: Step 1 Establishing the Goal of a Particular Discipline; Step 2 Reviewing the Extant Research Directed toward that Goal; Step 3 Identifying a Prominent Problem of the Discipline; Step 4 Identifying Selection/Evaluation Criteria of the Discipline Applicable to Any Proposed Solution to the Problem; and Step 5 Proposing a Solution to the Problem that Meets the Criteria. As Zappen (1983: 130) explained, in the RA Introduction, "the researcher addresses the goals, current capacities, problems, and criteria of evaluation that derive from and operate within that discipline". The Toulmin-Zappen model emphasized the importance of the collective audience-/readers-sensitivity in writing (the external contextual variables) and yet could not provide adequate explanations for the writers' own purposeful rhetoric (Swales & Najjar, 1987). Although it has a certain power of explanation for the rhetorical structure of the RA Introduction, this model is still vague and difficult to operationalise, and has therefore not been widely adopted in both genre analysis and the teaching of research writing.

Hoey's (1979) five-part rhetorical division looks simple and plausible, but its five categories (viz., "Situation", "Problem", "Solution", "Result" and "Evaluation") are abstract and overgeneralized, and there are no further steps and linguistic exponents to account for them. For instance, as Swales (1981: 84) observed, "the category of Situation masks the subtly different ways of Establishing the Field at Move 1" of his model. Another reason why the problem-solution schema is not easy to apply is that real introductory texts usually devote most space to "the Problem" with only a little or no mention of "the Solution" aside from a few peculiar cases where the researchers lay exceptionally strong emphasis on their new findings and contributions. This general tendency, however, is not explicitly suggested by the problem-solution model, which in contrast seems to indicate a balanced writing of "the Problem" and "the Solution" in the RA Introduction as its nomenclature suggests.

Based on the Toulmin-Zappen model, Najjar (1990) developed his alternative problem-solution model to account for the rhetorical structure of the Arabic RA introductions (45%) that departed from the CARS model by analyzing 48 Arabic RA introductions in agricultural sciences. Najjar's alternative problem-solution model is composed of four steps: Step 1 Identifying a Problem; Step 2 Identifying a Solution; Step 3 Presenting the Research Purpose; Step 4 A. Reviewing Previous Research, B. Indicating the Gap in Previous Research (optional). Unlike the Arabic RA introductions that generally fit the CARS model, those following Najjar's alternative problem-solution schema did not center on "establishing the niche" by reviewing previous research and identifying the concerning gaps (Lee, 2001).

Compared with Swales's CARS model and its revised version (Swales, 1990, 2004), various problem-solution schema are rather vague as they do not give clear and specific definitions of each "Step/Part", which actually corresponds to the "Move" in Swales's framework. Furthermore, most of them only contain the first-level overgeneralized category (i.e., "Step/Part") without more specific associated subdivided components included, which greatly limits their applicability and pedagogical usefulness. In addition to these limitations, Swales (1981: 84) pointed out that the inherent weakness of the above-mentioned problem-solution interpretations lies in their overemphasis on the "objectivity, logic and reason" in writing and structuring the RA Introduction, and their neglect of other important social functions and communicative purposes of the part-genre. In other words, "many RA introductions may on the surface be instances of problem-solution text types, but beneath that surface they are pleas for acceptance, and designed accordingly" (Swales, 1984: 82). Especially under the huge influence of the worldwide trend of commercialization and marketization, and the immense pressure on academics to publish internationally, RA writers tend to employ a variety of self-promotion strategies throughout the whole text (in particular in the introductory paragraphs). Consequently, the RA Introduction has multiple purposes and functions, and to solve the problem is only an optional one. In some disciplines such as biomedical science, the main duty of researchers is to observe something new and interesting, to record and explain their observations, and at times to pose new questions for future research, rather than to solve the existing problems or to answer research questions commonly set out at the start of the RA (Smith, 1987).

Second-storying model

Another interesting analogy for the writing of the RA Introduction is "second-storying" (Swales, 1981, 1984), which was originally an important concept in the field of ethnomethodology. A basic skill for giving a natural and proper new turn in daily conversation is that after one speaker tells a story or an anecdote, other conversational participants take the floor by giving another relevant story or anecdote with some further extension. The second-storying analogy compares the writing of the RA to this sort of conversation exercise, where the review of and comment upon the previous studies in the introductory portion is like telling "the first story", providing a basis for the writers' later elaboration on his/her own research and the findings thereof, constituting "the second story". At the very beginning, the writers need to establish the importance of "the first story" (viz., the review of the extant research), which is not yet complete and faultless. This leaves space for further development, which appears to be the main task of the writers' own research which is "the second story".

The second-storying model is enlightening as it points out that the RA Introduction is not simply a problem-solution discourse, and there are many social and contextual factors that need to be considered when we compose it. The writing of the RA Introduction is essentially a purpose-oriented social activity, governed by conventionalized rules of the disciplinary discourse community with the aim of gaining recognition from other expert members as well as the readers. Although this analogy-based model provides helpful general principles for handling the RA Introduction, it does not contain specific instructional guidelines for novice research writers on how to structure it.

To sum up, there is no point assessing which of the above alternative models is more advantageous as both are far from being completely successful and only reveal particular facets of the rhetorical organization of the RA Introduction. As Swales (1981) noted, they seem to have contrasting and yet somewhat complementary emphases: the problem-solution schema puts more weight on objectivity and reason involved in constructing the Introduction, which is more characterized by scientific and engineering discourse; in contrast, the second-storying analogy lays more emphasis on the social nature of the Introduction, which requires writers' compliance with an agreed upon set of rules of their discourse communities. Both models are therefore needed to help us to achieve a fuller and deeper understanding of organizational features of this important part-genre.

2.3.3.2 Variations in Rhetorical Structures of RA Introductions

Among all existing theoretical frameworks for the rhetorical structure of the RA Introduction, Swales's models (Swales, 1990, 2004) are widely-recognized as the most viable, robust and influential ones. However, subsequent studies have revealed some structural features not accounted for by them (or one of them—more often his 1990 original CARS model) as well as diverse variations in organizing this sub-genre across cultures, languages, disciplines and sub-disciplines.

In the existing literature, numerous studies have been undertaken on variations in schematic structures of the RA Introduction across different languages and cultures. There are fewer studies on inter-disciplinary and intra-disciplinary variations, and almost no systematic studies on rhetorical comparison of and generic interrelationship between the Introduction section and its related RA parts or other sections, except for Samraj (2005).

Table 2.1 lists all the major studies of rhetorical structures of the RA Introduction across different languages and cultures. Generally, they can be divided into three groups according to their main designs: the first group (Ahmad, 1997; Fakhri, 2004; Fredrickson & Swales, 1994; Jogthong, 2001; Najjar, 1990) focuses exclusively on the generic structure of introductions written in languages other than English, mainly using Swales's models as the analytical tool or for reference comparison; the second group includes the genre-based comparative rhetorical studies of the introductions written in English and in other languages (Duszak, 1994; Hirano, 2009; Loi, 2010; Loi & Evans, 2010; Zhang & Hu, 2010); and the last group is more complexly designed, comparing the structures of RA introductions composed by (usually three or four) different language groups (Huang, Xu, & Yang, 2010; Lee, 2001; Sheldon, 2011; Taylor & Chen, 1991).

As noted above, the first group of studies is principally concerned with whether the introductions written in other languages fit the CARS model, and if not, what the major variations are. On the one hand, different proportions of introductions were found to generally follow the CARS model in these studies, even with some inconsistent findings obtained (e.g., 56.3% for the Arabic introductions in Najjar's (1990) study in contrast to 39% for the Arabic introductions in Fakhri's (2004)

Table 2.1 Overview of schematic studies of the RA Introduction across different languages/cultures

Author(s)	Year	Model	Data (no. of RAs)	Language	Field(s)
Najjar	1990	CARS (1990) and the problem-solution model	48	Arabic	Agricultural science
Taylor and Chen	1991	Swales's 1981 four-move scheme	31	Chinese versus English	Science
Fredrickson and Swales	1994	CARS (1990)	26	Swedish	Art
Duszak	1994	CARS (1990)	40	Polish versus English	Language studies
Ahmad	1997	CARS (1990)	21	Malaysian	Agriculture, biological sciences, applied science and engineering
Jogthong	2001	CARS (1990)	40	Thai	Educational and medical fields
Lee	2001	CARS (1990)	160	Korean versus English	ESL/EFL education
Fakhri	2004	CARS (1990)	28	Arabic	Historical, political, social and economic issues
Hirano	2009	CARS (1990)	20	Brazilian Portuguese versus English	English for specific purposes
Huang, Xu, and Yang	2010	R-CARS (2004)	30	Chinese versus English	Material science
Zhang and Hu	2010	CARS (1990)	40	Chinese versus English	Medical science
Loi	2010	CARS (1990, 2004)	40	Chinese versus English	Educational psychology
Loi and Evans	2010	CARS (1990, 2004)	40	Chinese versus English	Educational psychology
Sheldon	2011	R-CARS (2004)	54	Spanish versus English	AL

study); on the other hand, the major deviations from the CARS model included the salient absence of the "gap-indication" step in Move 2 (e.g., Jogthong, 2001; Najjar, 1990) or the entire Move 2 ("Establishing the Niche") altogether (e.g., Ahmad, 1997; Fredrickson & Swales, 1994), and few evaluative discussions of previous research with sometimes the noticeable omission of Move1-Step3 ("Reviewing Items of Previous Research") in a number of Arabic (Fakhri, 2004; Najjar, 1990) and Thai introductions (Jogthong, 2001). While the former may stem from the lack of well-established conventions in the emerging research fields examined (Ahmad, 1997, Najjar, 1990) or that of severe competitions in local academic communities (Ahmad, 1997; Fredrickson & Swales, 1994; Jogthong, 2001), the latter for the most part characterized the culture-specific features in organizing this sub-genre.

The second group compares the accountability of Swales's models for the structure of RA introductions in English and in other languages, and examines the rhetorical differences between them. In general, English RA introductions followed more closely Swales's models (Duszak, 1994; Hirano, 2009; Loi, 2010; Loi & Evans, 2010; Zhang & Hu, 2010) than those written in other languages, one possible reason for which is that the CARS model was developed on the basis of RAs in English (Loi, 2010). The Brazilian Portuguese (Hirano, 2009) and Chinese introductions (Zhang & Hu, 2010) were rhetorically simpler than their counterparts in English as fewer moves with little cyclicity were used in them. While the prevailing absence of Move 2 ("establishing the niche") became the most distinctive structural feature of Brazilian Portuguese introductions (seven out of the ten) (Hirano, 2009), the indirect rhetorical style characterized by the employment of "strategies of avoidance" (Duszak, 1994: 303) was identified to be that of Polish introductions. Both features could be attributed to their native cultures and rhetorical traditions. For example, the Brazilian writers felt uncomfortable in pointing out the gaps in previous studies, especially those conducted by their colleagues in local academic communities, which was perhaps related to "solidarity" promoted in their own academic culture (Hirano, 2009: 245).

In Loi and Evans's (2010) and Loi's (2010)[2] comparative structural analyses of twenty RA introductions in English and Chinese in educational psychology, they observed their broadly similar communicative functions, for they all shared the three principal moves of Swales's (1990, 2004) CARS model and the three major features (viz., "explicitness", "specifying the value of research", and "taking a critical stance"). However, Chinese introductions in general made less use of the three features due to the Confucian philosophy, "high-context communication" and "the collective ethos" featured in Chinese social and cultural tradition, which is in sharp contrast with "the individual ethos", "low-context communication" and the Aristotelian rhetoric adhered by English NS writers. Loi also reported that Chinese introductions generally use the moves (Move 2 in particular) and their constituent steps less than

[2]It should be noted that Loi (2010) and Loi and Evans (2010) actually analyzed the same sets of data (i.e., 20 Chinese introductions and 20 English introductions in educational psychology, but interpreted the findings from different perspectives. Loi and Evans (2010) focuses more on cultural differences and philosophical values related to different rhetorical and structural styles of the introductions in two languages.

and differently to English introductions. In addition to revealing many similarities and differences between the rhetorical structure of the two sets of article introductions, Loi (2010: 271–272) identified in the data a few rhetorical steps (strategies) not accounted for in the CARS model (Swales, 1990, 2004), viz., Move 1 Step 2 Defining Terms/Concepts, Move 1 Step 3 Presenting the Theoretical Basis, Move 3 Step 2 Specifying the Focus of the Research and Move 3 Step 7 Introducing the Implication.

Only a few studies, which are classified as the third group, have investigated the textual organization of RA introductions produced by diverse (more than two) language groups, especially those of the NNS writers, e.g., the introductions written by the English L1 group, the Chinese L1 group and the English L2 group in Taylor and Chen (1991); those written by the English L1 group, the Spanish L1 group and the English L2 group in Sheldon (2011); those by the English L1 group, the local Korean L1 group, and the U.S.-educated (Korean L1)/(English L2) group in Lee (2001); and those by the English L1 group,[3] the Chinese L1 group and the English L2 group in Huang et al. (2010). The findings of these studies are complex and varied, and the most representative are: (1) whereas the English L2 introductions constructed by Spanish writers structurally resembled the English L1 introductions and the CARS schema (2004) to a considerable degree (Sheldon, 2011), those by Chinese writers were significantly different from the English L1 introductions both in terms of their rhetorical structures and referencing use (Taylor & Chen, 1991); (2) Swales's models seem to overemphasize the role of niche establishment realized mainly through a critical review of previous literature whilst ignoring other possibilities for writing the RA Introduction, including those indicated in Najjar's (1990) study and Golebiowski's (1999) study, such as referring to practical needs or existing problems in real situations (Lee, 2001); (3) in contrast, in both Korean L1 introductions (Lee, 2001) and Chinese L1 introductions (Taylor & Chen, 1991), less review of previous research with fewer references used was found than in English L1 introductions. The related reasons are detailed in Sect. 2.5.4; (4) Moreover, Spanish L1 introductions (Sheldon, 2011) and Chinese L1 introductions (Huang et al., 2010) favored less move cyclicity than English L1 introductions.

Compared to the rich body of literature on intercultural variations, there are to date only a few studies addressing cross-disciplinary (Bisenbach-Lucas, 1994; Crookes, 1986; Samraj, 2002, 2005; Swales & Najjars, 1987) and within-disciplinary variations (Ozturk, 2007) in rhetorical structures of the RA introductions (see Table 2.2). Among the studies listed, it should be noted that Bisenbach-Lucas's study (RAs vs. popularizations) and Samraj's (2005) study (Introduction vs. Abstract) are two special ones that involve both cross-disciplinary and cross-generic perspectives, which will be discussed later in this section.

[3]The group of writers in Huang et al. (2010) refer to the authors of the selected articles published in the international English journals in material sciences, and not all of them are necessarily NS writers of English. However, since their articles reach the international publishable level with relatively high research and writing quality and most of them are affiliated to Anglo-American institutions, this group is tentatively referred to as "the English L1 group" to parallel those in other studies of the same category.

Table 2.2 Overview of schematic studies of the RA Introduction across different disciplines and sub-disciplines

Author(s)	Year	Model	Data (no. of RAs)	Field(s)
Crookes	1986	Swales's 1981 four-move scheme	96	Hard sciences, biology/medical science, and social sciences
Swales and Najjar	1987	Swales's 1981 four-move scheme	110	Physical science and educational psychology
Bisenbach-Lucas	1994	CARS (1990)	12 (6 RAs and 6 popularizations)	Medicine, zoology, geology, biology, astrophysics and antiquity
Anthony	1999	CARS (1990)	12	Software engineering
Samraj	2002, 2005	CARS (1990)	24	Conservation biology and wildlife behavior
Ozturk	2007	CARS (1990)	20	Second language acquisition and second language writing within AL
Kanoksilapatham	2012	R-CARS (2004)	179	Civil, software and biomedical engineering

Similarly based on Swales's 1981 four-move schema, Crookes's (1986) study is one of the earlier empirical works focusing exclusively on the Introduction section while Swales and Najjar (1987) mainly studied the use of a particular move "announcing principal findings" ("APF") in introductions from two contrasting disciplines, viz., physics and educational psychology. By adopting both diachronic and cross-disciplinary perspectives, Swales and Najjar reported that physics RA introductions were often closed with an APF, a move that was optional and not common for educational psychological introductions. An increasing prominence of APF was observed in physics RA introductions over time: in 36% of all physics RAs in 1943 to 44% in 1963 and to 55% in 1983. However, this was not the case with educational psychological introductions, where there was still an occasional use of APFs despite their considerable length with many recycled structures observed, especially in the 1983 sample. Swales and Najjar also noted a prominent mismatch between published advice in style manuals and these actual practices in the two disciplines regarding the use of APFs in RA writing.

Noting problematic aspects of Swales's 1981 model (see Sect. 2.3.3.1) including inexplicit descriptions of moves (in particular Moves 1 and 2) and an overly rigid order of the four moves, Crookes (1986) made corresponding modifications of the system and adopted a stricter analytical procedure. On the whole, he found that the introductions examined generally conformed to Swales's model and most of them began with Move 1 and closed with Move 4. This roughly accords with Bisenbach-Lucas's (1994) conclusion about the rhetorical structure of the six RA introductions studied that all of them corresponded to the CARS model, and opened with Move 1 and ended with Move 3 [These two moves indeed respectively correspond with Move 1 and Move 4 in Swales's (1981) scheme, see Sect. 2.3.3.1]. Concerning disciplinary specific features, social sciences introductions tended to be longer with a greater amount of cyclicity used than their hard sciences and biology/medical science counterparts, which nevertheless exhibited a closer affinity to the CARS; the direct link between the length of the RA introduction and its structural complexity as well as the use of cyclicity suggested by him has, however, been refuted by subsequent studies (Sect. 2.3.3.1). In Bisenbach-Lucas's study, Move 2 was only absent in the astrophysics RA Introduction, and Move 1-Step 3 ("Reviewing Items of Previous Research") and Move 3-Step 1B ("Announcing Present Research") were identified as the two most frequently used steps, whose communicative purposes, as indicated in their nomenclature, rightly accord with the main function of the Introduction. The cycling, which was mostly found between the first move and the other two moves, occurred in as many as four out of the six introductions analyzed.

Two more significant studies that have inspired Swales's further revision of his CARS model are Anthony (1999) and Samraj (2002). Despite its modest data size, Anthony's study of software engineering introductions revealed some important features not yet accounted for in the CARS model, the most prominent being "*definitions of some important terms and examples to illustrate difficult concepts*" that extensively occurred after Move 1 steps (Anthony, 1999: 43) and "*evaluation of research*" as a newly devised step of Move 3 that appeared in all corpus introductions. However, the introductions examined in his study still fit well in the CARS framework as all of them used the three major moves.

Samraj (2002) conducted a comparative study of the generic structure of twelve introductions in two related fields (viz., wildlife behavior and conservation biology) and identified the following new features that she considered worthwhile being incorporated into the CARS: the multifunctional element "reviewing previous literature" can appear throughout the introduction; the research being reported can be justified not only by the gaps in the research world but also by problems in the real world; not as commonly used as the "gap-indication" step in the Introduction, positive justifications of the research are still employed for establishing the niche. One critical point she raised pertinent to the present study is that the element "reviewing literature" is not used simply for reviewing previous studies, but to fulfill diverse functions, e.g., to support the topic generalization or centrality claim made, to inform the background detail, and to justify the gaps identified by the researcher, which can perhaps account for its flexible placement. However, to what extent this element occurring in the Introduction is similar or dissimilar to the independent LR section within the same

RA, and whether there is any link between them are still unclear. These unsolved yet very intriguing issues are addressed in this study.

Another set of outcomes of her research relates to structural variations across the two disciplines. Firstly, centrality claims were more commonly used in conservation biology introductions for persuasive and promotional functions and often concerned the real world, whereas in wildlife behavior introductions, centrality claims were not frequent and the intended research was often justified by gaps in previous studies. Secondly, the hypothesis to be tested was included in some wildlife behavior introductions but generally absent in conservation biology introductions. Lastly, the species background description was uniquely used in wildlife behavior samples. All these notable differences, according to Samraj (2002), could be ascribed to the contrasting nature of the two disciplines:

> Conservation Biology is an applied field, whereas Wildlife Behavior is a theoretical field, the former is interdisciplinary, while the latter is disciplinary, and finally, the former is a relatively young field while the latter is field with historical depth. (Samraj, 2002: 14)

More recently, Kanoksilapatham (2012) examined variations in the rhetorical structure of article introductions from three engineering disciplines (viz., civil, biomedical and software engineering) and found that all the 179 introductions analyzed generally reflect the three-move structure set out in the CARS model (Swales, 1990). However, at the step level, two new elements for Move 3 were found, including "Step 6 Offering Procedural Justifications" which is used in introductions from all the three disciplines, and "Step 8 Describing Study Sites" which is only found in CE introductions. Step 8 is therefore a seemingly discipline-specific element. Disciplinary variations lie mainly in the use of some specific steps, which generally could be accounted for by the contrasting history and nature of the three disciplines, an interpretation similar to that of Samraj (2002). For example, the less frequent use of "Claiming Centrality" (Move 1 Step 1) in CE introductions is assumed to be the result of the maturity of this discipline, as CE is one of the oldest engineering disciplines. In contrast, researchers in software and biomedical engineering (two relatively new disciplines emerging in around the mid-20th century) feel more obliged to claim the importance of the research topic due to the younger age of these two fields. Also because of the immaturity of software engineering, the step for reviewing previous studies was less frequently used in introductions in this young discipline whilst the element for clarifying items is often adopted as more new terms are created or the meanings of existing terms are more frequently expanded. Different from that, there is greater use of the step for presenting positive justifications in biomedical engineering introductions, which according to Kanoksilapatham, is attributed to the fact that biomedical engineering is an interdisciplinary field merging medicine and engineering, mainly aiming to improve human health. Therefore, research proposed in this field usually needs to "be meticulously justified to avoid disastrous or unpleasant effects on humans."

Except for structural variations in RA introductions across different (Bisenbach-Lucas, 1994; Crookes, 1986; Kanoksilapatham, 2012) or related disciplines (Samraj, 2002), there is also significant variability documented between sub-disciplines within a single field (Ozturk, 2007). By comparing the rhetorical organization of ten RA introductions selected from *Journal of Studies of Second Language Acquisition* (SSLA) with that of another ten from *Journal of Second Language Writing* (JSLW), Ozturk observed apparent intra-disciplinary structural variations: in the SSLA corpus, M1-M2-M3 as the dominant move structure occurred in six out of the ten introductions while in the JSLW corpus, only one introduction was structured in this way and more deviations occurred from the conventional CARS model: the two move structures M1-M2-M1-M3 (40%) and M1-M3 (30%) accounted for 70% of the corpus and all the other three structural patterns (M1-M2-M1-M3-M1, M3-M1-M3-M1-M2-M3, and M1-M2-M3) only occurred once. He attributed this variation to the emerging-established field distinction, i.e., within the discipline of AL, second language writing is a less established area that is more of inter-disciplinary nature and customarily involves a wider range of diverse topics, compared with second language acquisition. He also cast doubt upon the direct relationship between the length of an RA introduction and the complexity of its move structure, which as mentioned earlier had been suggested in previous studies (e.g., Crookes, 1986). Although this study innovatively examined intra-disciplinary variations in the generic structure of the Introduction, its analysis was confined to the move level and its data size was relatively small. In the future, more sophisticated and fine-grained structural analyses in this regard should be preferably based on the data of a larger sample size from many other disciplines.

While generic interrelations remain a topic of ongoing interest in academic genre analysis, the limited existing work centers on comparisons between/among different genres in terms of their rhetorical structures [e.g., Nwogu (1990) on the structural comparison among the abstract, the RA, and the popularized version of the RA, as cited in Pho (2009), Adams Smith (1990), Fahnestock (1986) and Myers (1990) on that between academic RAs and popularizations] and those between/among related sub-genres that may constitute a genre set (Devitt, 1991) are fairly rare. Concerning the RA Introduction, Samraj's (2005) is thus far the only systematic study on the relationship between it and its related genres (viz., abstracts) regarding their generic structures.

Based on two groups of RAs respectively in conservation biology and wildlife behavior, Samraj (2005) not only made a cross-generic comparison between the Introduction and the abstract accompanying the RA structurally and functionally, but examined variations in their relationship across the disciplinary line. She concluded that in conservation biology, introductions bore a greater resemblance to abstracts than was the case in wildlife behavior. In both abstracts and introductions of conservation biological RAs, there was considerable use of centrality claims (a step in CARS that is originally used for the analysis of introductions) to promote the importance of the general topic, and real-world problems were frequently referred to in making these centrality claims as well as for justifying the proposed research. Different from that, in wildlife behavior, centrality claims were almost absent in abstracts while they appeared in half of the introductions examined. Furthermore, whereas the "Gap-indication" step was used in ten out of the twelve wildlife behavior introductions and all the gaps identified concerned the research world, it only occasionally occurred in the abstracts (two out of the twelve). Again, she attributed this difference in generic inter-relations between the introductions and the abstracts across the two disciplines to the contrasting disciplinary nature and history. However, the two genres in wildlife behavior still shared something in common, namely, the frequent use of a unique move labeled background on site or species (Samraj, 2005).

Overall, previous research has frequently studied the Introduction as a particular part-genre, and rarely compared it with its related part-genres or genres to ascertain their specific interrelationships either structurally, functionally or linguistically. Furthermore, as the LR section in the RA is still not a widely recognized part-genre in the EAP tradition, there is no comparative study of the LR and the Introduction either in terms of their schematic structures or language use, despite their partly shared content elements and language features (viz., the element "reviewing previous research" and citation use).

2.4 Other Introductory Parts in RAs

The decades-long preoccupation with IMRD in RA-related research and instruction has inevitably led to other possible sections in the introductory phase apart from the Introduction section being largely overlooked. Despite this fact, a most commonly invoked section that runs between I and M is LR. While some anecdotal evidence (as briefly mentioned in Chap. 1), a few writing reference books (e.g., Swales & Feak, 2000) and a limited number of empirical studies (Braine, 1995; Kwan et al., 2012; Yang & Allison, 2004) have alluded to the existence of an LR (with varied section headings and content foci) between I and M, its status in the whole RA is customarily underestimated by researchers, pedagogical practitioners and apprentice writers altogether. This section presents the existing knowledge about the LR section.

2.4.1 Literature Reviews (LRs)

2.4.1.1 Definitions and Forms of LRs

"Western definitions of the literature review are as numerous as they are varied"—this keen observation made by O'Connell and Jin (2001) from their extensive survey of more than one hundred guides and handbooks on academic writing and research—has best summarized the state of the art about interpretations of the concept LR. Among these numerous definitions, some well-cited ones are presented, from which the diversity and differing emphases in them can be clearly perceived:

> A literature review uses as its database reports of primary or original scholarship, and does not report new primary scholarship itself…The types of scholarship may be empirical, theoretical, critical/analytic, or methodological in nature. Second, a literature review seeks

> to ***describe, summarize, evaluate, clarify*** and/or ***integrate*** the content of primary reports (Cooper, 1988: 107);
>
> [A literature review] ***extracts*** and ***synthesizes*** the main points, issues, findings and research methods which emerge from a critical review of the readings (Nunan, 1992: 217);
>
> [A literature review can be defined as] the ***selection*** of available documents (both published and unpublished) on the topic, which contain information, ideas, data and evidence written from a particular standpoint to fulfill certain aims or express certain views on the nature of the topic and how it is to be investigated, and the effective ***evaluation*** of these documents in relation to the research being proposed (Hart, 1998: 13);
>
> A literature review is ***a narrative account*** of information that is already currently available, accessible and published, which may be written from a number of differing paradigms or perspectives, depending on the standpoint of the writer (Jesson & Lacey, 2006: 140);
>
> A literature review is ***a written document*** that presents a logically argued case founded on a comprehensive understanding of the current state of knowledge about a topic of study. This case establishes a convincing thesis to answer the study's question (Machi & McEvoy, 2009: 4).

The above definitions demonstrate previous researchers' dual approaches to LRs—the product-process view of LRs—either viewing LR as a process (literacy practice) or a (written) product (Kwan, 2005; Ridley, 2012). The term "literature review" as an indispensable part of the research process involves various activities in undertaking a review, including literature searching, selecting and classifying, reading, note-taking, and writing.

When viewed as a written product, LRs can at least be represented in three major forms: (1) a free-standing genre, i.e., review articles (Sect. 2.2.1); (2) a separate section of an array of genres such as RAs (Kwan et al., 2012), student project reports (Krishnan & Kathpalia, 2002), postgraduate theses (Kwan, 2006; Lang, 2004), dissertation proposals, grant applications and so on; (3) an element of a particular part-genre, e.g., "reviewing items of previous research" as Step 3 of Move 1 in the CARS model (Swales, 1990). LRs can also be integrated into RA discussions, various parts of theses, prospectuses and so on.

Indeed, Jesson and Lacey (2006: 140) noted different representation forms of LRs as well:

- a short section in a research proposal (showing the outcome of a preliminary search and review);
- the early chapter/s in a dissertation (here you need a more in-depth formal comprehensive review);
- **an introductory section in an academic paper**;
- a review in its own right (Brugha & Varvasovsky, 2000); and
- a systematic review to inform evidence-based policy or practice.

In the present study, LRs of the second form (LR sections in the RA) are chosen as the research focus. To be specific, the independent section(s) between I and M in the ERA that offer various kinds of "background" to the study such as that on the contextual, theoretical or methodological aspects are defined as the LR for this project. However, it is noted from the data that the intervening section(s) between I and M may contain propositional contents other than an integrated review of previous studies, e.g., a descriptive account of the research context. In such cases, LR might not be an entirely appropriate term representing these sections. In spite of that, as it is the most commonly invoked term whenever referring to the section(s) between I and M, the use of LR (as an umbrella term) is retained in this study. As such, I and LR may constitute the introductory phase of the ERA.

2.4.1.2 Functions of LRs

In the ESP tradition, the communicative purpose/rhetorical function as a core parameter of a genre/part-genre determines its propositional contents, constituent elements, organizational patterns and other generic features, and thus to conduct a schematic study of a particular genre or part-genre, the first fundamental step is to understand its main purposes/functions (Kwan, 2006).

In the emerging body of literature on the schematic structure of LRs, Kwan (2006: 32) as a forerunner determined that the principal communicative purpose of the LR in theses is to "justify the value of the research, and to show why it is distinct from what is documented in the literature." In Bruce's (1994) view, the LR chapter in the thesis aims to offer relevant background information and rationales for the proposed research. Although LRs in degree theses differ from those in RAs at least in their length and research scope, they might share something in common in their communicative purposes as they seem to belong to the same genre colony (Bhatia, 2001, 2004). Consequently, the communicative functions of LRs in theses numerated by previous researchers and manual writers can be referred to when we deliberate on those of LRs in RAs.

Indeed, like the well-researched Introductions in RAs, LRs also have multiple communicative functions as highlighted by Ridley (2012), Feak and Swales (2009) and many other EAP professionals. LR provides essential connections between the intended study and the existing body of literature; presents critical background details and rationales for the research to be conducted; expounds theoretical, methodological and empirical underpinnings; demonstrates a full command of the current state of knowledge about the research topic and an in-depth understanding of research problems; and helps to "generate and refine your own research ideas" (Jesson & Lacey, 2006: 140). Hart (1998: 27) listed as many as eleven purposes that a review of literature can serve, among which, "distinguishing what has been done from what needs to be done; discovering important variables relevant to the topic; synthesizing and gaining a new perspective; identifying relationships between ideas and practice; establishing the context of the topic or problem; rationalizing the significance of the problem and identifying the main methodologies and research techniques that have been used" are especially significant. After synthesizing these current understandings with my own perceptions of the real data, I propose the main purpose of the LR as an important section of the RA is to (further) contextualize the study, provide justifications for the necessity and significance of it and inform readers of what kind of premises on which it is based. This guides the follow-up schematic analysis of LRs in ERAs for this project.

In general, the rhetorical functions of the traditional Introduction and LR in research writing are somewhat similar in that they all orient the reader to the research to be presented, prepare for the arguments to be advanced, and relate the proposed study to the existent research. It has been empirically shown that the introduction chapter and the LR in postgraduate theses resemble each other in their rhetorical structures, confirming their membership of the same "genre agnation network" (Martin, 1992) or "the genre colony (Bhatia, 2001, 2004) of academic research introductions" (Kwan, 2006: 52). However, to what extent the Introduction and LR sections in (the same) RAs are similar or different in terms of their rhetorical structure and functions is still unclear and so far there has been no related empirical research conducted. Thus, the present study is an attempt to fill this void whilst pinpointing their interrelationships as well.

2.4.1.3 Genre Analysis of LRs

The review of previous literature is undeniably pivotal to conducting a research project, as Jankowitz (1995: 128–129) notes, "knowledge doesn't exist in a vacuum, and your work only has value in relation to other people. Your work and your findings will be significant only to the extent that they are the same as or different from other people's work and findings".

Overall, existing studies mostly concentrate on the process-view of LRs, i.e., novice writers' perceptions of, experiences and processes in writing literature review (Bruce, 1994; Kwan, 2008; Lang, 2004; Miguel & Nelson, 2007; Qian & Krugly-Smolska, 2008; Shaw, 1991, 1995), and practical techniques on and approaches to teaching how to construct a thoroughly researched literature review (Feak & Swales, 2009; Froese, Gantz, & Henry, 1998; Levy & Ellis, 2006; Liu & Houdek, 2006; Swales & Lindemann, 2002). In contrast, only a limited number of systematic structural analyses have been conducted of LRs as a written product, e.g., LRs in postgraduate theses (Kwan, 2006), LRs in student project reports (Krishnan & Kathpalia, 2002) and LRs as a separate section in RAs (Kwan et al., 2012; Tessuto, 2015). The fact that almost no genre research exists into the rhetorical structure of the LR in RAs except Kwan et al. and Tessuto could be partly accounted for by the long-term neglect of its importance and status as a major RA section (Sect. 2.2.2.2). The following are the reviews of a few studies on the rhetorical structure of LRs in various genres, which however have some reference value to the present research (Krishnan & Kathpalia, 2002; Kwan, 2005, 2006; Kwan et al., 2012; O'Connell & Jin, 2001; Tessuto, 2015).

Applying a genre approach to LR sections extracted from only ten final year student project reports written by NNS engineering undergraduates, Krishnan and Kathpalia (2002) determined the rhetorical structure of the report as follows: firstly there seems to be an overall structure of "Overview+Review"; then within the Review it had a substructure of "Opening+Citations+Closing". They found that student writers were basically able to apply relevant genre knowledge to structuring their LRs in reports, and yet there were still some weaknesses in their writing identified, e.g., the omission of certain essential functional elements. Some of them assumed that the "Overview" and the "Opening" element within the "Review" were overlapping and thereby omitted the latter. Indeed, the "Overview" offered a holistic preview of the content and the structure of subsections, contextualized and justified the research in very general ways while the major purpose of the "Opening" element was to orient the reader to the "Citation" element, a central yet difficult part of the "Review", and it may contain a specific definition and classification. However, while the focus of this study was students' coping strategies in writing LRs of their project reports and their related organizational problems in order to better inform teaching, no specific analytical procedures and criteria were expatiated on how the aforementioned generic structure of LRs were derived.

O'Connell and Jin's (2001) analysis of the rhetorical structure of five dissertation LRs written by Chinese postgraduates studying at British universities and comparison of their structural features with those of an effective LR written by a well-established NS academics was a bold initial attempt, for dissertation LRs are usually quite lengthy, complexly structured and difficult to analyze (Kwan, 2005). However, it is an online source and no details are given about how the structural model for the LR in dissertations they proposed was generated. The only known clue is that they employ "Moves" and "Elements" [first used by Nwogu (1997) and is similar to Bhatia's (2001) "Strategies"] as two-level analytical units for developing their LR model, which is theoretically based on Hoey's (1983) "Problem-Situation-Response-Evaluation", Swales's (1990) move analysis and Dudley-Evans's (1994) "move cycles".

In their LR model, there are five moves: Move 1: Statement of Problem Issues; Move 2: Findings Related to the Problem Issues; Move 3: Critical Analysis of Findings; Move 4: Identification of Gaps; and Move 5: Summation and Transitions to the Next Section. For each of these five moves, there are three to six associated elements, being too complex to detail here. Their analysis of five dissertation LRs written by Chinese postgraduates based on this LR model (which is deduced from the writing of the well-established western academics) revealed both strengths and weaknesses in their writing: like the well-written LR composed by the experienced NS writer, some of the five LRs included the comparison and contrast of previous writers' views and the identified theme at the beginning of the text; however, the major inadequacy in their writing was that none of them had employed an "argument and counter-argument" element in LRs, and they were weak in critically evaluating previous research work and voicing their own arguments. The reason, as they maintained, was that Chinese Confucianism and literary tradition advocate collectivism, collaboration and absolute deference without challenging the authority of ancient works, contradictory to expectations and requirements of the western academic community that values highly individualism and creativity. Although some useful practical implications were obtained from their analysis based on their self-developed LR model, the generation process for the model is not specified, as already mentioned, and the analytical procedure is vague and not sufficiently rigorous.

The most systematic schematic study of LRs thus far is that conducted by Kwan (2005, 2006). She applied a clearly-delineated semantic-functional approach with a coding scheme developed mainly by incorporating step-specific attributes identified in Lewin et al. (2001) and those in many other related genre studies (Anthony, 1999; Bunton, 2002; Kwan, 1996; Melander, 1998; Samraj, 2002; Swales, 1990) to her analysis of the rhetorical structure of LR chapters drawn from 20 ILMRD doctoral theses written by NS students in applied linguistics. The findings were compared with Bunton's (2002) revised CARS model for thesis introductions. As most of the 20 LR chapters embodied an "Introduction-Body-Conclusion" structure, Kwan divided all LR texts into such three parts (viz., "Introduction", "Body" and "Conclusion") accordingly for further analyses. It was observed that the introductory part primarily functions as an advance organizer whereas the concluding text summarizes all discussed content in the chapter and restates the research purpose. The body part is composed of multiple thematic sections, for which Kwan formulated a theme-bound CARS model (Fig. 2.4).

In this model, the two Move 2 sub-moves "*asserting the relevancy of the surveyed claims to one's own research*" and "*abstracting or synthesizing knowledge claims to establish a theoretical position or a theoretical framework*" (as indicated in italics in Fig. 2.4) are new elements identified in her study and apart from these, the remaining elements and the three major moves match with those posited in Bunton's (2002) revised CARS model for thesis introductions. These resemblances support Kwan's (2006: 52) assumption that the introduction chapters and the LR belong to "the genre agnation network (Martin, 1992) or a genre colony of academic research introductions (Bhatia, 2001, 2004)". However, being functionally distinguished, they do not entirely resemble each other in structural terms. The introduction chapter "has a more macro function of creating the research space for the thesis in more general terms"

Move 1	**Establishing one part of the territory of one's own research by**
Strategy A#	surveying the non-research-related phenomena or knowledge claims
Strategy B#	claiming centrality
Strategy C#	surveying the research-related phenomena
Move 2	**Creating a research niche (in response to Move 1) by:**
Strategy A	counter-claiming
Strategy B	gap-indicating
Strategy C	asserting confirmative claims about knowledge or research practices surveyed
Strategy D	*asserting the relevancy of the surveyed claims to one's own research*
Strategy E	*abstracting or synthesizing knowledge claims to establish a theoretical position or a theoretical framework*
Move 3 (optional)	**Occupying the research niche by announcing:**
Strategy A	research aims, focuses, research questions or hypotheses *
Strategy B	theoretical positions/theoretical frameworks*
Strategy C	research design/processes *
Strategy D	Interpretations of terminology used in the thesis *

* *Sub-strategy: justifying or claiming contributions*
# Strategy 1B tends to precede Strategy 1A when the two co-occur.

Fig. 2.4 A move structure for the thematic units in LR chapters (Kwan, 2006: 51)

(Kwan, 2006: 52) while the LR justifies the intended research in a specific manner and usually elaborates upon which aspects the proposed research differentiates from the existing studies. Structurally, the LR is far more complex than the introduction chapter, with "multi-chaptering", "multi-thematic sectioning", and the identified two theme-bound move structures as its major characteristic features. The two contrasting theme-bound move structures identified by Kwan are one more frequently-used linear progression of the three-move theme-bound structure and another less common mode consisting of several recursive cycles of the three-move theme-bound structure.

Another structural difference between thesis introductions [Bunton's (2002) revised CARS model] and thesis LRs is manifested in the new functional elements devised in the above model in Fig. 2.4. Among them, the most salient group is the affirmative strategies (i.e., Strategy C-E in Move 2), which suggest that the research niche can also be created by means of positive evaluations or practices.

Among the three moves, Move 3 was least favored while no move was actually obligatory. Since all constituent elements within each move neither had a 100% occurrence rate nor were sequenced in fixed orders, they only qualified as "Strategy" rather than "Step". The sophistication in the schematic patterning of LRs can be observed throughout the whole revealing process, and one representative revelation was the Move 1-2 pairing identified as the most commonly-used recursive combination configuration.

In brief, as noted already, Kwan's (2005, 2006) study is hitherto the most rigorous and meticulous genre analysis of LRs. Despite examining the rhetorical structure of LRs in theses rather than in RAs, Kwan's self-conceived theme-bound CARS model together with her division of the LR text into the three analytical units (viz., the introductory text, the concluding text, and the body part) will serve as a valuable reference for the present schematic analysis of the LR in ERAs.

The studies of direct relevance to the present research into the structure of LRs in ERAs are Kwan et al. (2012) and Tessuto (2015). While this study focuses on evaluation strategies associated with Move 2 for establishing the niche for the writer's study based on the CARS model and Hunston and Thompson's works on academic evaluations (Hunston, 1993a, b, 2000; Hunston & Thompson, 2000), a genre-based rhetorical structural analysis of LRs of 80 RAs in Information Systems was undertaken. Among these 80 articles, 40 follow a strong behavioral science research (BSR) paradigm and the other 40 show a strong design science research (DSR) paradigm. As assumed and then verified by Kwan et al., LRs in these 80 Information Systems RAs are rhetorically structured around the three moves of Swales's (1990) CARS model, with some new strategies identified, for example, the two DSR-specific Move 1 strategies "Listing Specific Artefacts Developed by Others" and "Listing and Describing Specific Artefacts", Move 2 strategy "Making Inferences", and Move 3 strategies "Making Comparison" and "Describing IT Artefacts". The statistical analysis performed reveals marked cross-paradigm differences in the use of move-specific strategies and the cross-sub-disciplinary qualitative analysis reveals contrasting evaluative entities/propositions and value parameters employed in the evaluations. As the present project is more concerned with the rhetorical structure of LRs, the major findings from the former analysis are reviewed in detail.

Specifically, in the BSR LRs, Move 1 strategies "Reviewing Items of Previous Research" and "Making Topic Generalizations", Move 2 strategies "Indicating a Requirement", "Claiming Relevancy or Importance of a Concept" and "Making Inferences", and Move 3 strategies "Announcing Own Research", "Introducing Variables", "Defining Constructs Used in the Study", "Describing the Research Model" and "Declaring a Thesis/a Hypothesis" have a stronger presence. In contrast, apart from the aforementioned two DSR-specific Move 1 strategies, "Suggesting a Solution" and "Counter-claiming" in Move 2, and "Describing IT Artefacts", "Appraising Own Work", and "Making Comparison" in Move 3 are significantly more often employed in the DSR LRs. The counts of all the other rhetorical strategies identified do not display any significant difference in LRs across the two domains. The different distribution of the strategies in the two sub-corpora can be mainly attributed to their research paradigms. For instance, the more frequent use of "Suggesting a Solution" and "Counter-claiming" in Move 2 in the DSR sub-corpora reflects clearly the problem-solving orientation of this domain, while that of the three evaluation strategies (viz., "Making Inferences", "Counter-claiming" and "Claiming Relevancy or Importance of a Concept") in the BSR LRs indicate an epistemological undertone of enhancing validity and certainty of theoretical modeling of IT-related behaviours.

While Kwan et al. (2012) has specified rhetorical strategies for the three moves used in the LRs of RAs in the two domains of Information Systems and presented cross-domain variations in the distribution of these move-specific strategies, it does not provide further details about the internal arrangement and combination of the moves and strategies. The reason is perhaps that its special focus is on evaluation strategies associated with Move 2 rather than on the entire rhetorical structure of this section. In addition, Kwan et al. have confirmed that the CARS model could be applied to the analysis of LRs in RAs of Information Systems, but whether this can be said of RA LRs in all disciplines remains unknown.

Another recent study that has touched on the structure of the LR section in ERAs is that conducted by Tessuto (2015). Informed by the ESP genre-based approach (Bhatia, 1993, 2004; Swales, 1990, 2004) and the SFL perspective on genre study (Martin, 1992), Tessuto examined the generic structure of 90 empirical law RAs selected from three highly-ranking journals. In this study, one of the ERA component units identified that are not represented in the IMRD model is the LR section (or the "Background Review" section in his words). Although Tessuto commented on the similar purposes of the Background Review section and the Introduction and thus adopted the three-move CARS model (Swales, 1990) to analyze the Background Review section, he did not present any details on the move and step configurations. Nor did he provide any information on the sequences and arrangement of these elements. Instead, he only presented quantitative findings on the use of each move and step: the three moves all occur in 88% of the ERAs examined and the step occurrence rates range from 29 to 61%. The only new element identified in the Background Review section seems to be Step 12A "Defining and Developing Methods, Theories, Concepts, Issues, Phenomena" in Move 3. However, no detailed explanation has been provided on this element. Hence, we still do not have clear ideas about the detailed internal structure of the LR section in ERAs and there is obviously a scarcity of research in this regard. In view of these gaps, a close examination of the rhetorical structure of LRs in CE and AL ERAs and the concerning cross-disciplinary variations in this study is of great significance.

As the introductory part is the primary site for introducing and reporting prior scholarship within the RA context, the use of citation in its two possible constituent units (viz., the Introduction and LR sections) is another major concern of the study, in addition to the detailed move and step analysis of its structure. The next section therefore gives an account of citation use in academic discourse (particularly in RAs as a special genre).

2.5 Citation Use in Academic Discourse

As an essential feature of contemporary published writing, the increasing use of citations over the years (Bazerman, 1988) reflects the booming academic world. Citations are generally considered as an effective means to trace the evolution of a research topic or a discipline. The quantified citation index is extensively applied as a "scientific" yardstick to measure the value of the research output of an individual, institution or the nation as a whole (Swales, 1986). However, as there exist negative citations and perfunctory citations, the validity of citing rates as an evaluation criterion is open to question. Hence, the use of citations in the texts in terms of their forms, classification, quality and functions has become a great concern of many analysts from all the aforementioned three disciplines. The subsections below review the literature on the following aspects of citations—citation forms (Sect. 2.5.1), citation signals (Sect. 2.5.2), citation functions (Sect. 2.5.3), and actual citation practices of diverse groups of writers working on different academic genres (Sect. 2.5.4).

2.5.1 Citation Forms

In terms of citation typology, citations can be classified on both formal/grammatical and functional parameters, namely, citation forms and citation functions (Petrić, 2007).

Citation forms as an important parameter of citation research can reflect the writer's stance or attitude towards the reported author or information (Sun, 2008; Yeh, 2010). The choice of different types of citation forms is a strategic rhetorical activity, influenced by a range of factors such as disciplinary conventions, the nature of the research, generic citation rules, the writer's rhetorical purpose, the theme of the sentence or the topic of the paragraph as well as the communicative function of the genre and its part-genre (Charles, 2006a; Hawes & Thomas, 1997). This sub-section reviews the typologies of citation forms proposed in the literature and relevant studies on inter-disciplinary differences, cross-generic variations and novice writers' difficulties in the choice of citation forms in academic writing.

On the basis of Moravcsik and Murugesan's (1975) framework, Swales (1986) proposed a characteristic scheme to categorize citations: A. short/extensive; B. evolutionary/juxtapositional/zero; C. confirmative/negational/zero. The latter two were more concerned with the semantic and content aspect of citational statements while the first category related to the form (length) of citation. As their names indicated, the extensive citation could extend over several sentences while the short citation was basically one sentence long or even shorter. Notwithstanding the apparent ease in operationalizing it, the first binary category did not have much application in later research due to its seemingly insignificant pedagogical value.

Swales's categorizations of citation forms proposed in 1981 and 1990 are more influential. However, they were always presented and discussed within a specific move or step of the introduction section by Swales (1981, 1990), i.e., the illustration and exposition of them was respectively confined to Move 2 of his 1981 four-part schema "Summarizing Previous Research" and Step 3 of Move 1 in his 1990 CARS model "Reviewing Items of Previous Research". Nevertheless, he acknowledged Samraj's (2002) important finding that referencing the previous research can indeed appear throughout the whole introduction or the entire RA in his 2004 R-CARS framework. According to Swales (1981: 41), there was a distinction in this move "Summarizing Previous Research" between three kinds of references to previous researchers on the basis of "author orientation", which have been termed as Strong Author Orientation (A-type), Weak Author Orientation (B-type) and Subject Orientation (C-type). The former two categories were usually marked by the use of the RV, contrasting with the absence of it in the final category. Therefore, the last category was characterized by its "Non-reporting Style" while the former two by their eminent "Reporting Style" (Swales, 1981: 41). Swales's dichotomy ("Reporting Style" vis-à-vis "Non-reporting Style") offered a basic template for much later research (e.g., Jacoby, 1987; Pickard, 1995; Shaw, 1992; Thompson, 2001).

In terms of their tense usage, Swales (1981) maintained that A-types are more associated with the past tense, B-types more with the perfective tense and C-types more with the present tense. Admittedly, this is a general statistical tendency rather than a stipulated rule; however, it has been largely corroborated in research papers from the hard-science discipline at least (Swales, 1981). In addition, B-types are more likely to refer to a broader range of previous research (than A-types), hence the perfective tense with a higher degree of generality is often used for this category (Swales, 1981). Nonetheless, in research writing practice, the relationship between citation forms and their tense choices is much more flexible and complicated than delineated here (Oster, 1981).

The above three categories outlined by Swales (1981) embodied some limitations in accounting for forms of citations in literary research papers (Jacoby, 1987). For example, four of six texts Jacoby examined did not use Harvard parenthetical system but the footnote/endnote format, which posed problems to Swales's (1981) categorization framework. Furthermore, she added another two categories (viz., "Summary

References" and "Contrastive Existential Orientation") and renamed Swales's (1981) "Subject Orientation" as "Existential Orientation" in order to capture the relationship between the authorial assertion and the previous research, and differentiate references to individual studies from those to consensus views in the discipline. In Jacoby's (1987) analysis of six literary RAs, she found Strong Author Orientation to be the most frequently used citation form, indicating that literary RAs gave more prominence to cited researchers rather than their research or findings. This may contradict with Swales's (1981) conclusion from his analysis that literary RAs lay more emphasis on previous research than their counterparts from other science or social science disciplines (Jacoby, 1987).

Prompted by Jacoby's (1987) criticisms, Swales (1990: 141) modified his categorization by reclassifying citation forms in a more general way into two types (viz., *integral* and *non-integral* citations). Integral citations are those where the name of the cited researcher appears in the referenced statement as a grammatical element while non-integral citations are those where references are made to the researcher in a parenthesis or by other means such as the use of a superscript number (Swales, 1990). The binary citation forms are most advantageous in their strong discriminatory power (Swales, 1990) and relative ease to work with. As sensibly commented by White (2004), working on this dichotomy primarily entails analysts' grammatical knowledge rather than any specialized domain knowledge. Thus, this classification is well-accepted and has been applied to much follow-up research such as Hyland (1999, 2002), Thompson (2001, 2005), Thompson and Tribble (2001), Mansourizadeh and Ahmad (2011), Jalilifar (2012), Samraj (2013) and Swales (2014). Admittedly, the most salient difference between the integral and the non-integral citations is formal. However, they do manifest contrasting functional emphases (Thompson, 2001): the former places more emphasis on the individual who has contributed the idea, the information or conducted the research, while the latter concentrates more on the proposition or the cited content (Hyland, 1999, 2002). A useful similar comment by Weissberg and Buker (1990: 44) is that they are respectively "author prominent" and "information prominent".

Drawing on Swales' (1990) seminal dichotomy, a number of previous studies have examined cross-disciplinary variations in the choice of citation forms in academic writing. For example, Hyland (1999) explored disciplinary differences in 80 RAs from eight subjects in terms of citation use. One of his findings was that non-integral citations have been prominently used in seven disciplines but not in philosophy, which is featured by its frequent employment of elaborate narratives that may involve many arguments of other scholars. In some science disciplines such as physics, research writers often employ numerical endnote systems in citing others' work as required by journals (Hyland, 1999). This leads to a significant reduction in the use of integral citations in their writing, an insightful viewpoint favored by Swales (1990) as well. However, the citation convention (the author/date convention vs. the number/endnote convention) is not the only factor behind the preponderance of either citation form. Charles (2006a) even demonstrated that there was no direct correlation between the number/footnote convention and the use of non-integral citations, and that between the author/date convention and the use of integral citations, since six out of seven theses from politics/international relations with the number/footnote citation convention unexpectedly had greater use of integral citations, and out of six theses from materials science with the author/date citation convention, one used equal amounts of integral and non-integral citations and two displayed low use of integral citations. As Charles (2006a: 317) explained, the selection of integral and non-integral citations is a complicated rhetorical act that may involve multiple factors such as "citation convention, genre, discipline and individual study type".

In Hyland's (1999) study of ten RAs from AL, it was found that the number of non-integral citations used far exceeded that of integral (65.6: 34.4 non-integral: integral). This preference of applied linguists for using non-integral citations was also reported in Yeh (2010), who however observed that Taiwanese applied linguists employed slightly fewer non-integral citations than their international colleagues (60.3% vs. 66.9%). In marked contrast, Pickard (1995) observed higher integral citation use (58: 42 integral: non-integral) in the eleven RAs published in *Hong Kong Papers in Linguistics and Language Teaching*. However, she did not provide specific reasons for it, and only regarded the citation patterns used by expert writers as models for student writers.

While Hyland (1999) discovered a common tendency for academics to use more non-integral citations in seven out of the eight disciplines selected, Thompson (2001) and Thompson and Tribble (2001) underlined important disciplinary variations in the use of citation forms in 16 theses from two contrasting disciplines (viz., Agricultural Botany and Agricultural Economics): academics from the former discipline preferred using non-integral citations whereas integral citations were favored by those from the latter discipline. Thompson (2001) and Thompson and Tribble (2001) attributed this to the different nature and lengths of the two genres: there could be more chances for the Agricultural Economics thesis writers to refer to previous literature in a more elaborate way with the cited author more often foregrounded than those article writers in Hyland's (1999) study. Another explanation is that between the two disciplines examined (Thompson, 2001; Thompson & Tribble, 2001), Agricultural Economics is of a more discursive nature, and this probably contributed to the writers' preferences for more prominence to the reported author in referencing.

To further explore the more subtle and in-depth differences in forms of citations employed by the thesis writers, Thompson and Tribble (2001), Thompson (2001) and Thompson (2005) extended Swales's (1990) binomial classification of citation forms into more sensitive schemes: **integral citations** were subdivided into three types: *verb-controlling*, where there is a lexical verb (frequently being RVs) in either passive or active voices to report the cited proposition; *naming*, where citations are represented as a noun phase or part of a noun phrase; and *non-citation*, where references are made to researchers without the publication year. **Non-integral citations** were further classified into *source*, which attributes the cited information or idea to a predecessor; *identification*, which makes the agent of the cited research action prominent and explicit; *reference*, which refers the reader to other texts where further and more complete information can be found by the frequent use of the directive "see"; and *origin*, which indicates the origin of the cited concept, theory, and technique. In addition to these four sub-types of non-integral citations proposed and analyzed by Thompson and Tribble (2001) and Thompson (2001, 2005), formulated another sub-category: *example*, which lists instances of studies that are referred to in the text sometimes with the use of typical markers such as "e.g." and "for example". This sub-category has been adopted and rephrased into "*exemplification*" in Petrić's (2007) comparative study of rhetorical functions of citations in high-rated and low-rated theses, as will be reviewed in detail in Sect. 2.5.3. However, these newly-developed and slightly different schemes further classified integral and non-integral citations on the basis of distinct criteria: integral citations on the formal/grammatical criterion; non-integral citations on the functional criterion (Mansourizadeh & Ahmad, 2011; Petrić, 2007). As a result, some recent functional studies of citations (Mansourizadeh & Ahmad, 2011; Petrić, 2007, see Sect. 2.5.3) extended such functional subcategories of non-integral citations to their analyses of all forms of citations in terms of their rhetorical functions in the discourse, including both integral and non-integral types.

By applying their proposed schemes of citation forms, Thompson and Tribble (2001) and Thompson (2001) further revealed more subtle inter-disciplinary, intra-disciplinary and cross-generic differences in their use, in addition to variations in using a particular type of the binary citation form by doctoral degree thesis writers from the two aforementioned disciplines (Agricultural Botany vs. Agricultural Economics). First of all, it was shown that Agricultural Botany thesis writers made far more frequent use of the non-integral *source* and *identification* citations whereas their counterparts in the field of Agricultural Economics favored integral *naming* types. Despite this preference of Agricultural Botany thesis writers, there remained a category of thesis in this field that had the prevalent use of integral verb-controlling citations (see Thompson & Tribble, 2001). By focusing only on the same eight theses in Agricultural Botany, Thompson (2005) noted that the patterned use of citation types in six out of the eight theses conformed to this tendency with only two exceptional cases identified which had the more frequent use of integral citations; in terms of the cross-generic differences, the Introduction and Discussion chapters were two part-genres of the thesis with the densest use of citations, in contrast to the Methods and Results chapters which had sparse referencing. The general tendency was that far more non-integral citations (*source* and *identification*) were used in the Introduction and Discussion chapters with *verb-controlling* integral citations occasionally used. Most of the citations employed in the Methods and Results chapters were also non-integral types (i.e., *reference* and *origin* in the Methods chapter and *source* in the Results chapter). Regarding the use of the integral *naming* citations, Agricultural Economics thesis writers employed over four times more of them than their colleagues in the discipline of Agricultural Botany did. Moreover, within the particular type of Preposition+Naming citations, the pattern "in X (Publication Year)" was far more frequently used in Agricultural Economics theses while another two patterns "of X (Publication Year)" and "by X (Publication Year)" were preferred in Agricultural Botany theses. Thompson and Tribble (2001) attributed this difference to the fact that Agricultural Botany writers were more concerned with scientific research activities whereas Agricultural Economics writers were more interested in specific prior texts and diverse concepts.

Both Samraj (2013) and Jalilifar (2012) adopted a cross-generic perspective to examine citation use in thesis and RA corresponding sections, but they yielded quite different findings. While Samraj revealed an overwhelming use of non-integral citations in discussion sections of both master's theses and RAs in biology, Jalilifar reported a significantly lower use of non-integral citations in M.A. thesis introductions and no significant differences in the quantitative use of integral versus non-integral citations in RA introductions in AL. However, in terms of the use of sub-types of the two citation forms, the two studies obtained similar findings: *source* citations were consistently found to be the most frequently used non-integral type, followed by *identifying* citations and then by *reference* citations; among integral citation sub-categories, the *verb-controlling* type remained being most preferred and the *naming* type occurred as the second most frequently used type. Compared with published writers, student writers tended to use integral citations more frequently in both studies, suggesting their preference for granting prominence to individual authors. Jalilifar attributed this disparate preference between student and published writers to their different knowledge about and experience of citation use in producing the two contrasting genres (i.e., theses and RAs) and student writers' focus on linguistic and grammatical features of theses whilst ignoring functional characteristics. However, student writers' preference for the use of integral citations has not been found in Swales (2014), who instead observed a percentual ratio of 73–27% for the use of non-integral versus integral citations in student papers in biology. Swales's finding seems to parallel Hyland's (1999) (viz., 90–10% found for published RAs in biology), indicating the more expert-like citation practices of the final year undergraduate and postgraduate student writers in Swales's study. On the other hand, the choice of citation forms is related to other factors, e.g., the length of the genre exemplar and novice writers' acquisition order of the two citation forms—"when students first learn to use references in their academic writing, they will be using integral forms" (Swales, 2014: 137) which may account for their preferential use of integral citations in degree theses as revealed by Samraj (2013) and Jalilifar (2012).

In addition to the above-mentioned inter-disciplinary, intra-disciplinary and cross-generic differences, scholarly attention has also been devoted to features of or existing problems in apprentice writers' or L2 research writers' use of citation forms in their academic writing. For example, Sun (2008) revealed that integral/reporting citations with cited authors as the grammatical subject were predominantly used by Chinese M.A. students in their thesis introductions. Their strong preferences for this citation form over others, claimed Sun (2008: 14), presumably "reflected students' lack of language variance". However, this assumption is open to doubt, as in Charles's (2006a) study of reporting clauses in theses written by native speakers, the integral citation with a human subject was also found to be the most frequently used pattern in their writing. Furthermore, Charles outlined some advantages of using this pattern, e.g., allowing research writers to freely and flexibly comment on individual research and researchers, which seemed to be a plausible explanation for the dominant use of this pattern. In Jiang's (2005) contrastive study of M.A. theses by L1 students and Chinese students in terms of citation use, she categorized citation forms into *integral, non-integral, non-citation, stative reporting, source reporting, elaborated reporting* and *quotation*. Based on this framework, she found that Chinese students generally used integral reporting while L1 students preferred non-integral reporting, which (as she assumed) might indicate that L1 students concentrated on previous findings or research whereas Chinese students paid more attention to the one who conducted the research. This perhaps resulted from cultural and ideological differences.

However, in Mansourizadeh and Ahmad's (2011) study of citation use in NNS expert and novice writing in chemical engineering, the novice NNS writers frequently used integral citations to compare their findings with others' while the seasoned NNS writers employed both types in their comparisons. Furthermore, the apprentice NNS writers used five times more of integral-verb controlling citations than integral-naming citations, which entailed more complex rhetorical and language skills. In contrast, the NNS expert writers had more even use of these two sub-types of integral citations. The above-mentioned differences reflected some weaknesses in novice writing, even though it was similarly featured by the overall greater use of non-integral citations (like expert writing), which might be a common characteristic of engineering RA writing.

In sum, most research into the use of citation forms has focused on either cross-disciplinary variations (e.g., Hyland, 1999, 2000, 2002) or apprentice writers' difficulties (e.g., Jiang, 2005; Mansourizadeh & Ahmad, 2011; Sun, 2008) while that on cross-generic variations is still somewhat limited. This constitutes one of the motivations for the present study.

2.5.2 Reporting Verbs

Closely related to citation forms are citation structures and components, among which citation signals are of particular interest to this study. According to Thompson (1994: 32), "a typical report structure consists of a reporting signal and a message." Reporting signals, or citation signals, are various, consisting of finite verbs (Hyland, 1999, 2000, 2002; Thompson & Ye, 1991), present participles, past participles, reporting adjuncts (Tadros, 1985), reporting nouns (Thompson, 1994), reporting adjectives and reporting clauses (Charles, 2006a, b).

Though studies in this area are relatively abundant, most of them focus on RVs. RVs, among the above-mentioned varied citation elements, are perhaps the most prominent reporting device and one of the clearest signals of attribution and the presence of (negative, neutral and positive) evaluation (Thompson & Ye, 1991). As one focus of this study, RVs are defined as the verbs that are used to report (and evaluate) the previous literature in any sentence that can be regarded as an actual citation.

In the ESP literature, RVs have been investigated from diverse perspectives: the use of tense (Lackstrom, Selinker, & Trimble, 1972, 1973; Malcolm, 1987; Oster, 1981; Salager-Meyer, 1992); the interaction between tense and voice (Hanania & Akhtar, 1985; Hawes & Thomas, 1997; Shaw, 1992); their roles in signaling evaluation (Hyland, 1999, 2000, 2002; Thompson, 1994; Thompson & Ye, 1991); the semantics of RVs and their discoursal function (Thomas & Hawes, 1994); and variations in the use of RVs across disciplines (Hyland, 1999, 2000, 2002; Thompson, 2001) and across different groups of writers (Neff et al., 2003). However, a close analysis of these studies reveals that the use of RVs has frequently been examined within the entire RA (e.g., Hyland, 1999, 2002) and rarely in its part-genres. Indeed, in this regard, more than a decade ago, Hyland (1999) pointed to the need for more research into variations in the use of RVs in subgenres, a fascinating point to be addressed in the present study.

Roughly in accordance with the evolution in approaches to reporting, RVs have been first examined in terms of their formal features (e.g., tense, aspect and voice) (Een, 1982; Oster, 1981; Swales, 1981, 1990) primarily with grammatical approaches, and later, increasing attention of citation researchers shifted to their semantic and functional aspects for such aspects are recognized as a major source of difficulties in apprentice writers' use of RVs in academic writing (Thompson & Ye, 1991).

In referenced statements, three tenses—the past, the present perfect and the present simple—can together account for more than 90% of all their finite verb usage (Swales, 1990). Swales (1990) summarized three main lines of early research into the tense use of citations: (1) "general rules" for the above-mentioned three tenses primarily related to time-lines and proximity of the reported message (Ard, 1985; Celce-Murcia and Larsen-freeman, 1983; Comrie, 1985); (2) more specific rhetorical concerns with tense meaning of citations in terms of degrees of their "generality" and "relevance" (Lackstrom et al., 1972; Oster, 1981); and (3) the third approach pointing to the way for introducing citation statements and their placement as major factors influencing tense/aspect use of citations (Een, 1982; Swales, 1981, 1990).

Given that tense usage is highly indicative of writers' stances towards the cited text or work, as well as the distance and relevance of reported messages to the present research, both "general rules" and "specific ones" are important and need to be taken into careful account in selecting tenses for citation statements (Swales, 1990: 153). In general, tense choices ranging from present to present perfect and then to past manifest a cline of increasing distance of the reported message to the present research. By investigating only two chemical engineering RAs, Oster (1981) formulated his hypotheses about tense use of citations as follows:

1. **The present perfect** commonly suggests generality about previous literature or continued discussions;
2. **The past simple** commonly indicates non-generality about previous literature or can refer to quantitative findings of previous research that could not lend support to the present study;
3. **The present simple** can refer to (instead of discussing) quantitative findings of previous research that countenance the present study or are irrelevant.

(Oster, 1981)

Although Swales (1981) could not verify Oster's (1981) claim that the present perfect could act as a grammatical signal for continued discussions in his data, Shaw (1992) found that non-integral citations where the present perfect verb in the passive is used would usually present generalizations that would be further expounded in subsequent sentences.

Another function of the present perfect tense, as outlined above by Oster (1981), was to indicate generality, contrasting with that of the past simple to suggest non-generality. This is generally in line with Lackstrom et al.'s (1972) finding that the present perfect tense generalizes previous literature whereas the past tense implies specificity in information to be reported with the present simple commonly making general claims. Indeed, Malcolm (1987) formulated similar hypotheses as well:

1. **The present tense** tends to be used in making generalizations.
2. **The past tense** tends to be used in reporting specific or individual previous studies.
3. **The present perfect** tends to be used in referring to the area under research.

Both her first and third hypotheses were validated as 74% true in her sample whereas the second hypothesis was 61% true. This generally conforms to Een's (1982) corollary that the tense usage in integral reporting citations is most varied with only half of all instances in his sample using the expected simple past tense. Swales (1990) attributed this to writers' possible preferences for strategically manipulating tense usages in reporting individual studies and their findings.

In correlating discourse functions of citations with their tense and aspect use, Hawes and Thomas (1997: 393) concluded that the integral reporting citations with RVs in the past tense tend to "provide particulars for a preceding generalization or the basis for a claim", citations with verbs in the present perfect tense claims high relevance of prior research to the present study and those with verbs in the present tense display a particular discourse function of "communicating generalized interpretations/conclusions" as well as suggesting the writers' commitment to the cited message. These conclusions are largely consistent with Malcolm's (1987) hypotheses. Along with these works, in Shaw's (1992) detailed examination of the interrelationship between the tense and voice of RVs and sentence functions, it was found that the voice selection and change was mainly decided by the higher-level discourse arrangement such as coherence and cohesion, the theme-rheme choice and information structure of the text. As such, making a sound choice of grammatical features of RVs (mainly their tenses and voices) involves taking a broad variety of factors into consideration, such as temporal distance, discoursal context, sentence function, and writers' rhetorical intentions.

The tense use of RVs has hitherto far more frequently been examined in scientific texts than in social sciences and humanities ones, as rightly pointed out by Thompson (2001). Despite this, extant research (Hawes & Thomas, 1997; Thompson, 2001) has proffered some significant findings as follows. Based upon eleven RAs from psychosomatic medicine, Hawes and Thomas (1997) observed that the preferred choices for the tense and aspect of referenced statements were the past simple tense and the present perfect tense, both being mainly in the active form. This finding has been in great part supported by that of Swales's (1981) research where in most of the cases he examined, the RVs were in the past tense with a minority in the perfective aspect. However, Thompson (2001) revealed partly different findings in his tense and voice data of RVs in two contrasting disciplines: Agricultural Botany thesis writers preferred past simple tense of RVs while Agricultural and Food Economics writers mostly favored present simple. Nevertheless, thesis writers from both disciplines preferred active voice to passive voice in their use of RVs. This disciplinary variation in tense use of RVs, like that in the use of citation forms (Sect. 2.5.1), was again attributed to the more discursive disciplinary nature of Agricultural and Food Economics in contrast to the more "experimental" nature of Agricultural Botany (where the thesis was likened to "the lens through which research work is seen" by a supervisor interviewed) (Thompson, 2001: 193).

In addition to tense choices, the classification of RVs regarding their denotative meaning and evaluation has also attracted considerable scholarly attention. Inspired by the concerns about student writers' difficulties in taking appropriate stances towards their cited propositional content with different sets of RVs, Thompson and Ye (1991) collected RVs from around 100 RA introductions in a variety of disciplines (e.g., AL, geology, public administration, engineering, and veterinary science) and for the first time systematically classified all RVs identified in terms of their denotation and evaluative potential (Fig. 2.5).

Dealing with "double voices" involved in the reporting act (Baynham, 1999; Groom, 2000), Thompson and Ye (1991) creatively made the useful distinction of the source of evaluation between the reported *author* and the reporting *writer*, which has been adopted by later researchers (Hyland, 1999, 2000, 2002) and will be maintained in the present study. The reporting *writer* refers to the writer of the present text; the reported *author* is the original owner and creator of the information or idea cited by the writer. Correspondingly, there are chiefly two denotation categories of RVs: Author act RVs and Writer act RVs. The former category involves "the existence of the author's text, to a more or less explicit degree… the responsibility for the process is ascribed to the author" while the latter refers to "processes for which responsibility is ascribed, as it were, covertly to the reporting writer" (Thompson and Ye, 1991: 370). Author act RVs are further classified into three subcategories according to the different nature of processes involved: **Textual** verbs (verbs referring to the process where verbal expression is essential, e.g., *state, write, term, challenge, underline, point out, name, deny*); **Mental** verbs (verbs mainly involving a cognitive

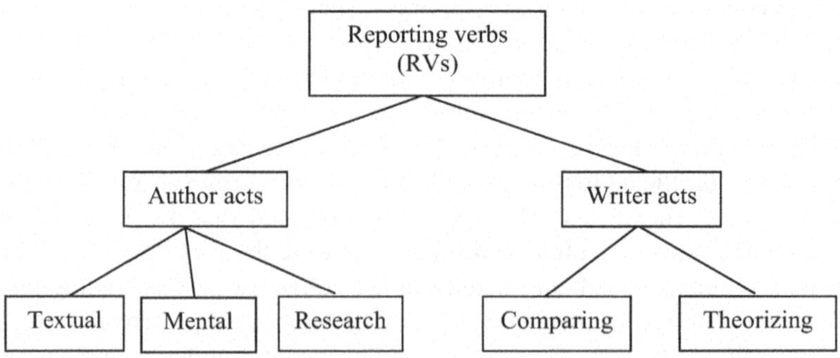

Fig. 2.5 Categorization of RVs in terms of denotation (Thompson & Ye, 1991: 372)

process, e.g., *believe, think, focus on, consider, prefer*); and **Research** verbs (verbs indicating either the physical or mental process involved in the research work, e.g., *measure, calculate, quantify, obtain, find*). As for Writer act RVs, there are two subtypes: **Comparing** verbs (verbs showing writers' views of the author's work within a certain disciplinary framework by means of comparison or contrast, e.g., *correspond to, accord with, anticipate, contrast with*) and **Theorizing** verbs (verbs suggesting the use made by the writer of the author's work in his/her own developing argument, e.g., *account for, explain, support*).

In terms of the evaluation categories of RVs, Thompson and Ye (1991: 372) provided a three-layer approach to show the important features of evaluation in RVs. The three approaches are termed **Author's stance** (**Positive, Negative and Neutral**), **Writer's stance** (**Factive, Counter-factive and Non-factive**) and **Writer's interpretation** (**Author's discourse interpretation, Author's behavior interpretation, Status interpretation and Non-interpretation**). The first two categories respectively indicate the authors' and the writers' views of the validity of the reported information and "Writer's interpretation, on the other hand, is related to various aspects of the status of the proposition". (Thompson & Ye, 1991: 373). The options under each category are encapsulated within the parentheses, and as noted, there are altogether as many as ten subcategories with possible overlap between them (Hyland, 2002), constituting a rather complicated system that could not be easily applied to the real analysis of RVs. Overall, although Thompson and Ye's (1991) pioneering work in classifying RVs embodied high rationality, yet was not watertight as they acknowledged.

However, Thompson and Ye's (1991) classification framework has inspired and served as an important stepping stone for subsequent research (Hyland, 1999, 2000, 2002; Thomas & Hawes, 1994). Based on only 11 RAs on psychosomatic medicine, Thomas and Hawes (1994) proposed a refined taxonomy of RVs. According to their taxonomy, there are three major groups of RVs: **Real-World or Experimental Activity RVs**, **Discourse Activity RVs** and **Cognition Activity RVs**, which respectively coincide with Research RVs, Textual RVs and Mental RVs in Thompson and Ye's classification scheme, as they themselves conceded. **Real-World or Experimental Activity RVs** (**Procedure verbs** and **Findings verbs**) and **Discourse Activity RVs** (**Qualification verbs**, **Tentativity verbs** and **Certainty verbs**) are further categorized by Thomas and Hawes into different sub-types as indicated within the above two pairs of parentheses, most of which however contain even finer sub-categories. This suggests that Thomas and Hawes's taxonomy is fine-grained, multi-layered, and even more complex than Thompson and Ye's in this regard. However, their scheme neither offers an explicit description of the evaluative potentials of RVs, nor always clearly distinguishes between the reported author and the reporting writer in terms of the source of the evaluation (Hyland, 2002).

By overcoming the aforementioned limitations of Thompson and Ye's (1991) and Thomas and Hawes's (1994) classification frameworks and incorporating his own observations of the data, Hyland (1999) proposed his modified taxonomy of RVs. He explicitly classified RVs in terms of their process and evaluative functions. According to their different process functions/denotation, RVs are categorized into three groups:

Research Acts verbs (which are primarily concerned with experimental actions or procedures, e.g., *observe, discover, notice, show, analyze, calculate, assay, explore, plot*, and *recover*), **Cognition/Mental Acts verbs** (which represent mental activities of researchers, e.g., *believe, conceptualize, suspect, assume,* and *view*) and **Discourse Acts verbs** (which are concerned with the verbal expression of research or cognitive activities, e.g., *ascribe, discuss, hypothesis, report,* and *state*) (Fig. 2.6). The three categories are similar to those in Thomas and Hawes (i.e., Experimental Activities RVs, Cognition Activities RVs and Discourse Activities RVs) and Thompson and Ye (i.e., Research RVs, Mental RVs and Textual RVs), and will be adopted in this study. However, RVs can not only refer to different types of activities, but the state (existence, development, etc.) of some phenomena, theories or other things in citations (e.g., appear, become, exist, remain, retain, occur, etc.). This particular category termed "Stative RVs" will be added to my analytical framework (see Fig. 2.6).

Hyland (1999) also clearly classified RVs from both the writers' and the authors' perspectives in terms of their evaluation (see Fig. 2.7). As Hyland explained:

> The writer may present the reported information as **true** (acknowledge, point out, establish), as **false** (fail, overlook, exaggerate, ignore) or **non-factively**, giving no clear signal. This option allows the writer to ascribe a view to the source author, reporting him or her as **positive**

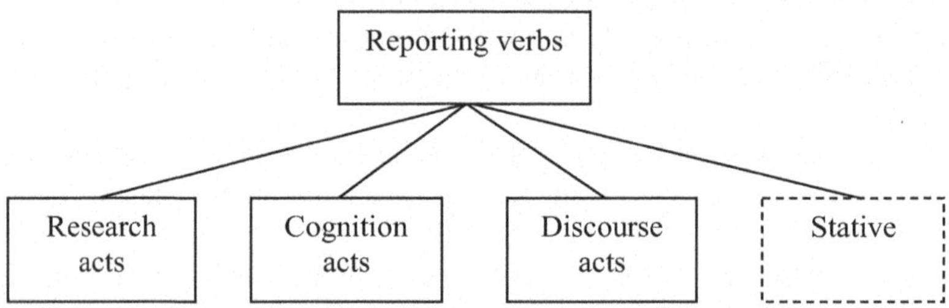

Fig. 2.6 Categorization of RVs in term of denotation (a modified version of Hyland, 1999)

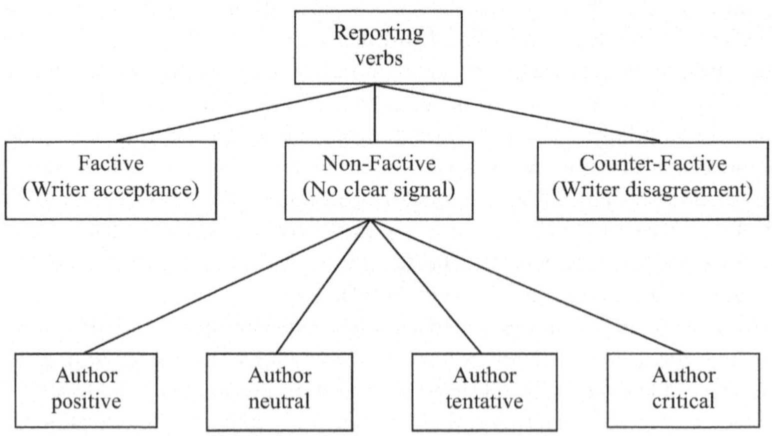

Fig. 2.7 Categorization of RVs in term of evaluation (Hyland, 1999: 350)

(advocate, argue, hold, see), **neutral** (address, cite, comment, look at), **tentative** (allude to, believe, hypothesize, suggest) or **critical** (attack, condemn, object, refuse). (Hyland, 1999: 350)

Given that Hyland's classification framework of RVs seems to be more clear-cut and easy to apply, a modified version of it will serve as the basis of my analysis of RVs. In other words, Hyland's taxonomy of RVs with a new category ("Stative RVs") added in terms of their denotation will be the analytical framework of the present research into the use of RVs in the introductory phase of 60 ERAs (see Figs. 2.6 and 2.7).

Previous studies have highlighted considerable difficulties encountered by novice writers (especially those NNS writers) (Jiang, 2005; Lang, 2004; Neff et al., 2003; Pickard, 1995; Sun, 2008) and disciplinary variations (Hunston, 1995; Hyland, 1999, 2000, 2002; Thompson, 2001) in the use of RVs with various functions. The problematic aspects in apprentice (L2) writers' use of RVs with different functions include (but are not confined to): the excessive use of RVs with the simple illocutionary force such as "*say*" (Jiang, 2005; Lang, 2004; Neff et al., 2003; Pickard, 1995), the employment of a narrow range of RVs (Jiang, 2005; Neff et al., 2003; Sun, 2008), their unawareness and/or incomprehension of subtle differences between RVs with partly similar semantic meanings such as *show*, *display* and *exhibit* (Lang, 2004), and their inability in taking proper stances towards the source text with RVs of different evaluative functions (Jiang, 2005; Lang, 2004; Sun, 2008). Possible contributing factors of these problems may be the negative transfer of L1 (Jiang, 2005), their low overall English language proficiency and small vocabulary sizes (Pickard, 1995), and their lack of awareness, knowledge and related skills of exploiting an adequately wide range of RVs with their varied semantic denotation and evaluative functions (Lang, 2004; Pickard, 1995).

Concerning disciplinary variations in the use of RVs, researchers in the hard sciences commonly employ a restricted repertoire of RVs (Hyland, 1999; Martinez, 2008) whereas those from more discursive disciplines (e.g., history) use a wider range of RVs (Hunston, 1995). According to Hyland (1999), this can be attributed to disparate structures of knowledge systems and epistemological traditions in the hard and soft disciplines. For instance, in scientific and engineering disciplines, there is a large amount of knowledge that has been traditionally shared and accumulated linearly. Therefore, research writers from these disciplines usually do not need to devote considerable rhetorical efforts in these aspects in their writing.

Apparent disciplinary variations in the use of RVs with diverse functions have also been noted by previous researchers such as Hyland (1999, 2000, and 2002) and Thompson (2001). Hyland revealed that Discourse Activity verbs were more frequently used in the soft disciplines such as sociology and AL than in the hard disciplines, while Research Acts verbs were more favored by academics in the fields of engineering and sciences. The writers in the field of marketing had strong preferences for Author Tentative verbs such as *suggest*. Moreover, he found that rather than directly voicing their stance towards the cited information, research writers in all disciplines preferred to indicate their positions by ascribing an attitude to authors. As a consequence, there was a higher occurrence of Writers' Non-Factive verbs in all the 80 RAs examined. Consistent with Hyland's findings, Thompson observed the preferences of Agricultural Botany thesis writers for Research RVs [using Thompson and Ye's (1991) terminology] contrasting with those of Agricultural Economics writers for Discourse and Mental RVs. Their divided preferences corresponded to their respective disciplinary nature: Agricultural Botany as an applied science discipline is grounded more on experimental or field research work whereas Agricultural Economics as an applied social science discipline is more reliant on discoursal activities and textual arguments (Thompson, 2001).

2.5.3 Citation Functions

Having evolved to be an almost "defining feature" of academic writing (Hyland, 2002: 115), citation is by no means a simple, mechanical act of formatting references by consistently abiding by a certain type of well-established referencing system as specified in style manuals to avoid serious plagiarism charges. Neither is it simply a decorative rhetorical device that marks modern scholarly writing. It is a strategic, complicated rhetorical activity shaped by a multitude of social, institutional, generic and private factors, to name just a few (Harwood, 2004).

The multiple functions of citations and complexities of the citing behavior have been increasingly recognized by analysts from three research camps: information science (Bornmann & Daniel, 2008; White, 2004), sociology of science (Bazerman, 1988; Becher, 1989; Kaplan, 1965; Latour & Woolgar, 1979; Myers, 1990) and AL (among others, Harwood, 2004, 2009; Harwood & Petrić, 2012; Martinez, 2008; Petrić, 2007). For many information scientists (e.g., Brooks, 1985; Chubin & Moitra, 1975; Vinkler, 1987), the lingering doubt about the validity of the evaluative citation analysis by means of citation indices stimulates their interests in content analysis of citations. Sociologists are more concerned with how social, cultural and disciplinary traditions and situational factors influence academic referencing behaviors (Mansourizadeh & Ahmad, 2011). Applied linguists have long focused on formal/grammatical features of citations, e.g., citation forms (Swales, 1986, 1990; Thompson, 2001, 2005; Thompson & Tribble, 2001), and citation structural elements such as RVs (Hyland, 1999, 2000, 2002; Thompson & Ye, 1991) and reporting clauses (Charles, 2006a, b), with far less scholarly attention paid to pragmatic purposes and rhetorical functions of citations until fairly recently (e.g., Harwood, 2004, 2009; Harwood & Petrić, 2012; Petrić, 2007; Samraj, 2013). The insights drawn from this particular body of research (into motivations/functions of citations) mostly conducted in information science and sociology of science may however illuminate current EAP literacy education, since they can be used to induct the apprentice writers into conscious and purposeful citation practices for which various social and personal factors need to be fully considered (Harwood, 2004).

Traditionally, there are two contrasting views of citations: the normative/reward hypothesis advocated by information scientists and the rhetorical/persuasion hypothesis by sociologists of scientific knowledge (Harwood, 2004; White, 2004). The former suggests that the overarching aim of citations is to acknowledge the indebtedness to the creator and the original owner of the borrowed ideas or words. In this normative view, "citation is above all an ethical practice" (Harwood, 2004: 81). In contrast, the latter argues that the principal purpose of referencing to previous works of special values is "persuasion" (see Gilbert, 1977; Harwood, 2004; Latour & Woolgar, 1979). Accordingly, the usually selective citation (i.e., the citing of one publication over another) aims to maximize the relevant rhetorical effects so as to make the present research work more convincing and acceptable to the wider readership. Indeed, the act of citing commonly plays both fundamental roles (i.e., to credit and to persuade) simultaneously, as demonstrated in Harwood's (2004) illustrative analyses of several corpus extracts; even more than that, it can perform a host of other rhetorical functions, as indicated in a good many associated classification schemes outlined and expounded by previous citation analysts (see Gilbert, 1977; Harwood, 2009; Peritz, 1983; Petrić, 2007).

The complexity of citing motivations/functions can therefore be perceived from these classification schemes. For instance, Garfield (1977) enumerated as many as fifteen categories of citing motives such as "Decorations", "Providing Justifications", "Demonstrating the Novelty of One's Results" and "Showing Knowledge of the Important Work in the Field"; Peritz (1983) listed eight categories of citation functions, i.e., "Setting the Stage for the Present Study", "Background Information", "Methodological", "Comparative", "Argumental, Speculative, Hypothetical", "Documentary", "Historical" and "Casual"; and Brooks (1985, 1986) proposed a scheme consisting of seven representative citing functions selected from the existing literature and applied it to his empirical analyses.

This notable complexity of functional aspects of citations is also reflected in the inconsistencies in terminologies relative to them in previous research work, making valid comparisons of their corollaries difficult. Despite this weakness, consistencies remain in some types of citation functions uncovered in prior studies even with different methodologies, e.g., the "Credit", "Signposting" and "Engaging" functions of citations derived from the emic accounts of computer scientists and sociologists in Harwood (2009) respectively corresponded to the citation functions "Source" and "Reference" theorized by Thompson (2000a, b, 2001, 2005) and "Evaluation" by Petrić (2007).

As such, this observation (that the categories of citation functions developed in the previous theorizing and empirical literature is consonant to some extent with those accounted by research writers themselves) confirms the validity of both methods—the textual-focused analysis and the emic, interview study to some extent, notwithstanding penetrating criticisms by Harwood (2008a, b, 2009) of the weaknesses of the text-based content/context analysis, which has prevailed in the traditional citation research.

With referencing interpreted as an idiosyncratic and private process by some citation analysts (Cronin, 1984, 2005; Harwood, 2008a, b, 2009; Petrić & Harwood, 2013), text-based content/context studies have been criticized for their large amount of subjective guesswork and speculations. In contrast, the discourse-based, semi-structured interview (especially without the ready-made functional checklist offered) has been repeatedly recommended (Harwood, 2008a, b, 2009; Harwood & Petrić, 2012) as an effective means to directly elicit the citers' insights into their own citation practices, which might not be revealed by other research methodologies. Furthermore, the adoption of this method can help to circumvent the "unreflexive" accounts of the informants to a maximum degree, for they are led to re-read and reflect on the citations they made in their writing (Harwood, 2009). Another advantage of the approach is that it does not impose any confinement or pre-set ideas on the informants, in contrast to some foregoing interviews with preconceived categories of citation functions provided (e.g., Bonzi & Synder, 1991; Brooks, 1985, 1986; Case & Higgins, 2000; Liu, 1993) and the questionnaire survey, whereby further explanations and more complete accounts of their views are hardly possible.

In spite of these merits, the discourse-based interview (Odell, Goswami, & Herrington, 1983), like all other kinds of interviews, suffers from the problems of "informant recall", the sometimes stubborn unreflective accounts, and inherent differences in individual competence of and preferences for introspection (Harwood, 2008a, b, 2009; Harwood & Petrić, 2012). However, it is worth reiterating that every research method has its limitations, and both the emic interview (Harwood, 2008a, b, 2009) and the discourse approach into rhetorical functions of citations (Mansourizadeh & Ahmad, 2011; Petrić, 2007) have generated many insightful findings. An integration of the etic findings from the rigorous discourse analysis and the emic accounts from the qualitative interview may provide us with a more comprehensive understanding of the citer motivation and citation functions. Such an approach is adopted in this study.

As mentioned earlier, although there is insufficient research on rhetorical functions of citations in the field of AL, different perspectives have been gradually taken on this issue, i.e., the comparison of the use of citation functions across disciplines (Harwood, 2009); different groups of writers [e.g., NNS student writers vs. NS student writers in Borg (2000); NNS high-rated thesis writers vs. NNS low-rated thesis writers in Petrić (2007); NNS expert writers vs. NNS novice writers in Mansourizadeh and Ahmad (2011)]; different part-genres within the RA (Kwan & Chan, 2014; Mansourizadeh & Ahmad, 2011; Martinez, 2008) and within the thesis (Petrić, 2007); and between the corresponding sections in RAs and in degree theses (Samraj, 2013).

Disciplinary specificity in the use of citations for different functions has been documented in Harwood (2009). Based upon the discourse-based interview transcripts of twelve informants from computer science and sociology, Harwood (2009) created a scheme of eleven categories of citation functions and observed considerable inter- and intra-disciplinary similarities and dissimilarities. In both disciplines, interviewees frequently attributed the functions "Position", "Support" and "Credit" to their citations, which accords with the findings of some previous studies (Case & Higgins, 2000; Frost, 1979; Shadish, Tolliver, Gray, & Sen Gupta, 1995) to different degrees. For instance, Frost (1979) found that "Review the Present State of Research" and "Support Statements or Claims" were the top two functional categories, which respectively correspond to "Position" and "Support" (Harwood, 2009). Shadish et al. (1995) reported that "Supporting an Assertion" and "Documenting the Source of a Method or Design Feature Used" were the two most frequently used categories, which are actually similar to "Support" and "Credit" (Harwood, 2009) respectively. Moreover, Case and Higgins (2000) concluded that the two most favorable categories in their study were "Reviewing Prior Work in the Area" and "Concept Markers", which are analogous to the "Position" function in Harwood (2009).

However, Harwood (2009) also found that the "Signposting" function, which is close to the "Reference" function in Thompson's (2000a, b, 2001, 2005) studies and "Refer to Further Reading" in Frost's (1979) research, was more often used in computing texts, whereas the "Engaging" function was more frequently employed in sociological texts. This result was in line with the frequently-revealed "discursive" and "disputational" nature of humanities/social sciences texts (Harwood, 2009: 515) in a great number of previous studies such as Hyland (1999, 2000, 2002), Becher and Trowler (2001), Whitley (2000) and Thompson and Tribble (2001). Substantial within-disciplinary variations in the use of citation functions have also been recorded in Harwood's interview-based study, which he attributed to a series of factors such as the "publication outlet" (Harwood, 2008b: 253), the readership and the nature of the text written (e.g., the empirical or theoretical nature) [see also the comparison of the full-length RA with the letter writing in Chubin and Moitra (1975)].

All these revealed cross- and within-disciplinary variations in the expert use of citation functions have largely indicated the interaction between disciplinarity and individuality with the combined effects from a range of other contextual factors. Previous studies have also uncovered similarities and differences in functional use of citations by different groups of writers (notably the NNS writers) (Borg, 2000; Mansourizadeh & Ahmad, 2011; Petrić, 2007) or different individual writers (Harwood & Petrić, 2012) from the same field. In Borg's comparative study of citation use in 11 non-assessed take-home essays of around 2500 words written by NNS students and in five essays of a similar nature written by NS students, it was observed that the NS and NNS student writers had actually similar patterns of citation functional use. One marked feature was that both groups made excessive use of Hortatory citations, which was assumed to be a common feature of the novice writing.

Within the field of gender studies, Petrić (2007) compared rhetorical functions of citations in eight high- and eight low-marked L2 master's degree theses in order to highlight effective citation strategies in successful student writing. One important motivation for this study, as she noted, was that expert scholarly writing has been deeply researched in order to inform EAP teaching; however, there may exist different citation needs between student and scholarly writing. While noting Thompson's (2001, 2005) mixed criteria (both functionally and formally) in further classifying integral and non-integral citations (Sect. 2.5.1), Petrić extended her three functional sub-types of non-integral citations ("Source" ("Attribution"), "Reference" and "Example") to the analysis of the functional use of all citations in student thesis writing, including both integral and non-integral ones. In addition to that, she identified the other six categories from her corpus data as a part of the entire analytical scheme. There were both quantitative and qualitative differences observed between the high- and the low-marked theses in the use of citations for various functions. A wider variety of rhetorical functions of citations and in particular the non-attribution functions were more frequently used in the high-rated theses than in the low-rated theses, both in the entire theses and in each thesis section.

Since "Attribution" was "rhetorically the simplest" and the most commonly used function in both sets of theses (Petrić, 2007: 247), knowledge-displaying seems to be a more noticeable feature of student writing than of expert writing. In individual thesis sections/chapters, the highly-rated thesis writers were also able to flexibly employ a greater number of non-attribution functions matching with their communicative purposes. For example, they frequently used "Evaluation" and "Establishing Links between Sources" in the Literature Review chapter, "Establishing Links between Sources" in the first move of the Introduction chapter, and "Evaluation" and "Statement of Use" in the latter two moves of the Introduction chapter according to the CARS model.

In marked contrast, the low-grade theses were characterized by their "descriptiveness" (Petrić, 2007: 248) which resulted from their writers' inability to exploit varied citation strategies for making knowledge claims. Other problems with these writers in thesis writing included their linguistic deficiencies in realizing citation functions explicitly and improper use of certain citation functions in the discourse context.

Like Petrić's (2007) study, Mansourizadeh and Ahmad (2011) focused on citation practices of a group of NNS writers (who work in a major research university in Malaysia). Nevertheless, they for the first time conducted a comparative analysis of both forms and functions of citations employed by seasoned and emerging writers of RAs from the same field of chemical engineering. Drawing on previous typologies of citation forms [i.e., the binary citation forms—integral vs. non-integral citations—introduced by Swales (1990) and the scheme for classifying integral citations proposed by Thompson and Tribble (2001)] and functions (Petrić, 2007; Thompson & Tribble, 2001) combined with a self-identified *Support* function of citation, they found that novice writers made far more frequent use of the rhetorically less-demanded forms (Sect. 2.5.1) and functions (Myers, 1990; Petrić, 2007). While no citations were used by both groups of writers in the Conclusion section, the main difference in the functional use of citations between them was in the other three major sections (viz., I, [RD] and M). A clear preference of the novice writers for the *Attribution* function was demonstrated throughout the three sections while the experienced writers were able to apply citations for more diverse functions suitable for the communicative purpose of these rhetorical sections. This marked distinction is similar to that between the high-rated thesis writers and the low-rated thesis writers in their functional use of citations in Petrić's study. For instance, in the Introduction section, expert writers most frequently used *Establishing Links* and *Identification*; in the [RD] section, the most favorable two citation functions for them were *Comparison* and *Support*; in the M section with the low density of citation use, expert writers had a dominant use of *Support* (around 46%) mainly for justifying the methods and procedures they adopted with relevant pre-confirmed knowledge cited.

Apparently, the main concerns of Mansourizadeh and Ahmad (2011) and Petrić (2007) were the similarities and differences between different groups of writers in their use of citations for various functions. However, the variations in the functional use of citations across part-genres of the RA (Mansourizadeh & Ahmad, 2011) and of the thesis (Petrić, 2007) can actually be perceived from citation practices of the more successful groups of writers, i.e., expert writers in Mansourizadeh and Ahmad (2011) and the proficient thesis student writers in Petrić (2007). The variations in their use of citations for different rhetorical functions across RA or thesis sections as detailed above indeed pointed to distinct communicative purposes of these part-genres (Kwan & Chan, 2014).

However, the specific interrelatedness between the functional moves of the particular genre or part-genre and the use of citations for different functions in them has been hardly addressed in the existing literature, except for Martinez (2008), Samraj (2013) and Kwan and Chan (2014). The latter two studies have indicated the association of citation roles with the communicative functions of the particular section and move where citation is located. However, they respectively focus on the discussion sections of theses and RAs and the results and the post-results sections of RAs while the present study centers on the introductory phase of ERAs. Therefore, the two studies are not reviewed in detail here.

As for Martinez's study (2008: 270), which focuses on the whole RA, she innovatively used the name of each move to represent the function the ("most central") citation located in them performed in her detailed examination of six biological published RAs. "The most central" citation, according to Martinez, referred to the one most explicitly relevant to the communicative function of the move, when the move contained multiple citations. It is argued here, however, that this treatment not only led to the loss of information as "the most central" citation needed to be subjectively determined at the expense of other citations used, but overlooked the fact that the name of each move indicates the major communicative purpose of this functional discourse unit rather than the role the citation in it plays, notwithstanding some certain relations existing between them. Furthermore, this treatment also precluded diversity in subtle functions that a citation could serve, which has been illustrated in previous typologies as mentioned before (Harwood, 2009; Petrić, 2007; Thompson & Tribble, 2001), and the possibility of multiple functions some citations could perform as documented in Petrić (2007) and Harwood (2009). Nevertheless, Martinez's (2008) pioneering study still revealed some interesting findings: the "functions" of citations were closely linked with the functional moves where they occurred and the distribution of moves with citations varied across the I, M, R and D sections of the RA.

Specifically speaking, the most frequently used two functional moves with citations were *Reviewing Items of Previous Research* and *Providing Information*, and while the use of the former was confined to a single Introduction section, the latter was indeed most widely used (i.e., throughout the four RA sections). As for the R and D sections, both were found to contain the comparative and interpretative rhetorical moves, but D was the section that included the most. However, as Martinez's (2008) research only involved six biology RAs, its findings need to be validated by further empirical studies.

As the above review demonstrates, the cross-generic/cross-sectional comparison of functional use of citations has been the subject of relatively little research in the EAP field and the comparative study of rhetorical functions of citations in two adjoining sections with partly overlapping communicative purposes and propositional content (such as "reviewing previous literature" in the Introduction and LR sections) within the same genre is not existent. The present study thus seeks to bridge this gap.

2.5.4 Previous Research into Citation Practices

The preceding sections have presented an overview of existing studies of the three aspects of citations (viz., citation forms, signals (RVs) and functions), which are selected as the main parameters for citation analysis of the introductory phase of the ERA in the present study. What follows is a focused review of the body of literature on the integrated citation practices, which can vary across cultures/languages (Adnan, 2004; Bloch & Chi, 1995; Taylor & Chen, 1991), disciplines (Hyland, 1999, 2000, 2002; Thompson, 2001; Thompson & Tribble, 2001), (part-) genres (Campbell, 1990; Thompson & Tribble, 2001; Yeh, 2010) and different groups of writers (Borg, 2000; Campbell, 1990; Dong, 1996; Sun, 2008; Yeh, 2010). As revealed in the last column of Table 2.3, a considerable number of studies (e.g., Adnan, 2004; Bloch & Chi, 1995; Thompson, 2001; Thompson & Tribble, 2001) have approached citation practices from a combination of the above-mentioned perspectives with a complex framework of multi-layered citation features.

Writing from sources is a challenging task for disciplinary neophytes, especially for those learning English as a second or foreign language (Borg, 2000; Lang, 2004). There is much literature available on problematic aspects of novice citation practices. In terms of frequency, citations seem to be more often used in expert writing than in novice writing (Mansourizadeh & Ahmad, 2011), in NS student writing than in NNS student writing (Bloch, 1988, 1990, cited in Bloch & Chi (1995); Borg, 2000). As stated earlier, many novice writers (in particular the L2 group) lack awareness about the importance of citing references in English academic writing as well as relevant knowledge about how to appropriately acknowledge source use and integrate their own evaluations into referencing. At worst, these may result in plagiarism, which however is mostly unintentional (Lang, 2004; Pecorari, 2003). Many NNS inexperienced writers have even greater difficulties in singling out their own voices from those of their sources and in appropriately positioning themselves in connection with their readership, their prior scholarship, their new findings and texts (Thompson, 2001; Thompson & Ye, 1991). Another noticeable weakness in their citation practices is that they tend to be well versed at knowledge display but not at knowledge transformation through the use of referencing. As shown in Sun's (2008) study, Chinese M.A. students tended to cite others' works merely as authoritative support for their research without taking critical stances towards them. This might be partly rooted in the traditional Chinese culture they had long cherished, which is colored by conservatism and strong "face-protection", with modesty and harmony promoted as its core value. Another important reason, as aptly expounded by Sun, may be these students' unfamiliarity with international (English) academic writing conventions

Table 2.3 Overview of major previous research into citation practices

Previous studies	Citation features examined	Data	Genres or part-genres concerned	Methods	Perspectives
Campbell (1990)	The amount of information from the background text; ways to present source material (original explanation; summaries; paraphrases; quotations; near copies and exact copies); citation functions (backgrounded vs. foregrounded)	30 in-class compositions written by three groups of writers (NS students, less proficient NNS students, and more proficient NNS students)	Student in-class essays	Textual analysis	L1 versus L2 (less proficient and more proficient groups) fresh students; cross-generic
Taylor and Chen (1991)	Citation density in the whole RA and in the Introduction section; **[Move structural analysis]**	31 (theoretical and empirical) RAs in four related fields of physics (11 for English/English, 10 for English/Chinese and the other 11 for Chinese/English)	RA introductions	Textual analysis	Cross-cultural

(continued)

Table 2.3 (continued)

Previous studies	Citation features examined	Data	Genres or part-genres concerned	Methods	Perspectives
Bloch and Chi (1995)	Citation density in the whole RA; citation dates; the functional use of citations (or rather, citation strategies); critical citation use	60 theoretical RAs in English and another 60 in Chinese in three disciplines from social science (economics, sociology and psychology) and three disciplines from physical science (physics, biology and engineering)	RAs	Textual analysis	Cross-cultural; cross-disciplinary
Dong (1996)	Citation density in each draft; the position of citations in the text; revisions of citations over several drafts and the related rationales in the view of advisors and students	All main drafts of the three Chinese scientific doctoral students' dissertations; interviews with students and their thesis advisors; observations of writing conferences	Thesis introductions	Textual analysis, interviews, and observations	L2 students
Hyland (1999, 2000, 2002)	Citation density in the whole RA; citation forms; the frequency, types, and evaluative functions of RVs; ways to present source material	80 1997 RAs from eight disciplines; interview data (with eight expert writers from these disciplines)	RAs	Textual analysis and semi-structured interview study	Cross-disciplinary

(continued)

Table 2.3 (continued)

Previous studies	Citation features examined	Data	Genres or part-genres concerned	Methods	Perspectives
Borg (2000)	Citation length, forms (extended, brief, a fragment; direct quotation vs. paraphrase/summary) and functions	16 non-assessed student take-home essays in the field of education	Student take-home essays	Textual analysis	L1 versus L2 MEd student writers
Thompson (2001), Thompson and Tribble (2001)	Citation density in the whole thesis; citation types (forms); the use of RVs (Thompson, 2001); ways to present source material	Eight Agricultural Biology doctoral theses and eight Agricultural and Food Economics doctoral theses written by L1 students at a UK university; interview data (with eight Ph.D. supervisors from these two departments) (Thompson, 2001)	Ph.D. theses	Textual analysis; semi-structured background interview study (Thompson, 2001)	Cross-disciplinary (both the inter- and intra-disciplinary perspective); cross-generic
Adnan (2004)	Citation density in the whole RA; citation forms and subject positions; the functional use of citations; the evaluative attitude to the cited information	30 Indonesian RAs from three humanities disciplines (education, linguistics, and social-political sciences)	RAs	Textual analysis	Cross-disciplinary, cross-cultural (compared with Hyland's (1999) study)

(continued)

Table 2.3 (continued)

Previous studies	Citation features examined	Data	Genres or part-genres concerned	Methods	Perspectives
Petrić (2007)	Citation density; rhetorical functions of citations	Eight high- and eight low-rated master's theses in gender studies	Master's theses	Textual analysis	Proficient student writers versus their less proficient fellows; cross-sectional
Martinez (2008)	Citation functions and forms, RVs, self-citation	Six "IMRD-structured" RAs in the biological sciences	RAs	Textual analysis	Cross-generic
Sun (2008)	Citation density, citation forms; placement of researchers' names in integrated citations; the frequency, type, range, function and tense use of RVs	100 English MA thesis introductions by Chinese students in AL	Thesis introductions	Textual analysis	L2 learners' perspective (Chinese MA students)
Yeh (2010)	Citation density in the whole RA and across the RA sections; citation forms; citation dates; Ways to present source material (short quote, block quote, summary/paraphrase, generalization)	20 English RAs written by Taiwanese scholars and 20 English RAs by international scholars in English language teaching	RAs	Textual analysis (discourse analysis)	Local writers versus international writers; cross-generic

(continued)

Table 2.3 (continued)

Previous studies	Citation features examined	Data	Genres or part-genres concerned	Methods	Perspectives
Mansourizadeh and Ahmad (2011)	Citation density; citation forms and functions	14 chemical engineering RAs written by non-native expert and novice writers	RAs	Textual analysis	L2 expert writing versus L2 novice writing; cross-sectional
Jalilifar (2012)	Citation density; citation forms (integral and non-integral citations and their sub-types); evaluative stance in the verb controlling type of integral citations	The introduction sections of 65 international RAs and 65 Iranian master's theses	RA introductions versus thesis introductions in AL	Textual analysis	Cross-generic
Samraj (2013)	Citation forms and functions	The discussion sections of eight master theses and eight RAs in the field of biology; two 1-h long interviews with specialist informants)	RA discussions versus thesis discussions in biology	Textual analysis and interviews	Cross-generic

(continued)

Table 2.3 (continued)

Previous studies	Citation features examined	Data	Genres or part-genres concerned	Methods	Perspectives
Swales (2014)	Citation density, citation forms, RVs, the occurrence of selected features such as the use of citees' first names	15 graduate student papers and 22 final-year undergraduate student papers in biology	Student papers	Textual analysis	Cross-sub-fields (molecular and evolutionary biology), comparison of citation practices in student writing of different levels (viz., undergraduate vs. graduate)
Kwan and Chan (2014)	Citation density, rhetorical functions and semantic content of citations (i.e., the types of knowledge cited)	40 RAs in the behavior science research paradigm published between 2008 and 2010 in a research journal and an applied-research journal	RA results and discussion sections	Textual analysis supplemented with informants' checks and accounts of their own and others' citation practices in this particular domain	Cross-sectional and cross-journal

and their lack of expertise in creating the essential research space for their studies by strategically using various sorts of citation techniques.

In addition to Sun's (2008) study, other representative investigations in this line include the case study of three Chinese Ph.D. students' acquisition of the process of referencing in writing the introductory chapter of their theses by Dong (1996), both quantitative and qualitative comparison of L1 and L2 students' amounts of and way of using prior texts in their essay writing by Campbell (1990) and Borg (2000), and the comparative analysis of Taiwanese and international expert citation practices by Yeh (2010). Dong's (1996) research revealed the process of how her three case subjects studying at a US university overcame their typical citation problems such as their insufficient use of citations and ineffective integration of prior literature into their writing for making new knowledge claims. With the help of their thesis advisors, the three students finally succeeded in presenting their new and reconstructed claims by employing different strategies: one gave a chronological account of the evolution of her research topic, another carved out the research space through contrastive argumentation, and the third transformed his experimental study into a story.

Although both Campbell (1990) and Borg (2000) compared L1 and L2 writers' use of citations in their assignment writing, Campbell analyzed 30 in-class compositions while Borg studied 16 take-home student essays to overcome Campbell's (1990: 221) self-acknowledged methodological limitation that "in-class writing may be less of a measure of actual writing ability than of other factors, such as the students' ability to follow instructions". However, both studies found that neither L1 nor L2 students had a full mastery of the proper acknowledgement of their sources. In Campbell's study, both language groups used copying as their main citation strategy, for they obviously had little knowledge about acknowledging sources with appropriate attributions. In Borg's (2000: 35) study, while L1 students "tended to have less difficulty making clear their stance towards their sources", they sometimes were found to over-quote sources. In contrast, L2 students generally used fewer citations and preferred the topics that required less source-writing. Additionally, they appeared to have more difficulties in separating their own voices from those of the cited authors while taking an evaluative stance appropriately and in using second-hand citations properly. Despite these revelations, the small size of the data collected from a single university in both studies inevitably limited their applicability and generalizability.

For the groups of local (Taiwanese) and international scholars in Yeh's (2010) study, both similarities and dissimilarities existed in their professional citation practices. To be specific, Taiwanese scholars and their international peers had similarly overwhelming preferences for non-integral citations, summary/paraphrase (from a single source) and generalization (from more than one source) over direct quotations, which was the same as most of the academics in Hyland's (1999, 2000, 2002) study. However, Taiwanese expert writers made less use of citations and favored more dated references. Yeh (2010: 57) attributed this to the phenomenon that "Taiwanese may not always aim to keep ahead of the fast-moving progress of information or include the most recent research updates in their papers".

Along with these studies, another body of research into citation features used by novice writers, especially (L1 or L2) student writers, concerns the issues of their source use/language reuse and plagiarism (e.g., Flowerdew & Li, 2007; Greene, 1995; Kennedy, 1985; Li, 2007; Li & Casanave, 2012; O'Brien, 1995; Pecorari, 2003, 2006; Pecorari & Shaw, 2012; Shi, 2004). This body of research is characterized by its cross-text analysis and comparison between their source reports and original sources, in addition to the other means (such as interviews with student writers, advisors, and course instructors) yielding important findings as well. It has great pedagogical significance in that it often clearly informs us of whether the novices have mastered the relevant citation strategies and techniques, and if not, where their problems lie. However, it does not approach citation in more meticulous ways in terms of its multi-layered features, with attention most frequently paid to the relationship between the source and the citation, rather than the discourse context per se where it occurs.

As can be seen in Table 2.3, researchers have also focused on cultural-specific features in using citations in academic writing (Adnan, 2004; Bloch & Chi, 1995; Taylor & Chen, 1991). Taylor and Chen (1991) conducted a systematic contrastive discourse analysis of move structures and citation use in 31 introductions to RAs written by three groups of physical scientists: NS (Americans) writing in English (English/English), Chinese writing in English (Chinese/English), and Chinese writing in Chinese (Chinese/Chinese). They found that in terms of the numbers of references used in the whole paper and in the Introduction section, the English/English group made the densest use of citations, followed by the Chinese/English group with the other group with the least common use of them. Most prominently, Chinese physicists writing either in English or in Chinese had more frequent omission of "Move 2" ("Summarizing the relevant previous research") (Swales, 1984) than their Anglo-American counterparts and the sparse use of critical citations. For these results Taylor and Chen (1991: 328) provided the following plausible explanations. On the cultural side, "the more 'Anglicized' the paper, the more space was devoted to summarizing the literature, with a 'quantum leap' from the Chinese/English papers to the Anglo-American/English papers". Influenced by the traditional culture and social ideological value, Chinese scientists were more reluctant to disclose and critique the weaknesses in others' work in public. On the practical side, Chinese scientists at that time indeed had little access to the international referencing resources.

By comparing citation practices of Chinese and American academics from social and physical sciences, Bloch and Chi (1995) revealed a set of complex results about the frequency, date and function of citations they used. With respect to citation frequency, English academics employed far more citations than their Chinese counterparts in their research writing. As Chinese academics traditionally attach more importance to the classics (than the new published work) and view them as the principal source material for constructing their own texts, they were found to use a far greater number of dated references than American academics in both areas, this discrepancy being more conspicuous in the social sciences. Chinese physical sciences texts were more like English ones in terms of the date and the function of citations used, for they had been more influenced by "Western thinking" (Bloch & Chi, 1995:

249). As such, considerably more recent citations were employed in them than in Chinese social sciences texts. For both language groups, the background citation was the most frequently used type, followed by the support citation with the critical citation least favored.

Most significantly, Bloch and Chi's (1995: 253) study did confirm that "Chinese writers can and do take critical positions, though not necessarily as often as the English-language writers do", which contradicted the observation of Taylor and Chen (1991) that Chinese writers seldom made criticisms publicly in their texts, as mentioned earlier. Nevertheless, Taylor and Chen's study focused on the introductions, and it was likely that Chinese writers were used to postponing their critical citations until their arguments had been made. Moreover, Chinese academics often made "indirect criticism" without people's names cited, and their critical positions were frequently introduced with the two expressions "it is worthwhile to reconsider and discuss" and "some people have said" (Bloch & Chi, 1995: 258). Their possible placement of critical citations in the later part of the RA and favorable use of "indirect criticism" also reflected the core Chinese social and cultural value—"harmony, courtesy, and concessions"—which had been long held by them (Bloch & Chi, 1995: 260).

Generally, the significant differences in citation use by Chinese and English academics in these two large areas covering six disciplines clearly revealed how culture influences language and that Chinese writers' difficulties in adapting themselves to the western academic writing system may be rooted in their L1 rhetoric traditions, social values, and cultural beliefs.

Similar to Chinese academics, the Indonesian professional writers writing in their own language from the field of the humanities in Adnan's (2004) study used far fewer citations than did the international scholars writing in English in Hyland's (1999, 2000, 2002) studies, and had the positive evaluations most often towards their cited work with criticisms yet rarely made. This could also be accounted for by the lack of resources available to them in their country and their less established academic tradition.

Compared with the substantial literature devoted to the problematic aspects of citation use by (both NS and NNS) novice writers, relatively little attention of the EAP academics has been paid to cross- and within-disciplinary variations in citation practices with far less to cross-generic differences in this regard.

A growing number of empirical studies (Adnan, 2004; Bloch & Chi, 1995; Thompson, 2001; Thompson & Tribble, 2001) have been conducted on discipline specificity in academic citation practices since the seminal work by Hyland (1999). Since disciplinary differences in the use of citation forms, RVs and citation functions have been detailed in the previous sections, these are not repeated here. Regarding the importance of citations in disciplinary academic writing, Hyland (1999) proposed a broad division between the hard disciplines with commonly less use of citations and the soft disciplines with generally more use of citations. This could be naturally attributed to different epistemological bases and knowledge structures between the hard and the soft disciplines. However, conflicting findings have been reported by Thompson and Tribble (2001), who observed that there was far less use of citations in

Agricultural Economics theses (a soft discipline) than in Agricultural Botany theses (a hard discipline), and by Bloch and Chi (1995) who also found that in both the English and Chinese RAs, more citations were used in the physical sciences than in the social sciences. In Adnan's (2004) study of academic citation practices of the Indonesian academics, those in education employed only half as many citations as their peers in the other two disciplines (viz., linguistics and socio-political sciences), which was explained by greater focus of education researchers on practical teaching issues (rather than theoretical ones), with their arguments being frequently built upon real world experience.

In terms of presentation forms of prior texts, "summary" (from a single source) and "generalization" (from multiple sources) are the two predominantly used in research writing (Hyland, 1999, 2000, 2002; Thompson, 2001; Thompson and Tribble, 2001) with direct quotations being least favored. The reason may be that the two most favorable ways for integrating sources into their texts can most effectively help them separate their voices from those of the cited authors. While academics in almost all disciplines display a similar preference for these two ways to present source information, there were disciplinary differences identified in the functional use of direction quotations: in Thompson and Tribble's (2001) study, the only one direct quotation used in Agricultural Botany thesis was a definition and many of those in Agricultural Economics theses were evaluative comments.

As for the functional use of citations, in physical science RAs, far more citations were used to provide background information, whereas in social science RAs, the citations were more frequently employed to support the writers' positions, as revealed by Bloch and Chi (1995). Likewise, in Adnan's (2004) study, all the Indonesian academics in the three disciplines of humanities were found to prefer "Support" citations to "Background" citations.

As mentioned before, there seemed to be no variations among the Indonesian academics from the three humanities disciplines in their evaluative attitudes towards the cited information (Adnan, 2004). However, Bloch and Chi (1995) observed some contrasting disciplinary differences. Within the group of English academics, those from the area of the social sciences employed more critical citations than their colleagues from the physical sciences. In contrast, within the group of Chinese academics, those from the area of the physical sciences used a greater number of critical citations than their counterparts from the social sciences.

Overall, among all research perspectives taken on the issue of academic citation practices, the cross-generic perspective has been least explored. This admittedly limited line of research however suggests salient variations in the dispersion of citations across rhetorical sections of the RA. The traditional Introduction section is frequently identified to be the one with the highest density of citations (Yeh, 2010), followed by the Discussion section or the coalesced Results and Discussion section (Mansourizadeh & Ahmad, 2011), and the Method section is usually a site where least referencing could be found (see Sun, 2008; Yeh, 2010). However, some partially different findings have also been documented in a few prior studies. For example, Martinez (2008) observed from his small data (i.e., the six published RAs in biological sciences) that among the four major conventional sections of the RA (viz., I, M, R and D), it was the Results section that contained the fewest citations and the Introduction section that contained the most; In contrast, Mansourizadeh and Ahmad (2011) reported that the Conclusion section was the one with the lowest percentage of citations (0%) in chemical engineering papers written by non-native expert and novice writers. The general tendency that referencing most often clusters in the Introduction section and the Discussion section (or its variants, such as the blended Result and Discussion section) with other sections (such as M, R, and C) usually containing far less of it can be accounted for by their distinct rhetorical needs and communicative purposes indicated by the hourglass RA model (Hill, Soppelsa, & West, 1982). In light of this model, "the Methods and Results sections are narrow, focusing on the research itself" (Thompson & Tribble, 2001: 98) whereas the Introduction section is a main location in which the writer establishes the links between "what has been done" with "what is new" (Sun, 2008: 12), and the Discussion section is the one in which what has been found by the writer is to be linked back with that by others. Hence, there is a considerable likelihood for the prior scholarship to be cited in these two sections I and D (or its varieties as mentioned above).

Nonetheless, as noted above, the small number of existing studies relative to cross-generic variations in citation use (e.g., Thompson, 2001; Thompson & Tribble, 2001; Yeh, 2010) has been mostly concerned with its proportional distribution in different rhetorical part-genres of the RA or the thesis. Apart from this sort of frequency analysis, various formal aspects of citation as well as the complex functional use of it across part-genres have been much less studied. Only Thompson and Tribble (2001) and Thompson (2001) have conducted detailed examinations of different citation types (classified based on both functional and formal criteria) used across the rhetorical sections of Agricultural Botany theses (Sect. 2.5.1), Martinez (2008) conducted an innovative study of the distribution of moves with citations for different rhetorical functions across the biological RA sections (Sect. 2.5.3), Samraj (2013) researched the functional and formal use of citations in thesis and RA discussions, and Kwan and Chan (2014) studied rhetorical functions and semantic content of citations in the results and post-results sections of ERAs. Therefore, more large-scale and in-depth explorations need to be conducted into the multi-layered citation features both in the functional and formal terms across different part-genres.

Further, although Martinez's (2008) initial attempts have demonstrated that the "functions" of citations were closely associated with the four major sections of the RA (i.e., I, M, R and D), some critical intrinsic limitations in her study have been critiqued in Sect. 2.5.3, and the specific relationship between the communicative purposes of the part-genres (with the dense use of citations) and the use of different citation features in them is still unclear. To fill this gap, the present study systematically examines the links between the identified moves and move elements in the two partly analogous RA sections (i.e., the Introduction and LR sections) and the frequency, forms, functions and signals (RVs) of citations used in them.

Finally, with regard to the methods selected for investigating citation practices, textual analysis is mainly used with others (such as qualitative interviews and case study) less often resorted to in the extant literature. Although discourse analysis is an important and effective approach that has generated revealing findings about citation use in the EAP literature, methods such as interviews and case studies can provide the insiders' unique views and perceptions of their own citation practices (Hyland, 1999, 2000, 2002) and even the process of their acquiring citation techniques in academic writing (Dong, 1996). For instance, in Hyland's (1999) study of reporting practices of published writers in eight disciplines as indicated in Table 2.3, eight seasoned writers from these disciplines were interviewed about their own referencing behaviors and the disciplinary practice, offering illuminating accounts of discipline-specific features in citing as well as important disciplinary variations in this respect. In a similar vein, eight Ph.D. supervisors from the two fields (viz., Agricultural Botany and Agricultural Food Economics) were invited to participate in a semi-structured interview in Thompson's (2001) study. These participants contributed substantial details on the background settings and disciplinary cultures where these Ph.D. theses were written. Their explanations undoubtedly enhanced our understandings of the students' citation practices in their thesis writing in these two departments, in addition to relevant findings derived from the analysis of their written work. Although Thompson (2001: 73) realized that valuable and enlightening insights could possibly be obtained by interviewing these student writers about their citation practices, this turned out to be impractical due to "the constraints of time, access and reliability". In view of the purpose and need of this study as well as the strengths and weaknesses of the above-mentioned methods, a combination of textual analysis and interview study is adopted in this study.

2.6 Summary

This chapter has reviewed five important topics which offer a theoretical basis for the current study. Here I summarize the important points which have emerged.

- Different types of RAs are introduced and the present study focuses on the ERA.
- The preoccupation with the conventional IMRD framework and little empirical research conducted on the macro-structure of the ERA has led to the long-term neglect of other major sections, including the LR in the opening phase of the ERA.
- The Introduction section is a much studied part-genre of the RA. However, a great number of previous studies have investigated the rhetorical structure of introductions written in different languages, with fewer ones on related disciplinary/sub-disciplinary variations. Almost no systematic studies have been undertaken on rhetorical comparison of and generic relation between it and its related part-genres, except for Samraj (2005).
- There is hardly any systematic research into the rhetorical structure of the LR as a particular part-genre in RAs, except for Kwan et al. (2012) and Tessuto (2015), two pioneering studies among the few whose work is of particular pertinence to the current study. Kwan et al.'s study has generated many insightful findings in that it specified move-specific strategies used in LRs of RAs in the two sub-disciplines of Information Systems and presented cross-domain variations in the

quantitative use and distribution of different types of strategies. However, maybe due to its focus on evaluation strategies associated with Move 2 (rather than aiming for a comprehensive view of the LR rhetorical structure), this study did not explore the internal structural flow of the LR, e.g., the co-occurrence patterns of moves and strategies and in what order moves and move-specific strategies are sequenced. Similarly, although Tessuto (2015) also confirmed that the LR section (or the Background Review section in his words) of the 90 empirical law RAs are structured around the three moves of the CARS model (Swales, 1990, 2004), he only presented quantitative findings on the use of each move and step. No specific information has been given on the move and step configurations and the preferred sequences in which these elements are arranged. Also, the new element identified (viz., Step 12A "Defining and Developing Methods, Theories, Concepts, Issues, Phenomena" in Move 3) has not been fully explained and illustrated. Hence, we still have a rather limited understanding of how this section is rhetorically structured; only a limited amount of research has been undertaken into that of the LR in other genres such as degree theses (Kwan, 2005, 2006; O'Connell & Jin, 2001) and student project reports (Krishnan & Kathpalia, 2002), among which, Kwan's (2005, 2006) study is an important reference. As such, both Swales' (1990, 2004) CARS model for RA introductions and Kwan's (2006) theme-bound CARS model for thesis LRs are used as references for comparison.

- A comprehensive and critical review of previous research on citation use has generated the following observations, with the relevant gaps identified. First, it has mainly focused on novice writers' (in particular L2 student writers') difficulties and the possible reasons accounting for them, while (part-)genre-specific and discipline-specific features have been comparatively less studied. Second, the existing citation studies have been chiefly concerned with the frequency distribution of it across rhetorical sections of the RA or the thesis, whereas the variations in the use of many multi-layered citation features in formal terms as well as its functions across these part-genres have been largely ignored. To date, no study has compared citation use in the Introduction and LR sections of ERAs. Third, studies of citation use have been mostly text-based. A combination of the text-based analysis with other supplemental ethonographic methods such as the interview study may offer a fuller and better understanding of the disciplinary citation practices.
- Swales's (1990) binary citation forms (integral vs. non-integral citation forms) has been frequently adopted or modified in subsequent analyses of citation forms (Thompson, 2001; Thompson & Tribble, 2001); several taxonomies of RVs have been created (Hyland, 1999; Thomas & Hawes, 1994), based on the work of Thompson and Ye (1991). Hyland's (1999) classification framework of RVs in terms of their denotation and evaluative stance with some modifications will be adopted in the present research.
- Citation functions have been intensively researched in information science and sociology of sciences but not in AL; applied linguists traditionally concentrate on grammatical features and formal aspects of citations and have started examining functional aspects of citations only recently. However, few analysts have examined cross-sectional variations in the functional use of citations (Kwan & Chan, 2014)

and no comparison has thus far been conducted of the rhetorical functions of citations in the Introduction and LR sections of ERAs in the EAP literature.

This chapter has provided the background to and rationale for the present investigation of the rhetorical structure of and citation use in the introductory phase of the ERA. The investigation will include textual analysis and interview study. The details of the methodology are presented in the next chapter.

References

Adams Smith, D. (1990). Source and derived discourse. In M. A. K. Halliday, J. Gibbons, & H. Nicholas (Eds.), *Learning, keeping and using language* (pp. 415–433). Amsterdam: John Benjamins.

Ädel, A., & Mauranen, A. (2010). Metadiscourse: Diverse and divided perspectives. *Nordic Journal of English Studies, 9*(2), 1–11.

Adnan, Z. (2004). Citing behaviours in Indonesian humanities research articles. *ASAA E-Journal of Asian Linguistics & Language Teaching, 6*. Retrieved December 24, 2011, from http://pandora.nla.gov.au/pan/21217/20050109-0000/languages.arts.unsw.edu.au/asaa_ejournal/Issue6/Adnan.pdf.

Adnan, Z. (2008). Discourse structure of Indonesian research article introductions in selected hard science. In S. Burgess & P. Martin-Martin (Eds.), *English as an additional language in research publication and communication* (pp. 39–64). Berlin: Peter Lang.

Ahmad, U. (1997). Research article introductions in Malay: Rhetoric in an emerging research community. In A. Duszak (Ed.), *Culture and styles of academic discourse* (pp. 273–304). Berlin: Mouton de Gryuter.

Allen, R. C. (1989). Bursting bubbles: "Soap opera", audiences, and the limits of genre. In E. Seiter, H. Borchers, G. Kreutzner, & E. Warth (Eds.), *Remote control: Television, audiences and cultural power* (pp. 44–55). London: Routledge.

Allison, D. (1999). Key concepts in ELT: Genre. *ELT Journal, 53*(2), 144.

Anthony, L. (1999). Writing research article introductions in software engineering: How accurate is a standard model? *IEEE Transactions on Professional Communication, 42,* 38–46.

Ard, J. (1985). Vantage points for the analysis of scientific discourse. *English for Specific Purposes, 4,* 3–20.

Arvay, A., & Tanko, G. (2004). A contrastive analysis of English and Hungarian theoretical research article introductions. *IRAL, 42,* 71–100.

Askerhave, I., & Swales, J. (2001). Genre identification and communicative purpose: A problem and a possible solution. *Applied Linguistics, 22*(2), 195–212.

Atkinson, D. (1992). The evolution of medical research writing from 1735 to 1985: The case of the *Edinburgh Medical Journal*. *Applied Linguistics, 13*(4), 337–374.

Atkinson, D. (1999). *Scientific discourse in sociohistorical context: The Philosophical Transactions of the Royal Society of London, 1675–1975*. Mahwah, NJ: L. Erlbaum Associates.

Bawarshi, A. S., & Reiff, M. J. (2010). *Genre: An introduction to history, theory, research, and pedagogy*. West Lafayette: Parlor Press.

Baynham, M. (1999). Double-voicing and the scholarly "I": On incorporating the words of others in academic discourse. *Text, 19*(4), 485–504.

Bazerman, C. (1984). Modern evolution of the experimental report in physics: Spectroscopic articles in *Physical Review*, 1893–1980. *Social Studies in Science, 14,* 163–196.

Bazerman, C. (1988). *Shaping knowledge: The genre and activity of the experimental article in science*. Madison, WI: University of Wisconsin Press.

Becher, T. (1989). *Academic tribes and territories: Intellectual enquiry and the cultures of disciplines*. Milton Keynes, UK: Open University Press.

Becher, T., & Trowler, P. R. (2001). *Academic tribes and territories: Intellectual inquiry and the culture of disciplines* (2nd ed.). Buckingham, UK: Open University Press.

Bhatia, V. K. (1993). *Analyzing genre: Language use in professional settings*. New York: Longman.

Bhatia, V. K. (1997). Genre-mixing in academic introductions. *English for Specific Purposes, 16*(3), 181–195.

Bhatia, V. K. (2001). Analyzing genre: Some conceptual issues. In M. Hewing (Ed.), *Academic writing in context: Implications and applications: Papers in honour of Tony Dudley-Evans* (pp. 79–92). Birmingham: University of Birmingham Press.

Bhatia, V. K. (2004). *Worlds of written discourse: A genre-based view*. London: Continuum.

Bhatia, V. K. (2012). *Critical reflections on genre analysis. Ibérica, 24,* 17–28.

Biber, D., & Conrad, S. (2009). Historical evolution of registers, genres, and styles. In D. Biber & S. Conrad (Eds.), *Register, genre, and style* (pp. 143–176). Cambridge: Cambridge University Press.

Bisenbach-Lucas, S. (1994). *A comparative genre analysis: The research article and its popularization*. Unpublished doctoral dissertation, Georgetown University.

Bley-Vroman, R., & Selinker, L. (1984). Research design in rhetorical/grammatical studies: A proposal optimal research strategy. *English for Specific Purposes, 3,* 37–46.

Bloch, J. G. (1988). *Academic writing in Chinese and English: Is there a difference?* Paper presented at the 1988 Conference on College Composition and Communication Convention, St. Louis, MO.

Bloch, J. G. (1990). *Universalism versus particularism: The relationship between Chinese and English rhetoric*. Paper presented at the 1990 Conference on College Composition and Communication Convention, Chicago, IL.

Bloch, J., & Chi, L. (1995). A comparison of the use of citations in Chinese and English academic discourse. In D. Belcher & G. Braine (Eds.), *Academic writing in a second language: Essays on research and pedagogy* (pp. 231–273). Norwood, NJ: Ablex.

Bonzi, S., & Snyder, H. W. (1991). Motivations for citation: A comparison of self citation and citation to others. *Scientometrics, 21,* 245–254.

Borg, E. (2000). Citation practices in academic writing. In P. Thompson (Ed.), *Patterns ad perspectives: Insights for EAP writing practice* (pp. 26–44). Reading: CALS, The University of Reading.

Bornmann, L., & Daniel, H.-D. (2008). What do citation counts measure? A review of studies on citing behaviour. *Journal of Documentation, 64,* 45–80.

Braine, G. (1995). Writing in the natural sciences and engineering. In D. Belcher & G. Braine (Eds.), *Academic writing in a second language: Essays on research and pedagogy* (pp. 113–134). Norwood, NJ: Ablex.

Brett, P. (1994). A genre analysis of the results section of sociology articles. *English for Specific Purposes, 13*(1), 47–59.

Brooks, T. A. (1985). Private acts and public objects: An investigation of citer motivations. *Journal of the American Society for Information Science, 36*(4), 223–229.

Brooks, T. A. (1986). Evidence of complex citer motivations. *Journal of the American Society for Information Science, 37*(1), 34–36.

Bruce, C. S. (1994). Research students' early experiences of the dissertation literature review. *Studies in Higher Education, 19*(2), 217–229.

Bruce, I. (2008). Cognitive genre structures in methods sections of research articles: A corpus study. *Journal of English for Academic Purposes, 7*(1), 38–54.

Bruce, I. (2009). Results sections in sociology and organic chemistry articles: A genre analysis. *English for Specific Purposes, 28*(2), 105–124.

Brugha, R., & Varvasovsky, Z. (2000). Stakeholder analysis: A review. *Health Policy Planning, 15*(3), 239–246.

Bunton, D. (2002). Generic moves in Ph.D. thesis introductions. In J. Flowerdew (Ed.), *Academic discourse* (pp. 57–75). London: Pearson Education.

Cacavas, J., & Kaplan, S. (1994). *The art of writing music: A practical book for composers and arrangers of instrumental, choral, and electronic music as applied to publication, films, television, recordings, and schools*. California: Alfred Music Publishing.
Campbell, C. (1990). Writing with others' words: Using background reading text in academic compositions. In B. Kroll (Ed.), *Second language writing: Research insights for the classroom* (pp. 211–230). Cambridge: Cambridge University Press.
Cargill, M., & O'Connor, P. (2009). *Writing scientific research articles: Strategy and steps*. Chichester: Wiley-Blackwell.
Case, D. O., & Higgins, G. M. (2000). How can we investigate citation behavior? A study of reasons for citing literature in communication. *Journal of the American Society for Information Science, 51,* 635–645.
Celce-Murcia, M., & Larsen-freeman, D. (1983). *The grammar book: An ESL/EFL teaching course*. Rowley, Mass: Newbury House.
Charles, M. (2006a). Phraseological patterns in reporting clauses used in citation: A corpus-based study of theses in two disciplines. *English for Specific Purposes, 25*(3), 310–331.
Charles, M. (2006b). The construction of stance in reporting clauses: A cross-disciplinary study of theses. *Applied Linguistics, 27,* 492–518.
Chubin, D. E., & Moitra, S. D. (1975). Content analysis of references: Adjunct or alternative to citation counting? *Social Studies of Science, 5,* 423–441.
Coe, R. M. (2002). The new rhetoric of genre: Writing political briefs. In A. M. Johns (Ed.), *Genre in the classroom: Multiple perspectives* (pp. 197–210). Mahwah, NJ: Lwarence Erlbaum.
Comrie, B. (1985). *Tense*. Cambridge: Cambridge University Press.
Cooper, C. (1985). *Aspects of article introductions in IEEE publications*. Unpublished master's thesis, University of Aston.
Cooper, H. M. (1988). Organizing knowledge syntheses: A taxonomy of literature reviews. *Knowledge in Society, 1,* 104–126.
Cronin, B. (1984). *The citation process: The role and significance of citations in scientific communication*. London: Taylor Graham.
Cronin, B. (2005). *The hand of science: Academic writing and its rewards*. Lanham, MD: Scarecrow Press.
Crookes, G. (1986). Towards a validated analysis of scientific text structure. *Applied Linguistics, 7,* 57–70.
Day, R. A., & Gastel, B. (2006). *How to write and publish a scientific paper* (6th ed.). Westport, CT: Greenwood Press.
Del Saz-Rubio, M. M. (2011). A pragmatic approach to the macro-structure and metadiscoursal features of research article introductions in the field of agricultural sciences. *English for Specific Purposes, 30*(4), 258–271.
Devitt, A. J. (1991). Intertextuality in tax accounting: Generic, referential, and functional. In C. Bazerman & J. Paradis (Eds.), *Textual dynamics of the professions* (pp. 336–357). Madison, WI: University of Wisconsin Press.
Dong, Y. (1996). Learning how to use citations for knowledge transformation: Nonnative doctoral students' dissertation writing in science. *Research in the Teaching of English, 30,* 428–457.
Dudley-Evans, T. (1986). Genre analysis: An investigation of the introduction and discussion sections of MSc dissertations. In M. Coulthard (Ed.), *Talking about text* (pp. 128–145). Birmingham: English Language Research, Birmingham University.
Dudley-Evans, A. (1994). Genre analysis: An approach to text analysis for ESP. In M. Coulthard (Ed.), *Advances in written text analysis* (pp. 219–228). London: Routledge.
Dudley-Evans, T., & Henderson, W. (1990). The organization of article introductions: Evidence of change in economics writing. In T. Dudley-Evans & W. Henderson (Eds.), *The language of economics: The analysis of economics discourse* (pp. 67–78). London: Modern English Publications/British Council.
Dudley-Evans, T., & Henderson, W. (1993). The development of the economics article: 1891–1980. *FINLANCE, 12,* 159–181.

Duszak, A. (1994). Academic discourse and intellectual styles. *Journal of Pragmatics, 21*(3), 291–313.

Een, J. A. (1982). Tense usage in reporting research in geotechnical writing. *Working Papers in ESL, 2,* 72–91. Minneapolis: University of Minnesota.

Eggins, S. (1994). *An introduction to systemic functional linguistics*. London: Pinter.

Fahnestock, J. (1986). Accommodating science: The rhetorical life of scientific facts. *Written Communication, 3,* 275–296.

Fakhri, A. (2004). Rhetorical properties of Arabic research article introductions. *Journal of Pragmatics, 36*(6), 1119–1138.

Feak, C. B., & Swales, J. M. (2009). *Telling a research story: Writing a literature review*. Ann Arbor: The University of Michigan Press.

Ferguson, G. (1997). Teacher education and LSP: The role of specialized knowledge. In R. Howard & G. Brown (Eds.), *Teacher education for languages for specific purposes* (pp. 80–89). Clevedon: Multilingual Matters.

Flowerdew, J. (2002). Genre in the classroom: A linguistic approach. In A. M. Johns (Ed.), *Genre in the classroom: Multiple perspectives* (pp. 91–104). Mahwah, NJ: Lawrence Erlbaum.

Flowerdew, J. (2011). Reconciling contrasting approaches to genre analysis: The whole can equal more than the sum of the parts. In D. Belcher, A. Johns, & B. Paltridge (Eds.), *New directions in English for specific purposes research* (pp. 119–144). Ann Arbor: The University of Michigan Press.

Flowerdew, J., & Li, Y. (2007). Plagiarism and second language writing in an electronic age. *Annual Review of Applied Linguistics, 27,* 161–183.

Flowerdew, J., & Wan, A. (2006). Genre analysis of tax computation letters: How and why tax accountants write the way they do. *English for Specific Purposes, 25*(2), 133–153.

Flowerdew, J., & Wan, A. (2010). The linguistic and the contextual in applied genre analysis: The case of the company audit report. *English for Specific Purposes, 29,* 78–93.

Fredrickson, K., & Swales, J. (1994). Competition and discourse community: Introductions from Nysvenska studier. In B.-L. Gunnarsson, P. Linell, & B. Nordberg (Eds.), *Text and talk in professional contexts: Selected papers from the international conference "Discourse and the Professions"* (pp. 9–21). Stockholm: ASLA.

Freedman, A., & Medway, P. (Eds.). (1994). *Genre and the new rhetoric*. London: Taylor & Francis.

Froese, A. D., Gantz, B. S., & Henry, A. L. (1998). Teaching students to write literature reviews: A meta-analytical model. *Teaching of Psychology, 25*(2), 102–105.

Frost, C. O. (1979). The use of citations in literary research: A preliminary classification of citation functions. *Library Quarterly, 49,* 399–414.

Futász, R. (2006). Analysis of theoretical research article introductions written by undergraduate students: A genre-based approach. *Acta Linguistica Hungarica: An International Journal of Linguistics, 53*(2), 97–116.

Garfield, E. (1977). Can citation indexing be automated? In E. Garfield (Ed.), *Essays of an information scientist* (pp. 84–90). Philadelphia, PA: ISI Press.

Gilbert, G. N. (1977). Referencing as persuasion. *Social Studies of Science, 7*(1), 113–122.

Golebiowski, Z. (1999). Application of Swales' model in the analysis of research papers by Polish authors. *International Review of Applied Linguistics in Language Teaching, 37,* 231–247.

Greene, S. (1995). Making sense of my own ideas: The problems of authorship in a beginning writing classroom. *Written Communication, 12*(2), 186–218.

Groom, N. (2000). Attribution and averral revisited: Three perspectives on manifest intertextuality in academic writing. In P. Thompson (Ed.), *Patterns and perspectives: Insights for EAP writing practice* (pp. 15–26). Reading: CALS, The University of Reading.

Halliday, M. A. K. (1994). *An introduction to functional grammar* (2nd ed.). London: Arnold.

Hanania, E., & Akhtar, K. (1985). Verb form and rhetorical function in science writing: A study of MS theses in biology, chemistry, and physics. *The ESP Journal, 4,* 49–58.

Hart, C. (1998). *Doing a literature review: Releasing the social science research imagination*. London: Sage.

Harwood, N. (2004). Citation analysis: A multidisciplinary perspective on academic literacy. In M. Baynham, A. Deignan, & G. White (Eds.), *Applied linguistics at the interface* (pp. 79–89). London: Equinox.
Harwood, N. (2008a). Citers' use of citees' names: Findings from a qualitative interview-based study. *Journal of the American Society for Information Science and Technology, 59*(6), 1007–1011.
Harwood, N. (2008b). Publication outlets and their effect on academic writers' citations. *Scientometrics, 77*(2), 253–265.
Harwood, N. (2009). An interview-based study of the functions of citations in academic writing across two disciplines. *Journal of Pragmatics, 41*(3), 497–518.
Harwood, N., & Petrić, B. (2012). Performance in the citing behavior of two student writers. *Written Communication, 29,* 55–103.
Hawes, T., & Thomas, S. (1997). Tense choice in citations. *Research in the Teaching of English, 31*(3), 393–413.
Hewings, A., Lillis, T., & Vladimirou, D. (2010). Who's citing whose writings? A corpus based study of citations as interpersonal resource in English medium national and English medium international journals. *Journal of English for Academic Purposes, 9*(2), 102–115.
Hill, S. S., Soppelsa, B. F., & West, G. K. (1982). Teaching ESL students to read and write experimental-research papers. *TESOL Quarterly, 16*(3), 333–347.
Hirano, E. (2009). Research article introductions in English for specific purposes: A comparison between Brazilian Portuguese and English. *English for Specific Purposes, 28*(4), 240–250.
Hoey, M. (1979). *Signaling in discourse*. Birmingham: English Language Research.
Hoey, M. (1983). *On the surface of discourse*. London: George Allen & Unwin.
Holmes, R. (1997). Genre analysis and the social sciences: An investigation of the structure of research article discussion sections in three disciplines. *English for Specific Purposes, 16*(4), 321–337.
Hopkins, A., & Dudley-Evans, T. (1988). A genre-based investigation of the discussion sections in articles and dissertations. *English for Specific Purposes, 7*(2), 113–121.
Hsieh, W. M., Tsai, T. C., Lin, M. C., Liou, H. C. U., & Kuo, C. H. (2006). Exploring genre sets: Research article sections in illustrative humanities and science disciplines. In *The 23rd International Conference on English Teaching and Learning in the ROC,* Taipei (pp. 249–262).
Huang, D., Xu, L., & Yang, X. (2010). A corpus-based genre analysis of Chinese and English research article introductions: Revisiting a symbolic trade in the new century. In *2010 International Conference on Artificial Intelligence and Education (ICAIE)*, 29–30 Oct 2010 (pp. 729–733). https://doi.org/10.1109/icaie.2010.5641508.
Hunston, S. (1993a). Evaluation and ideology in scientific writing. In M. Ghadessy (Ed.), *Register and analysis: Theory and practice* (pp. 57–73). London: Printer Publishers.
Hunston, S. (1993b). Professional conflict: Disagreement in academic discourse. In M. Baker, G. Francis, & E. Tognini-Bonelli (Eds.), *Text and technology: In honour of John Sinclair* (pp. 115–134). Philadelphia, PA: John Benjamins.
Hunston, S. (1995). A corpus study of some English verbs of attribution. *Functions of Languages, 2*(2), 133–158.
Hunston, S. (2000). Evaluation and planes of discourse: Status and values in persuasive texts. In S. Hunston & G. Thompson (Eds.), *Evaluation in text: Authorial stance and the construction of discourse* (pp. 176–205). Philadelphia, PA: Oxford University Press.
Hunston, S., & Thompson, G. (2000). Evaluation: An introduction. In S. Hunston & G. Thompson (Eds.), *Evaluation in text: Authorial stance and the construction of discourse* (pp. 1–27). Philadelphia, PA: Oxford University Press.
Hyland, K. (1999). Academic attribution: Citation and the construction of disciplinary knowledge. *Applied Linguistics, 20*(3), 341–367.
Hyland, K. (2000). *Disciplinary discourses: Social interaction in academic writing*. London: Longman Pearson Education.

Hyland, K. (2002). Activity and evaluation: Reporting practices in academic writing. In J. Flowerdew (Ed.), *Academic discourse* (pp. 115–130). Harlow: Pearson Education Limited.
Hyland, K. (2003). Genre-based pedagogies: A social response to process. *Journal of Second Language Writing, 12*(1), 17–29.
Hyon, S. (1996). Genre in three traditions: Implications for ESL. *TESOL Quarterly, 30,* 693–722.
Jacoby, S. (1986). *The inevitable forked tongue: An analysis of references to other researchers in literary research articles*. Unpublished master's thesis, The University of Birmingham.
Jacoby, S. (1987). References to other researchers in literary research articles. *ELR Journal, 1,* 33–78.
Jalilifar, A. (2012). Academic attribution: Citation analysis in master's theses and research articles in applied linguistics. *International Journal of Applied Linguistics, 22*(1), 24–41.
Jankowitz, A. D. (1995). *Business research projects*. London: Chapman Hill.
Jesson, J., & Lacey, F. (2006). How to do (or not to do) a critical literature review. *Pharmacy Education, 6*(2), 139–148.
Jiang, Y. C. (2005). *A corpus-based contrastive study on reporting in English M.A. thesis*. Unpublished master's thesis, Huazhong University of Science and Technology.
Jogthong, C. (2001). *Research article introductions in Thai: Genre analysis of academic writing*. Unpublished doctoral dissertation, West Virginia University.
Johns, A. M. (Ed.). (2002). *Genre in the classroom: Multiple perspectives*. Mahwah, NJ: Lawrence Erlbaum.
Johns, A. M. (2003). Genre and ESL/EFL composition instruction. In B. Kroll (Ed.), *Exploring the dynamics of second language writing* (pp. 195–217). Cambridge: Cambridge University Press.
Johns, A. M. (2011). The future of genre in L2 writing: Fundamental, but contested, instructional decisions. *Journal of Second Language Writing, 20*(1), 56–68.
Kanoksilapatham, B. (2005). Rhetorical structure of biochemistry research articles. *English for Specific Purposes, 24*(3), 269–292.
Kanoksilapatham, B. (2011). Civil engineering research article introductions: Textual structure and linguistic characterization. *The Asian ESP Journal, 7*(2), 55–84.
Kanoksilapatham, B. (2012). Research article structure of research article introductions in three engineering subdisciplines. *IEEE Transactions on Professional Communication, 55*(4), 294–309.
Kaplan, E. (1965). The norms of citation behavior: Prolegomena to the footnote. *American Documentation, 16*(3), 179–184.
Kennedy, M. (1985). The composing process of college students writing from sources. *Written Communication, 2*(4), 434–456.
Kinneavy, J. L. (1971). *A theory of discourse: The aims of discourse*. Englewood Cliffs, NJ: Prentice-Hall.
Körner, A. M. (2008). *Guide to publishing a scientific paper*. Abingdon: Routledge.
Krishnan, L. A., & Kathpalia, S. S. (2002). Literature reviews in student project reports. *IEEE Transactions on Professional Communication, 45*(3), 187–197.
Kuteeva, M., & McGrath, L. (in press). The theoretical research article as a reflection of disciplinary practices: The case of pure mathematics. *Applied Linguistics*.
Kwan, B. S. C. (1996). *Introductions in state-of-the-art, argumentative, and teaching tips TESL journal articles: Three possible sub-genres of introduction?* Unpublished master's thesis, City University of Hong Kong.
Kwan, B. S. C. (2005). *A genre analysis of literature reviews in doctoral theses*. Unpublished doctoral dissertation, City University of Hong Kong.
Kwan, B. S. C. (2006). The schematic structure of literature reviews in doctoral theses of applied linguistics. *English for Specific Purposes, 25,* 30–55.
Kwan, B. S. C. (2008). The nexus of reading, writing, and researching in the doctoral undertaking of humanities and social sciences: Implications for literature reviewing. *English for Specific Purposes, 27,* 42–56.

Kwan, B. S. C., & Chan, H. (2014). An investigation of source use in the results and the closing sections of empirical articles in Information Systems: In search of a functional-semantic citation typology for pedagogical purposes. *Journal of English for Academic Purposes, 14,* 29–47.
Kwan, B. S. C., Chan, H., & Lam, C. (2012). Evaluating prior scholarship in literature reviews of research articles: A comparative study of practices in two research paradigms. *English for Specific Purposes, 31,* 188–201.
Lackstrom, J., Selinker, L., & Trimble, L. (1972). Grammar and technical English. *English Teaching Forum, 10*(5), 3–14.
Lackstrom, J., Selinker, L., & Trimble, L. (1973). Technical rhetorical principles and grammatical choice. *TESOL Quarterly, 7*(1), 127–136.
Lang, H. L. (2004). *The use of reporting verbs in literature reviews of Taiwanese postgraduate business students.* Unpublished doctoral dissertation, The University of Manchester.
Latour, B., & Woolgar, S. (1979). *Laboratory life: The social construction of scientific facts.* Beverly Hills: Sage Publications.
Lee, S. (2001). *A contrastive rhetoric study of Korean and English research paper introductions.* Unpublished doctoral dissertation, University of Hawaii.
Lester, J. D., & Lester, J. D. (2006). *Writing research papers in the social sciences.* New York: Pearson/Longman.
Levy, Y., & Ellis, T. J. (2006). A systems approach to conduct an effective literature review in support of information systems research. *Information Science Journal, 9,* 181–212.
Lewin, B. A., Fine, J., & Young, L. (2001). *Expository discourse: A genre-based approach to social science research texts.* London: Continuum.
Li, Y. (2007). Composing citations through language reuse: A doctoral student of biomedicine writing a research paper. *Asian Journal of English Language Teaching, 17,* 1–27.
Li, Y., & Casanave, C. P. (2012). Two first year students' strategies for writing from sources: Patchwriting or plagiarism? *Journal of Second Language Writing, 21*(2), 165–180.
Lim, J. M. (2010). Commenting on research results in applied linguistics and education: A comparative genre-based investigation. *Journal of English for Academic Purposes, 9*(4), 280–294.
Liu, M. X. (1993). A study of citing motivation of Chinese scientists. *Journal of Information Science, 19,* 13–23.
Liu, C., & Houdek, R. (2006). Teaching computer science graduate students scholarly literature review techniques. In *36th Annual Frontiers in Education Conference* (pp. 14–19).
Loi, C. K. (2010). Research article introductions in Chinese and English: A comparative genre-based study. *Journal of English for Academic Purposes, 9*(4), 267–279.
Loi, C. K., & Evans, S. M. (2010). Cultural differences in the organization of research article introductions from the field of educational psychology: English and Chinese. *Journal of Pragmatics, 42*(10), 2814–2825.
Machi, L. A., & McEvoy, B. T. (2009). *The literature review: Six steps to success.* Thousand Oaks, CA: Corwin Press.
Macken-Horarik, M. (2002). "Something to shoot for": A systemic functional approach to teaching genre in secondary school science. In A. M. Johns (Ed.), *Genres in the classroom: Applying theory and research to practice* (pp. 17–42). Mahwah, NJ: Lawrence Erlbaum Associates.
Malcolm, L. (1987). What rules govern tense usage in scientific articles? *English for Specific Purposes, 6*(1), 31–44.
Malinowski, B. (1935). *The language of magic and gardening.* London: AllenUnwin.
Malinowski, B. (1946/1923). The problem of meaning in primitive languages. In C. Ogden & I. A. Richards (Eds.), *The meaning of meaning* (pp. 296–336). London: Kegan Paul.
Mansourizadeh, K., & Ahmad, U. (2011). Citation practices among non-native expert and novice scientific writers. *Journal of English for Academic Purposes, 10*(3), 152–161.
Martin, J. R. (1984). Language, register and genre. In F. Christie (Ed.), *Children writing: Reader* (pp. 21–29). Geelong, VIC: Deakin University Press.

Martin, J. R. (1985). Process and text: Two aspects of human semiosis. In J. D. Banson & W. S. Greaves (Eds.), *Systemic perspectives on discourse: Selected theoretical papers from the 9th International Systemic Workshop* (pp. 248–274). New Jersey: Ablex Publishing Corporation.

Martin, J. R. (1992). *English text: System and structure*. Philadelphia: John Benjamins Publishing Company.

Martin, J. R. (2009). Genre and language learning: A social semiotic perspective. *Linguistics and Education, 20*(1), 10–21.

Martin, J. R., & Rose, D. (2007). *Working with discourse: Meaning beyond the clause*. London: Continuum.

Martin, J. R., & Rose, D. (2008). *Genre relations: Mapping culture*. London and Oakville: Equinox.

Martinez, I. A. (2008). Building consensus in science: Resources for intertexual dialog in biology research articles. *Journal of English for Academic Purposes, 7,* 268–276.

Medway, P. (2002). Fuzzy genres and community identities: The case of architecture students' sketchbooks. In R. Coe, L. Lingard, & T. Teslenko (Eds.), *The rhetoric and ideology of genre: Strategies for stability and change* (pp. 123–153). Cresskill, NJ: Hampton Press.

Melander, B. (1998). Culture or genres? Issues in the interpretation of cross-cultural differences in scientific articles. In I. Fortanet, S. Posteguillo, J. C. Palmer, & J. F. Coll (Eds.), *Genre studies in English for academic purposes* (pp. 211–226). Castello de la Plana: Universitat Jaume I.

Miguel, C. S., & Nelson, C. D. (2007). Key writing challenges of practice-based doctorates. *Journal of English for Academic Purposes, 6*(1), 71–86.

Miller, C. (1984). Genre as social action. *Quarterly Journal of Speech, 70,* 151–167.

Moravcsik, M., & Murugesan, P. (1975). Some results on the function and quality of citations. *Social Studies of Science, 5,* 86–92.

Myers, G. (1990). *Writing biology: Texts in the social construction of scientific knowledge*. Madison: University of Wisconsin Press.

Najjar, H. (1990). *Arabic as a research language: The case of the agricultural sciences*. Unpublished doctoral dissertation, University of Michigan.

Neff, J., Dafouz, E., Herrera, H., Martínez, F., Rica, J. P., Díez, M., et al. (2003). Contrasting learner corpora: The use of modal and reporting verbs in the expression of writer stance. In S. Granger & S. Petch-Tyson (Eds.), *Extending the scope of corpus-based research: New applications, new challenges* (pp. 211–230). Amsterdam: Rodopi.

Nunan, D. (1992). *Research methods in language learning*. Cambridge: Cambridge University Press.

Nwogu, K. N. (1990). *Discourse variation in medical texts: Schema, theme and cohesion in professional and journalistic accounts*. Monographs in Systemic Linguistics (Vol. 2). University of Nottingham.

Nwogu, K. N. (1997). The medical research paper: Structure and functions. *English for Specific Purposes, 16*(2), 119–138.

O'Brien, T. (1995). Rhetorical structure analysis and the case of the inaccurate, incoherent source-hopper. *Applied Linguistics, 16*(4), 442–482.

O'Connell, F., & Jin, L. X. (2001). *A structural model of literature review: An analysis of Chinese postgraduate students' writing.* Paper presented at the BALEAP Conference, Sheffield Hallam University, Sheffield, UK. Retrieved January 23, 2012, from http://www.baleap.org.uk/baleap/conference-events/pims/pim-reports/focus-chinese-learners/opening-plenary-session/fionnuala-summary.

Odell, L., Goswami, D., & Herrington, A. J. (1983). The discourse-based interview: A procedure for exploring the tacit knowledge of writers in nonacademic settings. In P. Mosenthal, L. Tamor, & S. A. Walmsley (Eds.), *Research on writing: Principles and methods* (pp. 221–236). New York: Longman.

Oster, S. (1981). The use of tense in "reporting past literature" in EST. In L. Selinker, E. Tarone, & V. Hanzeli (Eds.), *English for academic and technical purposes: Studies in honour of Louis Trimble* (pp. 76–90). MA, Newburg House: Rowley.

Ozturk, I. (2007). The textual organization of research article introductions in applied linguistics: Variability within a single discipline. *English for Specific Purposes, 26*(1), 25–38.
Paltridge, B. (1995). Analyzing genre: A relational perspective. *System, 23*(4), 503–511.
Paltridge, B. (2001). *Genre and the language learning classroom*. Ann Arbor: University of Michigan Press.
Paltridge, B. (2007). Approaches to genre in ELT. In J. Cummins & C. Davison (Eds.), *International handbook of English language teaching* (Vol. 2, pp. 931–943). New York, NY: Springer.
Peacock, M. (2002). Communicative moves in the discussion section of research articles. *System, 30*(4), 479–497.
Pecorari, D. (2003). Good and original: Plagiarism and patchwriting in academic second-language writing. *Journal of Second Language Writing, 12,* 317–345.
Pecorari, D. (2006). Visible and occluded citation features in postgraduate second-language writing. *English for Specific Purposes, 25*(1), 4–29.
Pecorari, D., & Shaw, P. (2012). Types of student intertextuality and faculty attitudes. *Journal of Second Language Writing, 21*(2), 149–164.
Peritz, B. C. (1983). A classification of citation roles for the social sciences and related fields. *Scientometrics, 5,* 303–312.
Petrić, B. (2007). Rhetorical functions of citations in high- and low-rated master's theses. *Journal of English for Academic Purposes, 6*(3), 238–253.
Petrić, B., & Harwood, N. (2013). Task requirements, task representation, and citation functions: An interview-based study of the citing behavior of a successful L2 student writer. *Journal of English for Academic Purposes, 12,* 110–124.
Pho, P. D. (2009). Linguistic realizations of rhetorical structure: A corpus-based study of research article abstracts and introductions in applied linguistics and educational technology. In S. T. Gries, S. Wulff, & M. Davies (Eds.), *Corpus linguistic applications: Current studies, new directions* (pp. 135–152). Amsterdam: Rodopi.
Pickard, V. (1995). Citing previous writers: What can we say instead of "Say"? *Hong Kong Papers in Linguistic and Language Teaching, 18*(9), 89–102.
Posteguillo, S. (1999). The schematic structure of computer science research articles. *English for Specific Purposes, 18*(2), 139–160.
Pyrczak, F., & Bruce, R. R. (2007). *Writing empirical research reports: A basic guide for students of the social and behavioral sciences* (6th ed.). Glendale, CA: Pyrczak Pub.
Qian, J., & Krugly-Smolska, E. (2008). Chinese graduate students' experiences with writing a literature review. *TESL Canada Journal, 26*(1), 68–86.
Ridley, D. (2012). *The literature review: A step-by step guide for students* (2nd ed.). London: Sage.
Rosmarin, A. (1985). *The power of genre*. Minneapolis: University of Minnesota Press.
Salager-Meyer, F. (1992). A text-type and move analysis study of verb tense and modality distributions in medical English abstracts. *English for Specific Purposes, 11,* 93–133.
Samraj, B. (1989). Exploring current issues in genre theory. *Word, 40*(1–2), 189–200.
Samraj, B. (2002). Introductions in research articles: Variations across disciplines. *English for Specific Purposes, 21*(1), 1–17.
Samraj, B. (2005). An exploration of a genre set: Research article abstracts and introductions in two disciplines. *English for Specific Purposes, 24*(2), 141–156.
Samraj, B. (2013). Form and function of citations in discussion sections of master's theses and research articles. *Journal of English for Academic Purposes, 12,* 299–310.
Sayfouri, N. (2010). *SFL and ESP genre analysis of English research articles in Iranian and English-American medical journals: A contrastive study*. Unpublished doctoral dissertation, University of Tehran.
Shadish, W. R., Tolliver, D., Gray, M., & Sen Gupta, S. K. (1995). Author judgments about works they cite: Three studies from psychology journals. *Social Studies of Science, 25*(3), 477–498.
Shaw, P. (1991). Science research students' composing processes. *English for Specific Purposes, 10,* 189–206.

Shaw, P. M. (1992). Reasons for the correlation of voice, tense and sentence function in reporting verbs. *Applied Linguistics, 13,* 302–317.

Shaw, J. (1995). A schema approach to the formal literature review in engineering theses. *System, 23*(3), 325–335.

Sheldon, E. (2011). Rhetorical differences in RA introductions written by English L1 and L2 and Castilian Spanish L1 writers. *Journal of English for Academic Purposes, 10*(4), 238–251.

Shi, L. (2004). Textual borrowing in second language writing. *Written Communication, 21,* 171–200.

Smith, D. E. (1987). *The everyday world as problematic: A feminist sociology.* Boston, MA: Northeastern University Press.

Soler-Monreal, C., Carbonell-Olivares, M., & Gil-Salom, L. (2011). A contrastive study of the rhetorical organisation of English and Spanish Ph.D. thesis introductions. *English for Specific Purposes, 30*(1), 4–17.

Sollaci, L. B., & Pereira, M. G. (2004). The introduction, methods, results and discussion (IMRAD) structure: A fifty-year survey. *Journal of the Medical Library Association, 92*(3), 364–367.

Stanley, R. M. (1984). The recognition of macrostructure: A pilot study. *Reading in a Foreign Language, 2,* 156–168.

Stoller, F. L., & Robinson, M. S. (2013). Chemistry journal articles: An interdisciplinary approach to move analysis with pedagogical aims. *English for Specific Purposes, 32,* 45–57.

Sun, Y. H. (2008). Citation problems of Chinese MA theses and pedagogical implications. *The Journal of Asia TEFL, 5*(1), 1–27.

Swales, J. M. (1981). *Aspects of article introductions.* Birmingham: The University of Aston, Language Studies Unit.

Swales, J. M. (1984). Research into the structure of introductions to journal articles and its application to the teaching of academic writing. In R. Williams, J. Swales, & J. Kirkman (Eds.), *Common ground: Shared interests in ESP and communication studies* (pp. 77–86). Oxford: Pergamon.

Swales, J. M. (1986). Citation analysis and discourse analysis. *Applied Linguistics, 7,* 39–56.

Swales, J. M. (1990). *Genre analysis: English in academic and research settings.* Cambridge; New York: Cambridge University Press.

Swales, J. M. (1993). Genre and engagement. *Revue Belge de Philogie et d'Histoire, 71*(3), 687–698.

Swales, J. M. (1998). *Other floors, other voices: A textography of a small university building.* Mahwah, NJ: Lawrence Erlbaum Associates.

Swales, J. M. (2004). *Research genres: Explorations and applications.* Cambridge; New York: Cambridge University Press.

Swales, J. M. (2014). Variation in citational practice in a corpus of student biology papers: From parenthetical plonking to intertextual storytelling. *Written Communication, 31*(1), 118–141.

Swales, J. M., & Feak, C. B. (2000). *English in today's research world.* Ann Arbor: University of Michigan Press.

Swales, J. M., & Feak, C. B. (2004). *Academic writing for graduate students: Essential tasks and skills* (2nd ed.). Ann Arbor: University of Michigan Press.

Swales, J. M., & Lindeman, S. (2002). Teaching the literature review to international graduate students. In A. Johns (Ed.), *Genre in the classroom: Multiple perspectives* (pp. 105–119). Mahwah, NJ: Lawrence Erlbaum.

Swales, J. M., & Najjar, H. (1987). The writing of research article introductions. *Written Communication, 4,* 175–191.

Tadros, A. A. (1985). *Prediction in text.* Discourse analysis monograph no. 10. Birmingham: University of Birmingham.

Tardy, C. (2011). The history and future of genre in second language writing. *Journal of Second Language Writing, 20*(1), 1–5.

Tarone, E., Dwyer, S., Gillette, S., & Icke, V. (1981). On the use of the passive in two astrophysics journal papers. *The ESP Journal, 1,* 123–140.

Taylor, G., & Chen, T. (1991). Linguistic, cultural, and sub-cultural issues in contrastive discourse analysis: Anglo-American and Chinese scientific texts. *Applied Linguistics, 12*(3), 319–336.

Tessuto, G. (2015). Generic structure and rhetorical moves in English-language empirical law research articles: Sites of interdisciplinary and interdiscursive cross-over. *English for Specific Purposes, 37*(1), 13–26.

Thomas, S., & Hawes, T. P. (1994). Reporting verbs in medical journal articles. *English for Specific Purposes, 13*(2), 129–148.

Thompson, D. (1993). Arguing for experimental facts in science. *Written Communication, 10*(1), 106–128.

Thompson, G. (1994). *Collins COBUILD English guides 5: Reporting*. London: Harper Collins Publishers.

Thompson, G. (2000a). *Reporting*. Beijing: Foreign Languages Publishing House.

Thompson, P. (2000b). Citation practices in Ph.D. theses. In L. Burnard & T. McEnery (Eds.), *Rethinking language pedagogy from a corpus perspective*. Frankfurt: Peter Lang.

Thompson, P. (2001). *A pedagogically-motivated corpus-based examination of Ph.D. theses: Macrostructure, citation practices and uses of modal verbs*. Unpublished doctoral dissertation, The University of Reading.

Thompson, P. (2005). Points of focus and position: Intertextual reference in Ph.D. theses. *Journal of English for Academic Purposes, 4*(4), 307–323.

Thompson, P., & Tribble, C. (2001). Looking at citations: Using corpora in English for academic purposes. *Language Learning and Technology, 5*(3), 91–105.

Thompson, G., & Ye, Y. (1991). Evaluation in the reporting verbs used in academic papers. *Applied Linguistics, 12*(4), 365–382.

Tickoo, M. L. (1994). Approaches to ESP: Arguing a paradigm shift. In R. Khoo (Ed.), *LSP: Problems and prospects* (pp. 30–48). Singapore: SEAMEO Regional Language Centre.

Toulmin, S. (1972). *Human understanding: The collective use and evolution of concepts*. Princeton, NJ: Princeton University Press.

Valle, E. (1997). A scientific community and its texts: A historical discourse study. In B.-L. Gunnarsson, P. Linell, & B. Nordberg (Eds.), *The construction of professional discourse* (pp. 76–98). London: Longman.

Vinkler, P. (1987). A quasi-quantitative citation model. *Scientometrics, 12*, 47–72.

Weissberg, R., & Buker, S. (1990). *Writing up research: Experimental research report writing for students of English*. Englewood Cliffs, NJ: Prentice Hall Regents.

White, H. D. (2004). Citation analysis and discourse analysis revisited. *Applied Linguistics, 25*(1), 89–116.

Whitley, R. (2000). *The intellectual and social organization of the sciences* (2nd ed.). Oxford: Oxford University Press.

Williams, J. (1999). Results sections of medical research articles. *English for Specific Purposes, 18*(4), 347–366.

Yang, R. Y., & Allison, D. (2003). Research articles in applied linguistics: Moving from results to conclusions. *English for Specific Purposes, 22*(4), 365–385.

Yang, R. Y., & Allison, D. (2004). Research articles in applied linguistics: Structures from a functional perspective. *English for Specific Purposes, 23*(3), 264–279.

Yeh, C. (2010). Citation practices in TESL research articles: A comparative study. *Asian ESP Journal, 6*(2), 40–64.

Yunick, S. (1997). Genres, registers and sociolinguistics. *World Englishes, 16*, 321–336.

Zappen, J. P. (1983). A rhetoric for research in science and technology. In P. V. Anderson, R. J. Brockmann, & C. R. Miller (Eds.), *New essays in technical and scientific communication: Research, theory, practice* (pp. 123–138). Farmingdale, NY: Baywood.

Zhang, Y., & Hu, J. (2010). A genre-based study of medical research article introductions: A contrastive analysis between Chinese and English. *The Asian ESP Journal, 6*(1), 72–96.

Chapter 3
Research Design and Methods

3.1 Overview of the Research Design

The foregoing literature review shows that the sections not accounted for in the well-established "IMRD" framework, including the LR section, have long been overlooked by EAP researchers. The long-term dearth of research into identifying the major RA sections from the contemporary research writing practice leaves the status of such sections in the whole RA unclear, let alone their internal structural movements and rhetorical linguistic features. The review of the literature has led to a decision to focus on the introductory phase of the ERA in this project, whose main design is depicted in Fig. 3.1.

This project encompasses three related studies: two lead-in studies respectively from the cross-sectional and diachronic perspectives on the major structural format of ERAs and of their introductory phases in particular, verifying the importance of the independent LR as a major section of ERAs; and a third study on the rhetorical structure of and citation use in the introductory phase structured in the "I+LR" pattern.[1] As shown in Fig. 3.1, the two lead-in studies provide essential justifications for the follow-up focused analysis of the introductory phase formatted in "I+LR" in terms of its rhetorical structure and citation use.

The research design aims to answer the following research questions:

1. What are the dominant macro-structures and the major sections of ERAs, and particularly, what is the status of the LR section?
2. What is the macro-structural development of ERAs in Applied Linguistics (AL) and Civil Engineering (CE), and particularly, is the LR section a new development?
3. What are the rhetorical structure of and citation use in the introductory phase structured in the "I+LR" pattern in AL and CE?

---

[1] The "I+LR" pattern refers to the frequently-used yet rarely researched structural format for the introductory part of the RA that comprises two separate sections, namely, an Introduction section and a subsequent Literature Review section.

(Kathy). L. Lin, *Perspectives on the Introductory Phase of Empirical Research Articles*, Corpora and Intercultural Studies 5, https://doi.org/10.1007/978-981-32-9204-8_3

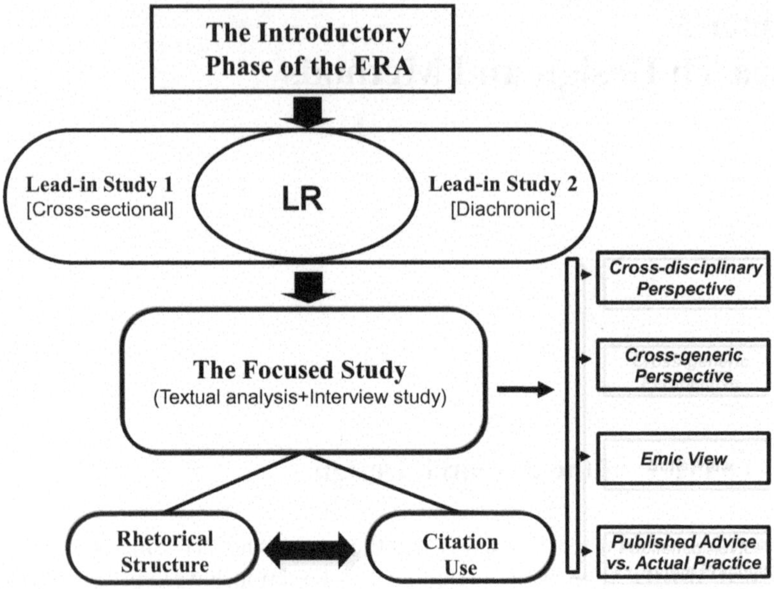

Fig. 3.1 Research design of the study

4. What are disciplinary academics' views and experience on structuring the introductory phase of the ERA and on using citations in it in AL and CE?

The design and rationale for each part of this study are as follows.

3.2 Lead-in Study 1: Cross-Sectional Analyses of ERA Macro-structure in 39 Disciplines

The first lead-in study investigates the macro-structure of the contemporary ERA from the cross-sectional perspective and identifies its major sections, with a particular focus on the structural form of its introductory phase and the status of the LR in the whole article. Its main findings and relevant implications are presented in Chap. 4.

The study involved compiling and analyzing a corpus of journal articles from every discipline taught at The Hong Kong Polytechnic University (24 in all) together with 15 fields (particularly in the social sciences and humanities) that are not currently offered at the institution, such as political science, music and history (see Appendix A). The corpus, which totals 5.6 million words and is available online at http://rcpce.engl.polyu.edu.hk/RACorpus/default.htm, is therefore representative of virtually all the major disciplines offered at comprehensive and application-oriented universities worldwide. Selected articles from the corpus were analyzed in the Swalesian tradition and the results of these analyses have been incorporated into instructional materials on RA writing. These materials (and the courses and workshops in which they are used) are essentially organized on the basis of IMRD; that is, each section in this pattern has its accompanying models, notes and tasks. What became apparent in the process of analyzing the corpus is that many ERAs did not conform to IMRD, which meant that certain aspects of RA writing, such as the division of the introductory phase into two clearly defined sections (i.e., Introduction and Literature Review), did not receive the attention they merited (a shortcoming that has subsequently been rectified). Recognition of this variation inspired the analysis described below.

3.2.1 *Data Collection*

The corpus consists of 780 full-length articles drawn from 20 leading international journals in each of the 39 disciplines. The selection of journals was based on the impact factors listed in the Journal Citation Report and the categorization in the University's journal list. The basic principle for the selection of RAs from these journals was that they should be the lead article of the first issue of 2007, except in occasional cases where the first article could not be extracted for some reason (e.g., its PDF format was not compatible with the Word operating system for format conversion), in which case the next article was selected. If this happened repeatedly in the first issue of 2007, the second issue in that volume was selected (and so on). To maximize variation in the corpus, no two RAs were written by the same author. As many of the RAs in the corpus were not empirical studies, the first stage of the analysis involved categorizing the RAs.

3.2.2 *Data Analysis*

3.2.2.1 Categorizing RAs

Based on the definitions of three categories of traditional RAs explicated in Sect. 2.2.1, 438 ERAs, 236 theoretical RAs and 106 review RAs were respectively identified in this study. As mentioned already, in the categorization process, RAs containing the heading Method (or variations on this theme, such as "Experimental", "Empirical design", "The study" and "Data and research design") were identified as empirical. Among the 438 RAs categorized as empirical, there are five without sectional labels. It should be noted that the remaining 433 sectionalized RAs are the focus of my analysis.

3.2.2.2 Analyzing ERAs

The second stage of the analysis involved a "manual" analysis of the main structural patterns in the 433 ERAs. Specific labels of sections and sub-sections provide some indication of the generic formats of such articles. On the basis of Yang and Allison's (2003: 369; 2004: 270) classification of section headings, the section headings were categorized into three groups, namely, "major standard headings", "varied functional headings" and "content headings".

The "major standard headings" are mostly conventional, viz. Introduction (I), Literature Review (LR), Method (M), Results (R), Discussion (D), and Conclusion (C). Among them, LR may require explanation when examined in the context of RAs as a genre. In this study, LR is used as an umbrella term to refer to a section or series of sections that occur between the introduction and the method which provide various kinds of "background" to the study. This background may be (inter alia) contextual, theoretical or methodological in nature, and may in some cases be in the form of a conventional literature review. In other words, the term is conceived more broadly here than is usually the case.

As noted earlier, some studies have imposed the IMRD framework on the RAs under review, with the result that, for example, LR and C have been treated as a part of I and D respectively despite being clearly different in both function and format. However, in the present study, as long as stand-alone sections not accounted for in the IMRD framework possessed their unique communicative purposes or distinct functional foci (in cases where they may have multiple communicative functions), they would be assigned an independent status rather than grouped as subcategories of their neighboring sections or those of the "conventional" sections encompassing partly overlapping elements with them. Likewise, this study neither adopted Yang and Allison's (2003) treatment of the Results and Discussion sections as a subgroup of Results nor regarded them as the equivalents or alternatives of the arrangements of the separate sections of Results and the subsequent Discussion. In fact, as the study has found, the above-mentioned elements are often merged into single sections, e.g., Results and Discussion [RD], Method, Results and Discussion [MRD] and Method and Results [MR]. Merging is represented in the present article with square brackets.

The "major standard headings" described above are largely self-explanatory and readily recognizable. This is not necessarily the case with "varied functional headings" and "content headings" as they are diverse, sometimes not rhetorically transparent and need to be judged by their specific function and content, as their designations suggest. For instance, instead of employing the "standard heading" D in their RAs, some authors labelled their discussion of findings with "varied functional headings" (e.g., "Discussion and critique", "Comment", "Beyond the evidence", "General discussion", "Interpretation of the findings") or "content headings" (e.g., "An example from the tobacco litigation", "Use of humour in the meetings", "Learning effort comparison").

In general, when analyzing sections with headings that were ambiguous (or even without headings altogether), the two analysts (a research associate and I) took full account of their discourse content, linguistic clues indicating section boundaries, their functions in the RA, the authors' apparent intentions as well as their overall communicative purposes. For instance, the opening sections of some ERAs in the corpus have no headings and yet the information elements embedded in them generally conform to the CARS model (Swales, 1990) and their role within the context of the entire RAs is primarily to establish the research background and state the research objectives. In such cases, it made sense to classify them as Introduction. In the process of analyzing sections, we also calculated the number of structural patterns for ERAs in each discipline and the frequency of each structural pattern in all disciplines (see Appendix A), which respectively reveal within-disciplinary variations and cross-disciplinary variations in macro structures.

After undergoing systematic training in the methods of analysis, the two analysts independently categorized the 780 RAs in the corpus (based, as noted above, on the presence or otherwise of M) and subsequently conducted a "manual" analysis of the 433 ERAs. This analysis was reasonably straightforward since most papers contained "major standard headings". Analyzing RAs with "varied functional headings" or "content headings" was rather more taxing and thus required repeated readings of the texts. Despite this, relatively high agreement rates of 93.9% and 90.2% were achieved respectively for the first and second stages of the analysis, suggesting that the two analysts were largely in accord in their judgments. In cases where initial disagreement arose, the two analysts reviewed and discussed the RAs in question and eventually reached an agreement.

3.3 Lead-in Study 2: Diachronic Studies of ERA Macro-structural Development in Two Contrasting Disciplines

One of the important contributions of the first lead-in study is the identification of AL and CE as two of the disciplines with the frequent use of LRs between I and M in contemporary ERAs. The second preparatory study thus focuses on the fields of AL and CE, and examines the recent macro-structural development of ERAs in them (1980–2010) with a particular focus on the evolution of the structural forms of their introductory phases. Two other important reasons for focusing on these two disciplines include: firstly, while previous diachronic RA studies mostly focus on traditional scientific disciplines such as physics (e.g., Bazerman, 1984) and medicine (e.g., Atkinson, 1992), AL and CE are two disciplines that have yet to be studied. Furthermore, since many existing studies only trace RA development in an individual discipline (e.g., Atkinson, 1992, 1999; Bazerman, 1984; Valle, 1997) and the related inter-disciplinary variations have rarely been researched, this study compares ERA structural development during the same period (1980–2010) in AL and CE. They are two disciplines with the contrasting nature and lengths of history: CE is a traditional engineering discipline with a long history (Wood, 2012), whereas AL is a less-established social science discipline. Hence, cross-disciplinary variations may exist in their ERA structural development (see Sects. 5.2–5.4). The following two subsections detail the procedures for this diachronic study.

3.3.1 ERAs Selected

To fulfill the purpose of this diachronic macro-structural study, ERAs should be firstly selected from all full-length, original English papers published in sampled volumes of the two leading journals respectively from AL and CE for the past thirty years. Regarding the number and the type of the journals selected, many diachronic RA studies (e.g., Atkinson, 1992, 1999; Bazerman, 1984; Valle, 1997) only choose a single high-impact, representative journal for analysis, given the considerable number of RAs involved. For this study, *Applied Linguistics (AL), TESOL Quarterly (TQ), Journal of Geotechnical and Geoenvironmental Engineering (JGGE)* and *Journal of Water Resources Planning and Management (JWRPM)* were selected as the source journals, for they all have a record of continuous publication and an excellent reputation, with their establishment years no later than 1980.

Textual changes are examined at five-year intervals during the 30-year period from 1980 to 2010, and thus the years sampled were 1980, 1985, 1990, 1995, 2000, 2005 and 2010. Altogether 1269 English RAs were gathered from all issues of the sampled volumes, with 301 from AL and the other 968 from CE. The difference in the number of RAs collected for the two disciplines is not surprising, as many scientific and engineering journals publish far more issues per year with each issue containing more papers than their counterparts in the social sciences. Of all the articles examined, 63.5% of AL RAs and 80.9% of CE RAs were found to be empirical ones; in other words, they report data derived from direct observation or experiments, usually to formulate and test theories, hypotheses and (computer-generated) models (Swales & Feak, 2004; Weissberg & Buker, 1990). All the other types of RAs including theoretical (234), review (45) and a few early articles that are engineering practice-based narrative accounts and teaching practice-based reports (only in AL) were identified and excluded.

The proportions of ERAs in these sampled volumes of the studied journals in AL and CE range respectively from 34.1% to 92.3%, and 64.3% to 88.3%, with a generally upward trend during the period under review. The large number of ERAs distributed across time in both disciplines makes the subsequent diachronic analysis of their macro-structure feasible.

3.3.2 Macro-structural Analysis of ERAs

Following Yang and Allison (2004), Pérez-Llantada (2013), and the macro-structural analytical methods used in the first lead-in study, a genre-based "manual" analysis of the macro-structure of the 974 in the two disciplines was conducted to examine the status of the IMRD pattern, to identify possible structural changes during the period under review, and to highlight pertinent cross-disciplinary variations. Since purpose is an important defining feature of genre or part-genre (Swales, 1990), the communicative function of the sections analyzed with reference to their roles in the whole RA context should be the principal concern in determining the overall structure of an ERA. Accordingly, the classic IMRD framework would not be imposed on the analysis but instead used as a descriptive reference point. Regarding the sections not accounted for in the IMRD model (e.g., LR, C and [RD]), they would be assigned an independent status on the condition that they have unique communicative purposes or functional foci (cf. Pérez-Llantada, 2013).

In addition to the communicative function of the sections and their roles in the entire articles, different section heading categories (viz. "major standard headings", "varied functional headings" and "content headings" firstly proposed in Yang and Allison 2003: 369, 2004: 270), linguistic signals and discourse content provide helpful indications of the generic structure of the RA and thus were taken into consideration in the analysis.

While utilizing all the above-mentioned clues, I also invited a CE post-doctoral researcher to assist with the analysis in that he mainly offered to explain some technical content and sectional relationship. After I completed the macro-structural analysis of all 974, around a half (95) of the AL ones and a third of the CE ones (260) were randomly chosen and emailed to a Ph.D. student with an ESP genre analysis background for another round of independent analysis. Our judgments were highly consistent (94.4%), suggesting the high reliability of the analysis. For a few disputed cases, we solicited the advice of the CE informant and subsequently reached agreement on their categories.

After the process of analysis, all the macro-structural patterns used over time were identified, with their frequencies of occurrences and the proportions of each pattern calculated, to document the cross-time and cross-disciplinary variations in macro-structures and to examine the status of the classic IMRD format in research writing during these years. Since the status and importance of the independent LR section is of particular interest in the present study, different structural patterns of the introductory phase across time were recorded with their frequencies and the proportions of each of them computed.

3.4 The Focused Study of the Introductory Phase

The two lead-in studies answer the first two research questions from the cross-sectional and diachronic perspectives respectively. As for the latter two research questions, they are answered by a focused study of an important yet hitherto unexplored type of introductory phase structured in "I+LR" in two contrasting disciplines (viz., AL and CE) through a combined method of textual analysis and interview study.

General procedures for this focused study are listed as follows:

Stage 1 Textual data collection and corpora compilation
Stage 2 Genre analysis of the introductory phase of ERAs in AL and CE
Stage 3 Citation analysis of the introductory phase of ERAs in AL and CE

Stage 4 Interviews with expert participants to elicit the insiders' views on structuring and using citations in the introductory phase of ERAs in the two disciplines.

3.4.1 Analysis of Structural and Citation Practices in the Introductory Phase

3.4.1.1 Rationale

As aforementioned, the two lead-in studies have provided compelling empirical evidence for the important status of LR in the entire ERA from two complementary perspectives (i.e., the cross-sectional and diachronic perspectives). Notwithstanding its status as a major section of the ERA, LR has seldom been examined in detail in terms of either its schematic structure or language use in the previous literature, and has hardly been accounted for in EAP writing workshops and instructional materials. For these reasons, a focused study of the entire introductory phase containing both the Introduction and LR sections was conducted as the core of this project in terms of their rhetorical structure and citation use.

3.4.1.2 Research Questions

Four specific research questions are explored in the focused analysis of the "I+LR" introductory phase:

1. What is the rhetorical structure of the introductory phase of ERAs with the format of "I+LR" in AL and CE?
2. How are citations used in the introductory phase of ERAs with the format of "I+LR" in AL and CE?
3. What are disciplinary variations in the rhetorical structure of and citation use in the introductory phase of ERAs with the format of "I+LR" in AL and CE?
4. What are differences between the Introduction section and the subsequent LR section regarding their rhetorical structure and citation use in AL and CE?

3.4.1.3 Corpus

This study employs two specialized corpora which respectively contain 30 introductory phases of ERAs structured in "I+LR" in the field of AL (hereafter CAL) and another 30 in CE (hereafter CCE), with texts associated with tables and figures, and relevant footnotes excluded. With impact factors listed in the Journal Citation Report and recommendations from disciplinary experts in these two fields taken into full consideration, *English for Specific Purposes, Language Learning, AL, TQ* and *Studies in Second Language Acquisition* were chosen as the five source journals for CAL and *Journal of Computing in Civil Engineering, Journal of Transportation Engineering, Transportation, JGGE* and *Journal of Composites for Construction* were those for CCE. Starting from the first RA of the first issue in 2011 volume, I collected six introductory phases that strictly follow the format of "I+LR" for each of these ten prestigious journals. In addition, special care was taken to select RAs written by different authors, and all special issues of the ten journals that consist of themed papers around a specific topic were not considered for data collection. Altogether 60 introductory phases of the ERA with an LR employed between I and M in AL and CE were selected for corpus compilation (see Appendix B for a list of source articles).

As the differences between the two part-genres "I" and "LR" with regard to their rhetorical structures and citation use were examined, CAL needs to be further divided into two sub-corpora: CALI (the sub-corpus for the Introduction section of ERAs from AL) and CALL (the sub-corpus for the Literature Review section of ERAs from AL). Likewise, CCE is separated into two related sub-corpora: CCEI (the sub-corpus for the Introduction section of ERAs from CE) and CCEL (the sub-corpus for the Literature Review section of ERAs from CE).

The particulars of the corpora CAL and CCE, and their sub-corpora CALI, CALL, CCEI, and CCEL are given in Table 3.1. The sizes of CAL and CCE are small (total 83,705 and 47,538 words respectively), but, as remarked by Hunston (2002: 26), "a small corpus can be valuable under certain circumstances" and one possible circumstance is to construct a specialized corpus for a particular research purpose. There are significant disciplinary variations in the lengths of the introductory phase and the LR section: the entire introductory part structured in the "I+LR" pattern in AL is much longer than that in CE (see both their average lengths in the corpora and their proportions in the full ERA); LR in AL is more than twice as long as that in CE, although the difference in their proportions in the full ERA is a little smaller. In contrast, the average length of the Introduction section and its proportion in the whole ERA in both disciplines are quite similar. Furthermore, the marked cross-generic differences in length can also be observed: in AL, the LR section averages 2,214 words (25.4% of the whole ERA), being approximately four times as long as the Introduction Sect. (555 words, 6.4% of the entire ERA); in CE, the average length of LR is 1,019 words (13.9% of the entire ERA), near twice as long as the Introduction (565 words, 7.7% of the whole ERA).

Table 3.1 The size of CAL, CCE, CALI, CALL, CCEI, CCEL, the average length of the introductory phase, I and LR, and their proportions in the full ERA

Disciplines	The introductory phase I+LR (average length, proportion)	I (average length, proportion)	LR (average length, proportion)
AL	83,705 (2769, 31.8%)	16,654 (555, 6.4%)	66,421 (2214, 25.4%)
CE	47,538 (1585, 21.6%)	16,958 (565, 7.7%)	30,580 (1019, 13.9%)

3.4.1.4 Data Analysis

After corpus compilation, a genre-based rhetorical structural analysis and a multi-layered citation research were conducted successively (see Stages 2-3 in general procedures outlined in Sect. 3.4).

Stage 2 Genre analysis of the introductory phase of ERAs in AL and CE

Sub-stage 1 Genre analysis of the rhetorical structure of the Introduction section

CALI and CCEI were used for the rhetorical structural analysis of the introductions with a following LR section. For ease of reference, each introduction in the two sub-corpora was assigned a number, CALI1 through CALI30 and CCEI1 through CCEI30 respectively.

All the 30 CE introductions are well-defined stand-alone sections headed "Introduction" except CCEI23 labeled "Introduction and background". In contrast, among the 30 AL introductions, 14 are headed "Introduction" whereas as many as 16 are non-labeled. This is because most of the source journals such as TQ, LL and SSLA require their submitted manuscripts to follow the specifications of the Publication Manual of the American Psychological Association (6th edition), which maintains that the introduction does not need to carry a heading that labels it as introduction due to its clearly identifiable position in the article. All these introductions have a distinguishable LR section employed after them.

Before identifying the move structure of the genre, it is essential to understand the overall rhetorical purpose of the texts in the genre (Biber, Connor, & Upton, 2007). After repeated readings of all the texts in both disciplines, the present researcher, with the help of my supervisor and an experienced research associate (with reference to the literature, the interview accounts of some CE and AL professionals, and our personal exchanges with some other professors and doctoral researchers in these two fields), discovered that, when there is a subsequent LR section, the introductions may be structured in different ways with their distinct major communicative functions. Among the 60 introductions with a subsequent LR collected from the two disciplines, a significant portion of them regularly reflect a two-move structure with the main functions of identifying the issue to be addressed and informing readers of the study to be presented. They serve as an orientation to the study that provides the general background, identifies an issue of potential value or interest in a very brief, general and straightforward manner, but usually does not involve detailed elaboration to establish a niche based on specific and critical reviews of individual studies. Therefore, an appropriate term—"the Orientation introduction"—is proposed to characterize them. Two example texts of the Orientation introduction are provided (see CCEI28 in Appendix C and CALI9 in Appendix D).

Functionally different from Orientation-type introductions, many of the other introductions display a close affinity to Swales's (1990, 2004) CARS model in that the three prototypical moves suggested in Swales's schema (viz., Move 1 Establishing a Territory, Move 2 Establishing a Niche, and Move 3 Presenting the Present Work) are all present in them. In contrast, five out of the 30 CE introductions exhibit a fairly different move structure from CARS (see Sect. 6.2.1.4) and mainly address practical problems related to construction materials and infrastructure management projects, despite the fact that they also mainly function to create a research space for the study. These five introductions are analogous to "Problem-focused" introductions described by Feak and Swales (2011) and diverge greatly from the traditional "Gap-focused" introductions. Accordingly, the introductions that follow the CARS model and the five CE introductions with structural resemblance to "Problem-focused" introductions (Feak & Swales, 2011) are respectively termed the "Research-oriented Traditional CARS (RT CARS)" type and the "Practical-problem Solving (PS)" type based on their different structural flows and the nature and orientations of the studies reported.

In addition to the RT CARS type, the Two-move Orientation type and the PS type, a special AL introduction termed "Building on the Writer's Own Previous Research" was identified. It is styled and structured very differently from the previous three types. As this is the only case identified in CALI and is absent in CCEI, it is not suited for genre analysis. However, some descriptions of its structural flow and style features are presented in Sect. 6.2.2.1 to give readers a sense of structural variability of the introductions with a subsequent LR section and for the reference of the future similar research of a larger scale in other disciplines.

Accordingly, the 60 introductions with a following LR section in CE and AL could be firstly classified based on their major communicative functions, structural flows, and the nature and orientations of the studies reported into the RT CARS type, the Two-move Orientation type, the PS type and the "Building on the Writer's Own Previous Research" type. The distribution of the different types of introductions in the two studied disciplines is shown in Table 3.2. From this table, it can be found that the RT CARS type and the Orientation type are the two dominant categories of introductions identified in both disciplines while the other two types are either absent or in a minority. Therefore, the two-tier rhetorical structural analysis (moves and sub-moves) is only conducted for the two major categories of introductions, i.e., the Orientation type and the RT CARS type in both disciplines.

Notably, the present study followed Stoller and Robinson (2013), using "moves" and "sub-moves" as two levels of units to describe the rhetorical organization of introductions. The reason for preferring "sub-moves" to "steps" and "strategies" is that "steps" (involuntarily) indicates the obligatory and sequenced presence of a move constituent and "strategies" (Bhatia, 1993, 2001) suggests the opposite, while "sub-moves" is a more inclusive term. Since not all move constituents identified in this study can be strictly qualified as "steps" or "strategies" (see Sects. 3.2–3.3), the term

Table 3.2 Classification of introductions followed by an LR section in CE and AL

Disciplines	RT CARS	Orientation	Practical-problem solving	Building on the writer's own previous research
CE	15	10	5	0
AL	18	11	0	1

"sub-moves" of an all-encompassing nature seems more appropriate to represent them. As such, the present author only resumed the use of "steps" and "strategies" when referring to relevant previous studies, which adopted them as the analytical unit.

Two other important principles were also adhered to: first, imperatives rather than gerunds and present principles were used to label the moves and sub-moves for foregrounding writers' actions, as practised in Stoller and Robinson (2013: 50). Second, in the coding analysis, for a few sentences reflecting more than one rhetorical function, only the most salient one was considered, a criterion widely adopted by previous studies (e.g., Crookes, 1986; Del Saz-Rubio, 2011; Holmes, 1997; Ozturk, 2007; Sheldon, 2011).

By following the general steps outlined in Biber et al. (2007) for conducting a systematic move analysis and incorporating the salutary input from the informants of the disciplinary fields, the researcher with the help of the aforementioned two experienced academic staff formulated a "Two-move Orientation" approach (Fig. 3.2) for the rhetorical structure of Orientation introductions. The reason for naming it as an "approach" rather than a "model" is that it is a preliminary scheme formulated for Orientation-style introductions and awaits future studies for validation. Given that it is a newly-developed scheme, the definitions and examples of its featured moves and sub-moves are presented and explicated in Sects. 6.2.1.2 and 6.2.2.2.

As for the RT CARS introduction, Swales's (1990, 2004) CARS models were used as the starting point for the analysis of its structure. Concerning the moves and steps conceptually shared by the two versions of CARS and present in the current data, their new labels as depicted in the 2004 model were adopted. While the three moves in Swales's schema were found prototypical in all RT CARS introductions in this study, the genre analysis at the sub-move level is more complex and challenging.

Move 1	**Identify the issue**
Sub-move 1.1	Survey non-research phenomena/practices or general knowledge claims of the field
Sub-move 1.2	Establish importance of the field
Sub-move 1.3	Suggest value of the issue
Move 2	**Present the study**
Sub-move 2.1	Announce research purposes, foci, research questions, or hypotheses
Sub-move 2.2	Summarize the methods and contextual conditions
Sub-move 2.3	Make definitional clarifications
Sub-move 2.4	Preview main findings
Sub-move 2.5	State the significance of the present research
Sub-move 2.6	Indicate the Literature Review content
Sub-move 2.7	Outline the article structure

Fig. 3.2 The Two-move Orientation approach

To facilitate the analysis, all move constituents indicated in Swales's schema as well as in other previous studies (e.g., Del Saz-Rubio, 2011; Loi, 2010) were used as important references. Related semantic attributes and linguistic signals suggested were also referred to during the identification and assignment of move elements. Finally, a framework was developed for the analysis of RT CARS introductions. As the development of the framework is grounded in Swales's schema and informed by other genre studies in the Swalesian tradition, it is termed as "the Integrated CARS model" (Fig. 3.3).

In accounting for the Integrated CARS model, the moves and sub-moves that were adopted from Swales's schema are not explicated to avoid unnecessary repetition (see all the elements except those in italics in Fig. 3.3). Nevertheless, the elements adopted from other genre studies and the element newly found in this study are detailed. In terms of Move 1, Del Saz-Rubio's (2011) practice of maintaining the three sub-moves for Move 1 (namely, Sub-move 1.1 "Claim Centrality", Sub-move 1.2 "Make Generalizations of Increasing Specificity", and Sub-move 1.3 "Survey Items of Previous Research") was followed. The reason is that Adnan (2008: 48) and many other genre analysts (e.g., Del Saz-Rubio, 2011; Sheldon, 2011) have pointed out that the single unitary step in Move 1 of Swales's (2004) revised CARS model (viz., "Topic Generalization of Increasing Specificity") seems somewhat over-generalized and may lead us to "miss interesting strategies employed by the authors". Also due to this concern, Samraj's (2002, 2005) further classification of "Claim Centrality" into two subcategories (i.e., Sub-move 1.1a "Claim Importance in Research World" and Sub-move 1.1b "Claim Importance in Real World") was adopted with reference to the present data.

Move 1	**Establish a territory**
Sub-move 1.1	Claim centrality
	1.1a Claim importance in research world
	1.1b Claim importance in real world
Sub-move 1.2	Make topic generalizations of increasing specificity
Sub-move 1.3	Survey items of previous research
Move 2	**Establish a niche**
Sub-move 2.1	Indicate a gap
	2.1a Indicate a gap in research
	2.1b Indicate a problem in or need from real world
Sub-move 2.2	Present positive justifications
Sub-move 2.3	*Suggest implicitly inconsistencies precluding gap signalling*
Move 3	**Present the present work**
Sub-move 3.1	*Announce research purposes, foci, research questions, or hypotheses*
Sub-move 3.2	Summarize research methods
Sub-move 3.3	*State theoretical frameworks/theoretical positions*
Sub-move 3.4	Preview main findings
Sub-move 3.5	State the significance of the present research
Sub-move 2.6	*Indicate the Literature Review content*
Sub-move 3.7	Outline the article structure

Fig. 3.3 The Integrated CARS model

Similarly, in Move 2, the first sub-move "gap-indication" was distinguished into two varieties: Sub-move 2.1a "Indicate a Gap in Research" and Sub-move 2.1b "Indicate a Problem in or Need from the Real World" (Samraj, 2002, 2005). The present researcher also found the sub-move "Suggest Implicitly Inconsistencies Precluding Gap Signaling", which was newly discovered by Del Saz-Rubio (2011), in the current data, thereby including it in the model. An instance of this sub-move is provided below:

> (1) ...**some recent studies that have investigated the issue of pragmatic and grammatical acquisition have found evidence in support of the hypothesis that** SL environments foster awareness of pragmatic appropriateness, whereas FL environments focus on grammatical accuracy (e.g., Bardovi-Harlig & Dornyei...**However, evidence has also been reported that** English FL (EFL) speakers showed a higher sensitivity to pragmatic errors than their English SL (ESL) counterparts (Niezgoda & Rover, 2001). These somewhat *controversial* findings in the existing research... (CALI1)

Regarding Move 3, Sub-moves 3.2, 3.4, 3.5 and 3.7 in the integrated CARS model were drawn from Swales's (1990, 2004) CARS model. Sub-move 3.1 (Announce Research Purposes, Focuses, Research Questions, or Hypotheses) is a combination of Step 1 (Announcing Present Research Descriptively and/or Purposively) and Step 2 (Presenting RQs or Hypotheses) of Move 3 in the revised CARS model. This combination practice performed by Kwan (2006) in her genre analysis of the Literature Review chapters of doctoral dissertations was found applicable to the present data analysis and was thus adopted. Two new special elements (Sub-move 3.3 "State Theoretical Frameworks/Positions" and Sub-move 3.6 "Inform the Literature Review Content") are added as the writers were found to employ them in presenting their research work. These two new elements are illustrated below respectively:

> (2)...**it is argued throughout the present article** that not only are multiword expressions much more common than popularly assumed, but they are also difficult for readers to both accurately identify and decode—even when they only contain very common words. (CALI18)

> (3) **Two areas of current literature will be reviewed.** First, the effect of practice on the acquisition of cognitive skills...Second, the effects of time distribution... (CALI 26)

However, the element for informing LR content is not existent in the CE RT CARS introductions, more details of which are presented in Sect. 6.2.1. After developing the integrated CARS model and the Two-move Orientation approach as coding protocols of the two major types of introductions through repeated pilot-coding exercises and substantial discussions with the specialist informants in the two disciplines and the two expert genre analysts as mentioned before, the researcher used WinMax's QDA program (MaxQDA, 2012) to code all texts. A trained coder who is an applied linguistics PhD candidate coded independently six texts (around 33.3%) from the RT CARS group and five texts (around 45.5%) from the Orientation group in AL and five each (altogether 40% of the texts) from the two major groups in CE for our inter-coder reliability check. Our agreement percentages range from 85 to 88%, generally indicating the validity of and consistency in our coding and analysis. Any remaining few discrepancies were resolved through discussion, criteria checking and further clarification.

Sub-stage 2 Genre analysis of the rhetorical structure of the LR section

CALL and CCEL were used for the ESP genre-based study of the LR section in ERAs. Similarly, each LR text in the two sub-corpora was assigned a number—CALL1 through CALL30 and CCEL1 through CCEL30—for convenience of analysis and ease of reference.

As mentioned before, the ESP genre-based approach adopted here is a top-bottom, function-based analytical method of studying cognitive move-structure of genres (Bhatia, 1993: 22–36). The first step in ESP genre-based analysis is to understand the overall rhetorical purpose of the texts in the genre (Biber et al., 2007). To assist the understanding and analysis of propositional content and communicative purposes of the LR texts, the source ERAs and their abstracts were first skimmed through to obtain necessary information on the study and the related disciplinary knowledge. Following this, a pilot function-based move analysis of the LR texts was conducted, which however revealed that the LR section in ERAs may involve different separate functional components: Advanced Organizer/Overview, Theoretical Review, Contextual Background, and Conclusion. The four separate, distinct functional components comprise the general rhetorical organization of the LR section in ERAs (see Fig. 3.4).

Among the four functional components, "Theoretical Review" is the only obligatory one in this part-genre whereas the other three are optional. These four functional components of different nature are expatiated on consecutively.

Somewhat similar to the LR chapters in doctoral theses (Kwan, 2005, 2006), a very small number of LRs in ERAs in the present study open with a concise introduction (i.e., "Advanced Organizer/Overview", see Example 4 below), which consists of only one to a few sentences.

(4) The review of relevant literature begins with a summary of the findings related to median width and median barriers in general followed by a literature discussion focused on cable barriers. (CCEL24)

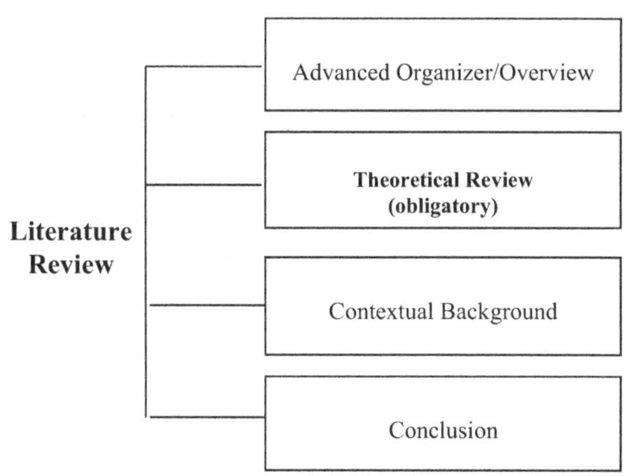

Fig. 3.4 The possible composition of the LR section

Also, a few other LRs examined in this study close with an obviously longer summary text, which often sums up the major content reviewed and sometimes prepares for the introduction of the present research work (see Example 5 below).

(5) **Summary**

In summary, the following has been argued thus far:

- Current estimates of how many words one needs to know in order to comprehend most texts may be inaccurate due to overinclusion of derived word forms and a total exclusion of multiword units of vocabulary.
- Contrary to some research, there is evidence in corpus data that the number of frequently occurring noncompositional multiword expressions in English ....
- Even when an expression is partly or even fully compositional....
- The claim that special attention to the 2,000–3,000 most common words in English is pedagogically sound....

It is therefore clear that there is a need for further investigation into how common words and the multiword units.... To that end, we conducted a study to answer the following research questions:

1. Are two texts, written with the exact same high-frequency words...?
2. Can the presence of multiword expressions in a text lead L2 learners to believe...? (CALL18)

The only predominant functional component is Theoretical Review, which is present in all 60 LRs. "Theoretical Review", as an inclusive term proposed in this study, refers to the review of "grand theories", "middle-range theories" and/or "background literature" (Bryman, 2008: 21–23). The three types of "theory" [including "background literature" as theory in Bryman (2008: 23)] with decreasing generality and abstractness are defined as follows: "Middle-range theories" are "intermediate to general theories of social systems which are too remote from particular classes of social behaviour, organization and change to account for what is observed and to those detailed orderly descriptions of particulars that are not generalized at all" (Merton, 1967: 39). This is a definition originally provided for sociology; in applied linguistics, an instance of "middle-range theories" is Functional Grammar (Halliday, 1985, 1994; Halliday & Matthiessen, 2004), which could be successfully applied to empirical inquiry of some language data but may still be a developing theory that continually incorporates amendments and more explanations of its associated concepts and systems. Compared to "middle-range theories", "grand theories" "operate at a more abstract and general level" (Bryman, 2012: 21). Grand theory usually does not guide empirical research; in contrast, middle-range theory can be the focus of empirical enquiry. A classic example of grand theory is Einstein's Theory of Relativity.

"Background literature as theory" is a concept grounded from the perception that, in many cases, background literature related to a research topic functions as the main impetus for the research work to be undertaken, thereby acting as "the equivalent of a theory" (Bryman, 2012: 23). Taken together, "Theoretical Review" in this study covers the review of theories, frameworks, hypotheses and all schemes of different degrees of abstractness and generality as well as all related other literature. As such, chronology of methodology, descriptions of theories and frameworks and the traditional "pure" literature review all belong to "Theoretical Review".

An example of the Theoretical Review component is the first section of CALL20 (see Appendix E), which is headed "Wikis and Academic Writing". This Theoretical Review component outlines a theoretical framework for the ensuing empirical study of collaborative writing on the wiki. More specifically, the definition of "wiki", related sociocultural theory, reader-oriented writing, the concept and taxonomy of metadiscourse, the writer-reader relationship, and the notion of the writer as a member of a given discourse community are reviewed. The purpose is to inform readers of theoretical background of this study and to establish links among collaborative learning theories, metadiscourse research and the philosophy behind collaborative writing on the course wiki.

Different from the Theoretical Review component, "Contextual Background" provides necessary details on the specific context or background setting for the study; this type of study is often particularly relevant to a social or educational context and the implications of its findings need to be interpreted and understood in this context. For instance, in CALL20 (see Appendix E), before the Method section, there is an additional section which follows the Theoretical Review "Wikis and Academic Writing" and can be categorized as a "Contextual Background" component. This section, as its heading "Background to the Study" suggests, details the contextual background of the study to the readers: the design, focus, and purpose of the course of Effective Communication in English at Stockholm University where wikis are applied to the teaching of academic and professional writing, how peer feedback and collaboration is performed in student assignment writing via the MediaWiki platform, and how the readership of the students' texts could be extended accordingly. This contextual background description fosters our understanding of the design and significance of this study, which adds to the emerging literature on the application of ICT to the teaching and learning of academic and professional writing.

Based on all the explanations above, it can be easily inferred that the rhetorical organization of CAAL20 is: "Theoretical Review + Contextual Background". This way of analyzing LR texts has also been applied to all the other LR data.[2] As mentioned above, the important findings of the analysis exercise is that Theoretical Review is the only obligatory, separate functional component in the LR section and the majority (90%) of the 60 LRs contain exclusively the Theoretical Review component. Consequently, a systematic genre-based study of the rhetorical structure of Theoretical Reviews was undertaken and all the other functional components were excluded from the detailed move-based study because of their limited numbers. However, some useful accounts of their rhetorical structure and communicative functions are presented in Sect. 6.3.1. Another point is that for the few LRs that contain both Theoretical Review and any other functional components (viz., "Advanced Organizer/Overview", "Conclusion" and "Contextual Background"), only Theoretical

[2]Note that all functional components identified in the 60 LRs are functionally-distinct, individual parts, thus there is no difficulty in the parsing exercise.

Reviews were analyzed. Accordingly, if we take CAAL20 again as an example, only the first section "Wikis and Academic Writing" as a "Theoretical Review" was analyzed using the ESP genre-based approach.

In the focused study of the rhetorical structure of Theoretical Reviews, sectional analyses, which have been used in Kwan's (2005, 2006) pioneering research into the schematic structure of the LR chapters in Ph.D. theses, were not adopted, due to the following concerns. First, Kwan's innovative attempts to analyze the LR chapters into different theme-bound sections and then to focus on the structure of these "thematic units" were inspired by her observations that thesis LR chapters comprise multiple sections on different themes and the CARS structure may occur and recur within such sections. However, in contrast to the LR chapter in research degree theses which is often much longer and covers as comprehensively as possible different dimensions of research background, the LR section in ERAs (or rather the Theoretical Review component) is often a more focused review of selected and synthesized literature (Machi & McEvoy, 2012). Hence, many of the 60 LRs collected (e.g., 20 out of the 30 CE LRs) do not contain multiple theme-bound sections like LR chapters in Kwan's study; they are instead purely stand-alone sections with no thematic subsections included (e.g., CCEL_TR3 in Appendix F). Given this, sectional analyses are not applicable to the present data. On the other hand, in AL, although there are more Theoretical Reviews displaying "multi-(sub-)sectional" structure than in CE, to keep the analysis consistent and to make cross-disciplinary comparison valid, sectional analyses were not conducted and the Theoretical Review component from each source ERA was analyzed as an individual unit.

Second, even within the group of Theoretical Reviews comprising multiple theme-bound sections/sub-sections, their thematic units may have different proportional content, nature, and functional contributions to the overall Theoretical Reviews or LR texts. Thus, it is not appropriate to treat them as the same basic unit of analysis, a practice which might also overlook the logical links among such thematic units and the element that provides a smooth transition for them (e.g., "Suggest the Subsequent Theme to be Reviewed" as a newly-identified element to be reported in Sect. 6.3.2.4). A good case in point is CALL19 (see Appendix G), where the two theme-bound subsections respectively cover related theories and hypotheses and the body of empirical research, as can be easily perceived from their headings ("Demonstratives, cohesion, and the problem with prescriptivism" and "Previous investigations into demonstratives as pronouns vs. determiners"). They thus function quite differently, with the first sub-section mainly aiming to provide theoretical underpinnings and contextualization and the second aiming to offer justifications or rationales for the study based upon the critiques of previous empirical studies. If we break this LR text into two parallel thematic units and then analyze them separately, we may have entirely neglected the featured information flow of Theoretical Reviews in ERAs: from theoretical to empirical (Wen, 2001). Therefore, to have a complete and more accurate representation of the rhetorical structure of Theoretical Reviews, sectional analyses were not conducted and all of them were instead analyzed as individual units based on different source ERAs they were drawn from. As the Theoretical Review component is present in all 60 LRs, there are 60 Theoretical Reviews to be analyzed in terms of their move structure. These 60 Theoretical Review components in the two disciplines are henceforth referred to as CALL_TR1 through CALL_TR30, CCEL_TR1 through CCEL_TR30 respectively for ease of reference.

Regarding the ESP genre-based study of Theoretical Reviews, a two-tier structural analysis ("moves" and "sub-moves") was conducted. This genre-based study mainly relied on cognitive judgment of the rhetorical purpose of Theoretical Reviews, the function of each textual segment in Theoretical Review in terms of its local purpose and its possible contribution to a functional unit of a higher class, and the interrelationship among adjacent textual segments. As both Tessuto (2015) and Kwan, Chan, and Lam (2012) contend that the LR section in RAs generally follow the CARS structure, this study also used the CAS model and its revised version (Swales, 1990, 2004) and all the semantic attributes, linguistic exponents and characterizing accounts of each move and move constituent reported in previous introduction studies (e.g., Anthony, 1999; Bunton, 2002; Del Saz-Rubio, 2011; Lewin, Fine, & Young, 2001; Loi, 2010; Loi & Evans, 2010; Ozturk, 2007; Samraj, 2002, 2005; Sheldon, 2011; Swales, 1990, 2004; Tessuto, 2015) and LR studies (Kwan, 2005, 2006) as important references.

Repeated readings of Theoretical Review texts and several rounds of manual coding and discussions on the nomenclature of some elements and on any disagreements in the coding were conducted by an expert genre analyst and the present researcher. After this taxing analytical process with continuous refinements, fine-tuning, and recoding of some textual segments, a four-move structure was eventually developed for the Theoretical Review component (see Fig. 3.5). It was then applied to the coding of all 60 Theoretical Reviews by the present researcher using MaxQDA 10 (MaxQDA, 2012). The same applied linguistics doctoral student who was once invited to code some introductions for the inter-rater reliability check independently coded four Theoretical Reviews from AL and another four from CE (altogether 13.3%). A comparatively high agreement rate (around 86.7%) was achieved between our coding. Apparent disagreements were resolved through our discussions and a few segments were re-coded afterwards. A few coding ambiguities will be detailed in Sect. 6.3.2.

As shown in Fig. 3.5, the four-move structure proposed indicates that the communicative function of the Theoretical Review component is to present theoretical, empirical and non-research background for the study, to situate and position the present study in this background and to outline it. Some elements in this four-move structure resemble those in the CARS structure. Nevertheless, many others particularly characterize the genre of the LR section (e.g., "Relevance-claiming" and "Theoretical framework-synthesizing") with some being newly discovered (e.g., "Assert the Irrelevance of the Surveyed Claims to One's Own Research to Specify the Scope of the Study"). All four moves and their constituents will be fully explicated and illustrated in Sect. 6.3.2, where findings on their frequency, combination patterns and sequential use are also reported. Kwan's (2005, 2006) structural model formulated for the theme-bound sections in thesis LR chapters and the CARS structure for article introductions (Swales, 1990, 2004) were used as the reference for comparison. Finally, a structural comparison between the LR sections in CE ERAs and

Move 1	Demarcate the research territory
Sub-move 1.1	Highlight significance of research issues/problems
Sub-move 1.2	Survey knowledge claims or provide an overview of the research area
Sub-move 1.3	Survey non-research-fronted phenomena or practices
Move 2	**Review key studies**
Move 3	**Position the present study**
Sub-move 3.1	Indicate explicitly a gap or problem 3.1a Indicate a research gap or a limitation in previous research 3.1b Indicate a problem in or need from the real world
Sub-move 3.2	Assert confirmative claims about knowledge or research practices surveyed
Sub-move 3.3	Assert the relevance of the surveyed claims to one's own research
Sub-move 3.4	Assert the irrelevance of the surveyed claims to one's own research to specify the scope of the study
Sub-move 3.5	Abstract, synthesize, or make inferences from knowledge claims to establish a theoretical position or framework
Sub-move 3.6	Indicate inconsistencies in findings/conclusions/claims from previous studies without explicit gap-signaling
Move 4	**Outline the present study**
Sub-move 4.1	Announce research aims, purposes, research questions or hypotheses
Sub-move 4.2	Announce theoretical positions/frameworks
Sub-move 4.3	Indicate research design/processes/methodology
Sub-move 4.4	Announce interpretations of terminology used in the study
Sub-move 4.5	State the value of the present study
Sub-move 4.6	Suggest the subsequent theme to be reviewed
Sub-move 4.7	Indicate the content of the Method section

Fig. 3.5 A possible structure for Theoretical Reviews in ERAs

those in AL ERAs was undertaken to provide more insights into discipline-specific LR writing.

Stage 3 Analysis of citation use in the introductory phase of ERAs in AL and CE

In citation analysis of the Introductions and LR sections in the two contrasting disciplines, citation density, citation forms, functions and RVs are selected as the research parameters. Before the analysis of these research parameters, the first step is to identify citations based on certain criteria, which are specified below.

Following the operational definitions of citation as detailed in Sect. 2.5.1, all citations in the corpora were carefully identified. During this identification process, there were some important notes that I complied with: firstly, as it is noted that the nature, function and purpose of self-citations is diametrically different from citations to others' works (see Berkenkotter & Huckin, 1995; Bonzi & Snyder, 1991; Myers, 1990), in this research, only references to others' works were analyzed; secondly, references to the specific or representative work of others rather than to the school of thoughts or ideas in general (e.g., "Swalesian" or "Freudian and post-Freudian theory") are regarded as the real citation (Hyland, 1999; Thompson & Tribble, 2001); thirdly, the second hand referencing is considered as a single citation. It is noted that all 60 introductory phases selected use Harvard System conventions rather than the footnote referencing system, which ensures their comparability for citation analysis (Swales, 2014).

Other criteria recorded in the literature (e.g., Mansourizadeh & Ahmad, 2011; Thompson, 2000, 2001) were also adopted:

a. No matter whether it is a single or a multiple reference citation, only one citation tag was inserted (see Mansourizadeh & Ahmad, 2011; Thompson, 2001);
b. Also, for the citation that is not limited to one sentence but further elaborated on in the subsequent lines of the text (see "extensive citations" in Swales (1986)), only one citation tag "<cit n = "*"> … </cit>" was inserted to enclose it (see Table 3.3), e.g.,

> (6) <cit n = 1> In addition, tests on GFRP reinforced beams performed by Laoubi et al. (2006) found no significant difference when comparing beams subjected to sustained loads at room temperature with the results of control specimens. **The writers also concluded that** the equation from ACI 440.1R-06 (ACI 2006) for the long-term deflection due to creep and shrinkage highly overestimates the deflections. </cit> (CCEL8)

c. According to Thompson's (2000, 2001) classification, "Non-citation", which usually appears after the researcher has been cited and does not have the publication year and page followed, is a special type of integral citation. e.g.,

Table 3.3 Tagging scheme

Tag	Use	Tag	Use
<cit n = "*">…</cit>	The text that is enclosed is a reported statement of a certain number of citations and "*" indicates the number of citations contained	<an/>	Author neutral RVs
<ic/>	Integral citations	<at/>	Author tentative RVs
<nc/>	Non-integral citations	<att/>	Attribution
<ivc/>	Integral verb-controlling citations	<fr/>	Further reference
<inc/>	Integral naming citations	<exa/>	Example
<rv/>	Reporting verbs (RVs)	<ori/>	Origin
<drv/>	Discourse RVs	<ide/>	Identification
<mrv/>	Mental RVs	<exe/>	Exemplification
<rrv/>	Research RVs	<sup/>	Support
<srv/>	Stative RVs	<gen/>	Generalization from multiple sources
<wf/>	Writer factive RVs	<com/>	Comparison and contrast between/among sources
<wc/>	Writer counter-factive RVs	<st/>	Statement of use
<wn/>	Writer non-factive RVs	<app/>	Application
<ap/>	Author positive RVs	<eva/>	Evaluation
<ac/>	Author critical RVs	<cos/>	Comparison of one's own study with other sources

(7) Accordingly, **Chen and Guo** suggested that Chinese should be classified as an equipollently-framed language, as suggested by Slobin. (CALL30)

Based on these principles, all citations were identified and hand-coded with Notepad++6.6.3. The manual coding with Notepad++6.6.3 was also applied to the analysis of citation forms, functions and RVs, though with different corresponding tags. The tagging scheme used in the citation study is shown in Table 3.3. As noted above in Example (4), "<cit n = "*">…</cit>" was used to indicate the beginning and ending of a citation. As for the other tags, those suggesting different types of citation forms and functions such as "<ic/>" and "<nc/>" were placed to the right of the citation, while those indicating different categories of RVs in terms of denotation and evaluative potential were inserted to the right of RVs. AntConc 3.2.4 was used to concordance all tags in corpora to quantify their use.

As mentioned earlier, citation frequency/density, signals (RVs), forms and functions are the main parameters of citation research in this focused study. After the identification of citations, the occurrences of citations in the two major sections of the introductory phase (viz., I and LR) in the two disciplines were recorded and compared. In addition to these raw numbers, the average numbers of citations per text and per 1,000 words of running text in CALI, CALL, CCEI and CCEL were calculated and compared.

As for citation forms, Swales's (1990) binary citation forms (integral vs. non-integral citation forms) were applied to the present analysis. As detailed in Sect. 2.5.1, Thompson and Tribble (2001) and Thompson (2001, 2005) have further classified the two citation forms into different subtypes, however based on different criteria—syntactical/grammatical criteria for integral citations and functional criteria for non-integral citations. Nevertheless, it is noted that some subtypes of non-integral citations they proposed based on functional criteria (e.g., "source", "reference" and "origin") have been successfully applied to a range of functional analyses of all citations identified in subsequent studies (e.g., Mansourizadeh & Ahmad, 2011; Petrić, 2007), including both integral and non-integral citations. Since citation function is another important research focus of this study, it is preferable to make formal and functional analyses of citations separate and distinct. Therefore, in the present study, all the identified citations were firstly divided into *integral* or *non-integral* (Swales, 1990: 141); as for those integral citations, they were further classified into *integral verb-controlling* and *integral naming* types by following Thompson and Tribble's (2001) and Thompson's (2001, 2005) typology. The definitions and examples of integral citations, non-integral citations, integral verb-controlling and integral naming citations are listed below.

I. **Citation types based on formal criteria**

(1) **Non-integral**: citations where references are made to the researcher in a parenthesis or by other means such as the use of a superscript number (Swales, 1990: 148).

(8) Research has shown that the acquisition of second-language (SL) grammar and pragmatics differs for foreign language (FL) and SL contexts **(Bardovi-Harlig & Dornyei, 1998; Kasper & Rose, 2002; Kasper & Schmidt, 1996; Schauer, 2006)**. (CALI1)

(2) **Integral**: citations where the name of the cited researcher appears in the referenced statement as a grammatical element (Swales, 1990). Integral and non-integral citations are respectively author prominent and information prominent (Weissberg and Buker, 1990: 44).

(9) **Kwon, Polinsky, and Kluender (2006),** for example, showed that there is a processing advantage for both the subject gap in Korean RCs and subject pro-drop in Korean adjunct clauses. (CALL2)

(2a) **Integral verb-controlling**: The name of the cited author was introduced by using a RV, either in the active or passive voice.

(10) **Grace et al. (1998) presented** experimental results of seven simply supported rectangular beams and seven continuously supported concrete beams with T-section. (CCEL11)

(2b) **Integral naming**: The citation works as a noun phrase (Example 11) or part of a noun phase (see Example 12 being a modifier).

(11) **Swales (2005)** is a second exception to the limitations mentioned above. (CALL19)

(12) The objective of this paper is to examine the effect that the type of GCL may have on the magnitude of shrinkage in an experimental program that represents a significant extension of **the work of Thiel et al. (2006)**. (CCEI17)

While non-citations (where the author is (re-)cited without re-mentioning the year of publication) is also a sub-type of integral citations (Thompson, 2001, 2005; Thompson and Tribble, 2001), they were found being used infrequently in the present data—the percentages of integral citations identified as non-citations in the four sub-corpora CALI, CALL, CCEI, and CCEL ranging from 0.3 to 6.8%. Such low occurrences of non-citations are perhaps attributable to space constraints of journal articles, the present research focuses only on the two part-genres rather than the article in its entirety, and the applied nature of the studied disciplines. In view of their low occurrences, non-citations were not considered in the analysis. Accordingly, in the analysis of citation forms, integral citations, non-integral citations, and the two major sub-types of integral citations (viz., integral verb-controlling and integral naming citations) were identified, hand-tagged and quantified. The proportions of these citation forms and their subtypes used in the two part-genres across AL and CE were then compared and contrasted, with frequently-used integral naming citation patterns (whose percentages occupying over 10%) recorded for each of the four sub-corpora (CALI, CALL, CCEI, CCEL).

Another aspect to be examined is the rhetorical functions of citations. After the identification of citations and the coding and analysis of citation types according to their formal criteria, the investigation of rhetorical functions of citations was undertaken. Following practical guidelines and strategies for qualitative data analyses (Auerbach & Silverstein, 2003; Bazeley, 2013; Miles, Huberman & Saldaña, 2014), the present study conducted an initial analysis of rhetorical functions of citations in the data using categories proposed in Thompson (2001, 2005), Petrić (2007) and Mansourizadeh and Ahmad (2011) as the starting point. However, the analysis of discourse functions of citations is an iterative, inductive process with the whole taxonomy continually revised and modified by incorporating insights drawn from the initial rounds of analyses of data. As more texts were (repeatedly) analyzed, new categories emerged and the need for revising, collapsing or sub-dividing some categories arose. When determining the rhetorical function of a citation, its context (e.g., eminent linguistic cues surrounding the citation) and context and the input from a post-doc CE informant (no specialist informant for AL as two analysts are specialized in this field) were fully considered to maximize the accuracy of the analysis. The finalized classification scheme was formed after the initial rounds of piloting analyses by two analysts and then applied to the whole data sets for a thorough and in-depth comparative study of the functional use of citations in Introductions and LRs of ERAs in the two contrasting disciplines.

In the functional typology of this study, there are 13 categories of citation functions which can be classified into two groups: the rhetorically simpler citation functions (*attribution, further reference, example, origin*, and *identification*) and the rhetorically complex citation functions (*exemplification, support, generalization from multiple sources, comparison and contrast between/among sources, statement of use, application, evaluation,* and *comparison of one's own findings/interpretations/design/methods with other sources*). The criterion for determining citation functions as rhetorically simpler or complex is whether they could be suggested within the citing sentence (i.e., citations indicating intra-sentential relationship) or beyond that sentence (i.e., citations indicating inter-sentential relationship). In this light, rhetorically complex citation functions can only be inferred by resorting to the larger discourse context (e.g., the surrounding sentences or other paragraphs or even other pieces of research works).

The five rhetorically simpler citation functions were drawn from Thompson's (2001) typology with the functional category *source* relabeled as *attribution* to avoid confusion with the cited source and *reference* renamed as *further reference* to better reflect the purpose of the citation (following Petrić's (2007) practice). As for the eight rhetorically complex citation functions, *exemplification*, *statement of use*, *application* and *evaluation* in Petrić's (2007) study and *support* in Mansourizadeh and Ahmad's (2011) study were found applicable to the present data and thus adopted. The category *comparison of one's own findings with other sources* originally devised by Mansourizadeh and Ahmad (2011) seems narrow in its scope and coverage, and somewhat section-specific in that it appears most common to the Results and Discussion part. To accommodate it to the need of the current data analysis that focuses on the introductory phase, it is refined as *comparison of one's own study with other sources* since we found the comparison could be made between the present study and the source not only in terms of their findings, but in terms of their various other aspects such as research designs, methods, views and arguments, or implicitly unnamed aspects.

This category is established to indicate the link between the present work and various sources. On the other hand, as the present study focuses on the two main sections of the introductory part (viz., Introduction and the LR section) which both foreground the importance and prevalence of the links between or among sources, it is interesting and necessary to further identify and compare the different nature of source links in functional use of citations in them. Given that *establishing links between sources* in Petrić's (2007: 245) study is too general considering the research purpose of this study, and the two types of source links suggested by her (namely *generalization from multiple sources* and *comparison and contrast between/among different sources*) are distinct and common in the data, *establishing links between sources* was further divided into these two categories (*generalization from multiple sources* and *comparison and contrast between/among sources*). The sub-division also makes the two new functional categories more parallel to others (e.g., *comparison of one's own study with other sources*) in terms of levels of generality and specificity. The list of citation functions with each illustrated by authentic extracts from the present data is provided below.

II. **Citation types based on functional criteria**

1. **Rhetorically simpler citation functions**

(1) **Attribution**

The citation attributes information, ideas, or propositions to a source. As Thompson (2001) clarified, in Attribution citations, the information is contained in a proposition, which contrasts with Origin citations that commonly refer to a noun phrase within the sentence.

> (13) **For Slaouti** (2002, p. 120), "the WWW deserves to find its place within our teaching but not simply as a resource for project work".

(2) **Further reference**

The citation directs the reader to a source for more information or exact details. It is usually preceded by imperatives such as "see" and "but see", but not necessarily (Thompson, 2001). This type of citation can be used as a space-saving strategy; the employment of this type of citation shows the writer's competence in distinguishing relevant information from additional one gleaned from sources (Petrić, 2007).

> (14) The aforementioned factors can be roughly divided into input features and learner factors **(see VanPatten et al., 2004, for details)** or…. (CALL27)

(3) **Example**

The citation is used to provide a number of example studies that are referred to in the sentence, usually being a non-integral citation. "E.g." or "for example" are typical markers (Thompson, 2001; Thompson and Tribble, 2001).

(15) A large range of research evidence based on behavioural research studies has now identified passenger responses to transport system changes for a range of service design aspects **(e.g. Balcombe 2004; Evans 2004; McCollom and Pratt 2004; Pratt and Evans 2004)**. (CCEL29)

(4) Origin

The citation is used to indicate the originator of a concept, technique, equation, or product. The difference between Attribution citations and Origin citations has been stated above and to keep the two categories separate also helps to identify cross-generic and cross-disciplinary variations in functional use of citations in this study. However, the identification of some Origin citations is not easy, which requires the researcher to seek for more information from relevant literature in the field or disciplinary insiders' input and confirmation.

(16) The hydraulic conductivity of saturated clean sands at maximum porosity has thus long been estimated using **the Hazen (1911) equation**, which is a function of the equivalent particle diameter d10.... (CCEL15)

(5) Identification

The type of citation identifies the actor or the agent within the cited sentence. It is commonly in an non-integral form with an RV used and the reported researcher de-emphasized. In the following example, the two Identification citations identify the agents for the RV "expanded" to be Kamat and El-Tawil (2007) and Behzadan and Kamat (2007).

(17) Recently, 3D/4D CAD research **was expanded to** make use of augmented reality for assessing earthquake-induced building damage **(Kamat and El-Tawil 2007)** and for improving construction simulation **(Behzadan and Kamat 2007)**. (CCEL3)

2. Rhetorically complex citation functions

(1) Exemplification

The citation is used to illustrate the writer's statement or argument by citing relevant sources as specific examples. As can be seen from Extract (18), Exemplification citations are used to illustrate and elaborate the main statement in the first sentence. Thereby, *exemplification* as one of the rhetorically complex citation functions, suggests the inter-sentential relationship. In contrast to Example citations that are usually in non-integral forms, Exemplification citations are commonly integral citations.

(18) **Similarly, organic matter in soil is known to affect stabilization using cements or fly ashes. For example, Tremblay et al. (2002)** evaluated how cement stabilization of an inorganic soil [a clay with plasticity index (PI) = 26] was inhibited by organic content by adding organic compounds to the soil, such as acetic acid, humic acid, tannic acid, ethylenediaminetetraacetic acid (EDTA), and sucrose. **Tremblay et al. (2002)** also suggested that pozzolanic reactions are likely to be inhibited if the pH of the soil-cement mixture is less than 9. (CCEL14)

(2) Support

Somewhat similar to the *supporting* function proposed in Harwood (2009) and Petrić and Harwood (2013), *support* in the present study means that the citation is used to justify (i) the significance of the topic and the writer's choice of it; (ii) the selection of the procedures and materials; (iii) the researchers' (i.e., the writer's or previous researchers') arguments and claims; and/or (iv) the findings of the study or one of the previous studies. Two examples are provided for space reason:

> (19) Chemical stabilization with binders such as cement, lime, and fly ash can be undertaken rapidly and often at low cost, and therefore chemical stabilization is becoming an important alternative **(Keshawarz and Dutta 1993; Sridharan et al. 1997; Kaniraj and Havanagi 1999; Parsons and Kneebone 2005)**. (CCEI14)

In the above example, as the topic of the study is stabilization of organic soils with fly ash, listing a number of sources within the parenthetical reference is to justify topic significance and value. In contrast, in Extract (20), the second citation which is a Support citation provides evidence for the view of Kane and Engle (2003), illustrating another use of the *support* function. However, what is worth noting here is that the citation function *support* in this study is broader in scope than *supporting* in Harwood (2009) and Petrić and Harwood (2013) and *support* in Mansourizadeh and Ahmad (2011) in that it also covers supporting or justifying previous studies' (not just the citing researcher's) selection of a research method or material, their arguments or findings, as can be seen from Extract (20). The functions *supporting* or *support* in the above-mentioned previous studies only focus on providing justifications for the topic, research methods, claims or findings of the citing writer's research. Broadening the scope and implicature of the *support* function in this study is to better capture the relationship between the citation and the citing sentences when the data (i.e., the introductory phases) emphases the links between/among the cited studies.

> (20) Kane and Engle (2003) described a similar view of working memory according to which working memory is equal to the sum of short-term memory, which is the amount of information that can be held in memory temporarily, and controlled attention, which is an individual's ability to direct attention to task relevant information (and away from task-irrelevant information). **This view is supported by evidence that** although working memory and short-term memory are highly correlated, only working memory is correlated with measures of higher order cognition, such as fluid intelligence **(see also Engle, Tuholski, Laughlin, & Conway, 1999, for an in-depth analysis of the relationship among these constructs)**. (CALL29)

(3) Generalization from multiple sources

The Generalization citation is used to indicate links between/among sources with similar findings, arguments, or research focus. Usually being a multi-reference non-integral citation, it helps to identify what is commonly recognized in the field and demonstrate the existing knowledge in the research area, as in the following example:

> (21) It has been widely argued that frequently occurring strings of language can be stored as whole units, 'chunks', in the long-term memory **(Pawley and Syder 1983; Bybee and Scheibman 1999; Wray 2002; Schmitt and Carter 2004)**. (CALL7)

(4) Comparison and contrast between/among sources

The Comparison citation in our corpus suggests similarities or differences between/among sources in terms of their findings, views or claims. As another way to link sources, this type of citation is commonly used in integral forms. Here is an example:

(22) Thompson has made **similar** claims about the use of citations. (CALL22)

(5) Statement of use

The function of this citation is to state which research works are going to be used in the study and for what purposes. In the introductory part of the ERA, by using this type of citation the writer declares prospective use of the cited works (Petrić, 2007), as in:

(23) Hyland and Tse's taxonomy, together with elements of Thompson's (2001), will form a basis for the ensuing analysis of interactional resources in the texts published by students on the wiki (further described in Sect. 3.4). (CALL20)

(6) Application

This type of citation is used to connect the cited source and the present work in that usually the concepts, terms, (theoretical) arguments, or research methodology or procedures are directly borrowed from previous works and used for the writer's own purposes, as in the following example:

(24) In Question 1, I defined L2 writing ability as an academic ability to write in "**pedagogical genres**" (Johns, 1997, p. 46) such as "the essay examination response, the term paper, or the pedagogical summary" (p. 46). (CALL14)

Note that "pedagogical genres" is a term borrowed from Johns (1997: 46) and used to define L2 writing ability in the study.

(7) Evaluation

The citation is used to engage either positive or negative evaluation of the cited source by using evaluative language such as Writers' Counter-factive RV (e.g., *fail, misuse, ignore, overlook*) and evaluative adjectives and adverbs. The following is an example of positive evaluation:

(25) However, in light of Geisler's work on academic expertise, Hyland and Thompson's work on the first-person pronoun and citation practices is **particularly insightful**. (CALL2)

(8) Comparison of one's own findings/interpretations/designs with other sources

This type of citation is used to compare similarities and/or differences between one's own study and the works of previous scholars regarding their findings, claims, research designs and method. Here is an example:

(26) **As in Tremblay and Garrison, this study** presents the benefits of grouping L2 learners by cloze-test level rather than by classroom level, but it also identifies specific cloze-test levels on the basis of a larger sample of L2 learners of French… (CALI3)

The corresponding tags for the 13 citation functions have been listed in Table 3.3. In the process of using tags to code and analyze the rhetorical roles of citations, all functions were ascribed to "multifunctional" citations rather than the most prominent one, as the latter is difficult to determine. Owing to this, the frequency of the rhetorical functions is much larger than the number of citations identified. Take the following excerpt as an example of "multi-functional" citations:

(27) In his **seminal** treatise "The Problem of Speech Genres", **Bakhtin (1986) wrote**:

from the very beginning, the utterance is constructed while taking into account possible responsive reactions, for whose sake, in essence, it is actually created.… Both the composition and, particularly, the style of the utterance depend on those to whom the utterance is addressed, how the speaker [or writer] senses and imagines his [or her] addressees, and the force of their effect on the utterance. (p. 94–95). (CALL22)

As we can see, the citation in the above extract has both rhetorical functions of *evaluation* and *attribution*. While the positive evaluation function is explicitly suggested by the evaluative adjective "seminal", the entire quote is attributed to the cited author, justifying it as an Attribution citation as well.

Another issue is ambiguous citations. Among 1956 citations identified in the four sub-corpora of this study, only 0.3% (six) of them are obscure cases: their rhetorical roles are heterogeneous and the relationship between them and the citing sentence is vague and difficult to determine. Thus, they were excluded from analysis. An instance of ambiguous citations is provided below:

(28) The results of the Hass-Klau and Crampton (2002) and Crampton (2002) analyses are worthy of further examination relative to this study. (CELL29)

While this sentence implies the relevance and importance of the two cited studies to the present research, the two citations clearly do not play the rhetorical roles of *comparison and contrast between/among sources*, or *comparison of one's own findings/methods/interpretations/design with other sources* (which are more often associated with citations in the Results and Discussion part), but only suggest the need to do further examination and comparisons in the introductory part. Since it is a heterogeneous case with an obscure link suggested between the citing sentence and the two citations, it is assigned into the group of "Other" and excluded from further analysis. As the number of ambiguous citations is very small, this practice would certainly not affect the main findings on the general distribution of citation functions in the two rhetorical sections (viz., the Introduction and LR sections) in AL and CE.

After the coding and analysis of citation functions, the total number of instances of each rhetorical function and their relative proportions were calculated for Introductions and LRs in AL and CE. The purpose is to understand the range of citation functions and the degree of importance each rhetorical function has in the two part-genres in the two disciplines. Any similarities or differences in functional use of citations in them are interesting, given that the two part-genres are conventionally assumed as the major locations for reviewing previous literature with partly overlapping communicative functions (e.g., positioning the study in the wider literature).

The final aspect to be examined is a most prominent citation signal (i.e., RVs). There are two main stages involved in the analysis of RVs: the identification and classification of RVs. The identification of RVs was undertaken in this study based on the following working definition: RVs are defined as verbs that are used to report (and evaluate) the previous literature in any sentence that can be regarded as an actual citation. In many cases, the identification of RVs is straightforward. However, some difficulties also emerged and the principles below were adhered to throughout the process.

a. RVs could be identified in places where a generalized or unspecified term for authors or studies is used in citation statements, e.g., "examined" in the first sentence of the following extract.

> (29) The effect of length of residence on pragmatic competence has also been **examined** by **a number of other studies**. These have **concluded** that SL speakers who have spent longer periods of time in the SL environment approximated NS appropriateness in the employment of speech acts such as refusals (Felix-Brasdefer, 2004) and requests and apologies (Blum-Kulka & Olshtain, 1986; Olshtain & Blum-Kulka, 1985), among others. Additionally, length of residence was **found** to be a stronger factor in pragmatic development than level of proficiency (Felix-Brasdefer). (CALL1)

b. In the "extensive" citation (Swales, 1986), RVs can usually be preceded by a personal pronoun which refers back to an author already cited in the previous text. For instance, "tested" used in the second sentence of Extract (30).

> (30) Chung et al. (2009; 2008) **developed** an ERP success model for construction firms on the basis of the technology acceptance model and DeLone and McLean's information systems success model. By **utilizing** regression analysis, **they tested** the relationships concerning ERP implementation and user adoption. (CCEL5)

c. Some verbs in "multifunctional reporting sentences" play a role more of introducing and generalising the entire body of research rather than reporting (Lang, 2004: 109). These verbs were not regarded as RVs and thus excluded. This is exemplified as follows.

> (31) Early studies have **focused on** determining the relationship between accelerometer readings and metabolic activities. (CCEL6)

d. In some ambiguous cases, when determining whether a verb is an RV, the researcher needs to go back to the cited source text to see whether the verbs used are to articulate the writers' own positions or to report what has been stated in the cited work. For instance, in the following extract, there could be two different interpretations of the verb "support": the main consistency between the findings of Bardovi-Harlig and Dornyei's (1998) study and those of Niezgoda and Rover (2001) may be either the writer's own interpretation and understanding or what has been claimed by Niezgoda and Rover. To ascertain whether it is an RV, Niezgoda and Rover's article was carefully checked and their original related statement was found: *"The findings of this study corroborate Bardovi-Harlig and Dornyei's results in one central aspect...however, we also found intriguing differences..." (Niezgoda and Rover, 2001: 76).* Therefore, "support" as reporting what Niezgoda and Rover has maintained in their paper in Extract (32) could be justified as an RV.

(32) Bardovi-Harlig and Dornyei's (1998) findings were in great part **supported** by the results of Niezgoda and Rover's (2001) study set in different ESL and EFL contexts. (CALL1)

In all, 1946 RVs were identified for the two corpora CAL and CCE. As outlined in Chap. 2 (see Figs. 2.6 and 2.7), Hyland's (1999) taxonomy with a slight modification (i.e., the addition of a new type of RVs—"Stative RVs"—in terms of denotative meaning of RVs) forms the basis for the ensuing classification and analysis of RVs. The detailed definitions and examples of different categories of RVs concerning their denotative meaning and evaluative stance are listed in Appendix H, serving as a general working guide for the current study. While previous scholars (e.g., Hunston, 1993a; John, 2012; Lang, 2004; Thompson, 2001; Thompson and Tribble, 2001) have pointed out that the analysis of a small number of RVs is somewhat problematic, the present researcher maximized all efforts to determine their categories by referring to the broader context where the RVs are used, resorting to all possible sources such as authentic dictionaries, previous relevant literature and in-text linguistic clues, and discussing with disciplinary experts.

Some noteworthy issues observed in the present analysis of RVs are raised for reference of future similar research. First of all, for a few RVs that are delexicalized (e.g., "make, present, offer, provide"), their classification relies mainly on their noun collocates which bear the essential part of the meaning. For example, "offer" in "**offered** detailed architectural *description*" (CALL17) is considered a discourse RV whereas that in "**offering** his own *judgments*" (CALL17) a mental RV. Following Ädel and Garretson (2006), the complex verb phrases with such delexicalized RVs were grouped with their corresponding simple RVs, e.g., "make the claim" with "claim" and "provide the explanation" with "explain".

Second, in a few cases, the same RV could possibly be categorized into different types regarding their evaluative functions in the specific discoursal context. For instance, "claim" could be an "Author Positive" yet "Writer Counter-factive" RV, suggesting the contrasting evaluative stance between the citing writers and the authors towards the source information (Extract 33); on the other hand, it sometimes does not help building up the writer's argument but indicates both writers' and authors' neutral stance towards the reported proposition, similar to the use of "say" (Extract 34). As such, the grouping of some particular RVs is not fixed, which entails more contextual discourse analysis.

(33) This language learning model has been challenged by a few authors who **claim** that SLA takes place mainly on the basis of implicit knowledge (Ellis, 2002; 2005) and that explicit (or declarative) knowledge cannot turn into implicit (or procedural) knowledge (Hulstijn, 2002; Krashen, 1981, 1985). Paradis (1994, 2004, 2009) has also **claimed** that explicit and

implicit knowledge are located in different areas of the brain and that practice of knowledge acquired explicitly can never become part of implicit competence. (CALL26)

(34) As Bahrick and Phelps (1987) **claimed**, "the optimum interval is likely to be the longest interval that avoids retrieval failures" (p. 349). (CALL26)

Lastly, in a very small number of "borderline cases", the RV is difficult to be neatly grouped into a particular category. For example, in the following extract, "provide a good overview" may involve both textual and mental activities of researchers in complex ways, thereby posing challenges to the classification. However, such cases found in the present data analysis are rare, which suggests that the general tendencies revealed on the use of different types of RVs regarding their denotation and evaluation in the two rhetorical sections (i.e., Introductions and LRs) across the two contrasting disciplines (i.e., AL and CE) would certainly not be affected.

(35) As far as general foreign language education is concerned, Karpati (2009) proposes a new educational paradigm for "social CALL" and **provides a good overview** of how different social web applications can be used by teachers and learners. (CALI20)

As aforementioned, by using Notepad++6.6.3, corresponding tags for different types of RVs in terms of their denotation and evaluation such as Discourse RVs ("<drv/>"), Writer Factive RVs ("<wf/>") and Author Tentative RVs ("<at/>") (see Table 3.3) were inserted to the right of the RVs. Then, AntConc 3.2.4 was employed to retrieve the number of occurrences and distribution of different types of RVs with regard to their denotative meaning and evaluation, in order to assess to what extent RVs are deployed differently when research writers with contrasting disciplinary backgrounds construct the two adjoining sections with partly overlapping communicative functions (viz., the Introduction and LR sections).

3.4.2 Interviews with Experienced Research Writers

3.4.2.1 Rationale

The advantages and disadvantages of textual analysis and the qualitative interview study have been explicated in Chap. 2. In addition to experienced applied linguists' interpretations and explanations of significant findings derived from discourse analysis, the insiders' voices need to be heard in order to obtain a more comprehensive understanding of the specific research issue and the validation of our initial understandings. Therefore, as a complement to the multi-layered text-based analysis, an emic, interview-based study of experienced research writers' views and perceptions towards their own structural and citation practices in ERAs (particularly in their introductory phases) as well as the entire disciplinary practice was undertaken. Experts' insights gleaned from the interview study were incorporated into the discussion of the diachronic textual findings (Chap. 5) and the findings from the focused study on the rhetorical structure of and citation use in Introductions and LRs (Chaps. 6 and 7).

3.4.2.2 Data Collection and Analysis

For the fourth/last stage of the focused study, altogether 12 experienced research writers from AL and CE were invited to participate in the 1hr-long face-to-face interviews. As the semi-structured interview can allow respondents to express themselves at some length, but offer enough shape to prevent aimless rambling and the responses from the interviewees could be compared on the key questions (Denscombe, 2010; Dörnyei, 2007; Gillham, 2005; Kvale & Brinkmann, 2009), the interviews with the 12 informants were based on an interview schedule. Among these interviewees, seven (identified as AL1-7) work in different research areas of AL such as corpus linguistics, second language acquisition and EAP/ESP, while the other five (identified as CE1-5) specialize in a range of CE areas such as hydrology, transportation, and geotechnical engineering. Although they have mixed backgrounds in terms of their nationalities (viz., UK, Singapore, Hong Kong, Turkey and Pakistan), working locations, mother tongues and educational experience, they are all experienced research writers with impressive track records of publishing their research. All of them are also manuscript reviewers for such journals and some serve as chief editors.

As the interviews were semi-structured, an interview guide with a mix of guiding questions was prepared in advance (see Appendix I). Based on this interview schedule, all the interviews were conducted in English. The interview questions cover the following major areas, e.g., expert writers' background and their learning and teaching experience on research writing, their macro-structural practices and related disciplinary norms, and their views on how to organize the introductory part and the respective functions of the two possible sections in the opening phase (i.e., Introduction and LR) and their relationship. Regarding citation use and RV use in Introductions and LRs, the interviewees were invited to comment on my findings from the corpus-based analysis of the present textual data (i.e., 60 introductory phases in AL and CE) about their disciplinary citation practices. Whenever necessary, an example text or more from my data would be referred to.

Considering that the adoption of the discourse-based interview approach (Odell, Goswami, & Herrington, 1983) can largely reduce or avoid interviewees' "recall error" or "lack of awareness" in responding to interview questions (Harwood, 2009: 500), the researcher also encouraged the participants to use some of their own published RAs or others' as "specific illustrations" of their viewpoints in the interview. All the journal articles they chose to discuss during the interview had to be sent to me in advance so that I can prepare relevant questions of potential importance and interest. Those participants whose recently published ERAs may contain both Introduction and LR sections were requested to email the researcher one or more of such ERAs that can typically represent their structural and citing styles in their own views. The use of citations and RVs in the introductory phases of these ERAs was analyzed in detail before the interviews. During the interviews, the interviewees were then asked to explain some interesting or potentially significant points found in their citation use and RV use in Introductions and LRs of their own ERAs, no matter whether the findings here are similar to or different from those derived from my data.

All the interviews were audio-recorded, transcribed verbatim and then analyzed and coded. Comments and notes were made both during and immediately after each face-to-face interview, which provide insights for subsequent formal analyses of the interview data. As for the interpretation and analysis of interview transcripts, the first step is to read through all of them to obtain a general sense of the information and to reflect on their overall meaning in the context. Then all transcripts were divided into different "meaning units" (Burnard, 1994: 113) with a certain number of "open codes" created (Merriam, 2009: 179). In the light of the guiding questions outlined in the interview protocol and the research purpose of the in-depth interview study, these open codes were grouped and integrated into an appropriate number of categories and sub-categories after repeated readings and considerable reflections. These identified categories and sub-categories generally capture the recurring overarching themes and important perspectives of the participants emerging from their responses. To facilitate the data analysis, a qualitative computer software package (viz., MaxQDA, 2012) was used mainly for sorting, organizing, and retrieving information, and helping with the discovery of the recurring "patterns". As mentioned earlier, findings from the interviews help to illuminate what we have obtained from the discourse analysis and are thus presented when related textual findings are discussed (see Chaps. 5–7).

3.5 Summary

This chapter describes the research design and methodology of this project, which consists of two lead-in studies and one focused study. The three studies are interconnected, in that the two lead-in studies verifying the importance of the LR section from the cross-sectional and diachronic perspectives respectively have justified the significance of the focused study and the selection of CE and AL to be investigated in it. Based on 60 introductory phases structured in the "I+LR" pattern, the focused study examines the rhetorical structure of and citation use in the two componential sections (viz., the Introduction and LR sections). Different corpora data have been used in these three studies and the major approaches applied include ESP genre-based analysis, corpus-based discourse study and the interview. The essential information has been tabulated below to give a clear overview of the methodology of this project.

Table 3.4 Overview of the methodology

Project	Data	Approaches	Foci
Lead-in study (1)	Corpus of RAs (780 RAs/433 ERAs from 39 disciplines, 2007)	Genre-based "manual" analysis	Major structural patterns; Major ERA sections
Lead-in study (2)	1269 RAs/974 ERAs from AL and CE (1980–2010)	Genre-based "manual" analysis	Macro-structural development; Changing shapes of the introductory phase
Focused study	60 ERA introductory phases structured in "I+LR" in AL and CE respectively (2011)	ESP genre-based approach (MaxQDA 10)	Rhetorical structure of I and LR sections
		Corpus-based discourse analysis (Notepad++6.6.3, AntConc 3.2.4)	Multi-layered citation features in I and LR sections
	12 face-to-face 1h-long interviews with experienced research writers (AL1-7; CE1-5)	Semi-structured interviews (MaxQDA 10)	Disciplinary insiders' views on structuring and using citations in the introductory phase

References

Ädel, A., & Garretson, G. (2006). Citation practices across the disciplines: The case of proficient student writing. In C. Perez-Llantada, R. Plo, & C.-P. Neumann (Eds.), *Academic and professional communication in the 21st century: Genres and rhetoric in the construction of disciplinary knowledge* (pp. 271–280). Zaragoza, Spain: Prensas Universitarias.

Adnan, Z. (2008). Discourse structure of Indonesian research article introductions in selected hard science. In S. Burgess & P. Martin-Martin (Eds.), *English as an additional language in research publication and communication* (pp. 39–64). Berlin: Peter Lang.

Anthony, L. (1999). Writing research article introductions in software engineering: How accurate is a standard model? *IEEE Transactions on Professional Communication, 42,* 38–46.

Atkinson, D. (1992). The evolution of medical research writing from 1735 to 1985: The case of the *Edinburgh Medical Journal. Applied Linguistics, 13*(4), 337–374.

Atkinson, D. (1999). *Scientific discourse in sociohistorical context: The Philosophical Transactions of the Royal Society of London, 1675–1975.* Mahwah, N.J.: L. Erlbaum Associates.

Auerbach, C. F., & Silverstein, L. B. (2003). *Qualitative data: An introduction to coding and analysis.* New York: New York University Press.

Bazeley, P. (2013). *Qualitative data analysis: Practical strategies.* London: Sage.

Bazerman, C. (1984). Modern evolution of the experimental report in physics: Spectroscopic articles in *Physical Review*, 1893–1980. *Social Studies in Science, 14,* 163–196.

Berkenkotter, C., & Huckin, T. (1995). *Genre knowledge in disciplinary communication: Cognition, culture, power.* Hilldale: Lawrence Erlbaum Associates.

Bhatia, V. K. (1993). *Analyzing genre: Language use in professional settings.* New York: Longman.

Bhatia, V. K. (2001). Analyzing genre: Some conceptual issues. In M. Hewing (Ed.), *Academic writing in context: Implications and applications: Papers in honour of Tony Dudley-Evans* (pp. 79–92). Birmingham, U.K.: University of Birmingham Press.

Biber, D., Connor, U., & Upton, T. A. (2007). *Discourse on the move: Using corpus analysis to describe discourse structure*. Amsterdam: John Benjamins.
Bonzi, S., & Snyder, H. W. (1991). Motivations for citation: A comparison of self citation and citation to others. *Scientometrics, 21,* 245–254.
Bryman, A. (2008). *Social research methods* (3rd ed.). Oxford: Oxford University Press.
Bryman, A. (2012). *Social research methods* (4th ed.). Oxford: Oxford University Press.
Bunton, D. (2002). Generic moves in Ph.D. thesis introductions. In J. Flowerdew (Ed.), *Academic discourse* (pp. 57–75). London: Pearson Education.
Burnard, P. (1994). Searching for meaning: A method of analyzing interview transcripts with a personal computer. *Nurse Education Today, 14*(2), 111–117.
Crookes, G. (1986). Towards a validated analysis of scientific text structure. *Applied Linguistics, 7,* 57–70.
Del Saz-Rubio, M. M. (2011). A pragmatic approach to the macro-structure and metadiscoursal features of research article introductions in the field of agricultural sciences. *English for Specific Purposes, 30*(4), 258–271.
Denscombe, M. (2010). *The good research guide: For small-scale social research* (4th ed.). Buckingham: Open University Press.
Dörnyei, Z. (2007). *Research methods in applied linguistics: Quantitative, qualitative and mixed methodologies*. Oxford: Oxford University Press.
Feak, C. B., & Swales, J. M. (2011). *Creating contexts: Writing introductions across genres*. Ann Arbor: University of Michigan Press.
Gillham, B. (2005). *Research interviewing: The range of techniques*. Maidenhead, England: Open University Press.
Halliday, M. A. K. (1985). *An introduction to functional grammar*. London: Arnold.
Halliday, M. A. K. (1994). *An introduction to functional grammar* (2nd ed.). London: Arnold.
Halliday, M. A. K., & Matthiessen, C. M. I. M. (2004). *An introduction to functional grammar* (3rd ed.). London: Arnold.
Harwood, N. (2009). An interview-based study of the functions of citations in academic writing across two disciplines. *Journal of Pragmatics, 41*(3), 497–518.
Holmes, R. (1997). Genre analysis and the social sciences: An investigation of the structure of research article discussion sections in three disciplines. *English for Specific Purposes, 16*(4), 321–337.
Hunston, S. (1993). Evaluation and ideology in scientific writing. In M. Ghadessy (Ed.), *Register and analysis: Theory and practice* (pp. 57–73). London: Printer Publishers.
Hunston, S. (2002). *Corpora in applied linguistics*. Cambridge: Cambridge University Press.
Hyland, K. (1999). Academic attribution: Citation and the construction of disciplinary knowledge. *Applied Linguistics, 20*(3), 341–367.
John, S. (2012). Identity without the 'I': A study of citation sequences and identity in literature review sections of dissertations. In R. Tang (Ed.) *Academic writing in a second or foreign language: Issues and challenges facing ESL/EFL academic writers in higher education contexts*. London: Continuum.
Kvale, S., & Brinkmann, S. (2009). *Interviews: Learning the craft of qualitative research interviewing*. Thousand Oaks, CA: Sage.
Kwan, B. S. C. (2005). *A genre analysis of literature reviews in doctoral theses*. Unpublished doctoral dissertation, City University of Hong Kong.
Kwan, B. S. C. (2006). The schematic structure of literature reviews in doctoral theses of applied linguistics. *English for Specific Purposes, 25,* 30–55.
Kwan, B. S. C., Chan, H., & Lam, C. (2012). Evaluating prior scholarship in literature reviews of research articles: A comparative study of practices in two research paradigms. *English for Specific Purposes, 31,* 188–201.
Lang, H. L. (2004). *The use of reporting verbs in literature reviews of Taiwanese postgraduate business students*. Unpublished doctoral dissertation, The University of Manchester.

Lewin, B. A., Fine, J., & Young, L. (2001). *Expository discourse: A genre-based approach to social science research texts*. London: Continuum.
Loi, C. K. (2010). Research article introductions in Chinese and English: A comparative genre-based study. *Journal of English for Academic Purposes, 9*(4), 267–279.
Loi, C. K., & Evans, S. M. (2010). Cultural differences in the organization of research article introductions from the field of educational psychology: English and Chinese. *Journal of Pragmatics, 42*(10), 2814–2825.
Machi, L. A., & McEvoy, B. T. (2012). *The literature review: Six steps to success* (2nd ed.). London: Sage.
Mansourizadeh, K., & Ahmad, U. (2011). Citation practices among non-native expert and novice scientific writers. *Journal of English for Academic Purposes, 10*(3), 152–161.
MAXQDA. (2012). *VERBI software*. Sozialforchung, GmbH, Berlin, Germany: Consult.
Merriam, S. B. (2009). *Qualitative research: A guide to design and implementation*. San Francisco, CA: Jossey-Bass.
Merton, R. K. (1967). On sociological theories of the middle range. In R. K. Merton (Ed.), *On theoretical sociology: Five essays old and new* (pp. 39–72). New York: Free Press.
Miles, M. B., Huberman, A. M., & Saldaña, J. (2014). *Qualitative data analysis: A methods sourcebook* (3rd ed.). Thousand Oaks, CA: Sage.
Myers, G. (1990). *Writing biology: Texts in the social construction of scientific knowledge*. Madison: University of Wisconsin Press.
Odell, L., Goswami, D., & Herrington, A. J. (1983). The discourse-based interview: A procedure for exploring the tacit knowledge of writers in nonacademic settings. In P. Mosenthal, L. Tamor, & S. A. Walmsley (Eds.), *Research on writing: Principles and methods* (pp. 221–236). New York: Longman.
Ozturk, I. (2007). The textual organization of research article introductions in applied linguistics: Variability within a single discipline. *English for Specific Purposes, 26*(1), 25–38.
Pérez-Llantada, C. (2013). The article of the future: Strategies for genre stability and change. *English for Specific Purposes, 32*(4), 221–235.
Petrić, B. (2007). Rhetorical functions of citations in high- and low-rated master's theses. *Journal of English for Academic Purposes, 6*(3), 238–253.
Petrić, B., & Harwood, N. (2013). Task requirements, task representation, and citation functions: An interview-based study of the citing behavior of a successful L2 student writer. *Journal of English for Academic Purposes, 12,* 110–124.
Samraj, B. (2002). Introductions in research articles: Variations across disciplines. *English for Specific Purposes, 21*(1), 1–17.
Samraj, B. (2005). An exploration of a genre set: Research article abstracts and introductions in two disciplines. *English for Specific Purposes, 24*(2), 141–156.
Sheldon, E. (2011). Rhetorical differences in RA introductions written by English L1 and L2 and Castilian Spanish L1 writers. *Journal of English for Academic Purposes, 10*(4), 238–251.
Stoller, F. L., & Robinson, M. S. (2013). Chemistry journal articles: An interdisciplinary approach to move analysis with pedagogical aims. *English for Specific Purposes, 32,* 45–57.
Swales, J. M. (1986). Citation analysis and discourse analysis. *Applied Linguistics, 7,* 39–56.
Swales, J. M. (1990). *Genre analysis: English in academic and research settings*. Cambridge, U.K.; New York: Cambridge University Press.
Swales, J. M. (2004). *Research genres: Explorations and applications*. Cambridge, U.K.; New York: Cambridge University Press.
Swales, J. M. (2014). Variation in citational practice in a corpus of student biology papers: From parenthetical plonking to intertextual storytelling. *Written Communication, 31*(1), 118–141.
Swales, J. M., & Feak, C. B. (2004). *Academic writing for graduate students: Essential tasks and skills* (2nd ed.). Ann Arbor: University of Michigan Press.
Tessuto, G. (2015). Generic structure and rhetorical moves in English-language empirical law research articles: Sites of interdisciplinary and interdiscursive cross-over. *English for Specific Purposes, 37*(1), 13–26.

Thompson, G. (2000a). *Reporting*. Beijing: Foreign Languages Publishing House.

Thompson, P. (2000b). Citation practices in PhD theses. In L. Burnard & T. McEnery (Eds.), *Rethinking language pedagogy from a corpus perspective*. Frankfurt: Peter Lang.

Thompson, P. (2001). *A pedagogically-motivated corpus-based examination of Ph.D. theses: Macrostructure, citation practices and uses of modal verbs*. Unpublished doctoral dissertation, The University of Reading.

Thompson, P. (2005). Points of focus and position: Intertextual reference in Ph.D. theses. *Journal of English for Academic Purposes, 4*(4), 307–323.

Thompson, P., & Tribble, C. (2001). Looking at citations: Using corpora in English for academic purposes. *Language Learning and Technology, 5*(3), 91–105.

Valle, E. (1997). A scientific community and its texts: A historical discourse study. In B.-L. Gunnarsson, P. Linell, & B. Nordberg (Eds.), *The construction of professional discourse* (pp. 76–98). London: Longman.

Weissberg, R., & Buker, S. (1990). *Writing up research: Experimental research report writing for students of English*. Englewood Cliffs, N.J.: Prentice Hall Regents.

Wen, Q. F. (2001). *Applied linguistics: Research methods and thesis writing*. Beijing: Foreign Languages Teaching Research Press.

Wood, D. M. (2012). *Civil engineering: A very short introduction*. Oxford: Oxford University Press.

Yang, R. Y., & Allison, D. (2003). Research articles in applied linguistics: Moving from results to conclusions. *English for Specific Purposes, 22*(4), 365–385.

Yang, R. Y., & Allison, D. (2004). Research articles in applied linguistics: Structures from a functional perspective. *English for Specific Purposes, 23*(3), 264–279.

Chapter 4
Lead-in Study 1: The Macro-structure of Contemporary ERAs

4.1 Introduction

In Sect. 2.2.2.1, a comprehensive review of previous literature on the macro-structure of ERAs is presented with relevant gaps outlined. Some of such gaps include the dearth of research into RA macro-structures, the preoccupation with the "established" IMRD framework in both EAP research and published advice, the long-term oversight of other important sections with distinct communicative purposes that are not fully accounted for in the conventional IMRD framework.

In an attempt to fill these gaps as well as pave the way for the main design of this project, a close "manual" analysis of the major generic structures of 433 recent ERAs from high-impact English-language journals in 39 disciplines in the fields of engineering, applied sciences, social sciences and the humanities was conducted. This analysis reveals that while many ERAs follow the "standard" IMRD pattern, this structure is not the default option for organizing such studies. The findings indicate that the most frequently used structural pattern is Introduction-Literature Review-Method-Results and Discussion-Conclusion (ILM[RD]C). The other prominent patterns found in the corpus are Introduction-Method-Results and Discussion-Conclusion (IM[RD]C), Introduction-Method-Results-Discussion-Conclusion (IMRDC), Introduction-Literature Review-Method-Results-Discussion-Conclusion (ILMRDC) and Introduction-Literature Review-Method-Results-Discussion (ILMRD). This lead-in study identifies and highlights the importance of the sections that are not fully accounted for in the conventional IMRD framework, namely the LR, the merged (as opposed to separated) Results and Discussion [RD], and the C sections, and emphasizes the need to research into the relationship between the adjacent sections in the introductory and concluding parts.

(Kathy). L. Lin, *Perspectives on the Introductory Phase of Empirical Research Articles*, Corpora and Intercultural Studies 5, https://doi.org/10.1007/978-981-32-9204-8_4

4.2 The Major Structural Patterns of ERAs

This section identifies the major generic structural patterns found in the 433 ERAs. Three key points are worthy of note. First, as shown in Fig. 4.1, the most common structural pattern is ILM[RD]C, followed by IM[RD]C and three other configurations with similar percentages, viz. IMRDC, IMRD and ILMRDC. The "conventional" IMRD pattern is used in only 53 of the 433 ERAs analyzed. IMRD is therefore far from being the default option for organizing contemporary ERAs. In fact, patterns that have traditionally been regarded as "peripheral" variants of IMRD (Cargill & O'Connor, 2009), such as ILM[RD]C and IM[RD]C, are more prevalent among the empirical studies in the corpus. The remaining ERAs in the corpus (19.7%) comprise a multiplicity of less conventional patterns such as IL[MRD]C (3.7%), I[MRD]C (2.1%) and ILMRC (1.4%).

These findings partly accord with those of Yang and Allison (2004), who noted the inapplicability of the IMRD framework to a considerable number of the applied linguistics RAs they examined. Among the four chosen journals in their research, *English for Specific Purposes (ESP)* published RAs which were most likely to conform to IMRD, whereas *Applied Linguistics (AL)*, *Tesol Quarterly (TQ)* and *English Language Teaching Journal (ELTJ)* had different proportions of RAs with their macro-structures deviating from it. The most typical instances occurred in the *ELTJ* articles which had the same IMRC structure and, in some cases, an additional "pedagogical implications" at the end but no section devoted to a discussion of theory or to a review of the literature. Such a structure reflects the journal's primary concern with practical issues in English language teaching rather than theory-oriented research. Yang and Allison (2004) accounted for their findings, in particular the relative unimportance of IMRD, by pointing to the modest size of their corpus (20 primary RAs) as well as the inclusion of other kinds of ERAs (e.g., ones reporting case studies) whose findings required less conventional methods of presentation. In contrast, findings from the present research indicate that rather than being confined to individual

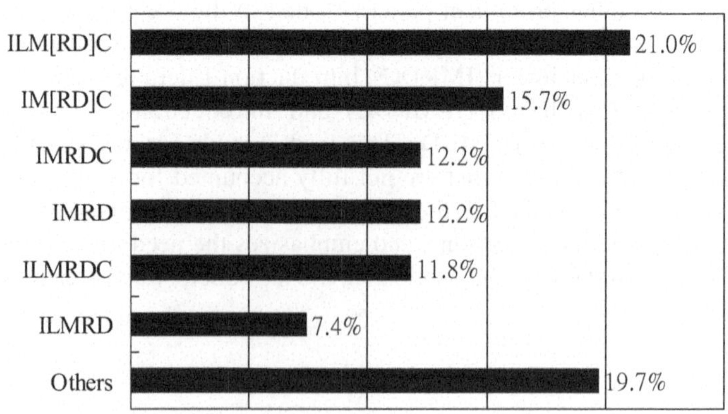

Fig. 4.1 The macro-structural patterns of ERAs

RAs, a large proportion of them do not follow the IMRD framework, and thus it is by no means the predominant schematic model for structuring ERAs.

Second, the findings indicate that C, LR and [RD], which are not fully accounted for in the IMRD framework, are important independent sections in contemporary RAs. However, as noted earlier, these sections—as discrete sections—have been the subject of little systematic research in ESP; such work that has been conducted into aspects of these sections has typically been contextualized within one of the four sections in the IMRD model. For example, various aspects of the LR either in terms of its schematic structure or representative language use (e.g., the use of citations, RVs) have been often positioned under the sectional heading "introduction". Nonetheless, the finding of this study points to the need for a detailed inquiry into textual properties of this newly-identified part-genre as well as the interrelationship between it and the partly analogous Introduction section, which will be an important objective of this project.

Similarly, quintessential components of independent "conclusion" sections (e.g., summary of findings) have been discussed in the context of apparently all-encompassing "discussion" sections. This lead-in study accordingly presents an initial analysis of the communicative purposes and functions of C, LR and [RD] and attempts to determine how these sections contribute to the patterns presented in Fig. 4.1 (see Sects. 4.3–4.5).

Third, among the six major macro-structures in Fig. 4.1, none essentially plays a dominant role and enjoys an overwhelming preponderance; instead all of them have similarly moderate proportions, suggesting that RA writers have comparatively diversified choices for structuring their articles and that there exist discernible disciplinary variations in this regard (as discussed in Sect. 4.6).

4.3 The Major Sections of ERAs

Figure 4.2 presents the most common independent sections in the RAs under review. The evidence suggests that I is an obligatory section followed by the quasi-obligatory M and C sections. D, LR and R appear in around a half of the RAs in the corpus while 170 of the 433 ERAs present findings in a merged [RD] section. These findings therefore reinforce the point made in Sect. 4.2, viz. that C, LR, and [RD] have important roles in modern research writing and thus merit the same degree of scholarly attention that has previously been devoted to I and, to a lesser extent, M, R and D.

These results are largely congruent with those of Posteguillo (1999), who found that I (100%), R (55%) and D/C (85%) were the most commonly used sections in the 40 computer science RAs he studied. They also accord to some degree with the findings of Yang and Allison (2004), Cooper (1985) and Belcher and Braine (1995). Yang and Allison (2004) observed from their research into the structures of 20 applied linguistics RAs that I, M and R were the three most common sections; Cooper (1985) concluded that I and C were the two sections most frequently used by scholars in computer technology; and Braine (1995) reported from their comparison

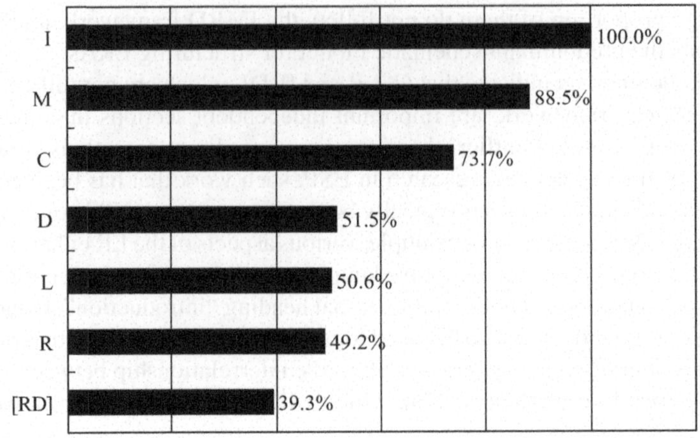

Fig. 4.2 The major sections in ERAs

of formats of six empirical reports offered by instructors in botany and five engineering disciplines that only I and R were common to all of the reports with D being absent in four of them, M omitted in one, the innovative "theory" section added in three and the extra "conclusion" used in as many as four.

As indicated in the hour-glass diagram for the overall organization of RAs (Hill, Soppelsa, & West, 1982), the introductory and closing phases of the RA respectively offer the transition from the general research context to the specific research issue and the transition from "specific findings to wider implications" (Swales, 1990: 133). Correspondingly, the information generally moves from the general to the specific and from the specific back to the general in the two phases of the RA. The current research reveals that most deviations from the IMRD framework essentially occur in these two "moving" processes of ERAs. In contrast, the central phase of RAs, specifically the method section, seems to be relatively fixed within the overall framework of empirical studies (Holmes, 1997). This finding contrasts with what Posteguillo (1999) concluded from his detailed examination of the schematic structure of 40 RAs in computer science that the central part of RAs contained irregular structural patterns and was thus the principal location for departures from IMRD.

Although every ERA in this corpus has an introduction, a sizeable number (93; 21.5%) do not have the corresponding section heading. Nevertheless, these unlabelled RA openings display all the characteristic features of an introduction and serve the relevant communicative functions, and were therefore accordingly categorized as I. Indeed, it is not uncommon for clearly sectionalized RAs, including those in leading journals, to omit the section heading for the introduction. For example, Yang and Allison (2004) noted the omission of the term "introduction" in RAs in *TQ*, which they attributed to the specific macro-structural requirement of the APA style sheet it recommends to contributors.

It should be noted that the frequency of M as a separate section is analyzed here rather than that of all its occurrences. All ERAs, except one from the field of archaeology, have clearly distinguishable M elements, with 383 instances of M as a stand-alone section, 33 cases of M merged with R and D [MRD], 14 cases of M coalesced with R [MR], one case of M combined with I [IM], and one unorthodox applied linguistics RA with two sections comprising M elements, the format of which is I[MRD]MRDC. Descriptions of methods are unsurprisingly a distinctive feature of ERAs, although, as Holmes (1997) points out, the M section is generally omitted in history RAs based on archival research. The present study is unable to confirm Holmes's (1997) finding since only one of the 20 history RAs was judged to be primarily empirical in nature. The only ERA in the corpus without a recognizable M element is from the field of archaeology. In this case, information about the "method", which involved the excavation of ancient tombs at Mowaihat in the United Arab Emirates, is briefly described in the introduction.

As might be expected, the vast majority of ERAs in the corpus have a separate M section. Of these, ten place M at the end of the article. Six of these ten RAs are from applied biology and chemical technology, two are from health technology and informatics, and the remaining two respectively from applied physics and textiles and clothing. Several diachronic studies of RAs as a genre (Bazerman, 1988; Berkenkotter & Huckin, 1995) have reported the tendency in recent decades of downgrading the importance of M whilst upgrading that of R and D. In this regard, Cargill and O'Connor (2009) note that the IRDM pattern is typically used in RAs in elite scientific journals such as *Nature* and *Science* to stress the highly significant new contributions or advances made by the research. Apart from placing it at the end of the article, other ways of de-emphasizing M include simplifying the content, employing a smaller font and even omitting the section altogether. These simplified M elements are frequently encapsulated in conflated sections such as [MRD], [MR] and [IM]. Regarding the unconventional applied linguistics RA where M components appear in two individual sections, the researchers firstly present the unexpected findings derived from a comparison of two transcribed extracts of children participating in a "role play" and a "rule play" in order—we assume—to stimulate the interest of the reader, to underscore the necessity for and significance of the research, and to pave the way for further analysis of the wider data base to obtain more general findings.

The findings indicate that C is a significant section in contemporary RAs, as around three-quarters of the writers employ it in the closing phase of their articles as a self-promotion strategy to highlight the value and contribution of their research (Katz, 2009). Notwithstanding its prevalence in ERAs, the conclusion—as a functionally distinct section—has received little attention in the ESP literature apart from in Yang and Allison's (2003) study of applied linguistics articles and in a handful of studies (e.g., Bunton, 2005) on conclusion chapters of theses and dissertations. The high occurrence of C can be attributed to the growing complexity and length of modern RAs and the increasing use of blended [RD] sections prior to it (see Sect. 4.5). As regards its placement, C can appear either as the final section (95.3%) or the penultimate section (4.70%) with M, D or other separate closing sections concerning directions for future research, implications, limitations, or applications as subsequent sections.

As noted by Swales (2004), the conception of the function of D remains somewhat blurry despite the increasing number of studies of it in recent years (e.g., Holmes, 1997; Peacock, 2002). This can largely be attributed to the fact that it has been mostly treated as an umbrella term to encompass C, [RD] and other optional sections in the closing phase of RAs such as Implications, Directions for Future Research, Limitations and Applications. However, the minimal difference in the proportions of RAs with separate R and D sections (45.9%) and blended [RD] sections (39.3%) found in the present study highlights the limitations of this approach and indicates the growing inclination of scholars in certain disciplines to depart from the conventional IMRD configuration in organizing their empirical studies.

Around a half of the RAs in the corpus include an LR between I and M. This finding largely accords with that of Yang and Allison (2004), who identified independent LR sections in three of the five primary RAs in *AL* and in four of the six RAs in *TQ*. Similarly, in Holmes's (1997) study, the employment of an LR after I occurred so frequently in political science and sociology RAs (but not history) that it might be regarded as a core component of the ERA in the social sciences. However, this newly-identified part-genre with its increasing use in a range of disciplines has not received due scholarly attention and therefore this project aims to fill this gap by investigating the specific structure of and the citation use in it, as well as its relationship with the adjoining sections in these aspects.

4.4 The Relationship Between Introduction and LR

As noted in Sect. 4.3, deviations from IMRD generally occur in the two "moving" processes in the opening and closing phases of ERAs. Regarding the first process (i.e., general to specific), the relationship between I and LR is intriguing and complex. Given the increasing employment of an independent LR section in modern research writing, there is clearly a need for detailed research into the functions and structure of LR vis-à-vis I through (inter alia) move-based analyses and case studies involving experienced RA writers. The following account of the I-LR relationship is therefore necessarily preliminary and, in places, speculative.

With the exception of the ten RAs which place M at the end and one archaeology RA without an M, there are 422 ERAs structured in the standard sequences and containing the main organizational components indicated in the hour-glass RA macro-structure. An analysis of these RAs reveals the following general patterns of the first "moving" process (i.e., from general background to specific focus): 218 RAs (51.7%) with an individual LR section between I and M and 204 RAs (48.3%) without such a section. Furthermore, in 25 of the 39 disciplines, more than 50% of their ERAs include an individual LR section and in disciplines such as management and marketing, industrial and systems engineering, accounting and finance, electronic and information engineering, and logistics, the LR section is used in more than 80% of the RAs. Therefore, providing an LR seems to be a major trend in many disciplines, and can be regarded as an important means of demonstrating a researcher's mastery of "specialist knowledge" (Ferguson, 1997) and promoting credibility in order to maximize the chances of their RAs being published.

As well as being a self-promotion strategy, the inclusion of a separate LR section appears to be desirable when there are several conflicting or contentious theoretical or practical issues in a particular research field, or the targeted journal is particularly interested in theoretically oriented research (Yang & Allison, 2004), or there is a voluminous literature in a well-established research area. In some social science disciplines, LR is frequently used to provide essential background for readers unfamiliar with the societal or institutional context in which an investigation has been conducted. The increasing use of LR as an often lengthy independent section may help to explain a trend that seems to be at work in a number of disciplines, namely, the practice of providing a brief, prologue-style introduction that simply indentifies the topic, purpose and structure of the RA, but makes no attempt to "create a research space" along Swalesian lines. In such RAs, LR is where the author engages in the crucial rhetorical work that has traditionally been located in I (i.e., CARS). This work necessarily includes a focused, gap-creating review of the literature.

In Swales's (1990) CARS model, Step 3 of Move 1 "reviewing items of previous research" seems to overlap with LR to a certain degree and, indeed, as Samraj (2002) observes, sketching in essential background information and reviewing previous research are generally not confined to a single step in one move in the introduction, but tend to appear throughout it. Despite this slight overlap, the fundamental differences between the adjoining I and LR sections lie in their foci and communicative purposes (Yang & Allison, 2004), that is, I focuses on establishing the research landscape, niche and identifying the research gaps in a more general way, while LR recreates and refines the research space initially cleared in I and prepares the ground for the study that is subsequently described in M.

As the section between I and M involves not only a literature review but also various kinds of contextual, theoretical and methodological material, it might be more appropriate to adopt an all-encompassing term rather than "Literature Review" to more accurately capture its coverage. One disadvantage of the term "Literature Review" is that it inevitably has connotations with the substantial, survey-like chapter that appears in research-degree theses. The use of the term in the context of RA writing instruction for research students might inadvertently convey the impression that such students, in preparing their RAs, simply need to "copy and paste" from their theses. Students who adopt such a strategy will inevitably come unstuck, since—as should be made clear in such classes—there are fundamental differences between RAs and theses. Despite these limitations, the use of "Literature Review" will be retained in this project for it is still the most commonly used term in referring to the section between the Introduction and Method sections.

4.5 The Relationship Between Results, Discussion and Conclusion

Besides the introductory parts, variations from the IMRD model also occur in the final phases of RAs. This section presents an account of the similarities, differences and interrelatedness of the major sections (i.e., R, D, C) based on my initial analysis and in light of the findings of previous research. Although the relationship between Results, Discussion and Conclusion seems not directly relevant to the project, it is still worth discussing for on the one hand, as with I and LR, detailed empirical research is required to further uncover their relationship, and on the other, some preliminary findings in this regard have already been obtained from this complete large-scale cross-sectional macro-structural study, which provides valuable insights into all major sections including LR not accounted for in the classic IMRD framework.

Despite the likely recycling structure shared by R and D, and the optional overlapping elements in them (e.g., the commentaries on results in R and the summary of results in D), these two sections have distinct emphases, purposes and natures. R focuses on new knowledge and aims to convert findings to textual form whereas D makes connections between the new knowledge or understanding reported in R and previous studies in the field, offers possible explanations for the findings and occasionally makes claims about the contribution, limitations and future avenues of the research. According to Swales and Feak (2004: 269), R mainly deals with "facts" and is of a "descriptive" nature and thus contrasts with D, which deals with "points" and is of an "interpretive" nature. As noted above, a substantial number of ERAs in the corpus employ [RD], thereby enabling the authors to move directly into the discussion of findings and perhaps to initiate more detailed comments.

Whereas D is more concerned with comments on specific results, C summarizes the general findings and highlights overall tendencies (Yang & Allison, 2003). A key finding from the present study is that C is more likely to be present in RAs in which R and D are merged (with other sections), e.g., [RD], [MRD] and [MR]D. The vast majority of RAs (89.4%) with a blended [RD] section make C its subsequent section, whereas 50.5% of those with independent R and D sections include a C section. Some 70.6% of RAs with an [MRD] section and 57.1% of those with an [MR]D pattern include a subsequent C section. The high occurrence of C in patterns involving merging appears to substantiate the point made in relation to the [RD] section, namely, that since such a section is likely to contain detailed comments on the results, it is necessary to provide an additional C section to synthesize the major findings and related discussion points. This is another area that requires detailed research.

In addition to the major sections in the closing phase of RAs, there are other noteworthy independent sections with their particular communicative emphases such as Implications, Directions for Future Research, Limitations and Applications, which however have traditionally been analyzed as a part of D or C (Nwogu, 1997; Swales, 2004). Around 10.2% of the RAs in our corpus feature such separate sections outside the IMRD framework in their final phases, which, like LR, [RD] and C, merit closer attention than they have previously received from ESP researchers. Interestingly, these sections mostly occur as the penultimate section followed by C (47.7%) and as the last section following D (31.8%) rather than, as might be supposed, as the final section following C (13.6%). To date, little research has been conducted into them other than by Yang and Allison (2003), who noted the presence of an independent "Pedagogic Implications" section in the applied linguistics RAs they studied, a tendency they attributed to the practical classroom concerns of professionals in this discipline. Consequently, the nature and orientation of the research appears to determine the choice of components in such sections.

4.6 Disciplinary Variations in ERAs

The present study represents the first attempt to explore variations in ERA macrostructures across a wide range of disciplines. However, it is important to acknowledge that, despite its ambitious scope and scale, the study analyzed only 20 RAs in each discipline and not all of these articles were categorized as empirical. Nevertheless, it is believed that the most prominent disciplinary preferences revealed by the present study are potentially useful for ESP practitioners who work with apprentice RA writers in particular disciplines.

Before analyzing disciplinary variations, it would be helpful to report the distribution of ERAs in each discipline. As can be seen in Appendix A, over three-quarters of the RAs in many applied science and engineering disciplines and in some social science disciplines were categorized as empirical. By contrast, most RAs in humanities disciplines and in several social science disciplines were not empirical in nature. No ERA was found in the field of history of art, which is thus excluded from the analysis.

The ERAs in the remaining 38 disciplines are remarkably varied in their overall organizations. In terms of within-disciplinary variations, most of the disciplines with less than half of their RAs identified as empirical ones (e.g., anthropology, logistics, design, applied mathematics and law) do not have frequently-used "major" structural patterns (see Appendix A). Aside from such disciplines, there are other disciplines with relatively high proportions of ERAs and yet extremely large variations in the macro structure of their ERAs, such as hotel and tourism, applied linguistics/ELT, and industrial and systems engineering. In these disciplines, no or few "major" structural patterns could be identified. Appendix A lists the numbers of structural patterns (as an indication of within-disciplinary variations in organizing empirical studies) and "major" structural patterns employed in each discipline. This list may have considerable reference value for disciplinary apprentice writers as well as ESP professionals and practitioners.

As for the cross-disciplinary variations in use of the six major patterns identified in Fig. 4.1, ILMRD and IMRD are used in less than half of the disciplines analyzed, indicating their comparatively limited applicability. In this regard, it is worth emphasizing that frequency of use does not necessarily equate to breadth of use. For instance, despite being the most frequently used pattern, ILM[RD]C is not the most widely used one. Instead, IM[RD]C, which was adopted by academics in as many as 27 different disciplines, ranks first in terms of its applicability across disciplines. ILM[RD]C, IM[RD]C and IMRD tend to be confined to a narrow range of disciplines, whereas IMRDC, ILMRDC and ILMRD seem to be more dispersed.

The IMRD pattern is most frequently employed in RAs in many applied science disciplines (e.g., health technology and informatics, applied biology and chemical technology, rehabilitation sciences) and two social science disciplines (viz., psychology and education), but is rarely used in engineering and humanities disciplines. Previous research (Brett, 1994; Holmes, 1997; Nwogu, 1997) indicates that the vast majority of ERAs in medicine, sociology, political science and applied linguistics conformed to the IMRD format. However, this conclusion is not borne out by the present study.

The most prevalent pattern, ILM[RD]C, is mainly distributed in RAs in engineering and social science disciplines such as industrial and systems engineering, civil and structural engineering and management and marketing, whereas academics in the applied sciences and humanities use it only occasionally. The second most frequently used pattern, IM[RD]C, is generally used in the area of textiles and clothing, where 14 of the 18 ERAs are structured in this way. This pattern is also common in building services engineering, applied physics, building and real estate, land surveying and geoinformatics and mechanical engineering.

The IMRDC format is most commonly used in a number of applied science disciplines such as applied biology and chemical technology, rehabilitation sciences and health technology and informatics. The ILMRDC and ILMRD patterns are most frequently adopted in social science disciplines, but in different subject areas. For example, ILMRDC is more likely to be employed by academics in applied linguistics/ELT, management and marketing and theoretical linguistics, whereas ILMRD tends to be used by scholars in applied social sciences, archaeology, education and sociology. The distinctive characteristics and significant cross-disciplinary variation in macro-structures revealed by the present study are not meant to be prescriptive; but they do nevertheless offer pointers for ESP practitioners who design and teach courses on RA writing.

4.7 Summary

As Swales (1990: 110) has observed, "like all living genres, the RA is continually evolving" and thus periodic, cross-disciplinary reviews of its structural patterns are essential if ESP professionals are to meet the needs of apprentice research writers. The present study has presented a detailed analysis of the principal macro-structures found in a sample of 433 ERAs published in 2007 and a preliminary account of variation across the 39 disciplines represented in the corpus. The study has found that the "standard" IMRD pattern is still one of the major structural patterns in

ERAs, but is by no means the default option for organizing such studies. Instead, the most frequently used pattern in the corpus is ILM[RD]C, and there are many other predominant structural patterns such as IM[RD]C, IMRDC, ILMRDC and ILMRD. The relatively diverse choices for structuring ERAs, as well as the presence of the major sections—LR, C, [RD]—not fully accounted for in the traditional IMRD model demonstrate that scholars' writing practices are far more complex than might be guessed from the principles set out in many research writing manuals and style guides.

The disciplinary variations uncovered by the present study highlight the need for research students to select high quality RAs in their disciplines as starting points in the process of disciplinary acculturation. ESP practitioners are thus advised not to give undue attention to the IMRD model in courses and materials in certain disciplines, but instead should encourage students to reflect on and understand the basis of the practices of professionals in their own fields (Paltridge, 2002). Studying authentic, discipline-specific texts is likely to be an effective means to enable students to appreciate the flexibility they may enjoy when structuring their RAs, particularly in the opening and closing phases.

The gap between "published advice" and "actual practice" in thesis and dissertation writing has been discussed at length in Paltridge's (2002: 125) research. A similar gulf exists in the area of RA writing, since many writing manuals and reference books (e.g., Körner, 2008; Pyrczak & Bruce, 2007) confine their accounts of RA structures to the conventional IMRD framework or the simplest "Introduction-Body-Conclusion" ("IBC") model and thus tend to overlook other—evidently more important—structural patterns such as ILM[RD]C and IM[RD]C. It is hoped that the findings of the present study will encourage the writers of such guides to provide a more complete account of structural patterns in ERAs and to place greater emphasis on disciplinary variation.

In particular, more prominence should be given to LR, C and [RD] in RA writing guides and courses since these sections, as the present study indicates, play a key role in contemporary research writing. Such materials need to be informed by detailed analyses of the structures, functions and communicative purposes of these sections, particularly the relationship between I and LR and R, D, [RD], and C.

In sum, the present analysis provides empirical evidence for the importance and prominence of frequently-used structural patterns other than the conventional IMRD pattern and for that of the LR section used at the outset of the ERA from the cross-sectional perspective. In the following chapter, a diachronic perspective will be adopted for further examining ERA macro-structural changes in two particular disciplines (i.e., applied linguistics and civil engineering), offering more justifications for the focused study of the introductory phase comprising both Introduction and Literature Review sections in them.

References

Bazerman, C. (1988). *Shaping knowledge: The genre and activity of the experimental article in science*. Madison, WI: University of Wisconsin Press.

Belcher, D. D., & Braine, G. (1995). Academic writing in a second language: Essays on research and pedagogy. Norwood, NJ: Ablex Pub. Corp.

Berkenkotter, C., & Huckin, T. (1995). *Genre knowledge in disciplinary communication: Cognition, culture, power*. Hilldale: Lawrence Erlbaum Associates.

Braine, G. (1995). Writing in the natural sciences and engineering. In D. Belcher & G. Braine (Eds.), *Academic writing in a second language: Essays on research and pedagogy* (pp. 113–134). Norwood, NJ: Ablex.

Brett, P. (1994). A genre analysis of the results section of sociology articles. *English for Specific Purposes, 13*(1), 47–59.

Bunton, D. (2005). The structure of Ph.D. conclusion chapters. *Journal of English for Academic Purposes, 4*(3), 207–224.

Cargill, M., & O'Connor, P. (2009). *Writing scientific research articles: Strategy and steps*. Chichester: Wiley-Blackwell.

Cooper, C. (1985). *Aspects of article introductions in IEEE publications*. Unpublished master's thesis, University of Aston.

Ferguson, G. (1997). Teacher education and LSP: The role of specialized knowledge. In R. Howard & G. Brown (Eds.), *Teacher education for languages for specific purposes* (pp. 80–89). Clevedon: Multilingual Matters.

Hill, S. S., Soppelsa, B. F., & West, G. K. (1982). Teaching ESL students to read and write experimental-research papers. *TESOL Quarterly, 16*(3), 333–347.

Holmes, R. (1997). Genre analysis and the social sciences: An investigation of the structure of research article discussion sections in three disciplines. *English for Specific Purposes, 16*(4), 321–337.

Katz, M. J. (2009). *From research to manuscript: A guide to scientific writing* (2nd ed.). Dordrecht: Springer.

Körner, A. M. (2008). *Guide to publishing a scientific paper*. Abingdon: Routledge.

Nwogu, K. N. (1997). The medical research paper: Structure and functions. *English for Specific Purposes, 16*(2), 119–138.

Paltridge, B. (2002). Thesis and dissertation writing: An examination of published advice and actual practice. *English for Specific Purposes, 21*(2), 125–143.

Peacock, M. (2002). Communicative moves in the discussion section of research articles. *System, 30*(4), 479–497.

Posteguillo, S. (1999). The schematic structure of computer science research articles. *English for Specific Purposes, 18*(2), 139–160.

Pyrczak, F., & Bruce, R. R. (2007). *Writing empirical research reports: A basic guide for students of the social and behavioral sciences* (6th ed.). Glendale, CA: Pyrczak Pub.

Samraj, B. (2002). Introductions in research articles: Variations across disciplines. *English for Specific Purposes, 21*(1), 1–17.

Swales, J. M. (1990). *Genre analysis: English in academic and research settings*. Cambridge; New York: Cambridge University Press.

Swales, J. M. (2004). *Research genres: Explorations and applications*. Cambridge; New York: Cambridge University Press.

Swales, J. M., & Feak, C. B. (2004). *Academic writing for graduate students: Essential tasks and skills* (2nd ed.). Ann Arbor: University of Michigan Press.

Yang, R. Y., & Allison, D. (2003). Research articles in applied linguistics: Moving from results to conclusions. *English for Specific Purposes, 22*(4), 365–385.

Yang, R. Y., & Allison, D. (2004). Research articles in applied linguistics: Structures from a functional perspective. *English for Specific Purposes, 23*(3), 264–279.

Chapter 5
Lead-in Study 2: The ERA Macro-structural Development in Civil Engineering (CE) and Applied Linguistics (AL)

5.1 Introduction

In the preceding chapter, a cross-sectional study of macro-structure of ERAs in as many as 39 disciplines in social sciences, humanities, applied sciences and engineering was reported on, and discussed. The study found a number of often-used structural patterns other than the classic IMRD framework, e.g., those with an independent LR section used. To provide further justifications for the focused study of the introductory phase consisting of both Introduction and Literature Review sections, this chapter presents an analysis of the recent macro-structural development of ERAs in the two representative disciplines (viz., AL and CE) over the past thirty years (1980–2010). A particular focus is placed on the evolution of the structural forms of their introductory phases. The related textual findings derived will be complemented with and illuminated by our interviewees' valuable insights on how to structure the ERA in these two studied disciplines and whether and when they would use a discrete LR section. Therefore, both insightful textual findings on structural changes and related cross-disciplinary variations, and insiders' accounts contribute together to our better understanding of the disciplinary structural practices and raise questions about the current research-writing pedagogical practice and materials writing.

This diachronic study firstly examines the status of IMRD (Sect. 5.2), and then tracks the changing development of the macro-structure of ERAs in these two contrasting disciplines (Sect. 5.3). As aforementioned, the changing structural forms of the introductory phase of ERAs (Sect. 5.4) is a special focus of this study, as it aims to offer additional empirical evidence for the LR becoming an important major section in contemporary research writing in AL and CE. In this sense, it will convincingly account for the necessity for and significance of research into this section and its relationship with the Introduction in the follow-up focused study. To conclude the chapter, a summary of the key findings of this study is provided (Sect. 5.5).

(Kathy). L. Lin, *Perspectives on the Introductory Phase of Empirical Research Articles*, Corpora and Intercultural Studies 5, https://doi.org/10.1007/978-981-32-9204-8_5

5.2 The Status of IMRD

Before specific macro-structural changes of ERAs in the two disciplines over the years studied are presented, we firstly examine the status of the "standard" IMRD format in expert writing practices. To our surprise, this study shows that none of the CE ERAs published in the two chosen journals in the past 30 years follow the long-established IMRD structure, and in AL, only 12 out of the 191 ERAs have this pattern. This suggests that although this traditional model is often espoused as "the simplest and most logical way to communicate research results" (Day & Gastel, 2006: 9), there is indeed a great deal of deviation from it in expert writing in the two disciplines.

In terms of the distribution of the 12 IMRD-structured AL ERAs (Fig. 5.1), nine of them are from the first ten-year period (i.e. 1980–1990) with six published in the year 1985. However, none of them are from the year 2010. This indicates that although the IMRD pattern is not widely used in both disciplines, AL ERAs of the earlier period (approximately before the 1990s) tend to be comparatively more frequently structured in this conventional four-part model than their contemporary counterparts.

While previous historical RA studies focusing on traditional scientific disciplines such as medicine (e.g., Atkinson, 1992; Sollaci & Pereira, 2004) and physics (e.g., Bazerman, 1984) have documented an overall trend for (empirical) RAs towards the IMRD-standardization starting in the early or mid-20th century and continuing up till the 1980s, the present study shows the rare use or even absence of the canonical IMRD model in empirical research writing in the two far less studied disciplines in the diachronic literature (i.e., AL and CE) since the 1980s. This contrast, as a possible display of the cross-time and cross-disciplinary structural variations, may mainly be attributed to the ever-evolving nature of the genre of ERAs, and the changing conventions and expectations of research writing in different disciplinary contexts (Atkinson, 1999).

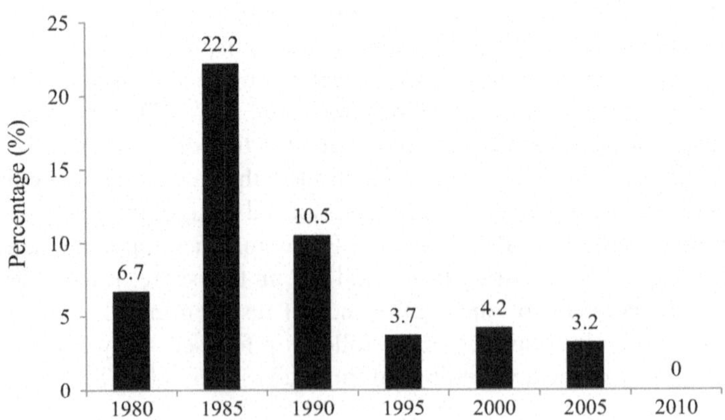

Fig. 5.1 Changing proportions of ERAs with the conventional IMRD structure across the 30 years in AL

The present findings are generally consistent with those of the first lead-in study (Chap. 4): the use of the IMRD pattern is least preferred in engineering and humanities disciplines but most favored in many applied science disciplines (e.g., applied biology and chemical technology, rehabilitation sciences). Recent studies such as Pérez-Llantada (2013) and Stoller and Robinson (2013) have addressed discipline-specificity or even journal-specificity in RA macro-structural use. In these studies, the classic IMRD has often been found as a not particularly prominent pattern and instead disciplinary writers have a variety of other preferred structural choices (e.g., IMR[DC] and IM[R(DC)] for chemistry writers). This indicates that the IMRD is not a "one-size-fits-all" model that should be recommended to apprentice writers with quite varied disciplinary backgrounds and aiming for successful publication in different categories of journals.

Emphasizing discipline-/(sub-discipline-)specificity or sometimes journal-specificity in RA macro-structure use and distinguishing what have evolved into predominant patterns other than the canonical IMRD format from what are just "peripheral variants" (Cargill & O'Connor, 2009) are perhaps of more direct and practical value to student writers. Nevertheless, the current reality is that numerous research writing reference books and instructional manuals still confine their accounts of (empirical) RA structure to either the restrictive IMRD format (e.g., Körner, 2008; Lester & Lester, 2006) or to the simplest and general three-component structure "IBC" ("Introduction"—"Body"—"Conclusion") (e.g., Dees, 2000; Soles, 2010). The discrepancy between published advice and disciplinary practice has been raised by Paltridge (2002) and Stoller and Robinson (2013) for attention of EAP scholars and practitioners.

What is significantly different from the simplistic and impractical published advice is our experts' insider perceptions and experience as well. Most of them agreed that there is no strong convention in structuring current ERAs in their own fields as "there are different ways for people to do it" (AL6). Even the only two interviewees explicitly recommending IMRD as the "standard" way of writing ERAs emphasized that "there is a certain amount of creativity and flexibility allowed" (CE3) and "good writers don't need to follow this convention very closely" (AL7). What they perceived is that competent writers would be much more likely to write in their own ways while noting some contributors' pages to ensure that they would not diverge too far from that. This perhaps explains why the non-IMRD articles are found to be the majority.

The overall impression from the interviews is that expert insiders considered structuring ERAs as a complex issue, which should be based on the particular nature of their investigations. As noted by AL2, it is essentially a question of "content and form matching" whilst considering fully and making the best of the communicative purpose or functional foci of each part-genre (Swales, 1990) to make the paper a logical and well-connected whole. The classic IMRD pattern is important but constitutes only a small part of the reality concerning expert actual structural practices; it is only one of the many potential choices available to expert writers who only select the best one to fit their needs.

5.3 Development in the Macro-structure of ERAs

To track ERA macro-structural development in AL and CE (1980–2010), all "frequently-used" structural patterns for each sampled year are listed in Table 5.1. "Frequently-used" patterns are those used in no less than 10% of ERAs in each selected volume, given a variety of macro-structural patterns recorded for them with most patterns enjoying relatively moderate proportions. Generally, it shows that expert writers in both disciplines have apparently varied and diverse structural

Table 5.1 The frequently-used structural patterns in AL and CE across the 30 years

Year	AL	%	CE	%
1980	Unsectioned	13.3	IS[MRD]C	16.1
	IM[RD]	13.3	IMRC	14.5
	IMRC	13.3	IM[RD]C	14.5
			IMRDC	12.9
			IL[MRD]C	11.3
1985	IMRD	22.2	IMRC	16.2
	IMRC	11.1	IM[RD]C	14.7
	IMRDC	11.1	IMRDC	13.2
			IS[MRD]C	11.8
			ILM[RD]C	11.8
1990	IMRDC	15.8	IMRC	15.8
	ILMRC	15.8	IM[RD]C	15.0
	ILMRDC	10.5	IMRDC	12.5
	ILM[RD]C	10.5	IS[MRD]C	12.5
	IMRDC	10.5	ILM[RD]C	10.0
	IBC	10.5		
1995	ILMRDC	25.9	IS[MRD]C	18.9
	ILM[RD]C	18.5	ILM[RD]C	15.1
	IMRDC	11.1	IM[RD]C	13.2
2000	ILMRDC	45.8	ILM[RD]C	13.8
	ILMRC	12.5	IMRC	11.9
	ILMRD	12.5	IMRDC	11.9
			ILMRC	10.1
			ILMRDC	10.1
			IS[MRD]C	10.1
2005	ILM[RD]C	19.4	IM[RD]C	18.5
	ILMRDC	16.1	IS[MRD]C	15.2
	ILMRD	12.9	ILM[RD]C	13.2
	IM[RD]C	12.9	IMRDC	12.6
			ILMRDC	10.6
2010	ILMRDC	33.3	IM[RD]C	25.7
	ILM[RD]C	22.9	ILM[RD]C	15.0
	ILMRD	10.4	IS[MRD]C	13.2

Notes I=Introduction; S=Simulation Model; LR=Literature Review; M=Method; R=Results; D=Discussion; C=Conclusion; [RD]=the blended Results and Discussion section; [MRD]=the coalesced Method, Results and Discussion section; B=Body choices such as IM[RD]C and ILM[RD]C, rather than using the canonical IMRD as the default or predominant pattern. This is broadly congruent with the findings of recent cross-sectional studies of RAs such as Stoller and Robinson (2013). One crucial reason for this is that disciplinary expert writers do not usually write to the formula, but consider more their actual needs and the principle of "article content, form, and function matching" (AL2), as astutely noted by our expert insiders (see more explanations in Sect. 5.2).

They also reported an array of other factors that could influence their structural decisions, most prominently the types of research conducted. For example, a report of a case study might be structured quite differently from that of an experimental reading test. Intuitively speaking, journal policy is another concern, which however turns out to be not particularly relevant for this study. Among the 12 IMRD-structured AL ERAs, eight are from *TQ* and the other four from *AL*. *TQ* recommends its submissions to conform to the requirements of the APA Publication Manual (2010), which suggests the possibility of using the combined Results and Discussion section, in addition to the four traditional sections set out in the IMRD model. *AL* neither has such recommendation nor specifies the structure submitted papers should follow. As such, it is not certain whether there is a link between the journal and the structure employed. Regarding the two CE journals, they are ASCE (American Society of Civil Engineering) journals. According to the ASCE Author Guide, all the submitted full-length papers should consult the Chicago Manual of Style. However, neither the author's guides in the two journals nor the Chicago Manual of Style (2010) have specific instructions on how to organize a full-length technical paper. Consequently, journal regulations may not play a decisive role in shaping authors' plans. Despite this, journal editors and reviewers could make suggestions for restructuring the article due to various concerns, which makes the fixed use of a standard structure such as the IMRD virtually impossible.

In addition to structural diversity, another noticeable feature is that, as aforementioned, these varied patterns revealed across time mostly share similarly moderate proportions except that in the recent decade the pattern with the LR section like ILM-RDC (45.8% in 2000, 33.3% in 2010) has been noticeably more prevalent among applied linguists. This implies to some extent the increasing importance of the LR section in AL research writing, a trend which will be explicated later.

Among these frequently-used macro-structural patterns, "IS[MRD]C", where "S" represents the section devoted to descriptions of the simulation model, is a distinct one consistently used by CE writers. It may entail some explanations. This is the common pattern for CE empirical simulation articles. In the present study, empirical simulation articles or simulation articles that are empirically based, are those RAs featured by the use of a real experiment or a set of specific empirical case studies for testing and evaluating the formulated model in real sites; they report simulation studies that represent specific real-world situations or whose key parameters are set (and calibrated) based on data from real situations. Hence, they are considered to be empirical in nature and thus assigned into the group of ERAs (Shafer & Smunt, 2004).[1] In "IS[MRD]C", "I" and "S" respectively refer to an independent Introduction section and a stand-alone section presenting details of the computer simulation model; "[MRD]" represents a single section where the elements of method, results and discussions are coalesced (usually for a real experiment or a set of case studies in real sites to test the validity of the computer simulated model), which is always followed by a final stand-alone "Conclusion" section.

The practice of categorizing empirical simulation articles as a special type of ERA is conducted for both the convenience of analysis and foregrounding this prominent pattern featured in CE writing. This preliminary analysis has considered the purpose of the study, their salient empirical nature and features, and the advice of the specialist informant. However, it should be noted that hitherto there has been little or no EAP research explicitly addressing simulation articles and the determination of their category. This may be open to discussion and entail more future investigations.

From the diachronic perspective, the detailed cross-time comparison of macro-structural use in the two disciplines (Table 5.1) suggests both the evolving (Berkenkotter, 2007; Swales, 1990) and the inherent "stabilized-for-now or stabilized-enough" nature (Schryer, 1994: 108) of the genre of ERAs. The former is reflected in changes in the preferential use of some patterns and major sections. For example, the IMRC pattern was generally more favored in the early periods in both disciplines: it was frequently used in CE ERAs on and before 2000[2]; in AL, it was only frequently used in the 1980s. Another case in point is that, in 1980, there are still a considerable number of unsectioned ERAs (13.3%) in AL, where indeed more complex patterns have gradually appeared since the 1990s with a dramatic increase in the use of the LR section and macro-structural patterns associated with it. This macro-structural development is, however, not found in CE, and the cross-disciplinary variation may be attributed to the contrasting nature, epistemology, and lengths of history of the two disciplines. As aforementioned, CE is one of the oldest engineering disciplines with a long research history and tradition and a vast body of literature (Wood, 2012). In contrast, AL is a less-established social science discipline that emerged in the mid-20th century. Many premier journals such as *Applied Linguistics* and *English for Specific Purposes (ESP)* were founded in the 1980s, a period when both the disciplinary research knowledge base and writing conventions were beginning to take shape. Consequently, there may have been little literature to review at that time, a possible reason for the rare use of the substantial LR section and complicated organizational patterns associated with it. Based on this finding, it can also be argued that there might be some limitations in Swales's (1990, 2004) models for journal article introductions, which are derived from his 1981 four-part schema. This four-part schema, as he clearly stated (Swales, 1981: 9), was developed

[1] In contrast to empirical simulation articles, a small number of pure mathematical modeling papers and computer simulation papers that are not empirically-based but characterized by logical inferences and argumentation (Swales & Feak, 2004) found in CE were categorized as theoretical RAs in this study.

[2] For the year 1995, IMRC used in 10 out of the 106 CE ERAs is nearly a "frequently-used" structural pattern.

from his analysis of 48 short article introductions (of usually between 100 and 500 words) published in the late 1970s and early 1980s. An updated understanding of the structure and communicative purposes of this evolving part-genre (i.e., the Introduction section) thus seems essential.

In addition, it is found from the present analysis that the generic context for RA introductions may change (i.e., a prominently increasing use of an independent LR section after introductions has been found in AL but not in CE). This indicates that the rhetorical structure and communicative functions of this part-genre (viz., introductions) may have evolved and could be different from what Swales has perceived from his source data (i.e., the 48 article introductions written in the late 1970s and early 1980s as aforementioned) and proposed afterwards (Swales, 1981, 1990, 2004). The reason is that Swales did not specify whether the 48 introductions he examined were the independent Introduction without a subsequent LR section ("I") or the Introduction with such a following functionally distinct section ("I+LR") (Swales, 1981). Therefore, whether Swales's (1981) four-part schema and his follow-up CARS model (Swales, 1990, 2004) could account for the rhetorical structure of the introductions that are followed by a substantial LR section is unknown (or at least dubious, considering that the Introduction and LR sections are two part-genres with possibly partly-overlapping communicative purposes and structural constituents). Finally, Swales's (1981: 9) source data also include an introduction to a survey article in education, despite his concern that introductions to survey articles might be structured and functioned differently from those to other types of articles. His statement about the categories of all the other 47 articles from which the remaining introductions were selected was vague, but as he clarified, they mostly have a feature in common, i.e., they are the RAs "in which the DPR [viz., Describing Previous Research] was in some way a springboard for the presentation of new research…Again exclusions were few" (Swales, 1981: 9). By adopting a stricter criterion in data selection for the focused study of the rhetorical structure of the introductions (see Sect. 6.2) (i.e., only focusing on the introductions with a following LR section in ERAs), the present research aims to yield some interesting findings and make some useful contributions to the introduction studies where currently the CARS model (Swales, 1990) prevails.

ERAs as a research genre with their inherent "stabilized-for-now or stabilized-enough" nature regarding their purposes (Schryer, 1994: 108) could be partly perceived from writers' generally consistent use of conventional structural units such as "I" and "M" and a newly-identified section "C" not accounted for in the IMRD model with their typical underlying functions in both disciplines. While the first preparatory study (Chap. 4) noted that deviations from the IMRD generally occur in both the opening and closing phases of ERAs, those occurring towards the end such as C and [RD] seem to have grown as common sections frequently employed in ERAs as early as in the 1980s in the two disciplines. As mentioned earlier, in the APA Publication Manual (2010), [RD] is recommended for papers with a relatively concise and straightforward discussion. The C section, which was traditionally considered and analyzed as a part of the Discussion (Hsieh et al., 2006), has been increasingly recognized as an independent, essential structural component of a manuscript, as specified by journals such as *ESP* and *Journal of English for Academic Purposes*.

However, the advice for employing a discrete LR section is generally lacking in all journal guidelines and style manuals, and the reason is presumably that reviewing previous literature has long been regarded as a part of the Introduction, as indicated in the well-known CARS model (Swales, 1990). The long-standing preoccupation with the IMRD macro-structural framework and the overwhelming scholarly attention devoted to the CARS-related studies of introductions, result in the stand-alone LR section being "overshadowed" by the Introduction and the very likely reduced value of research into it (Kwan, 2005).

Despite the limited research into these important sections outside the IMRD framework, they are well-noted and flexibly employed by all our expert insiders in their writing. Many of them prefer using the blended Results and Discussion section to "make articles condensed and concise" (CE3). As for the C section, they mostly viewed it as a common section that shares some elements and features of the traditional D section. Nonetheless, they attached great importance to the particular "promotional" function of it, where the most important findings and contribution of the study should be highlighted. Concerning the LR section, it was named by some interviewees as "Background". However, many of them were acutely aware that the review of the background can either be embedded within the Introduction or used as a discrete second section, and their relevant accounts about this flexibility are discussed in the next sub-section.

5.4 Development in Structural Forms of the Introductory Part

As more evident development seems to occur in the opening phase of ERAs (especially the obviously growing use of more complex patterns with the independent LR section in AL), this sub-section focuses on the evolution of its structural patterns. Among the 974 ERAs, 964 have the introductory phases organized in the two major patterns: 543 (55.7%) of them contain only a single Introduction ("I") before M whereas 421 (43.2%) have both the Introduction and the independent LR section ("IL"). The other ten cases are exceptions, with three AL ERAs of the 1980s being continuous texts, a special AL case with the LR and M merged together subsequent to the Introduction (i.e. I[LM]), and another two AL and four CE articles written in the 1980s and 1990s containing the coalesced Introduction and Method section (i.e. [IM]).

Figure 5.2 shows the changing proportions of ERAs with the two predominant forms of the introductory part (i.e. "I" vs. "IL") in AL and CE from 1980 to 2010. Generally, compared with their colleagues in the 1980s, contemporary research writers in both disciplines employ far more frequently "IL" before the M section, which confirms LR as an increasingly prominent RA section in the past 30 years. However, the use of the two predominant forms in these two disciplines still exhibits somewhat different patterns. In AL, only 13.3% of the ERAs used "IL" before M while

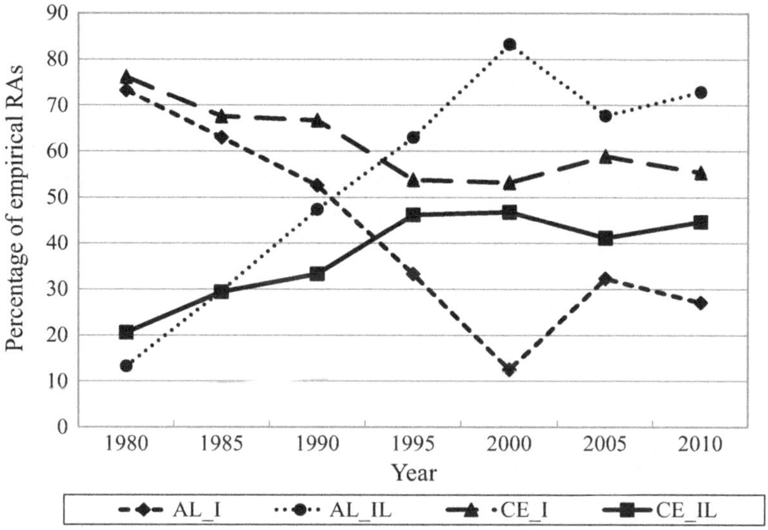

Fig. 5.2 The development of the two dominant structural forms of the introductory phase in AL and CE (1980–2010)

73.3% employed only a single Introduction in 1980. This contrast had been almost reversed in the past 30 years: in 2010, around 73% of the ERAs used "IL" whereas just over 27% used only a stand-alone Introduction without a subsequent LR. In CE, the initial contrast in the proportions of ERAs with the two structural forms of the opening phase was very similar to that in AL in 1980. However, by 2010, the gap had been largely reduced and around 55.4% and 44.6% of the ERAs respectively used "I" and "IL" as their introductory parts. Specifically, in AL, during the first 20 years, from 1980 to 2000, the pace of "IL" increments was rapid, from 13.3 to 83.3%. Although there was a noticeable fluctuation in using "IL" during the following ten years, the proportions of ERAs with "IL" as the introductory part stayed constantly above 65%. In CE, the proportion of ERAs with "IL" rose gradually during the first two decades (i.e., almost doubled from 1980 to 2000), and then similarly fell slightly in 2005 (41.1%) but rose again to 44.3% in 2010. Such different development patterns for the use of the two predominant forms (or rather, the LR section) between AL and CE is inextricably bound up with the contrasting nature and history of the two disciplines, as explicated in Sect. 5.3.

While this study provides for the first time the diachronic evidence of the increasing importance of the independent LR section since the 1980s, sporadic accounts of its existence (with varied section headings and content foci) between I and M have been given in a number of earlier studies [e.g., the "Theory" section observed in Braine (1995), and separate sections for "Literature Review" and "Theoretical Basis" in Yang and Allison (2004)]. Its status as one of the major sections outside the IMRD framework has been suggested in a few recent cross-sectional studies of RAs from various disciplines (e.g., Kwan et al., 2012). In Kwan et al. (2012), the

LR section, defined as the section(s) between the introduction and the methodology sections where previous literature is reviewed, is found to be a quasi-obligatory RA part-genre in the field of information systems (i.e., being used in over 80% of the RAs in its four source journals). With the macro-structure of 433 ERAs from a multitude of disciplines studied, my first lead-in study (Chap. 4) reported that over half (51.7%) of the ERAs examined use both the I and LR sections in their opening phases. For the two disciplines similar to those studied in this paper (i.e., AL/English language teaching, and civil and structural engineering), the major macro-structural patterns used are respectively "ILMRDC" and "ILM[RD]C", the two patterns with a functionally distinct LR between I and M.

Being a more recent development of the ERA, the appearance of the separate LR section is clearly evidence of its evolving nature. Whereas the early papers of the first two centuries were mostly random observational reports of events or phenomena without any literature reviewed for contextualization, contemporary papers focus on quite tightly defined research problems for which literature is selectively and purposively cited. Indeed, the present-day independent LR section may sometimes go beyond the scope of a traditional focused, gap-creating literature review by offering other background information such as that on the research setting, which suggests that the term "Literature Review" is probably not the most appropriate description of these sections. Similar views were expressed by our expert insiders, who held that the LR section may indeed contain varied content like the introduction of key concepts or theoretical models or hypotheses, and contextual descriptions that would work better for the kind of research while it is making some claims about social practices or when its findings and significance are closely related to the particular setting.

As our focus is on the entire introductory phase, one interesting question for the interviewees is when they would embed the element of reviewing previous literature into the Introduction without using a subsequent LR section and when they would prefer to provide a separate section. For this question, they expressed the following concerns: firstly, it depends on "how much data-driven the study is, and how much contextualization is needed" (AL2). As AL2 further explained, for example, if there is a great deal of data to be presented in the paper, then the writers probably do not have enough space to review the literature. However, if it is a "theory-driven" (rather than "data-driven") article, research writers usually need to review a considerable body of previous literature and models in order to contextualize their studies and build their own frameworks.

Secondly, for a number of informants (e.g., AL1, AL4, AL7, CE1, CE2 and CE4) who often prefer to use "IL" as the pre-methodology sections, they put reader experience and the distinctive functions of the two sections as major concerns. In their view, the usually short and persuasive Introduction in "IL" seeks to "sell" the paper by "explaining what and why" to the readers (CE4) without "boring them with the extremely theoretical and technical details" (AL7). This echoes what CE2 described: "usually in the Introduction (before the LR), we are talking about the nature of the problem, and then get into the scale of the problem, when some very general background or statistics from government reports might be asserted, before you carry on straight into the literature review in the second long section." So to them, the Introduction (before the LR) is simply for scene-setting and identifying the problem/issue, being a kind of "set-up" (AL1), while the LR section is functionally a "build-up" mainly for further developing the arguments and rationales based on a focused, critical review of the literature, and developing the theoretical frameworks or conceptual/methodological basis. In this sense, the Introduction in "IL" serving as a "general overview" (AL4, CE1) functions somewhat differently from the traditional introductions without a subsequent LR section, especially those suggested by the CARS model (Swales, 1990). However, this entails systematic function-oriented genre-based analyses for verification (see Chap. 6).

Thirdly, while it is assumed that the extremely rapid information flow and the accelerated accumulation of the literature in the present-day research world may contribute to the use of a separate LR section to some extent, our interviewees emphasized that there are different ways of representing the literature, and for articles, only the most relevant and important literature should be reviewed in detail. In other words, although the term "Literature Review" sounds like "a ritual or a perfunctory step" (AL4), this section in RAs should be purpose-oriented and "everything reviewed should be related to research questions explicitly or implicitly" (AL7). It is quite different from the LR chapter in research degree theses, which is commonly a comprehensive survey of all possible aspects on the research theme partly in order to demonstrate the students' knowledge of the field. This point is however often neglected by apprentice writers who develop their first articles based on their thesis work, with sometimes unfortunate consequences (Peters, 2011). Some CE informants also expatiated on the difficulties in writing up the LR for the interdisciplinary study, when quite diverse literature in different fields needs to be reviewed, synthesized and strategically integrated. For instance, the following quote from CE1, who is a professor in transportation research, has vividly captured the complexities involved in this regard:

> …sometimes when you've got quite diverse literature, which crosses disciplinary boundaries…Transport does that quite a lot: you're pulling information from different fields essentially and getting that material together, and then writing that in a coherent way which makes sense to be informed from different disciplines. It's not straightforward. You know, we are doing some work at the moment on futures [*sic*], looking at future scenarios for transport in urban areas in the UK and that draws in a wide range of information from all areas. You've got geography, you've got engineering perspectives, and you've got lots of futurologists, counter-perspectives…You've also got some different people who are writing about kind of things of periphery. You don't know whom the editors are going to send your articles to…. Quite a lot will go to diverse disciplines…. And then you get comments from people who clearly come from one of the disciplines, so you have to cover this literature. Therefore, you need to get it revised and spend time reading additional materials and incorporating that into the review. That can be quite time-consuming and complicated. Sometimes you don't have space to write that sort of the review, because you pull different things and read some of them for quite a short time, and you want to cover what you did as well. So it can be very complicated. There is also an updating job. You know, lots of this stuff is…it dates quite quickly. So about the time you've got two referees' [comments], how long may it come back to you?

Finally, as a part of the macro-structural practices, whether to use an independent LR section also hinges on some circumstantial factors, such as space concern, editors' or referees' suggestions, and co-writing experience (i.e., co-authors' re-structural decisions). As AL1 explained explicitly, although she always favors drafting two sections before Method (i.e., "IL"), the first section she will revise is the LR section if she needs to reduce the article length for the space reason. Therefore, during the editing and revising process, the initial separate Introduction and LR may be significantly reduced and eventually incorporated into one section. To CE informants, the reviewers may give suggestions in terms of the organization of articles as well. However, this is not common and they attach more importance to scientific technical content, as CE4 commented, "…you get a lot of comments from referees typically, but they don't usually pick you up on whether you use a separate section between I and M. They tend to pick you up on the sort of scientific technical content, say, whether it is right or wrong, or whether someone else has done that already…".

5.5 Summary

The study reported in this chapter is a contribution to the literature by providing a diachronic perspective on the recent macro-structural development of ERAs (1980–2010) in two contrasting disciplines (i.e., AL and CE). Also, emic perspectives on some essential aspects thereof, for example, macro-structural diversity and flexibility, and the increasing use of an independent LR section are also included. A real picture of much more complex disciplinary expert structural practices in these years is thus revealed, which confirms that there seems to be some movement away from the "standard" IMRD pattern after the uniform trend towards the IMRD-standardization commencing in the early or mid-20th century. However, this requires further research perhaps conducted in other disciplines for verification.

The study reveals both cross-time structural changes and related cross-disciplinary variations. For example, in both disciplines, the IMRC pattern was generally favored in the earlier period. While there is an absence of the IMRD pattern in CE empirical research writing, it was more frequently used in AL empirical RAs before the 1990s. An increasing use of much more complex patterns with the LR section (e.g., ILM-RDC and ILM[RD]C) has been found in AL, which may be related to the nature and history of this discipline; however, this macro-structural development is not revealed in our CE diachronic data. In contrast, a discipline-specific pattern "IS[MRD]C" is discovered for a distinct type of CE ERAs (i.e., empirical simulation articles). Other characteristic patterns consistently used in CE throughout most of the period (1980–2010) include IM[RD]C and IMRDC. In addition to the dynamic and evolving nature, the genre of ERA also embodies its inherent "stabilized-enough" nature (Schryer, 1994: 108) regarding its purpose. This could be partly perceived from disciplinary writers' generally consistent use of conventional structural units such as the Introduction and M sections and a section not accounted for in the IMRD framework (i.e., the C section), with their typical underlying communicative functions, and their shared understanding of many functions of the newly-identified LR section.

References

APA Publication Manual. (2010). *Publication manual of the American Psychological Association* (6th ed.). Washington, DC: American Psychological Association.

Atkinson, D. (1992). The evolution of medical research writing from 1735 to 1985: The case of *the Edinburgh Medical Journal. Applied Linguistics, 13*(4), 337–374.

Atkinson, D. (1999). *Scientific discourse in sociohistorical context: The Philosophical Transactions of the Royal Society of London, 1675–1975*. Mahwah, NJ: L. Erlbaum Associates.

Bazerman, C. (1984). Modern evolution of the experimental report in physics: Spectroscopic articles in *Physical Review*, 1893–1980. *Social Studies in Science, 14,* 163–196.

Berkenkotter, C. (2007). Genre evolution? The case for a diachronic perspective. In V. K. Bhatia, J. Flowerdew, & R. H. Jones (Eds.), *Advances in discourse studies* (pp. 178–191). London: Routledge.

Braine, G. (1995). Writing in the natural sciences and engineering. In D. Belcher & G. Braine (Eds.), *Academic writing in a second language: Essays on research and pedagogy* (pp. 113–134). Norwood, NJ: Ablex.

Cargill, M., & O'Connor, P. (2009). *Writing scientific research articles: Strategy and steps*. Chichester: Wiley-Blackwell.

Day, R. A., & Gastel, B. (2006). *How to write and publish a scientific paper* (6th ed.). Westport, CT: Greenwood Press.

Dees, R. (2000). *Writing the modern research paper* (3rd ed.). Boston: Allyn and Bacon.

Hsieh, W. M., Tsai, T. C., Lin, M. C., Liou, H. C. U., & Kuo, C. H. (2006). Exploring genre sets: Research article sections in illustrative humanities and science disciplines. In *The 23rd International Conference on English Teaching and Learning in the ROC,* Taipei (pp. 249–262).

Körner, A. M. (2008). *Guide to publishing a scientific paper*. Abingdon: Routledge.

Kwan, B. S. C. (2005). *A genre analysis of literature reviews in doctoral theses.* Unpublished doctoral dissertation, City University of Hong Kong.

Kwan, B. S. C., Chan, H., & Lam, C. (2012). Evaluating prior scholarship in literature reviews of research articles: A comparative study of practices in two research paradigms. *English for Specific Purposes, 31,* 188–201.

Lester, J. D., & Lester, J. D. (2006). *Writing research papers in the social sciences*. New York: Pearson/Longman.

Paltridge, B. (2002). Thesis and dissertation writing: An examination of published advice and actual practice. *English for Specific Purposes, 21*(2), 125–143.

Pérez-Llantada, C. (2013). The article of the future: Strategies for genre stability and change. *English for Specific Purposes, 32*(4), 221–235.

Peters, S. (2011). Asserting or deflecting expertise? Exploring the rhetorical practices of master's theses in the philosophy of education. *English for Specific Purposes, 30*(3), 176–185.

Schryer, C. F. (1994). The lab vs. the clinic: Sites of competing genres. In A. Freedman & P. Medway (Eds.), *Genre and the new rhetoric* (pp. 105–124). London: Taylor and Francis.

Shafer, S. M., & Smunt, T. L. (2004). Empirical simulation studies in operations management: Context, trends, and research opportunities. *Journal of Operations Management, 22,* 345–354.

Soles, D. (2010). *The essentials of academic writing* (2nd ed.). Boston, MA: Wadsworth.

Sollaci, L. B., & Pereira, M. G. (2004). The introduction, methods, results and discussion (IMRAD) structure: A fifty-year survey. *Journal of the Medical Library Association, 92*(3), 364–367.

Stoller, F. L., & Robinson, M. S. (2013). Chemistry journal articles: An interdisciplinary approach to move analysis with pedagogical aims. *English for Specific Purposes, 32,* 45–57.

Swales, J. M. (1981). *Aspects of article introductions*. Birmingham: The University of Aston, Language Studies Unit.

Swales, J. M. (1990). *Genre analysis: English in academic and research settings*. Cambridge; New York: Cambridge University Press.

Swales, J. M. (2004). *Research genres: Explorations and applications*. Cambridge; New York: Cambridge University Press.

Swales, J. M., & Feak, C. B. (2004). *Academic writing for graduate students: Essential tasks and skills* (2nd ed.). Ann Arbor: University of Michigan Press.
The Chicago Manual of Style. (2010). (16th ed.). Chicago: The University of Chicago Press.
Wood, D. M. (2012). *Civil engineering: A very short introduction*. Oxford: Oxford University Press.
Yang, R. Y., & Allison, D. (2004). Research articles in applied linguistics: Structures from a functional perspective. *English for Specific Purposes, 23*(3), 264–279.

Chapter 6
Rhetorical Structure of the Introductory Part

6.1 Introduction

This chapter presents the results of the genre analysis of the Introduction section (Sect. 6.2) and the LR section (Sect. 6.3). As stated in the Methodology chapter, the introductions used before the LR section show structural and functional variability, with the two major types identified (viz., the "Research-oriented Traditional CARS (RT CARS)" type and the "Two-move Orientation" type), in addition to the "Practical-problem Solving (PS)" type in CE and the "Building on the Writer's Own Previous Research" type in AL. The findings on the move and sub-move analysis of these two dominant types of introduction are a major focus of this chapter. In the second half of this chapter, findings on the rhetorical structure of the LR section are presented and discussed, with related cross-disciplinary variations outlined. The similarities, differences and interrelationship between the Introduction and the LR sections are expounded so as to provide a comprehensive understanding of the communicative functions and rhetorical organization of the introductory phase structured in the "I+LR" format.

6.2 The Introduction Section

This section describes in detail the rhetorical structure of the introductions that are followed by an independent LR section. Although the RT CARS type and the Two-move Orientation type are the two dominant categories of introduction identified in both disciplines, there are still other different types of introduction found in CE and AL, as stated in Sect. 3.4.1.4. Therefore, this section firstly reports the findings in the two disciplines respectively and then compares them in order to ascertain the structural features of the introduction with a subsequent LR section across disciplines and the possible cross-disciplinary variations concerned.

(Kathy). L. Lin, *Perspectives on the Introductory Phase of Empirical Research Articles*, Corpora and Intercultural Studies 5, https://doi.org/10.1007/978-981-32-9204-8_6

6.2.1 Rhetorical Structure of CE Introductions

6.2.1.1 Different Types of Introductions

As mentioned in Sect. 3.4.1.4, three types of introductions (viz., the Two-move Orientation type, the RT CARS type and the PS type) were identified based on their major communicative functions, structural flows, and the nature and orientations of the studies reported in CE. Before studying their detailed structural features, I firstly examined their distribution and average length, and their length in relation to the entire ERA.

As revealed in Table 6.1, among the 30 introductions, one third of them are Orientation introductions while a half of them are RT CARS introductions and the other five are PS introductions. In terms of their average length, RT CARS introductions and PS introductions are similar, and in both cases are considerably longer than Orientation introductions. This tendency largely accords with their proportions in the whole articles. Nonetheless, all of them occupy less than 10% of the entire articles in terms of word length, indicating that the introductions are not a substantial section when they are followed by a usually elaborate LR section.

There are three possible reasons for the much shorter length of Orientation introductions compared to the other two types of introduction. Firstly, the main purpose of Orientation introductions is to introduce the issue and present the research work, which determines their two-move structure (Fig. 3.2). They commonly do not contain the detailed elaboration to establish the niche; in contrast, the other two types of introduction mainly function to create a research space for the study and usually engage in a great deal of rhetorical work in the "persuasion" process, which suggests that niche-establishment is their core component. Second, as indicated in the Integrated CARS model, RT CARS introductions with the longest average length frequently contain a detailed survey of items of previous research (Sub-move 1.3 Survey Items of Previous Research), which is usually characterized by the frequent use of integral citations. Nevertheless, this is lacking in all Orientation introductions and is usually postponed to the subsequent LR. Finally, Orientation introductions are often straightforwardly and linearly structured whereas RT CARS introductions are much more complexly organized with more cyclicity involved (see Sects. 6.2.1.2

Table 6.1 Different types of CE introductions identified: Their frequencies, average lengths and proportions in the full ERAs

Types of introductions	Orientation	Research-oriented traditional CARS	Practical-problem solving
No. of introductions	10	15	5
Ave. length per text (no. of words)	380	658.3	648.8
Proportion of the RA (%)	5.1	9.5	7.8

and 6.2.1.3). All these points will be further elaborated in the discussion of their rhetorical structures in the next two sub-sections.

6.2.1.2 Two-Move Orientation Introductions

The Orientation introduction is very different from the conventional introductions studied in previous research in both structural and functional terms. It is identified among the introductions with a subsequent LR and its major function is not to create a research space for the study but to identify the issue to be addressed and to inform the readers of the study to be discussed. As mentioned in Chap. 3, an example text of the Orientation introduction in CE (CCEI28) is provided as Appendix C.

The Two-move Orientation approach (Fig. 3.2) is proposed for the discourse structure of Orientation introductions. It consists of two prototypical moves: Move 1 Identify the Issue and Move 2 Present the Study. In CE, Move 1 is present in all introductions studied, which may reflect its obligatory nature. However, Move 2 is not an obligatory move as two out of the ten Orientation introductions do not contain it. Overall, the two moves are considered important and prominent in performing their rhetorical functions in this type of introduction.

The eight introductions with a Move 2 were found to follow the linear sequential pattern of "Move 1-Move 2" with no cyclicity involved. The remaining two introductions (i.e., CCEI11 and CCEI12) are single-move ones (viz., Move 1 only). The findings suggest that Orientation introductions are rather simply and straightforwardly structured. This is in marked contrast to the complex structure of the traditional introductions without a subsequent LR that involve much cyclicity of moves (e.g., the introductions studied in the IMRD context in Kanoksilapatham, 2005).

In the forthcoming subsections, the content of the two moves is detailed and the focus is on the typical move constituent that may characterize this type of introduction as well as this particular discipline. However, the elements that may largely correspond to the ones described in the CARS model will not be accounted for given space limitations. This is also applied to our explication of the moves and sub-moves of RT CARS introductions in Sect. 6.2.1.3.

(1) *Move 1 Identify the issue*

In the present corpus, all CE Orientation introductions open with Move 1 for identifying an issue of potential interest. Move 1 contains three sub-moves, as indicated in the Orientation approach (Fig. 3.2).

Sub-move 1.1 (Survey Non-research Phenomena/Practices or General Knowledge Claims of the Field) functions to contextualize the study by providing general background knowledge on the existing state of research or foundational theoretical constructs, or the definitions of some important terms, or describing non-research relevant phenomena or application activities. Take CCEI28 (Appendix C) as an example, in the first textual segment representing this sub-move that comprises the first four sentences of the text, Sentences 1–3 introduce the key concept of "car-sharing" while Sentence 4 presents non-research-related general knowledge on the advantages of carsharing compared to traditional car rentals or taxi service. This sub-move is analogous to Step 1.2 (Making Topic Generalizations) of the CARS model in terms of the propositional content and semantic attributes and does not include detailed reviews of the specific research studies. Some previous studies (e.g., Kwan, 2006; Samraj, 2002) have commented on the difficulties in distinguishing Step 1.2 and Step 1.3 (Reviewing Items of Previous Research) of the CARS model. However, in the present analysis, this kind of difficulty generally does not exist. The reasons are as follows: out of the 18 instances of this sub-move in this study, 14 are pure accounts of the non-research-related phenomena or engineering applications, which reflects the application-oriented nature of this discipline. The other four instances include general statements on both research-related and non-research-related background of this field. The research-related background information provided in three of them is simply a brief definition of relevant terms such as the case mentioned earlier in CCEI28, while that in the remaining single case is a general comment on the state of research in the field, as illustrated below:

(1) The moment redistribution behavior of concrete beams reinforced with steel was extensively studied and is well established. (CCEI11)

Therefore, all instances of this sub-move in the current data clearly do not embody the semantic attributes and features of the element "reviewing items of previous research". The detailed review of previous research items are indeed commonly postponed to the subsequent LR section, which accounts for the brevity and structural simplicity of Orientation introductions.

Sub-move 1.2 (Establish Importance of the Field) is similar to the centrality-claim step in the CARS model. Corresponding to the frequent reference to the non-research phenomena or practices by Sub-move 1.1, this sub-move in the present data predominantly (10 out of the 12 instances) functions to establish importance in the real world rather than in the epistemic world of research:

(2) Shear-wave velocity (Vs) estimates obtained from nonintrusive surface-wave techniques **are becoming increasingly popular** and **are widely used throughout the world for many applications**. (CCEI13)

This largely accords with Samraj's (2002, 2005) findings from her genre study of RA introductions and abstracts in two related fields (viz., wildlife behavior and conservation biology) that the two part-genres in conservation biology far more frequently refer to the real-world matters to claim centrality as well as to justify the research than those in wildlife behavior. She attributed this to the contrasting nature and lengths of history of the two fields: unlike wildlife behavior, conservation biology is an applied, interdisciplinary and relatively new field.

Sub-move 1.3 (Suggest Value of the Issue) is the featured element in Orientation introductions. Although Orientation introductions do not have a separate and substantial move for establishing a niche for the study as suggested in the CARS model, they instead commonly include only one or two sentences briefly indicating the potential significance of the research issue, which is worth investigating. For example, in CCEI28 (Appendix C), the sentence "one key aspect… (Schuster et al.,

2005)" generally and briefly indicates an important issue that is worth studying (i.e., whether carsharing can save money for people). This sub-move is often immediately followed by Sub-move 2.1 (Announce Research Purposes, Foci, RQs, or Hypotheses). In CCEI28, for instance, after suggesting the issue of potential value, the author states the specific research work to be conducted.

As indicated in the Two-move Orientation approach (Fig. 3.2), the detailed rhetorical work needed to establish a niche is generally lacking in Orientation introductions. This suggests that a significant portion of the introductions with a subsequent LR in this study do not contain detailed niche establishment, whereas in Kanoksilapatham's (2012) study, the majority of the 60 CE introductions studied have it. This difference might be attributed to the different generic context of the introductions studied, i.e., whether or not the introductions are followed by an independent LR. The introductions analyzed in Kanoksilapatham's study were very likely selected from the IMRD-structured RAs (i.e., the introductions without a subsequent LR), as could be observed from her statement "Because this report…aims to analyze the move structure of the four traditional sections (introduction, methods, results, and discussion), all selected articles had to contain these four sections" (Kanoksilapatham, 2012: 299). In contrast, in this study, all introductions selected had to be followed by a clearly distinguishable LR which commonly involves a focused, gap-creating review of the literature. Hence, the detailed elaboration to create the niche and the specific, critical reviews of the literature may be frequently shifted to the subsequent LR.

Figure 6.1 illustrates the frequency of occurrence of the sub-moves that constitute the two prototypical moves enacted in Orientation introductions. The three sub-moves have very high occurrence rates (100%, 80% and 90% respectively) in all

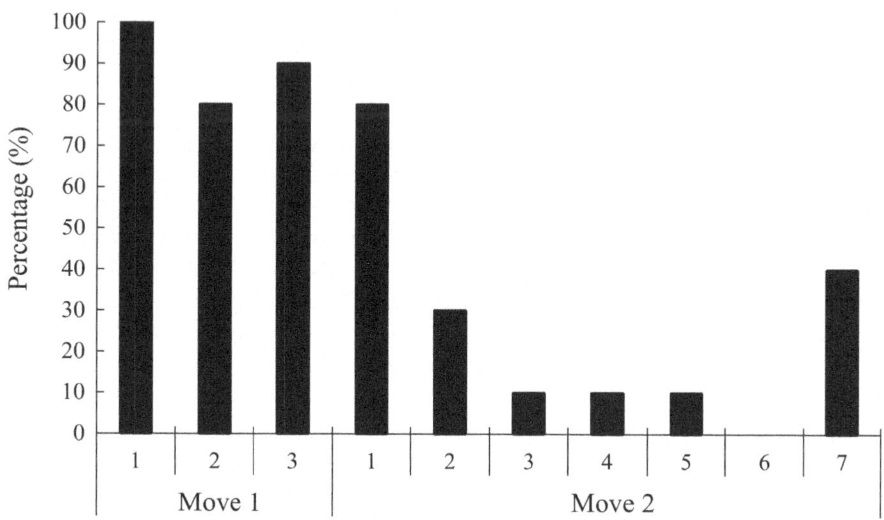

Fig. 6.1 Sub-move frequency within moves in the CE Orientation introductions

Table 6.2 Different combinations of sub-moves within Move 1 in the CE Orientation introductions

Observed sub-move patterns	Examples
Two sub-move configurations	
1-3	CE12
1-3-1	CE29
2-1-2	CE20
Three sub-move configurations	
Regular (2-1)n-3	2-1-3 [CE13, 19]
	2-1-2-1-3 [CE22]
Regular (1-2)n-1-3	1-2-1-3 [CE11, 14]
	1-2-1-2-1-3 [CE27, 28]

Orientation introductions, suggesting that they are all prominent elements through which Move 1 is realized.

The three sub-moves occur in a variety of combination patterns (Table 6.2). However, the co-occurrences of Sub-move 1 and 2 (i.e., sub-move combinations "1-2" or "2-1" without implying their sequential orders) have strong presence in the ten CE Orientation introductions examined (80%). The sub-move configuration "1-3" has been used even more frequently, i.e., in nine out of the ten introductions. Further, 60% of Orientation introductions commence with Sub-move 1 whereas the others begin with Sub-move 2. Generally, the three sub-moves are arranged flexibly yet fairly simply in Orientation introductions.

(2) *Move 2 Present the study*

Move 2 can be realized in seven sub-moves according to the Two-move Orientation approach (Fig. 3.2). Sub-move 2.1 (Announce Research Purposes, Foci, RQs, or Hypotheses) is actually an integration of Step 1 (Announcing Present Research Descriptively and/or Purposively) and Step 2 (Presenting RQs or Hypotheses) of Move 3 in the revised CARS model. This is indeed also the first sub-move for the move "Present the Present Work" in RT CARS introductions. The present researcher actually has the same reason for adopting this integration practice here, which has been stated in Sect. 3.4.1.4.

Sub-move 2.2 (Summarize the Methods and Contextual Conditions) is developed from the original Step 4 (Summarizing the Methods) in Swales's revised CARS model. The reason for including "contextual conditions" is that in two of the Orientation introductions, there is an extended description of the real site of the study, which per se is an important variable influencing the experimental result, as illustrated in the following extract:

> (3) Experimental ReMi results from three separate study sites are included in this article. These three sites generally classify as shallow bedrock geologic profiles (i.e., relatively thin/soft soil over bedrock), which are traditionally difficult subsurface profiles for surface-wave methods. Two of the sites are located in an area with a distinct passive noise source (near an interstate), whereas the third site is located in a quiet, rural area. The influence of different receiver array orientations was investigated in each of these environments. (CCEI13)

As the site condition is a parameter of the research method, the researcher considers the description of it functionally embedded within the Method sub-move. Therefore, one possibility is to retain the original label for this sub-move "Summarize the Methods", which could encompass the research site description. However, in order to highlight the particular importance of the real settings in some field studies in this applied discipline (Kanoksilapatham, 2012), the researcher renamed this sub-move as "Summarize the Methods and Contextual Conditions". Another noteworthy point is that the site description element here is functionally different from the "site/species description" sub-step identified in Samraj (2002). She found that this sub-step in her corpus is used to facilitate the author's moving on from a general introduction of the research work to a more detailed specification of the aims of the study, which justifies her categorization of it as one part of Step 1 (Outlining Purpose/Announcing Present Research).

Sub-moves 2.3-2.5 and Sub-move 2.7 are generally the same as those posited in the revised CARS model (Swales, 2004). Sub-move 2.6 (Inform the Literature Review Content) is a featured element identified in both the RT CARS introductions and the innovative Orientation introductions in AL (Sect. 6.2.2) but not in CE (see Fig. 6.1).

Among the seven sub-moves, Sub-move 1 has been found in 80% of the Orientation introductions, followed by Sub-move 7 (40%) and Sub-move 2 (30%) (Fig. 6.1). The rest are all rarely used (i.e., occur in only one introduction). Swales (2004) has classified the step for announcing the research descriptively and/or purposively as the only obligatory one. This is largely in line with the finding on the Orientation introduction in CE that Sub-move 1 is present in all the introductions except the two that do not employ Move 2.

A close examination of the sub-move combinations (Table 6.3) reveals that although the writers have varied choices in this move, they do not structure it complexly by repeatedly using some move elements or employing the cycled structure. Five out of the eight Orientation introductions with a Move 2 use no more than two sub-moves and CCEI20 uses the largest number of sub-moves, which is only four.

Table 6.3 Different combinations of sub-moves within Move 2 in the CE Orientation introductions

Observed sub-move patterns	Examples
Single sub-move	
Sub-move 1 only	CCEI14, 28
Two sub-move configurations	
1-5	CCEI22
1-7	CCEI27, 29
Three sub-move configurations	
1-2-4	CCEI13
1-2-7	CCEI19
Four sub-move configurations	
1-3-2-7	CCEI20

They are all featured by using Sub-move 1 as the opening element, in addition to their simple yet flexible structures.

6.2.1.3 Research-Oriented Traditional CARS (RT CARS) Introductions

RT CARS introductions share some functions with the other types of introductions (e.g., Orientation introductions) such as contextualizing the study and informing the readers of the background knowledge of the field. However, their more salient function is to justify the research and create the essential space for the study.

Accordingly, they display all the three moves presented in the CARS model and their rhetorical organization can be accounted for by the Integrated CARS model (Fig. 3.3). Table 6.4 shows the frequency distribution of the three moves, which have been found in all the 15 RT CARS introductions. Thus, they are all obligatory moves in this type of introduction, which resembles the traditional CARS introductions reported in previous studies to a considerable degree.

Compared to Orientation introductions, the move combination patterns in RT CARS introductions are far more complex. As demonstrated in Table 6.5, one third of them follow the strict M1-M2-M3 pattern set out in the CARS model. The rest have a recycled structure mostly with the repetition of two (e.g., 1-2-1-2-3 (CCEI8, 15, 26); 1-2-1-2-1-3 (CCEI23, 25)) or three moves (e.g., 1-2-1-2-1-3-1-3 (CCEI24); 1-2-1-2-1-2-3-1-2-3 (CCEI4)). While the alternation between Move 1 and Move 2 is a prominent feature in many of this category of introduction, all of them commence with Move 1 and conclude with Move 3, with large variations often occurring in the medial parts. Only one introduction (CCEI30) shows a radical departure from Swales's CARS model while all the others generally follow it.

At the sub-move level, most of the elements identified are exactly the same as those postulated in Swales's (1990, 2004) models and are thus not discussed here. However, Sub-move 2.3, the element newly discovered in Del Saz-Rubio (2011) and also present in the current data, and Sub-move 3.3, which is an element newly found and proposed in this study are exemplified below:

Table 6.4 Frequency counts of the three moves in the CE RT CARS introductions

Moves	Individual counts	No. of introductions with the move (%)
Move 1 Establish a territory	33	15 (100%)
Move 2 Establish a niche	26	15 (100%)
Move 3 Present the present work	21	15 (100%)

Table 6.5 Examples of the move configurations in the CE RT CARS introductions

Observed patterns	No. of articles	%	Examples
Introductions following Swales's CARS model			
1-2-3	5	33.3	CCEI3, 5, 16, 18, 21
1-2-1-2-3	3	20.0	CCEI8, 15, 26
1-2-1-2-1-3	2	13.3	CCEI23, 25
1-2-1-3	1	6.7	CCEI17
1-2-1-2-1-3-1-3	1	6.7	CCEI24
1-2-1-2-1-2-3-1-2-3	1	6.7	CCEI4
1-2-1-3-2-1-3-1-2-3	1	6.7	CCEI9
Introductions deviating from the strict Swales's CARS model			
1-3-1-3-2-3	1	6.7	CCEI30
Total no. of RAs	15	100	

Sub-move 2.3 Suggest implicitly inconsistencies precluding gap signaling

(4) Recently, a few researchers have noted that design elements, such as shoulder or lane width could follow a U-shaped relationship with safety, where the crash risk could be higher both for narrow and wide widths…On the other hand, others have found sinusoidal relationships between crash risk and lane and shoulder widths (Hauer 2004; Gross and Jovanis 2007a, b). (CCEI21)

Sub-move 3.3 State theoretical frameworks/theoretical positions

(5) The objective of this study consists of assessing the application of generalized additive models (GAMs) for estimating AMFs….GAMs are a new type of models that have been recently introduced in the statistical community to model observed data…GAMs can still generate statistically interpretable results, similar to GLMs. (CCEI21)

However, another newly-proposed element (i.e., Sub-move 3.6) is not found in the RT CARS introductions in CE either. In contrast, it is present in both the RT CARS type and the Orientation type of introductions in AL and thus it is perhaps more characteristic of the discipline of social sciences, which needs to be verified by future research.

As for retaining the separation of "Make Topic Generalizations of Increasing Specificity" (Sub-move 1.2) and "Survey Items of Previous Research" (Sub-move 1.3), the reasons have mostly been expounded in Sect. 3.4.1.4. In addition to these reasons, after the move and sub-move analysis, the present author found it relatively easy to distinguish the two in the current data. Maybe because of the application-oriented nature of CE and the introductions being followed by a substantial LR, most of the generalization statements are descriptions of the real-world phenomena or engineering applications. Only a few of them are about the summarized research state or explanations of theoretical concepts or constructs, similar to the instances of Sub-move 1.1 (Survey Non-research Phenomena/Practices or General Knowledge Claims of the Field) in Orientation introductions. However, no research site description was found in CE RT CARS introductions, hence the term for Sub-move 3.2 remaining "Summarize Research Methods".

Figure 6.2 shows the occurrence rates of each sub-move within the three moves. In Move 1, only Sub-move 2 that generalizes the relatively established knowledge claims and the non-research phenomena/practices is an obligatory one, which is the same as that in the CE Orientation introductions. Therefore, it strongly suggests that in the introductions with a subsequent LR section such as the CE Orientation introductions and RT CARS introductions, this generalization element is perhaps the most characteristic and important one in contextualizing the study and providing the background knowledge of the field.

However, "Survey items of previous research" (Sub-move 1.3) has been used in just over a half (53.3%) of the CE RT CARS introductions and not in any of the CE Orientation introductions. Very different from this finding, Kanoksilapatham (2012) found that around 93.3% of the 60 CE introductions studied employ the element for reviewing individual studies. Consequently, disciplinary influence could be excluded in this regard. In addition, unlike computer science which has a relatively short history (Posteguillo, 1999), CE is a long-established discipline with comparatively abundant literature. Thus, the most likely reason for the much less use of this element in the CE RT CARS introductions and the complete absence of it in CE Orientation introductions is that many detailed reviews of individual research items have been postponed to the subsequent LR. In some cases, this is explicitly signaled in the metalanguage such as the emboldened words of the following extract:

(6) Therefore, it is not surprising that a large number of studies have investigated the formation and behavior of dry bulk freight (charter) rates, chartering decisions and policies, transportation strategies, and fleet deployments and operations of the dry bulk shipping industry **(see "Review of literature")**. (CCEI30)

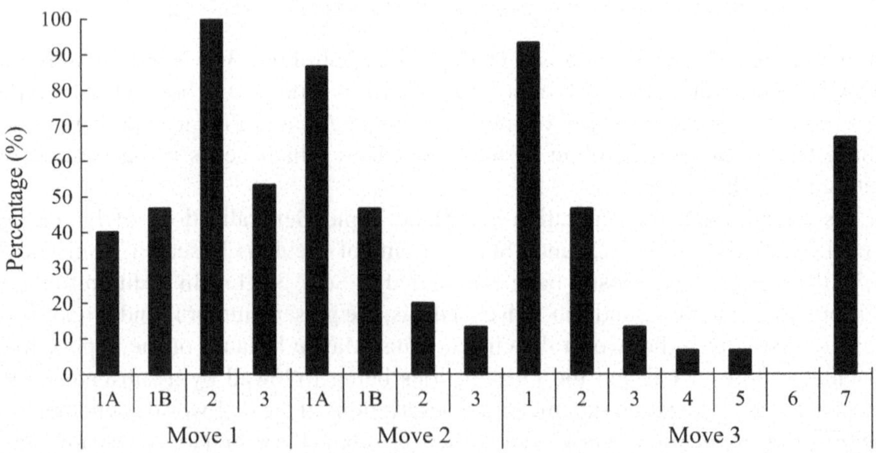

Fig. 6.2 Sub-move frequency within moves in the CE RT CARS introductions

Interestingly, in the subsequent LR section, the relevant individual studies were detailed by using a number of integral citations:

> (7) Studies by **Hawdon (1978), Strandenes (1984), and Beenstock and Vergottis (1989, 1993),** among others, argue that the shipping freight rate is determined through the interaction between the supply of and demand for sea transportation. **They find that** …More recent studies by **Dikos et al. (2006) and Randers and Goluke (2007)** also use macroeconomic variables…to model and forecast ship freight rates…Moreover, **studies such as that of Kavussanos and Alizadeh (2001)** investigate the seasonal behavior of dry bulk shipping freight rates …These studies utilize macroeconomic data in an attempt to capture the dynamics and fluctuations in shipping freight rates…(CCEI30)

Similar cases are also found in the CE Orientation introductions. With regard to the two centrality-claim sub-moves, "Claim Importance in Real World" (46.7%) is a little more frequently used, reflecting the applied nature of CE. The same percentage of introductions were found to indicate the problem in or need from real world; in contrast, far more (13 out of the 15 or 86.7%) introductions suggest the gap in previous research. Overall, "gap-indication" is the most common realization of Move 2, which is congruent with Kanoksilapatham's (2012) study that found approximately 86.1% of the 60 CE introductions have the "gap-indication" step. Only three CE RT CARS introductions employ the "positive" warrants (Sub-move 2.2) and two suggest implicitly inconsistencies in the findings or conclusions of previous studies precluding gap signaling.

Similar to the CE Orientation introductions, the most frequent realization of the move "Present the Present Work" is Sub-move 3.1 (93.3%), followed by Sub-move 3.7 (66.7%) and Sub-move 3.2 (46.7%). There are only two introductions that state theoretical frameworks (CCEI21 and CCEI24) and only one introduction that has respectively previewed the main findings (CCEI9) and made the value-claims for the study (CCEI16).

Generally, many frequently-used sub-moves within each of the three moves are often employed singly, as can be seen from Table 6.6. This table presents all the sub-move combination patterns that are found to be repeatedly used. That the most prevalent sub-move configurations within the three moves are all a single element (S1.2 in M1, S2.1a in M2, and S1 in M3) and the number of the sub-move units that integrate these "frequently-used" patterns only range from one to three suggest that RT CARS introductions in CE are also not so densely and complexly structured. All these identified frequently-used patterns have high reference and pedagogical value.

6.2.1.4 Practical-Problem Solving Introductions

Five out of the 30 CE introductions with a subsequent LR section are identified as the PS type. As aforementioned (Sect. 3.4.1.4), this type of introduction, as its name suggests, mainly addresses a problem in the real world rather than a niche in the existing research. Since this group is small, a systematic genre analysis of them could not have been conducted by quantifying the occurrences of the moves and sub-

Table 6.6 Frequently-used sub-move combination patterns within the three moves of the CE RT CARS introductions (no. of occurrence ≥ 2)

	Configurations of sub-moves	Count no.	% of introductions
M1	S1.2 (Make topic generalizations of increasing specificity)	13	53.3
	S1.3 (Survey items of previous research)	5	20
	S1.1b+S1.2 (Claim importance in real world + Make topic generalizations of increasing specificity)	2	13.3
	S1.1a (Claim importance in research world)	2	13.3
M2	S2.1a (Indicate a research gap)	14	60
	S2.1b (Indicate a problem or need in the real world)	5	20
	S2.1a+S2.3 (Indicate a research gap + Suggest implicitly inconsistencies precluding gap signaling)	2	13.3
M3	S3.1 (Announce research purposes, foci, RQs or hypotheses)	9	53.3
	S3.1+S3.7 (Announce research purposes, focuses, RQs or hypotheses + Outline the article structure)	3	20
	S3.1+S3.2+S3.7 (Announce research purposes, foci, RQs or hypotheses + Summarize methods + Outline the article structure)	2	13.3

moves used in them. However, the researcher closely examined their structures and found that only two of them largely follow the move-structure proposed by Feak and Swales (2011) for the "Problem-focused" article introductions: Move 1 Establishing the background; Move 2 Highlighting a problem that has emerged; Move 3. Outlining how the problem will be examined; Move 4 Proposed solution to the problem; and Move 5 Outlining the paper. The former three moves are obligatory while the other two are optional. One PS introduction (CCEI2) in the present data that displays this move-structure is provided for reference (Appendix J). In this introduction to the ERA on the assessment of weathered aggregates, the writers provide all the background information and establish the significance of the topic in the first four paragraphs (Move 1). Then, they identify the problem in using existing approaches (e.g., "the petrographic analysis" and "mechanical tests") to detect and evaluate weathered aggregates efficiently in Paragraph 5 (Move 2). In the last paragraph, the researchers propose the solution (i.e., a new approach named "the automatic method") and preview the positive result of applying this new method in their study (Moves 3 and 4).

The other three introductions are much more complexly structured. They all devote a substantial portion to the comparison of the conventional and the new approach or that between two types of material to highlight the advantages of their proposed ones (see an example text in Appendix J). However, this "comparison" move has not been covered in Feak and Swales's (2011) move structural model for their "problem-focused" introductions. More interestingly, all three introductions contain after this "comparison" move the "research gap-indication" element, one example of which can be seen from the last paragraph of the introduction in Appendix J. This indicates that the research described in these PS introductions is actually not only motivated by the observed problem or disadvantage of the conventional approach or material, but sometimes also by the absence of the relevant research testing their recommended ones. Whatever the source of the need identified for the research, the major aim of this type of introduction is essentially to create a space for the study. All of them are, however, more closely related to solving the problem in the real world.

6.2.2 Rhetorical Structure of AL Introductions

6.2.2.1 Different Types of Introductions

As suggested in Sect. 3.4.1.4, in addition to the two major types of the introduction identified (i.e., the RT CARS type (60%) and the unconventional Orientation type (36.7%), see Table 6.7), there is a special introduction displaying a completely different structure among the 30 AL introductions with a subsequent LR section. Although it is only a single case and not suited for genre analysis, its structural and stylistic features are worth mentioning as this "Building on the Writer's Own Previous Research" introduction is also seen in ERAs of other social sciences or humanities disciplines that are mainly based on a discursive research tradition according to my academic reading experience.

This unique case seems a "relaxed, story-telling" type that starts by introducing the present study and then recounts the author's whole research experience and process. In accounting for his research story, the author firstly stated what he did on the topic previously, then pointed out the link of his previous study to the initial design of the present one, and finally described how he further reshaped his research design by integrating his observations and thoughts during the research process. The entire introduction as a self-narrative account is not like the traditional CARS type of an argumentative nature, which usually emphasizes "niche-establishment" and proposes the study grounded on a critical review of the existing literature. While this introduction shows that the study it reports builds on the writer's own previous

Table 6.7 Different types of AL introductions identified: their frequencies, average lengths and proportions in the full ERAs

Categories of introductions	Research-oriented traditional CARS	Orientation	Building on the writer's own previous research
No. of introductions	18 (60%)	11 (36.7%)	1 (3.3%)
Ave. length per text (no. of words)	700.7	343	331
Proportion in the full RA (%)	7.9	4.1	3.7

research, in its subsequent LR section, the writer did review numerous previous studies by others and point out the gaps filled by his study.

Corresponding to its special structure, this "Building on the Writer's Own Previous Research" introduction is stylistically featured by the strong authorial voice and the intense use of the first person pronoun "I" (11 times) and its accusative case "me". This is in contrast to a widely-reported feature of contemporary academic writing, i.e., impersonal presentation of information represented by the use of language features such as passive voice and the inanimate subject (Biber & Conrad, 2009a).

This special kind of introduction seems more likely constructed by disciplinary experts with considerable authority and substantial research experience on particular topics, which enable them to confidently show the readers that their studies are an accumulation of experience in particular lines of research. It may also occur when there is a subsequent LR section that could afford a large space for reviewing others' works in the field, which is an essential element prompting any research work nowadays.

As for the two major types of the introductions, their major communicative purposes and structural components have been accounted for when the pertinent findings on CE introductions with a subsequent LR are reported. Consequently, they are not repeated here.

As displayed in Table 6.7, the Two-move Orientation introductions and the "Building on the Writer's Own Previous Research" introduction constitute nearly half of the RT CARS introductions both in terms of their lengths and their proportions in the whole ERAs. After the systematic move and sub-move analyses were undertaken of the two major types of introductions in AL, it is found that the differences in their lengths and proportions in the entire ERAs could be attributed to their different content elements and structural components, which is further explicated in the next two sub-sections.

6.2.2.2 Two-Move Orientation Introductions

As mentioned before, different from the traditional CARS introductions, the Two-move Orientation introductions do not function to create a research space for the study but mainly to identify the issue to be addressed and inform the readers of the research to be undertaken. They are essentially the brief, prologue-style introduction as described in Chap. 4. An example text of the Orientation introduction in AL (CALI9) is provided in Appendix D.

According to the Two-move Orientation approach (Fig. 3.2), there are two prototypical moves in this type of introductions: Move 1 Identify the Issue and Move 2 Present the Study. Move 2 is obligatory as it is used in all the 11 Orientation introductions while Move 1 is present in ten of them as CALI15 is a single-move (viz., Move 2) introduction. Therefore, the two moves are essential in realizing the communicative functions of the Orientation introductions.

In terms of move configurations, after CALI15 containing only a Move 2 excluded, eight out of the other ten Orientation introductions follow strictly the standard pattern

"M1-M2". As for the other two introductions, CALI7 (M1-M2-M1-M2) and CALI13 (M2-M1-M2) display the cyclical structure. In all, this new type of introductions displaying the two-move structure is mostly regularly and rather simply structured at the move level.

(1) *Move 1 Identify the issue*

In the Orientation approach, Move 1 can be divided into three sub-moves. Sub-move 1.1 (Survey Non-research Phenomena/Practices or General Knowledge Claims of the Field) shares mostly the propositional content and semantic attributes of Sub-move 1.2 "Make Topic Generalizations" in the traditional CARS model. The instances of this sub-move are commonly general statements on the research state of the field, explanations of the key theoretical constructs or concepts, accounts of the general beliefs on the theme, or descriptions of the non-research phenomena, practices or activities. In CALI9 (Appendix D), there are two segments illustrating this sub-move.

Generally, the element of the specific review of individual studies does not exist in this type of introductions in AL and thus there is no difficulty in distinguishing Sub-move 1.1 and the specific literature review element either. It is not surprising since this group of brief, prologue-style introductions simply identifies the topic, purpose and structure of the paper and does not engage in a focused, gap-creating review of the literature, which has become a major task of the subsequent LR section. In this regard, CALI9 again provides a good example. It does not contain any review of previous studies on the theme (viz., the usefulness of imagery in the form of pictorial illustrations and etymological notes in idiom dictionaries), which is however included in the subsequent LR section. One extract from the LR illustrates this:

> (8) Extensive research **has been conducted by Boers and his colleagues** into the effects of mental imagery evoked by etymological elaboration…**Gallese and Lakoff (2005: 4) propose** that in order to understand a concept such as grasp, 'one must at least be able to imagine oneself or someone else grasping an object…A positive influence of etymological elaboration on form and meaning retention **has been reported in Boers (2001)**…The question whether the strategy of etymological elaboration is equally effective…**is addressed by Boers et al. (2004a)**…**In Boers et al. (2008),** students' position on the verbalizer/imager continuum was correlated with their scores on the idiom comprehension and recollection tasks…**Boers et al. (2008) conclude** that pictures serve semantic elaboration rather than structural elaboration… (CALI9)

Owing to the absence of the detailed review of previous studies and the substantial niche-establishment move as well as much fewer complex recursive move patterns in these Orientation introductions, their length and proportions in the whole article are around a half of the RT CARS introductions (see Sect. 6.2.2.1).

Sub-move 1.2 (Establish Importance of the Field) resembles the centrality-claim element in the CARS model. However, among the ten instances of this sub-move, only one establishes importance in the research world and the other nine claim importance in the real world, which contrasts with what is revealed in the RT CARS introductions in this field (see Sect. 6.2.2.3).

Sub-move 1.3 (Suggest Value of the Issue) is the featured element in this type of introductions. Although the Orientation introductions do not have a substantial niche-establishment move for justifying the study, they often use one or two sentences concisely indicating the potential value of a research issue which is worth studying. Though it is absent in CALI9 (Appendix D), a text example is provided to illustrate this sub-move:

> (9) Although the data were collected from the KEPT, a test not widely used, the way in which raters assess lexis in writing **is an area which should be of interest to** a broad range of English language educators. (CALI13)

After suggesting the value of a research issue, the author usually immediately declares what he or she is going to do, hence this sub-move is often followed by Sub-move 2.1 (Announce Research Purposes, Focuses, RQs, or Hypotheses).

The three sub-moves are prototypical constituents of Move 1 since they have been used in a majority of the Orientation introductions (63.6%, 72.7% and 72.7% respectively) as revealed in Fig. 6.3. However, they co-occur in varied patterns and only AL28 uses them in the canonical linear pattern of "1-2-3" (see Table 6.8); in nine out of the 11 Move 1 instances, the number of sub-moves integrating Move 1 is no more than three and only four Move 1 instances involve cyclicity. All these suggest that the Move 1 structure of the Orientation introductions is very flexible and irregular but not heavily information-loaded.

(2) *Move 2 Present the study*

Among the seven realizations of Move 2, Sub-move 2.3 (Make Definitional Clarifications) is absent in AL Orientation introductions (Fig. 6.3), although it is an element suggested in Swales's (2004) revised CARS model. However, Sub-move 2.6 (Indicate the Literature Review Content) is a unique element found in AL introductions with a subsequent LR section, including both the Orientation type and the RT CARS type. It is different from the element "Outlining the Paper", which serves as a roadmap for the readers by briefing the content of each major part of the RA. It only indicates what will be presented in the forthcoming LR section, as illustrated below:

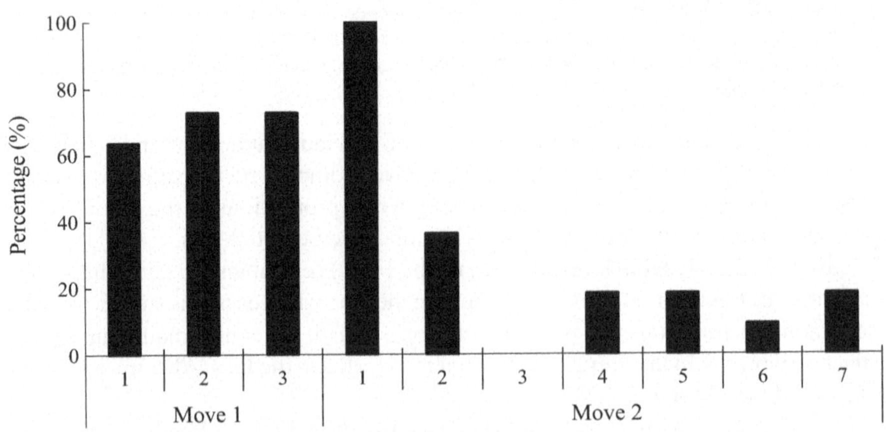

Fig. 6.3 Sub-move frequency within moves in the Orientation introductions in AL

Table 6.8 Different combinations of sub-moves within Move 1 of the Orientation introductions in AL

Observed sub-move patterns	Examples
Single sub-move	
Sub-move 3 only	CALI7
Two sub-move configurations	
1-3	CALI8, 27
1-2-1	CALI9
1-2-1-2-1	CALI7
2-1	CALI29
2-3	CALI11, 12
3-2-3	CALI13
Three sub-move configurations	
1-2-3	CALI28
1-2-1-2-3	CALI24

(10) The sections below review key theoretical concepts and various studies which have investigated creativity and language play for language learning. (CALI8)

The sub-moves for Move 2 in the Orientation introductions is basically the same as those for Move 3 in the RT CARS introductions in AL (Sect. 6.2.2.3) except that the element "State Theoretical Frameworks/Positions" is absent in these much shorter innovative introductions. The tendency in using sub-moves for presenting the study in the Orientation-style introductions is also similar to that in the RT CARS introductions: Sub-move 1 as an obligatory element is most frequently used, followed by the method statement (S2.2, 36.4%). All the other sub-moves are only used in a few introductions.

As for the sub-move combinations within Move 2, they are greatly varied, as can be seen from Table 6.9. However, "Sub-move 1 only" is the most frequently used configuration and the number of sub-moves integrating this move in most of its

Table 6.9 Different combinations of sub-moves within Move 2 of the Orientation introductions in AL

Observed sub-move patterns	Examples
Single sub-move	
Sub-move 1 only	CALI7, 13, 24, 27, 28
Two sub-move configurations	
1-2	CALI13, 29
1-5	CALI12, 15
1-7	CALI7, 9
Three sub-move configurations	
1-2-4	CALI11
Four sub-move configurations	
1-4-2-6	CALI8

instances is only one or two. These confirm again that the rhetorical structure of this new type of introduction is mostly flexible yet simple, similar to what we have found in CE Orientation introductions. In all the 11 AL Orientation introductions, Sub-move 1 is invariably present despite the different sub-move combination patterns used within Move 2, which also indicates the importance and prominence of this element. These frequently used patterns identified for the two moves further our understanding of this innovative type of introduction used before the LR section and have high reference value for the teaching of introduction writing in EAP classrooms.

6.2.2.3 RT CARS Introductions

Previous studies have mostly confirmed the strong explanatory power of Swales's (1990, 2004) CARS model in that it is generally stable at the move level with modifications mainly suggested to the sub-move level by other genre scholars (e.g., Anthony, 1999; Samraj, 2002). In line with this, the three moves of the CARS model are found prototypical in the RT CARS introductions in AL, though only Move 1 is obligatory, as shown in Table 6.10. This suggests that a noticeable number of AL introductions still bear a structural resemblance to the CARS model even when they are followed by a usually lengthy LR section that could possibly take over some communicative roles originally performed by them.

Only two out of the 18 CARS introductions (CALI2, 30) have Move 2 missing while the only introduction without a Move 3 is CALI22, which is characterized with four consecutive alternations between Move 1 and Move 2 (see Table 6.11). Although a few introductions omit either Move 2 or Move 3, the repeated use of the three moves are common, as can be seen from their individual counts.

Table 6.11 summarizs the move structure of this group of introductions. Generally congruent with the findings reported in most previous introduction studies on a similar discipline or sub-disipline (e.g., Ozturk, 2007 on second language acquisition and second language writing, Hirano, 2009 on English for specific purposes and Lee, 2001 on English education), this study found that a significant proportion (66.7%) of the RT CARS introductions in AL involve cyclicity, mostly with the repetition of two (e.g., 1-2-1-2-3 (CALI18, 23); 1-2-3-2-3 (CALI3)) or three moves (e.g., 1-2-1-

Table 6.10 Frequency counts of the three moves in the AL RT CARS introductions

Moves	Individual counts	No. of introductions with the move (%)
Move 1 Establish a territory	36	18 (100%)
Move 2 Establish a niche	30	16 (88.9%)
Move 3 Present the present study	22	17 (94.4%)

Table 6.11 Examples of the move configurations in the RT CARS introductions in AL

Observed patterns	No. of articles	%	Examples
Introductions following Swales's CARS model			
1-2-3	4	22.2	CALI1, 16, 17, 19
1-2-1-3	2	11.1	CALI4, 25
1-2-1-2-3	2	11.1	CALI18, 23
1-2-3-2-3	1	5.6	CALI3
1-2-3-1-2-3	1	5.6	CALI21
1-2-1-2-3-2-3	1	5.6	CALI10
1-2-1-2-1-2-1-3	1	5.6	CALI20
1-2-1-2-1-2-1-2	1	5.6	CALI22
1-2-1-2-1-2-1-2-3	1	5.6	CALI5
Introductions deviating from the strict Swales's CARS model			
1-3	2	11.1	CALI2, 30
1-3-1-2-3	1	5.6	CALI6
1-3-1-2-1-3	1	5.6	CALI26
Total no. of RAs	18	100	

2-3-2-3 (CALI10)). However, the archetypal 1-2-3 structure is still the most common pattern and another three structures gaining prominence are 1-2-1-3, 1-2-1-2-3 and 1-3. As stated before, only two introductions do not contain a Move 2, highlighting the central role played by this core component in the RT CARS introductions. Despite four introductions showing salient deviations from Swales's CARS model and the existence of varied move structures, all AL RT CARS introductions commence with Move 1 and conclude with Move 3, except CALI22 comprising four alternations between Move 1 and Move 2, as aforementioned.

Figure 6.4 displays the frequency of sub-moves within each major move in AL RT CARS introductions. Within Move 1, the generalization element (S1.2) is the only obligatory sub-move, suggesting the importance of providing general background knowledge and contextualizing the research study in general sense in the introductions used before the LR section. As for reviewing specific research activities, this element is frequently moved to LR and only used in just over half (55.6%) of the introductions. This contrasts with the obligatory nature of this element maintained in Swales (1990) and recorded in many follow-up structural analyses of the introductions without a subsequent LR section such as the Introduction in the IMRD context studied in Kanoksilapatham (2005). Therefore, much less use of reviewing individual research items to establish the territory is a prominent feature of the introductions with a following LR section, even though they reflect mainly the communicative function and move structure of the CARS model. The following text excerpts illustrate typically how the author just referred to the previous studies by listing them in a non-integral citation when summarizing the research state of the field in Introduc-

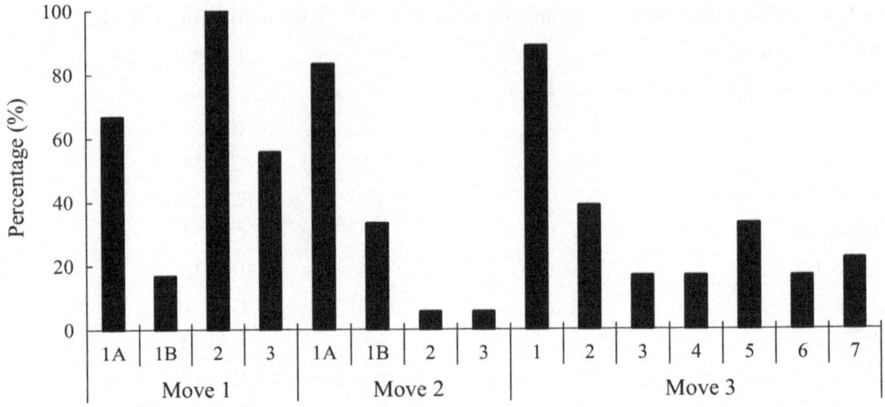

Fig. 6.4 Sub-move frequency within moves in the RT CARS introductions in AL

tion (Example 11) while reviewing at length and critically the cited studies in the subsequent LR section (Example 12):

(11) The few studies that have addressed unattended *this* **(Moskovit, 1983; Steinberg, Kaufer, & Geisler, 1984; Geisler et al., 1985)** have focused on prescriptive uses and reader interpretations, with little empirical focus on the linguistic environment surrounding such structures. (CALI19)

(12) Few studies have focused specifically on the use of demonstratives in anaphoric reference and in relation to text cohesion. The studies that do exist primarily focus on the pronominal use, which may be a consequence of the prescriptive rules that exist. For example, **Moskovit (1983) seeks to** determine when pronominal *this* constitutes 'broad reference'...**Moskovit attempts to** determine when broad reference is unclear by examining 28 examples of pronominal *this*...**Steinberg et al. (1984) and Geisler et al. (1985)** question Moskovit's interpretations and conclusions...Although **these early studies** offer a starting point, they focus on establishing prescriptivism, a practice which has in some circles fallen out of fashion. In addition, the research methodologies are problematic...Furthermore, these studies focus primarily on the use of pronominal *this*, and little (if any) attention is paid to demonstrative determiners.... (CALI19)

In the LR section, the detailed review of the studies referred to in the preceding Introduction establishes the link between the two sections and recreates the research space for the study. The linking of this sort is frequently found in the introductions with a following LR, including the RT CARS type and the Orientation type.

Regarding the two varieties of centrality claims, "Claim Importance in Research World" (66.7%) is much more frequently employed than "Claim Importance in Real World" (16.7%). Although a similar tendency occurred in writers' choices of two gap-indication sub-moves (i.e., research gap indication is far more favored), Sub-move 2.1b (33.3%) is still a prominent element, reflecting the great concerns of this discipline with real-world language-related problems. This could also be perceived from the frequently-cited definition of Applied Linguistics by Chris Brumfit (1995: 27):

> [applied linguistics is] the theoretical and empirical investigation of real-world problems in which language is a central issue.

Both the "positive" warrant and Sub-move 2.3 are used in only one RT CARS introduction. Of the seven variations realizing Move 3, Sub-move 3.1 (Announce Research Purposes, Focuses, RQs, or Hypotheses) is most frequently employed (88.9%), followed by the method statement (38.9%) and the statement on announcing research significance (33.3%). As for the two new elements identified in the present study, Sub-move 3.3 and Sub-move 3.6 are respectively used in 16.7% of the introductions. Their degrees of importance need to be further examined by using a larger data in this discipline.

Table 6.12 demonstrates the frequently-used sub-move configurations within each move in RT CARS introductions in AL. The fact that the number of the sub-moves integrating these patterns is mostly either one or two and the most frequently used patterns for the three moves are all a single sub-move structure occupying a large share, indicating that the RT CARS introductions used before LR are not densely structured. However, there are a wide range of choices in the combined use of different sub-moves within each move, suggesting that these introductions are flexibly structured at the sub-move level.

Table 6.12 Frequently-used sub-move configurations within the three moves in the AL RT CARS introductions (no. of occurrence ≥ 2)

	Configurations of sub-moves	Count no.	% of introductions
M1	S1.2 (Make topic generalizations of increasing specificity)	13	50
	S1.1a+S1.2 (Claim importance in research world + Make topic generalizations of increasing specificity)	4	22.2
	S1.3 (Survey items of previous research)	3	16.7
	S1.2+S1.1a (Make topic generalizations of increasing specificity + Claim importance in research world)	3	16.7
	S1.1b (Claim importance in real world)	2	11.1
	S1.3+S1.2+S1.3 (Survey items of previous research + Topic generalizations + Survey items of previous research)	2	11.1
M2	S2.1a (Indicate a research gap)	22	72.2
	S2.1b (Indicate a problem in or need from real world)	4	11.1
	S2.1b+S2.1a (Indicate a problem in or need from real world + Indicate a research gap)	2	11.1
M3	S3.1 (Announce research purposes, focuses, RQs or hypotheses)	6	33.3
	S3.1+S3.5 (Announce research purposes, focuses, RQs or hypotheses + State the significance of the present research)	2	11.1
	S3.1+S3.6 (Announce research purposes, focuses, RQs or hypotheses + Inform the Literature Review content)	2	11.1

6.2.3 Comparison of the Introductions in CE and AL

To the best of my knowledge, this is the first study of the rhetorical organization of introductions that are all followed by a subsequent LR section. CE and AL, as two applied and interdisciplinary disciplines chosen as the focus of this study, have been documented with the high frequency use of the LR section. Therefore, it is significant to study the discourse structure of this particular group of introductions in them to expand our present knowledge of this research part-genre as well as the disciplinary writing.

Through the detailed structural and functional analyses, we can find that there exist considerable similarities in the rhetorical structure and communicative function in the introductions with a subsequent LR in the two disciplines. First, the two major types of the introduction (viz., the Orientation type and the RT CARS type) could be identified in the data collected in both disciplines, although there are other minority types of introductions found in them. This indicates the importance of the two structural models for the two dominant types of introduction, which provide pointers for the teaching of writing RA introductions that are used before a usually elaborate LR section. Second, in both disciplines, a considerable number of introductions with a subsequent LR section actually largely conform to the classic CARS model, although there are some new elements found at the sub-move level, e.g., "Indicating the Literature Review Content" and "State Theoretical Frameworks/Positions", which may characterize the particular generic context of the introductions (i.e., being followed by an independent LR section) as well as the chosen disciplines.

Third, the Two-move Orientation introductions are rather simply and straightforwardly structured. In contrast, the RT CARS introductions are much more complexly structured with much cyclicity at the move level. This is the common feature found in the data from the two disciplines. In addition, at the sub-move level, writers' preferences for using some particular sub-moves within each move in both types of introductions are rather similar in the two disciplines, as is the case with their combined use of some move constituents. For instance, in the Orientation introductions in both disciplines, all the three sub-moves within Move 1 are prototypical elements, and within Move 2, Sub-move 2.1 (Announce Research Purposes, Focuses, RQs, or Hypotheses) is the most frequently used element and the sub-moves about method statements and outlining RA structure are also another two elements favoured by published writers. The sub-move combination patterns within the two moves are generally flexible, varied with no dense use of elements, partly accounting for the relatively shorter length of this new type of introduction.

However, there are still a few salient differences in the use of sub-moves in the two dominant types of introductions across the two disciplines. For example, the newly identified element "Indicating the Literature Review Content" was found in both the RT CARS introductions and the innovative Orientation introductions in AL but not in any of these two types of introductions in CE. Thus, this element is perhaps more characteristic of the discipline rather than the generic context shared by the introductions examined in the two disciplines (i.e., being followed by a stand-alone

LR section). However, this is only an assumption and needs to be further examined by future research. Another interesting difference is that the sub-move "Claim Centrality in Research World" is more frequently used in AL RT CARS introductions than the sub-move "Claim Centrality in Real World" while the opposite is true for the RT CARS introductions in CE. However, the elements for indicating the importance in real world and for suggesting real-world problems or need for the research are all prominent ones used in the two dominant categories of introductions in both disciplines. Finally, although the general tendencies in using the moves and sub-moves in the two types of introductions are very similar in both disciplines, the specific frequencies for using particular sub-moves/moves and some combination patterns are understandably different.

The similarities and differences discussed above about the rhetorical structure of the introductions with a subsequent LR section in the two contrasting disciplines could further our understanding of this important part-genre used in a new generic context (i.e., being followed by a usually lengthy LR section). In addition to the identification of an innovative type of introduction (i.e., the Two-move Orientation introductions), the present study also reveals other important structural features of this particular group of introductions with a following LR section: they employ far less elements for specific reviews of individual research items, which have often become a major task of the subsequent LR section; for those introductions that generally follow the Two-move Orientation approach, they do not use the substantial "niche-establishment" move for creating the research space for the study. Instead, they simply identify a research issue of high value and present the work to be undertaken, being more of the informative nature rather than the argumentative nature. Finally, they usually have certain intriguing links with the subsequent LR section either in terms of their content/functions and language use, which have been demonstrated and expounded in this section. In all, the influence from the use of an independent LR section on the rhetorical structure and communicative function of the Introduction is discernible.

6.3 The Literature Review Section

As Bhatia's (1993: 85) argument on "the individual status of literature review" has been verified (see the two studies reported in Chaps. 4 and 5), a genre-based, function-oriented study of its rhetorical structure has been conducted. Findings of the analysis of the LRs into different functional components and on the rhetorical organization of the Theoretical Review component are respectively reported in Sects. 6.3.1 and 6.3.2. Related cross-disciplinary variations in organizing this part are presented and the four-move structure postulated for the Theoretical Review component is explicated and compared with Kwan's (2005, 2006) structural model formulated for the theme-bound sections in thesis LR chapters and the CARS structure for article introductions (Swales, 1990, 2004).

6.3.1 The General Organization and Functional Components of Literature Reviews

The Method chapter has outlined two stages for analyzing the rhetorical structure of the LR section: the analysis of the general organization of the LR section and the genre-based study of the Theoretical Review component (see Sect. 3.4.1.4). This sub-section reports the findings from the first stage of the analysis.

The present study reveals that the LR section in ERAs contains four major functional components: Advanced Organizer/Overview, Theoretical Review, Contextual Background, and Conclusion. These four functionally distinct, separate components have been expounded and illustrated in Sect. 3.4.1.4 and a figure depicting the general organization and composition of the LR section in ERAs is thus proposed (Fig. 6.5).

While Theoretical Reviews as the only obligatory component in the LR section of ERAs were analyzed systematically using the ESP genre-based approach and findings relating to their schematic structure are presented in the next sub-section, all the other three functional components are small in number and thus not subjected to genre analysis. However, their major functions, structural features and frequency distribution are reported below in order to give readers some sense of what they are and what kind of roles they play in the entire LR sections.

In general, clear variations exist in the general organization of the LR sections between the two disciplines. First, most of the LR sections in AL are multi-thematic sections containing different numbers of sub-sections on various themes (see CALL_TR24 as an example in Appendix K) and only eight of them are single Theoretical Reviews without further sub-division. In contrast, as many as 20 out of the 30 LR sections in CE are stand-alone Theoretical Reviews (see CCEL_TR3 as an example in Appendix F). The contrasting structural forms of the LR sections in these two disciplines is an important reason why Kwan's (2005, 2006) approach to the LR chapters in research degree theses in AL is not applicable to the present data (i.e., first

Fig. 6.5 The possible composition of the LR section

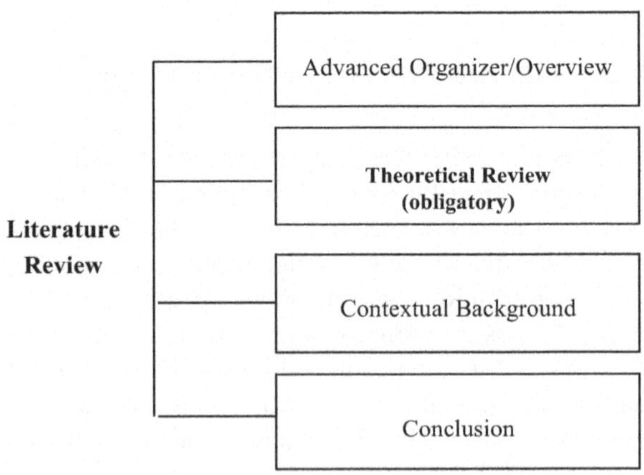

to analyze the LRs into different "thematic units" and then to study the schematic structure of these "thematic units") (see also other reasons in Sect. 3.4.1.4).

Second, only three out of the 60 LR sections open with an "Advanced Organizer/Overview" and they are all from CE (viz., CCEL9, 16, and 24). None of the LR sections of AL ERAs contain this component. This is in stark contrast to Kwan's (2005, 2006) observation of the LR chapters in doctoral theses in AL: around 72% of the LR chapters open with a unit commonly headed as "Introduction" and functioning as an advanced organizer.

"Advanced Organizer/Overview" is relatively short, compared with Theoretical Reviews, being usually confined to one paragraph. A close examination of the three "Advanced Organizer/Overview" components reveals that they indeed can be generally categorized into two types: the first type functions exactly as an "Advanced Organizer" (see CCEL24 in Example 4 in Sect. 3.4.1.4) to inform readers about the scope of the review and its sequential arrangement. The other two cases (viz., CCEL9 and 16, see Examples 13 and 14 below) display the CARS-like structure: they either start with centrality claims (e.g., the first three sentences in Example 13) or topic summarization (e.g., the first sentence in Example 14), which are immediately followed by a declaration of the niche to be occupied by the study (see the emboldened words in both Examples 13 and 14). CCEL9 does not announce the theme to be reviewed in this section, but CCEL16 does so (see the italicized part in the final sentence in Example 14).

(13) FRP materials have gained considerable popularity as a reinforcement alternative to steel in the preceding decade. The corrosion resistance of FRP materials is one of the most important advantages of this type of reinforcement in comparison to steel. This advantage has motivated extensive research in the area of strengthening of concrete structures by using FRP materials [Nanni and Norris 1995; American Concrete Institute (ACI) 2007]. Although extensive information is available for the use of FRP materials to strengthen concrete beams, **only limited research has specifically addressed FRP strengthening of concrete poles (Chahrour and Soudki 2006). Also, research on FRP strengthening of wood structures is comparatively limited, and has primarily focused on flexural strengthening with FRP strips (Gilbert et al. 2003). Notably, there is little or no research on the strengthening of deteriorated wood elements, nor for wood members with circular cross sections, such as the Gulfport crossarms where FRP wrapping and flexural strengthening may be employed.** (CCEL9)

(14) Clay mineralogy identification in soils has been pursued by researchers in the field of soil science and agronomy (Sridharan et al. 1988; Mitchell and Soga 2005). **Very few geotechnical engineers have focused on clay mineralogy aspects of the soils**, and their main focus is in the correlation of clay mineralogy with interpretation of engineering properties (Sridharan et al. 1988; Sridharan and Prakash 1999; Cerato and Lutenegger 2002; Mitchell and Soga 2005). One of the applications of clay mineralogy can be found in the stabilizer design guidelines and *the following section describes how the clay mineralogy can be used for better design of stabilizers for ground treatment.* (CCEL16)

Third, while "Advanced Organizer/Overview" are only present in the LR sections in CE, the Conclusion component was found in only two LR sections in AL (i.e., CALL18 and CAAL21). None of the CE LRs close with such a Conclusion component. This component usually summarizes what has been reviewed, highlights insights from previous studies, and sometimes reiterates the research questions or purposes of the study (see Example 5 in Sect. 3.4.1.4).

Finally, "Contextual Background" is not a common functional component either, and it was found in only two LR sections in AL (i.e., CALL20 and CAAL21) and in none of the LRs in CE. One of the two instances of this functional component (viz., CALL20) has been fully explained in Sect. 3.4.1.4, and it can be clearly seen that the use of this component is closely related to the nature of the study (i.e., whether the study is particularly associated with a social or educational context). More specifically, if the significance of the study and the implications of its findings are supposed to be understood and interpreted in this context, it is very likely that writers would provide a detailed account of contextual background for the study.

The general organization formulated based on the present data for the LR section and the accounts of the three optional functional components and the related cross-disciplinary variations provide valuable pedagogical input for EAP classroom teaching of LR writing. The next sub-section presents findings on the rhetorical structure of the predominant functional component of the LR section, i.e., the Theoretical Review component.

6.3.2 Rhetorical Structure of the Theoretical Review Component

As stated in Sect. 3.4.1.4, the repeated multi-rounds of function-based, top-down ESP-genre-based analyses of all Theoretical Review components in the two disciplines have identified a prototypical structure for this part-genre. Before we introduce it, a point worthy of special attention should be raised: as few genre studies have attempted to analyze the structure of the LR section in ERAs and the present study is a pioneering effort in this regard, the structure proposed for Theoretical Reviews based on the current data is a preliminary finding that requires further research for validation. However, the structure posited below serves as a potentially useful point of reference for future LR studies and has the potential to become an effective pedagogical tool that facilitates student writers' understanding and mastery of this hitherto underexplored part-genre.

The study reveals that the major communicative functions of Theoretical Reviews are to provide substantial theoretical, empirical and non-research background to the study, to contextualize and position the study against this background by suggesting various links between the study and its background (e.g., offering rationales for the study by critiquing key prior studies or suggesting its theoretical underpinnings or what kind of premises on which it is based), and to outline the present research work. In line with these principal communicative purposes of this functional component, a four-move structure is proposed based on the analysis of the data (see Fig. 6.6). Two examples of this analysis respectively from CE (CCEL_TR3) and AL (CALL_TR24) are provided in Appendices F and L for reference.

Move 1		**Demarcate the research territory**
Sub-move	1.1	Highlight significance of research issues/problems
	1.2	Survey knowledge claims or provide an overview of the research area
	1.3	Survey non-research phenomena or practices
Move 2		**Review key studies**
Move 3		**Position the present study**
Sub-move	3.1	Indicate explicitly a gap or problem 3.1a Indicate a research gap or a limitation in previous research 3.1b Indicate a problem in or need from the real world
	3.2	Assert confirmative claims about knowledge or research practices surveyed
	3.3	Assert the relevance of the surveyed claims to one's own research
	3.4	Assert the irrelevance of the surveyed claims to one's own research to specify the scope of the study
	3.5	Abstract, synthesize, or make inferences from knowledge claims to establish a theoretical position or framework
	3.6	Indicate inconsistencies in findings/conclusions/claims from previous studies without explicit gap-signaling
Move 4		**Outline the present study**
Sub-move	4.1	Announce research aims, purposes, research questions or hypotheses
	4.2	Announce theoretical positions/frameworks
	4.3	Indicate research design/processes/methodology
	4.4	Announce interpretations of terminology used in the study
	4.5	State the value of the present study
	4.6	Suggest the subsequent theme to be reviewed
	4.7	Indicate the content of the Method section

Fig. 6.6 A possible structure for Theoretical Reviews in ERAs

According to the proposed structure, the four prototypical moves of the LR section in ERAs are: Move 1 Demarcate the Research Territory, Move 2 Review Key Studies, Move 3 Position the Study, and Move 4 Outline the Present Study. Move 1 maps out the research area by highlighting the significance of research issues or problems and presenting general research and non-research background. Move 2 makes close-up surveys of the most relevant (usually empirical) studies which frequently serve as the springboard for the research to be undertaken. While the first two moves deal with the background and the body of literature in the research area, the latter two gradually foreground the study by suggesting the links between the present study and the background literature and outlining different aspects of the current research.

Among the four moves, the former three are the predominant ones found in the present data, although the weight given to them varies slightly between the two disciplines (see Table 6.13). In contrast, there is a greater disparity with Move 4 (Outline the Present Study), as 93.3% of Theoretical Reviews in AL use it compared to only 63.3% in CE. This indicates that Move 4 is not predominant in CE Theoretical Reviews. An important reason for this is that, while applied linguists prefer drawing together reviews of the literature from different research strands before outlining the present study at the end of Theoretical Reviews, CE researchers commonly favor constructing a comparatively short and concise review of the literature. Notably, CE researchers instead often attach much more importance to the results of their own studies and related discussions. The different preferences in the employment of Move

Table 6.13 Frequency counts of the four moves in the Theoretical Review Component in CE and AL

Moves	Disciplines	Individual counts	No. of Theoretical Reviews with the move (%)
Move 1 Demarcate the research territory	CE	100	29 (96.7)
	AL	180	30 (100)
Move 2 Review key studies	CE	86	29 (96.7)
	AL	95	28 (93.3)
Move 3 Position the present study	CE	91	28 (93.3)
	AL	154	30 (100)
Move 4 Outline the present study	CE	29	19 (63.3)
	AL	80	28 (93.3)

4 by researchers from CE and AL also partly account for the contrasting length of the LR sections in these two disciplines: the LR sections in AL is twice the length of those in CE (see Table 3.1 in Sect. 3.4.1.3). A final point is that the individual counts of the four moves displayed in Table 6.13 suggest probably high degrees of cyclicity in Theoretical Reviews in both disciplines, to which findings on move configurations presented in Tables 6.14 and 6.15 lend strong support.

Tables 6.14 and 6.15 display the frequency distribution of a variety of move configurations in Theoretical Reviews in CE and AL respectively. They show that, in both disciplines, no single move patterns were found, and in AL, all Theoretical Reviews comprise either three or four moves. 60% of CE Theoretical Reviews and over 85% of AL Theoretical Reviews are four-move configurations. All these imply that Theoretical Reviews may be a substantial part of the ERA with varied content and dense information involved.

While the overwhelming presence of the four moves in 60 Theoretical Reviews as shown in Table 6.13 is evidence that they are prototypical moves of this component, Tables 6.14 and 6.15 demonstrate the sophistication and intricacy of its structure mainly on account of the cycled use of move units. Complications in organizing Theoretical Reviews are clearly embodied in the far greater number of move units integrating most patterns, as compared with the much shorter Introduction sections within the same ERAs (see Sect. 3.4.1.3). While only four out of the 30 Theoretical Review components in AL use less than eight move units, as many as 40% of those in CE do so, suggesting different discursive practices of expert writers in these two disciplines. Specifically, applied linguists often write much longer and complexly structured Theoretical Reviews than CE researchers (see Table 3.1 for the comparison results of the average length of the LRs in AL and CE and their proportions in the entire ERAs in terms of length).

A number of regular move configurations are identified in Theoretical Reviews in both disciplines (see Tables 6.14 and 6.15), and many more are sophisticatedly structured with "irregular" patterns. These mostly unique, "irregular" patterns are indeed regular to some extent, as they predominantly open with Move 1 and close

Table 6.14 Examples of the move configurations in Theoretical Reviews in CE

Observed pattern	% of Theoretical Reviews	Examples
Two-move configurations	10	
Regular $(1\text{-}2)_n$	6.7	1-2-1-2 (CCEL_TR8)
		1-2-1-2-1-2 (CCEL_TR19)
Regular $(1\text{-}3)_n$	3.3	1-3-1-3-1-3-1-3-1-3-1-3-1-3 (CCEL_TR1)
Three-move configurations	30	
Regular $(1\text{-}2)_n$-1-3-2	6.7	1-2-1-3-2 (CCEL_TR30)
		1-2-1-2-1-3-2 (CCEL_TR7)
Irregular 1/2/3	20	1-2-3-2-3-2 (CCEL_TR17)
		1-3-**1-1**-3-2-3 (CCEL_TR28)
Irregular 2/3/4	3.3	2-3-4 (CCEL_TR10)
Four-move configurations	60	
Regular $(1\text{-}2\text{-}3)_n$-4	3.3	1-2-3-1-2-3-4 (CCEL_TR15)
Regular 1-$(2\text{-}3)_n$-4	3.3	1-2-3-2-3-2-3-4 (CCEL_TR4)
Irregular 4-move	53.3	1-3-1-2-4 (CCEL_TR2)
		1-3-1-2-1-3-4 (CCEL_TR11)
		1-2-3-2-3-2-1-3-4 (CCEL_TR22)
		1-3-2-4-1-2-3-2-3-1-4 (CCEL_TR13)
		3-2-3-**4-4**-1-3-4-1-2-1-3-1-2 (CCEL_TR5)

Note 1. Following Kwan (2005, 2006), "n" denotes the times for the likely repeated use of a combined pattern, e.g., "$(1\text{-}2)_2$" stands for "1-2-1-2". 2. Slashes used between each two move numbers suggest co-occurrence of these two moves without indicating the sequence of their occurrence. For example, an irregular 1/2/3 can be realized in a configuration of "1-3-**1-1**-3-2-3" (CCEL_TR28)

with Move 4, with variations and recurrence of one or more moves in the medial parts. The "irregularity" and "complications" in their structure is understandable, as the study may cover different research strands/parameters and the review touches on various sub-themes (e.g., CALL_TR24 in Appendix K) and almost all of Theoretical Reviews involve different degrees of cyclicity. In addition, the LR section has multiple, complicated communicative functions to be realized, such as providing theoretical underpinnings, delimiting research scope, and contextualizing and positioning the study.

In all, the strong cyclical nature is a most salient feature of Theoretical Reviews in both disciplines, with the repetition of one (e.g., CALL_TR12 in Table 6.15), two (e.g., CCEL_TR17 and CCEL_TR30 in Table 6.14), three (e.g., CALL_TR18 and CALL_TR24 in Table 6.15) or four (e.g., CCEL_TR13 and CCEL_TR5 in Table 6.14) of the moves. The cyclic patterns of most Theoretical Reviews lead to the high percentages of "irregular, unique" move configurations revealed as mentioned

Table 6.15 Examples of the move configurations in Theoretical Reviews in AL

Observed pattern	% of Theoretical Reviews	Examples
Three-move configurations	13.3	
Regular (1-3)n-4	6.7	1-3-1-3-4 (CALL_TR11)
		1-3-1-3-1-3-1-3-1-3-4 (CALL_TR20)
Irregular 1/2/3	6.7	**1-1**-3-1-2-1 (CALL_TR12)
		1-2-3-1-3-2-3-2-1-3-1-3-1-3-1-3-2-1-2-3 (CALL_TR18)
Four-move configurations	86.7	
Irregular 4-move		1-2-3-1-2-3-4 (CALL_TR24)
		1-3-1-2-1-4-1-4-1-3-2-4 (CALL_TR10)
		1-3-1-3-1-3-1-3-2-3-2-3-2-1-2-3-4 (CALL_TR19)
		3-1-**3-3**-1-2-3-1-2-1-2-3-4 (CALL_TR3)
		4-1-3-1-2-1-2-1-4-1-4 (CALL_TR21)
		1-3-2-3-4-1-2-3-4-1-2-1-3-4-1-4-1-3-4-1-4-1-2-3-2-3-4-1-4-1-3-4-1-3-4 (CALL_TR13)

before (e.g., over 50% of four-move configurations for CE Theoretical Reviews and over 80% of those for AL counterparts being "irregular" patterns). The finding echoes (Kwan's, 2005, 2006) observation that as many as 42.52% of theme-bound sections of the LR chapters in applied linguistics doctoral theses are irregularly structured with the three moves ("Territory-establishment", "Niche-creation", and "Niche-occupation").

Despite the strong cyclical tendency of the moves resulting in the wide variety of move configurations and structural complexity of Theoretical Reviews, it is the comparatively stable, repeated use of regular pairings of move units that are most prominent. This is also an important reason for which a prototypical structure still can be revealed for this part-genre. For instance, Moves 1 and 3 tend to co-occur in a sequential order within many Theoretical Reviews with "irregular" four-move patterns, as can be seen from some of the examples listed in the two tables. The pairings of Move 1 and Move 3 ("1-3") are often employed by writers when they attempt to provide theoretical underpinnings for the study and then draw the links between the existing theories and their studies, or they position their studies via critiquing the empirical scholarship in a general manner for reasons such as space concern or rhetorical need. Other interesting findings include: a high concentration of the sequenced use of Move 1-Move 2-Move 3 ("1-2-3") being found in AL Theoretical Reviews with "irregular" four-move patterns (over 50%) and the combined use of

Moves 2 and 3 being often observed in Theoretical Reviews in CE (e.g., 1-2-3-2-3-2-1-3-4 (CCEL_TR22) and 2-3-2-3-2-1-2-3-4-2-1-2-1-2-3-4-1-2 (CCEL_TR20)). The high recursiveness of the moves and the relatively stable recurrence of such regular pairings of move units in Theoretical Reviews in both disciplines closely relate to their length (see Table 3.1) and the nature of the study (e.g., whether it is an interdisciplinary research that entails reviews of different body of literature, or whether it is a complex study that draws on insights from various research strands).

Another structural feature of the LRs in ERAs is that, in some Theoretical Reviews that may cover different themes around a research topic, the ending move of a sub-section on one particular theme may be the same as the opening move of a second sub-section on another theme. Thereby, in some move configurations, a move number may be repeated consecutively [e.g., 1-3-**1-1**-3-2-3 (CCEL_TR28); **1-1**-3-1-2-1 (CALL_TR12); 3-1-**3-3**-1-2-3-1-2-1-2-3-4 (CALL_TR3)].

In the forthcoming sub-sections, the elements that are encapsulated under each of the four moves are described and illustrated. Particular attention is drawn to those newly discovered and the ones that characterize the LR section. Among these elements, some of them are obligatory or quasi-obligatory and qualified as "steps", while some others are "strategies" (Bhatia, 1993, 2004) in that they are neither fixed placed or co-occur with each other in any predictable patterns. Therefore, a more inclusive term "sub-moves" is used to refer to these elements with mixed nature identified in Theoretical Reviews.

6.3.2.1 Demarcate the Research Territory

As discussed in the last section, most of the 60 Theoretical Reviews start by sketching and demarcating the research landscape by foregrounding the significance of research issues or problems (Sub-move 1.1), surveying knowledge claims or making topic summarization (Sub-move 1.2), and/or presenting non-research background information for the study (Sub-move 1.3). The non-research background refers to accounts of the non-epistemic phenomena, practical application activities or engineering practices that serve as parts of the background to the study. For instance, for a study on the structure of English RAs such as the present case, the increasing importance of English as a language for academic communication and the intense pressure on university academics to publish in world-renowned (mostly English) journals in their fields need to be briefly described to inform readers about the general background/settings for the study (see Sect. 1.1).

The three sub-moves have clearly distinguishable communicative purposes, propositional content and semantic attributes. The first sub-move is analogous to "centrality-claims" in the CARS structure (Swales, 1990, 2004), which can be used to foreground the importance of either research issues or problems in the real-world. For instance, Example (15) below relates the importance of a non-epistemic phenomenon (i.e., "reporting what other people have said" as an aspect of personal communicative skills). In contrast, the first textual segment of CCEL_TR3 (Appendix F) highlights the significance and value of the research into 3D/4D CAD development and its application to construction practices through emphasizing intense research efforts that have been devoted to this area.

Sub-move 1.1 Highlight significance of research issues/problems

(15) Reporting what other people have said is performed **frequently** in oral and written discourse and thus constitutes an **important** aspect of a speaker's communicative skills. (CALL_TR1)

Sub-move 1.2 Survey knowledge claims or provide an overview of the research area

(16) **Connectionist theories** (e.g. Rumelhart et al., 1986) provide a model for how probability of this sort might be realized at the lower levels of 'implementation' (Jurafsky, 2003). **Such theories** propose that knowledge in the brain is represented by numerous inter-connected units and that it is through experience (i.e. repeated exposure) that these connections are strengthened. Probability may thus be encoded as weights on connections or resting activations. (CALL_TR7)

(17) **Most studies into written definitions** have taken a taxonomic approach, providing lists of semantic properties and syntactic features and showing the variation in form according to subject areas (Bramki & Williams, 1984; Chaudron, 1982; Chung & Nation, 2003; Darian, 1981; Flowerdew, 1992; Selinker, Trimble, & Trimble, 1976; Wignell, 1998). (CALL_TR28)

Sub-move 1.3 Survey non-research-fronted phenomena or practices

(18) The construction worker performs activities that involve body movements that are distinct for different phases in the work cycle. Walking, kneeling, fetching, lifting, placing, aligning, holding, and pushing are common and often repeated movements for a construction worker, but each class of activity has a different combination of these movements. (CCEL_TR6)

(19) In addition to reducing vehicle usage, the total number of vehicles in a city can be reduced through carsharing and, thus, the amount of land and infrastructure needed for parking can be reduced. This could decrease the cost of development, open up more space for development and, in the long run, reduce the spatial footprint of a city. (CCEL_TR28)

Sub-move 1.2 surveys existing knowledge claims (e.g., theoretical constructs, terminological definitions, models, hypotheses or other previous research claims) (see Example 16 above) and/or gives generalized statements on previous research (see Example 17 above). Sometimes it is difficult to differentiate whether a segment is surveying existing knowledge claims or giving an overview of the research area, especially when a summarized statement on previous research is cited from another source, as exemplified below:

(20) In the last decade, **the main focus of researchers** in this field **has been on** the number of sensors… **(X, Year1)**. (CCEL_TR6)

As can be seen from this case (Example 20), it is obviously a general overview of previous research conducted in the past ten years; at the same time, it is also a survey of X's claim, as the summarized statement on previous research in the last decade was originally made by X in his work published in Year1. This largely explains why this sub-move combines two sub-elements (i.e., "Survey knowledge claims" and "Provide an overview of the research area"). More importantly, they all serve the purpose of demarcating or delineating the research landscape in a general sense.

Sub-move 3.1 presents non-research background information for the study. This element is used because CE and AL are both applied disciplines. Examples 18 and 19 (see above) are two cases in point.

Figures 6.7 and 6.8 present sub-move frequency within three moves (i.e., Moves 1, 3, and 4) in Theoretical Review components in CE and AL respectively, as Move 2 is a single element that is not further divided into different types of sub-moves. By comparing the two figures, it is found that frequency distribution of the three sub-moves within Move 1 is quite similar between the two disciplines. In Theoretical Reviews from both disciplines, Sub-move 1.2 is the most commonly and widely used element, followed by Sub-move 1.1. Sub-move 1.3 was, however, found to have been employed only in very few Theoretical Reviews. In AL, Sub-move 1.2 is a mandatory element for writers to construct Theoretical Reviews. This suggests the paramount importance of surveying previous knowledge claims such as theories, models or definitions of some concepts and providing an overview of the research area in literature review in this discipline.

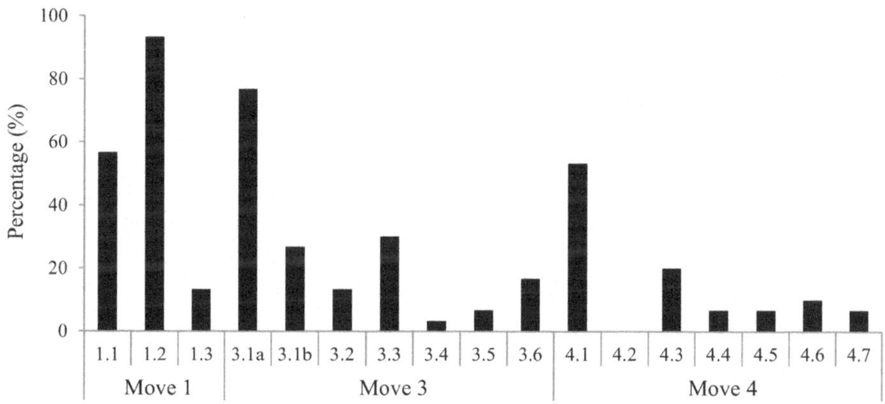

Fig. 6.7 Sub-move frequency within three moves in Theoretical Reviews in CE

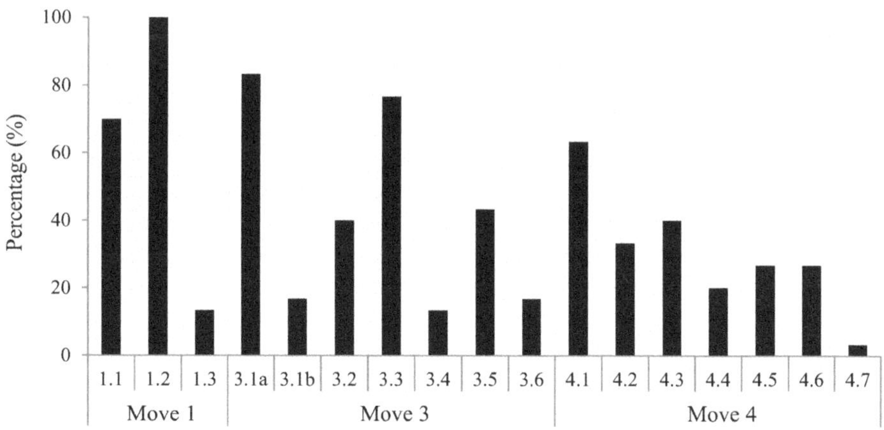

Fig. 6.8 Sub-move frequency within three moves in Theoretical Reviews in AL

Tables 6.16 and 6.17 outline frequently-used sub-move configurations in the three moves and their frequency counts and distribution in Theoretical Reviews in CE and AL respectively. In both disciplines, the configuration "Sub-move 1.2" is overwhelmingly used (93.3% for CE and 96.7% in AL), followed by various combined use of the first two sub-moves (e.g., "Sub-move 1.1+Sub-move 1.2" and "Sub-move 1.2+Sub-move 1.1+Sub-move 1.2"). The Move 1 configuration "Sub-move 1.3" is a prominent one used in Theoretical Reviews in CE; however, this element is never used singly in Theoretical Reviews in AL. In both CE and AL Theoretical Reviews, the configuration "Sub-move 1.1" is identified as a frequently-used pattern.

6.3.2.2 Survey Key Studies

After delineating a research landscape (Move 1), writers often conduct close-up surveys of key studies, which is the main task of the second move in the four-move structure formulated for Theoretical Reviews. "Close-up surveys" is a term inspired by Rudestam and Newton's (2007) comparison of the process of reviewing the literature to the three kinds of shots in film-production ("long shots", "medium shots" and "close-ups"). The main difference among these three kinds of shots lies in the distance between the camera and the subject matter; their metaphorical differences in the review of literature consist in their degrees of detail, scope, the extent to which they are related to the present research, and their functions in the whole literature review. Regarding this, Wen (2001: 82) has presented explicit accounts of what they are when they are used to describe literature review:

> A long shot or background review usually provides your project with a general framework or theoretical definitions of certain variables; a close-up or foreground review focuses on the details of some specific studies on which the design of your study is based; a medium-shot gives a description of empirical studies on the topic in general.

As such, a medium-shot seems to refer to "topic summarization" or an overview of a research area, while a close-up or foreground review is actually the review of key studies which motivates the present study and are most pertinent to it. It is usually the critiques of such key studies that provide rationales for the present research. A long shot or background review covers mainly theoretical underpinnings and the general research and non-research background information. However, as pointed out by Wen (2001: 82), "the differences among these three kinds of reviewing are relative" and they need to be understood with reference to specific cases and context.

Concerning the four-move structure we propose for Theoretical Reviews in ERAs, its first move indeed includes both "long shots" and "medium shots". When writers proceed from Move 1 (Landscaping) to Move 2 (Close-up Surveys), information flows from the most distantly related to the study to the most closely related to the study, from the general to the specific, from the theoretical to the empirical, and from the abstract to the concrete (Ridley, 2012). Based on the analysis of the present data, some linguistic exponents that are helpful for identifying Move 2 are garnered, e.g., "for instance", "for example", "…most relevant…", "to illustrate", "…are particu-

Table 6.16 Frequently-used sub-move configurations in three moves in Theoretical Reviews in CE (no. of occurrence ≥ 3)

	Sub-move configurations	Count no.	% of Theoretical Reviews
M1	S1.2 (Survey knowledge claims or provide an overview of the research area)	71	93.3
	S1.1+S1.2 (Highlight significance of research issues/problems + Survey knowledge claims or provide an overview of the research area)	7	20
	S1.1 (Highlight significance of research issues/problems)	7	13.3
	S1.2+S1.1+S1.2 (Survey knowledge claims or provide an overview of the research area + Highlight significance of research issues/problems + Survey knowledge claims or provide an overview of the research area)	5	13.3
	S1.3 (Survey non-research-fronted phenomena or practices)	4	6.7
M3	S3.1a (Indicate a research gap or a limitation in previous research)	47	70
	S3.3 (Assert the relevance of the surveyed claims to one's own research)	13	30.0
	S3.1b (Indicate a problem in or need from the real world)	10	16.7
	S3.6 (Indicate inconsistencies in findings/conclusions/claims from previous studies without explicit gap-signaling)	5	10
	S3.2 (Assert confirmative claims about knowledge or research practices surveyed)	5	6.7
	S3.1a+S3.2 (Indicate a research gap or a limitation in previous research + Assert confirmative claims about knowledge or research practices surveyed)	3	6.7
M4	S4.1 (Announce research aims, purposes, research questions or hypotheses)	14	33.3
	S4.1 + S4.3 (Announce research aims, purposes, research questions or hypotheses + Indicate research design/processes/methodology)	3	10
	S4.3 (Indicate research design/processes/methodology)	3	6.7

Table 6.17 Frequently-used sub-move configurations in three moves in Theoretical Reviews in AL (no. of occurrence ≥ 3)

	Sub-move configurations	Count no.	% of Theoretical Reviews
M1	S1.2 (Survey knowledge claims or provide an overview of the research area)	148	96.7
	S1.1+S1.2 (Highlight significance of research issues/problems + Survey knowledge claims or provide an overview of the research area)	13	40
	S1.2+S1.1+S1.2 (Survey knowledge claims or provide an overview of the research area + Highlight significance of research issues/problems + Survey knowledge claims or provide an overview of the research area)	6	20
	S1.1 (Highlight significance of research issues/problems)	3	10
	S1.2+S1.1 (Survey knowledge claims or provide an overview of the research area + Highlight significance of research issues/problems)	3	10
M3	S3.1a (Indicate a research gap or a limitation in previous research)	71	73.3
	S3.3 (Relevance-claiming)	35	66.7
	S3.5 (Abstract, synthesize, or make inferences from knowledge claims to establish a theoretical position or framework)	13	36.7
	S3.2 (Assert confirmative claims)	9	23.3
	S3.1a+S3.2 (Indicate a research gap or a limitation in previous research + Assert confirmative claims)	4	13.3
	S3.1b (Indicate a problem in or need from the real world)	4	10
	S3.4 (Assert the irrelevance of the surveyed claims to one's own research to specify the scope of the study)	3	10
M4	S4.1 (Announce research aims, purposes, research questions or hypotheses)	22	36.7
	S4.3 (Indicate research design/processes/methodology)	13	26.7
	S4.6 (Suggest the subsequent theme to be reviewed)	9	23.3

(continued)

Table 6.17 (continued)

	Sub-move configurations	Count no.	% of Theoretical Reviews
	S4.2 (Announce theoretical positions/frameworks)	7	20
	S4.4 (Announce interpretations of terminology used in the study)	5	13.3
	S4.1+S4.3 (Announce research aims, purposes, research questions or hypotheses + Indicate research design/processes/methodology)	4	13.3
	S4.5 (State the value of the present study)	4	10

larly insightful", "as a case in point…", and "specifically…". An extract illustrating this move is provided below:

> (21) **Two recent studies come to mind in this connection. The first**, using an RST as a measure of WM capacity, tested the interaction between WM capacity and topic familiarity in text recall of L2 learners of Spanish **(Leeser, 2007)**. It was found that both WM capacity and topic familiarity associated with domain knowledge significantly affected learners' text recall. Although the interaction between these factors was not statistically significant (p 5 0.058), post-hoc comparisons showed that learners benefited from higher WM capacity only if they were familiar with the topic. This was interpreted as support for the rich-getricher hypothesis. However, these findings should be viewed with caution, because the overall F test was not statistically significant, casting a shadow on the researcher's overall conclusion. **The second study (Payne et al., 2009),** done with adult native speakers of English learning Spanish, provides further evidence in support of the independent influences model, in agreement with the findings of Hambrick and his colleagues. Measuring WM capacity through a counting span task and operationalizing domain knowledge as domain experience (the number of Spanish courses taken and the years spent actively learning Spanish), the researchers found that these two factors make significant yet independent contributions to L2 reading comprehension. In sum, research on the combined effects of WM capacity and domain knowledge on L2 reading comprehension is scarce, and findings are inconclusive at best. (CALL_TR17)

This move often follows a topic summarization/an overview of the research area. An important observation of the above extract illustrating Move 2 is that, despite many details being given to key studies with a dense use of reporting verbs, the citation forms used are actually non-integral ones. Therefore, although some citation studies (e.g., Hyland, 1999, 2002; Swales, 1990) have concluded that non-integral citations are more often used in summary statements on the findings of a group of previous studies and integral citations are usually employed to describe details of individual studies (see the Move 2 instance in CCEL_TR3 in Appendix F), the use of citation forms is by no means the decisive criterion for determining a textual segment as a Move 2 or not. In the analysis of the present data, it is found that the boundary between Move 1 and Move 2 is generally explicit, although there are still a few ambiguous segments, the coding of which is resolved through substantial discussions between the two coders. For example, in the second Move 2 instance in CALL_TR24 (Appendix

L), there is a sentence "Once the lexical coverage…is decided, we need a tool to calculate the vocabulary size needed to reach the predetermined lexical coverage" (see p. 486), which poses some difficulties in analysis. The discussion between the two coders centred on whether it also should be assigned into Move 2. The first look of this sentence gave the impression that it seems to function as a transition between two research (sub-)themes, thus creating the temptation to code it as Sub-move 4.6 (Suggest the Subsequent Theme). However, obviously it is not a segment unfolding some aspects of the present study, to which Sub-move 4.6 should contribute to. Further, the entire sub-section reviews previous studies focusing on vocabulary levels and vocabulary size necessary for a certain degree of comprehension of different types of texts, as can be perceived from its heading and first sentence. This confusing sentence indeed does provide a transition to the review of the tool used for calculating vocabulary size, which is still a part the literature on vocabulary levels and vocabulary size covers. Therefore, it is more appropriate to consider it as being subsidiary to Move 2, i.e., the review of key studies on a particular theme.

As discussed before (see Sect. 6.3.2), this move is a quasi-obligatory or prototypical element of Theoretical Reviews in both disciplines. However, as it is not subdivided into various constituents, the discussion of findings on sub-move frequency and combination use is confined to the other three moves.

6.3.2.3 Position the Present Study

Move 3 (Position the Present Study) locates the present study in the background and establishes the links between the study and the literature beyond finding rationales for it. In other words, Theoretical Reviews, as a major functional component in the LR section, have multiple tasks and establish various connections between the present study and the body of the literature in order to offer insights from previous studies to the present research and/or to delimit the scope of the study. Therefore, an important difference between this four-move structure for Theoretical Reviews and the CARS structure is that, while the CARS model emphasizes the role of article introductions in establishing the niche for the study (Lee, 2001), the four-move structure highlights the multi-functions of the LR section in establishing various links between the study and the background literature. As such, Move 3 in this proposed structure for Theoretical Reviews encompasses three groups of constituents with different characteristics.

The first group evaluates the literature in a negative sense either explicitly or implicitly in order to locate the niche to be occupied by the study. It includes Sub-move 3.1 (Indicate Explicitly a Gap or Problem) and Sub-move 3.6 (Indicate Inconsistencies in Findings/Conclusions/Claims from Previous Studies without Explicit Gap-signaling). The instances of Sub-move 3.1 can be further classified into two types, based on whether gaps or problems identified are epistemic or non-epistemic orientations (Samraj, 2002, 2005; Kwan, 2005, 2006). Specifically, the first type suggests a gap or a limitation in previous research (Sub-move 3.1a, see Fig. 6.6) and the other type points out a problem in or need from the real world (Sub-move 3.1b, see Fig. 6.6). CCEL_TR3 in Appendix F contains two segments which belong to the two types respectively: Segment 1 suggesting the need to explore further the functionality of 3D/4D models or Building Information Modeling from the point of view of engineering practitioners (Sub-move 3.1b); and Segment 2 enumerating a list of (primarily) gaps and problems in previous research into 3D/4D CAD application in construction processes (Sub-move 3.1a).

Sub-move 3.6 is similar to the element "Suggesting Implicitly Inconsistencies Precluding Gap Signaling" discovered by Del Saz-Rubio (2011) in Agricultural Sciences RA introductions. Through presenting inconsistencies in previous findings or claims, the need for the study is implied, as illustrated below:

(22) One study found no statistical relationship between median width and severity (Noland and Oh 2004), whereas another study concluded that an increase in median width is associated with a decrease in the frequency of severe crashes (Hadi et al., 1995). A more recent study, which utilized an ordered multinomial logit model, found that the proportion of severe crashes increased as median width increased for median-related crashes (Miaou et al., 2005). (CCEL_TR24)

(23) Even though previous studies indicated that SA experiences tend to have positive impacts on participants' motivation (e.g., Simões, 1996), some studies reported otherwise (e.g., Allen, 2002). (CALL_TR14)

The second group either expresses writers' positive evaluation of previous claims explicitly (Sub-move 3.2 Assert Confirmative Claims about Knowledge or Research Practices Surveyed) or suggests implicitly their acceptance through Relevance-claiming (Sub-moves 3.3) and Theoretical Framework-Synthesizing (Sub-move 3.5). These elements were referred to as "affirmative strategies" by Kwan (2005, 2006) in her structural analysis of thematic units in the LR chapters of doctoral theses, who firstly discovered "Relevance-claiming" and "Theoretical Framework-Synthesizing" as two new elements particularly featured in the LR text. The three sub-moves are also present in Theoretical Reviews in ERAs in both disciplines and they are respectively illustrated below with some semantic attributes highlighted in boldface:

Sub-move 3.2 Assert confirmative claims about knowledge or research practices surveyed

(24) A reason why the time use approach **is appealing** is that the individual or activity episode is the unit of analysis, which greatly facilitates the inclusion of any relevant contextual information. Time use approaches **share a vital connection with** the activity-based approach to transportation analysis. (CCEL_TR25)

Sub-move 3.3 Assert the relevance of the surveyed claims to one's own research

(25) One of their findings **which has implications for this study** is the fact that the amount of time spent in different types of activities affect the amount of time spent in other activities... (CCEL_TR27)

Sub-move 3.5 Abstract, synthesize, or make inferences from knowledge claims to establish a theoretical position or framework

(26) **In the present study,** all participants were English (L1) dominant; **therefore**, English is the language that would need to be inhibited most strongly for accurate performance in Portuguese. (CALL_TR29)

Example (24) is extracted from an independent LR section headed "Time Use Approaches". This segment foregrounding the strength of the time use approach can indeed be considered as "positive warrants" for the time-use investigation of shopping participation in three Canadian cities. In terms of the realization of Sub-move 3.3, in Example (25), one of the previous studies is relevant to the present research in that one of its findings sheds some light on the study. Regarding Sub-move 3.5, Example (26) as an illustrative instance is an inferential hypothesis made by the writer based on a classic model surveyed (i.e., Green's (1998) Inhibitory Control (IC) model). According to this model, for unbalanced bilinguals, the dominant language will be inhibited most severely as L1 lemmas are more active than L2 lemmas, hence the prediction made by the writer (see Example 26 above). Another example of this sub-move is offered in CALL_TR24 (see Appendix L), where the writer infers from the literature that 95% and 98% are perhaps two coverage points representing respectively the lower and upper boundaries with respect to lexical threshold. In this segment, the phrase "taken together" is an obvious linguistic exponent for the sub-move.

The third group only contains one move constituent, i.e., Sub-move 3.4 (Assert the Irrelevance of the Surveyed Claims to One's Own Research to Specify the Scope of the Study). As a non-evaluative statement, this sub-move aims to position the study by announcing which part of the background literature is not pertinent to the present research and thus specifies its research scope after a relatively comprehensive review of the entire background. This is a new element emerging from the present data. Two instances are provided from CE and AL respectively:

(27) The UG debate over whether there is a representational deficit or not **is peripheral to the main goals of this article**, which examines online and offline responses to Spanish gender nonagreement, comparing natives with L2 learners of two proficiency levels. (CALL_TR25)

(28) The analysis of the factors controlling the bond strength **was beyond the scope of the research presented in this paper**. (CCEL_TR9)

Among all these Move 3 constituents, Sub-move 3.1a (Gap-indication/Counter-claiming) is the most frequently used element in both disciplines (being present in 76.7% of CE Theoretical Reviews and 83.3% of AL Theoretical Reviews), suggesting that one of the most important communicative functions of this component is to locate a niche to be filled by the study (see Figs. 6.7 and 6.8). In AL Theoretical Reviews, Sub-moves 3.3 (Relevance-claiming), 3.5 (Theoretical Framework-Synthesizing), and 3.2 (Positive Warrants) are prominent elements, while they are used much less frequently in CE Theoretical Reviews. This marked cross-disciplinary variation relates to the fact that applied linguistics research much more often draws on theoretical models, hypotheses, frameworks and other theoretical conceptualizations posited by previous researchers than that in CE, which often necessitates suggesting the links between such frameworks and the study. This implies that there are far more chances for AL writers to employ these three sub-moves. In contrast, CE writers use Sub-move 3.1b (Indicate a Problem in or Need from the Real World) more often than AL writers (26.7% vs. 16.7%), the instances of which are all concerned with engineering practices, material properties and applications, or transportation issues. As both disciplines examined in this study are of somewhat applied nature, Sub-move 3.1b is present in a number of Theoretical Reviews from both CE and AL. However, the other two elements (viz., Sub-move 3.4 Irrelevance-claiming and Sub-move 3.6 Inconsistencies-indication) are only used in a few Theoretical Reviews in both disciplines.

In terms of frequency distribution of different Move 3 configurations in the two disciplines, as revealed in Tables 6.16 and 6.17, the most common ones are those with one sub-move only. Among the instances of single-sub-move, those with Sub-move 3.1a only are the most common, followed by those with Sub-move 3.3, in both disciplines. Other frequently used sub-move configurations shared in the two disciplines are those such as Sub-move 3.1b and Sub-move 3.2. The most common composite Moves 3 are the "Sub-move 3.1a+Sub-move 3.2" combination (used in 6.7% of the 30 CE Theoretical Reviews and in 13.3% of the 30 AL Theoretical Reviews). Despite many similarities in the use of Move 3 configurations between the two disciplines, there are still some obvious differences. For instance, the use of the configuration "Sub-move 3.5 (Theoretical Framework-synthesizing) only" appears to be more discipline-specific, i.e., this single-sub-move configuration is only frequently used in Theoretical Reviews in AL (36.7%). While the configuration with only Sub-move 3.6 (Inconsistency-indication) is frequently used in CE but not in AL, there is a much higher frequency of the Sub-move 3.3 configuration (Relevance-claiming) in Theoretical Reviews in AL (66.7%) than in those in CE (30%). All these significant differences could be attributed to the contrasting nature of the two disciplines (namely, CE as an engineering/a hard discipline vs. AL as a social science/soft discipline) and their distinct knowledge structure and research orientations, as discussed before.

6.3.2.4 Outline the Present Study

Move 4 (Outline the present study) is used as the concluding move in a majority of Theoretical Reviews, indicating the likely embedding of move structures. It resembles the last move of the CARS model for article introductions (Present the Present Study) (Swales, 1990, 2004); however, it contains constituents that particularly characterize the LR section (e.g., Sub-move 4.6 Suggest the Subsequent Theme to be Reviewed and Sub-move 4.7 Indicate the Content of the Method section). Correspondingly, some other elements appear to be exclusively used in the Introduction (e.g., "Preview Main Findings" and "Outline the Article Structure").

Sub-move 4.1 (Announce Research Aims, Purposes, Focuses, RQs, or Hypotheses) is a combination of Step 1 (Announcing Present Research Descriptively and/or Purposively) and Step 2 (Presenting RQs or Hypotheses) of Move 3 in the revised

CARS model (Swales, 2004). Having been found by Kwan (2005, 2006) in the LR chapters of doctoral theses in applied linguistics, it is also frequently present in the LR section of ERAs. The final segments in CCEL_TR3 and CALL_TR24 in Appendices 6 and 12 are two cases in point. In addition, other aspects of the study such as theoretical positions/frameworks to be adopted, research methods or design, and definitions of some terminologies are also probably outlined (see the emboldened words below):

Sub-move 4.2 Announce theoretical positions/frameworks

(29) **Hyland and Tse's taxonomy, together with elements of Thompson's (2001), will form a basis** for the ensuing analysis of interactional resources in the texts published by students on the wiki (further described in Sect. 6.4). (CALL_TR20)

Sub-move 4.3 Indicate research design/processes/methodology

(30) ...**accident reduction potential approach** with at least 3-year crash histories was applied in this research. (CCEL_TR20)

Sub-move 4.4 Announce interpretations of terminology used in the study

(31) The term 'language creativity' or 'creative language use', **in the present study**, **is defined as** the playful use of language to construct new/unknown meanings, transforming one's current linguistic and conceptual world and involving several types of creative thinking.

(CALL_TR8)

Sub-move 4.5 State the value of the present study

(32) **This study contributes not only to** creativity research by exploring the processes involved in creative thinking and their contribution to language development **but also to** the current view of language as evolving/emerging in context. (CALL_TR8)

Different from Kwan's (2006) finding that value-claiming is a sub-strategy in the LR chapter of research degree theses, it is a stand-alone move constituent that does not often co-occur with other Move 4 elements in the LR section of ERAs. Another instance of it is given below, which is employed in an LR section that contains a Contextual Background component as well:

(33) **...while this study focuses on a particular context, it may have wider implications in terms of** both writer backgrounds and the content areas. (CALL_TR21)

The other two sub-moves functioning as signposts either provide transitions between different theme-bound (sub-)sections (Sub-move 4.6 Suggest the Subsequent Theme to be Reviewed) or prepare for introducing method details in the forthcoming section (Sub-move 4.7 Indicate the Content of the Method section).

Sub-move 4.6 Suggest the subsequent theme to be reviewed

(34) **The next section** will examine the effects of time distribution on learning, in general, and on foreign language learning, in particular.

(CALL_TR26)

Sub-move 4.7 Indicate the content of the Method section

(35) **The next section** describes the characteristics of the data. (CCEL_TR21)

Sub-move 4.6 is often used at the end of a theme-bound (sub-)section to offer a smooth transition to the next (sub-)section. For instance, in CALL26, there are two sub-sections encapsulated under the major heading of "Review of the Literature". Note that the formatting features the writer originally used are reproduced here to display the relation among the headings.

Review of the Literature

Practice in Cognitive Psychology and in SLA

Time Distribution in Cognitive Psychology and in SLA

Example (34) (see above), which is the last sentence of the first subsection in this LR text with the heading "Practice in Cognitive Psychology and in SLA", explicitly inform the readers of the main content or theme of the subsequent sub-section, which is also signaled by its own heading ("Time Distribution in Cognitive Psychology and in SLA").

The frequency distribution of these seven sub-moves are somewhat different in Theoretical Reviews across the two disciplines (see Figs. 6.7 and 6.8), notwithstanding Sub-moves 4.1 and 4.3 being registered as the two most frequently used elements within this move in both disciplines. As these two move constituents are also most common in the niche-establishment move of many introductions preceding the LR section (see Sect. 6.2), stating research purposes/focuses/hypotheses/methods and some method details are some major purposes of the introductory part of the ERA. However, significant cross-disciplinary variations exist in the use of other sub-moves. Firstly, the element of announcing theoretical frameworks or positions (Sub-move 4.2) is used in 33.3% of Theoretical Reviews in AL but is absent in all 30 Theoretical Reviews in CE, which reflects the special importance of theoretical arguments and frameworks to the study in AL as a social science discipline. Second, due to disciplinary influence as well (Hyland, 2004), the elements of terminological interpretations (Sub-move 4.4) and value-claiming (Sub-move 4.5) are more frequently used in Theoretical Reviews in AL than in those in CE. This embodies the different epistemological orientations and knowledge structure in these two disciplines: CE attaches much importance to factual findings and experimental designs, in contrast to the more discursive nature of AL. Further, while the writers in both disciplines occasionally suggest the content of the Method section (Sub-move 4.7) at the end of Theoretical Reviews, Sub-move 4.6 (Suggest the Subsequent Theme to be Reviewed) is clearly more often used in Theoretical Reviews in AL, as many of them are multi-thematic sections. Only three counts of this sub-move were found in Theoretical Reviews in CE, the reason for which is obvious: as many as 20 out of the 30 Theoretical Reviews in CE are stand-alone sections without further sub-division, suggesting that there is no need to use it to help to transit between theme-bound sub-sections.

In terms of the use of sub-move patterns, most frequently-used sub-move configurations within this final move are single elements, as shown in Tables 6.16 and 6.17. The single Sub-move 4.1 is the most often used pattern in Theoretical Reviews in both disciplines, followed by the single Sub-move 4.3 configuration delivering information on research design or methods (26.7%) in AL Theoretical Reviews and by the combined use of such two elements in a sequential order (10%) in CE Theoretical Reviews. There are, however, a wider variety of frequently-used sub-move configurations in Theoretical Reviews in AL. In addition to the above-mentioned three frequently-used sub-move configurations, the others found in AL Theoretical Reviews include S4.6 (Suggest the Subsequent Theme to be Reviewed), S4.2 (Announce Theoretical Positions/Frameworks), S4.4 (Announce Interpretations of Terminology Used in the Study), and S4.5 (Value-claiming) (see Table 6.17). All these single sub-move patterns being only frequently used in AL are suggestive of the nature of this soft discipline, as discussed before, and thus have high value for the teaching of discipline-specific LR writing.

6.4 Comparison and the Interrelationship Between Introductions and Literature Reviews

Based on the study of the schematic structure of 20 applied linguistics doctoral theses, Kwan (2005, 2006) advanced the possibility of considering both LRs and Introductions as members of the same genre colony (i.e., the colony of academic introductions) (Bhatia, 1993). In the same line, several recent studies (Kwan et al., 2012; Tessuto, 2015) have contended that the CARS structure is applicable to the analysis of the LR section in RAs. However, the present study reveals a much more complex reality than is assumed. The data shows that the LR section in ERAs in CE and AL comprises four possible functionally distinct components (viz., Advanced Organizer/Overview, Theoretical Review, Contextual Background and Conclusion). Therefore, the CARS model (Swales, 1990, 2004) apparently could not fully account for the structure of this part-genre with complicated and somewhat flexible compositions. Among the four functional components, Theoretical Review is the only obligatory one, and for its rhetorical structure, a prototypical four-move scheme ("Land-scaping" → "Close-up Surveys" → "Positioning of the Study" → "Presentation of the Study") is formulated.

While it is acknowledged that the LR section and the Introduction may share some communicative purposes (e.g., to provide background to and contextualize the study) and hence a number of moves (e.g., "Outline the Present Study") and sub-moves (e.g., "Highlight the Significance of the Study" and "Indicate a Gap/Problem"), there are significant differences between them in terms of their functions and structure. Firstly, while the core function of article introductions is to establish a niche for the present study (Lee, 2001), the LR section (or rather Theoretical Reviews) aims to "position the study", which has a broader connotation than just niche-establishment. To locate the present study in the background, the research writer either creates a detailed space for it via seeking for "negative" or "positive" warrants, or establishes other links of a different nature between it and the background literature, e.g., specifies the irrelevance of a part of the background literature to the present research in order to delimit its research scope.

Second, if we compare the Introduction with the LR sections within the same ERAs, as the present data shows, they are quite different in terms of their structural forms and communicative functional foci. As detailed in the preceding sub-section,

Theoretical Reviews as a major component of the LR sections in ERAs show complex, multi-thematic-sectional structure with varied content and dense information involved, particularly in AL (66.7%). In contrast, article introductions used before the LR section demonstrate structural variability with different types of them identified based upon their major communicative functions, structural flows, and the nature and orientations of the studies reported. A considerable number of them embody the relatively simpler, two-move structure with the main purposes of identifying the issue and presenting the research study. Although some of them exhibit the traditional CARS-like structure, generally speaking, when there is a subsequent LR section, the introductions are fairly flexibly yet simply structured with no dense use of sub-moves.

In addition to the multi-thematic-sectional structure, Theoretical Reviews mostly display a substantial amount of cyclical patterns, resulting in the wide variety of their move configurations and the high occurrences of the "irregular" patterns. In contrast, many of the introductions preceding the LR section follow a linear sequential pattern with no cyclicity involved, especially the Two-move Orientation introductions. The Orientation introductions are rather simply and straightforwardly structured, and some of them are of a single-move structure. While a number of the RT CARS introductions do involve cyclicity in their move structure, the number of move units integrating their move configurations is much smaller than that of move units constituting patterns for most of the Theoretical Reviews. This accounts for the fact that the LR section is far longer than the Introduction in both disciplines. The discrepancy in their length is particularly salient in the discipline of AL, where the LR section is around four times as long as its preceding Introduction.

Third, in both major types of introductions used before the LR section (viz., the Orientation introductions and the RT CARS introductions), the generalization element appears to be the most characteristic and important one in contextualizing the study and offering the background knowledge of the research field. In contrast, the element of "Survey Items of Previous Research" is only present in around half of the RT CARS introductions and is completely missing in all Orientation introductions in both disciplines. However, in Theoretical Reviews, "Survey Key Studies in Detail" has become an independent, prototypical move, and functions as a springboard for the advancement of the present study. It has been used in nearly all Theoretical Reviews in both disciplines. This suggests that the LR section is functionally a "build-up" mainly for further developing the arguments and rationales based on a focused, critical review of the literature, and/or developing the theoretical frameworks or conceptual/methodological basis, when the preceding Introduction becomes a kind of "set-up" (AL1) simply for scene-setting and identifying the problem/issue. One of the crucial connections between these two sections is the shift of the use of this element from the Introduction to the LR section, along with their changing communicative functional foci. This is also an important difference between the conventional CARS model for article introductions (Swales, 1990, 2004) and the four-move structure for Theoretical Reviews: the element of reviewing items of previous research is merely a step embedded within the first move ("Establishing the Territory") of the CARS model while the similar element "Survey Key Studies" is a distinguishable move.

Identifying "Survey Key Studies" as one of the prototypical moves in Theoretical Reviews helps to distinguish this part-genre from the Introduction section, showing it as one of the major functions of the LR section/Theoretical Reviews. In contrast, the Introduction section is often much shorter with "contextualization the study" generally as an inclusive function encompassing both elements (i.e., "reviewing items of previous research" and "topic generalization").

Other important differences lie in some elements exclusively used in the Introduction section (e.g., the steps of "Outline Article Structure" and "Announce Principal Outcomes") and some others characterizing the LR section/Theoretical Reviews (e.g., Sub-move 3.4 Irrelevance-claiming for Specifying the Research Scope, Sub-move 4.6 Suggest the Subsequent Theme to be Reviewed, and Sub-move 4.7 Indicate the Content of the Method section). The identification of Sub-move 4.6 only in Theoretical Reviews confirms many of them containing multiple theme-bound (sub-)sections, suggesting their structural sophistication and extended length.

In addition to the similarities and differences between the Introduction and LR sections in terms of their communicative functions or functional foci and rhetorical structure, there also exist important links between these two adjacent sections. One essential link is functional connection between the LR section and its preceding Introduction section as mentioned before: after the Introduction section acts as a kind of "set-up" (AL1) simply for scene-setting and identifying the problem/issue, its subsequent LR section further develops the arguments or rationales briefly mentioned in the Introduction, functioning as a "build-up". This functional support rendered by the LR section is also reflected in the fact that sometimes the references encapsulated within a non-integral citation in the Introduction section are further reviewed at length and critically in the form of integral citations in the LR section. Some interesting examples have been shown and discussed in Sect. 6.2. In some other cases, the detailed reviews of individual research studies have been postponed to the LR section, which is explicitly signaled in the Introduction section by using some metalanguage.

6.5 Summary

This chapter has examined the rhetorical structure of the two major sections in the opening phase of ERAs, viz., the Introduction and LR sections. Related cross-disciplinary variations (CE vs. AL) in structuring the two sections, and the possible similarities, differences, and interrelationship between them in terms of their communicative functions and structure have been presented and discussed. The major findings are summarized as follows:

1. In both CE and AL, the introductions preceding the LR section demonstrate structural variability. Different types of introductions have been identified based on their major communicative functions, structural flows, and the nature and orientations of the studies reported, e.g., the "Two-move Orientation" type and the "Research-oriented Traditional Creating a Research Space" ("RT CARS")

type in both disciplines, the "Practical-problem Solving" ("PS") type in CE and the single case of "Building on the Writer's Own Previous Research" in AL. The former two types are dominant categories identified among these 60 introductions with a subsequent LR section.

2. The Two-move Orientation approach is proposed for the schematic structure of the Orientation introductions with the major functions of identifying the issue/problem and presenting the present research. For the RT CARS introductions, an integrated CARS model is developed to capture their rhetorical organization. Two elements are identified that have not been reported in previous introduction studies (i.e., "Indicate the LR Content" and "State Theoretical Frameworks/Positions"), which may have characterized the special generic context of the introductions examined (i.e., all of them being followed by a substantial LR section) and/or the nature of the particular disciplines studied.
3. Both major types of introductions show substantial similarities in the frequency use of some particular sub-moves and sub-move combination patterns between the two disciplines. However, a number of noticeable cross-disciplinary variations exist in organizing these two dominant categories of introductions. For instance, the newly-discovered element "Indicate the Literature Review Content" was used in both RT CARS introductions and Orientation introductions in AL but not in any of the introductions in CE. Another observed difference lies in the use of the two sub-moves ("Claim Centrality in the Research World" and "Claim Centrality in the Real World"): while applied linguists prefer using the former to the latter in the RT CARS introductions, the opposite is true of the choices of CE experts.
4. The LR section comprises four possible functional components: Advanced Organizer/Overview, Theoretical Review, Contextual Background, and Conclusion. A "formula" accounting for the general organization of the LR section in ERAs is thus proposed: Literature Review = (Advanced Organizer/Overview) + Theoretical Review + (Contextual Background) + (Conclusion). The three functional components encapsulated within parentheses are optional whereas Theoretical Review is present in all LR sections.
5. Theoretical Reviews are the only obligatory functional component in the LR sections in ERAs and their rhetorical structure has been analyzed using the ESP genre-based approach. A four-move structure ("Landscaping" —> "Close-up Surveys" —> "Positioning of the Study" —> "Presentation of the Study") has been proposed for Theoretical Reviews to capture their major communicative functions.
6. The analysis shows high degrees of cyclicity in the move structure of most Theoretical Reviews. This most salient structural feature, together with their usually substantial length, both contribute to the occurrences of a considerable variety of move configurations and to the fact that the majority of such configurations appear "irregular". However, the four moves are found to be prototypical in the 60 Theoretical Reviews and the comparatively stable, repeated use of some "regular" pairings such as "Move 1-Move 3" ("1-3") and "Move 1-Move 2-Move 3" ("1-2-3") is prevalent. These demonstrate to some extent the validity of the proposed

four-move structure. There is much in common in the frequency use of some sub-moves and sub-move configurations in Theoretical Reviews between the two disciplines. However, the related marked cross-disciplinary differences also exist, e.g., the single sub-move patterns (S3.5 "Theoretical Framework-synthesizing" and S3.4 "Irrelevance-claiming") are frequently used in AL Theoretical Reviews but not in CE Theoretical Reviews. While Theoretical Reviews in both disciplines display a strong cyclical tendency in their move use, at the sub-move level, most frequently-used configurations only contain a single element.

7. Similarities, differences, and the interrelationship between the Introduction and the LR section in terms of their functions and structure have been addressed and accounted for. One of their important connections is that the use of the element "Survey Items of Previous Research" has often been shifted to the LR section, which corroborates the Introduction and the LR sections within the same ERA often functioning as a "set-up"/a "general overview" and a "build-up" respectively, as commented by our interviewees (e.g., CE1, AL1, and AL4).
8. The analyses of the pre-methodology phase consisting of Introduction and LR sections reveal that the classic CARS model could not accurately and fully represent their rhetorical structure and could hardly capture structural and functional differences and the interrelationship between the two distinct part-genres with their own communicative functional foci. The CARS model can only describe one type of pre-LR introductions (viz., RT CARS introductions, as opposed to Two-move Orientation introductions, PS introductions and Building on the Writers' Own Previous Research introduction) and thus could not account for structural and functional variability of introductions employed before the LR sections. While the CARS model prevails in the current introduction studies, and a few recent studies (Kwan et al., 2012; Tessuto, 2015) have suggested that LRs in ERAs are rhetorically structured around the three moves of CARS, the present study reveals much more complex possible compositions of the LR section. The four-move structure formulated for its only obligatory functional component (i.e., "Theoretical Reviews") embodies its communicative functions beyond finding rationales for the study, which is the core function of the CARS model (Swales, 1990, 2004). Indeed, it aims to contextualize and position the study (against the research (and contextual) background) through establishing various links between the study and the background, e.g., to delimit the research scope of the study by indicating the irrelevancy of parts of the literature to it.

References

Anthony, L. (1999). Writing research article introductions in software engineering: How accurate is a standard model? *IEEE Transactions on Professional Communication, 42,* 38–46.

Bhatia, V. K. (1993). *Analyzing genre: Language use in professional settings.* New York: Longman.

Bhatia, V. K. (2004). *Worlds of written discourse: A genre-based view.* Continuum.

Biber, D., & Conrad, S. (2009). *Register, genre, and style.* Cambridge: Cambridge University Press.

Brumfit, C. J. (1995). Teacher professionalism and research. In G. Cook & B. Seidlhofer (Eds.), *Principle and practice in Applied Linguistics* (pp. 27–41). Oxford: Oxford University Press.
Del Saz-Rubio, M. M. (2011). A pragmatic approach to the macro-structure and metadiscoursal features of research article introductions in the field of agricultural sciences. *English for Specific Purposes, 30*(4), 258–271.
Feak, C. B., & Swales, J. M. (2011). *Creating contexts: Writing introductions across genres*. Ann Arbor: University of Michigan Press.
Hirano, E. (2009). Research article introductions in English for specific purposes: A comparison between Brazilian Portuguese and English. *English for Specific Purposes, 28*(4), 240–250.
Hyland, K. (1999). Academic attribution: Citation and the construction of disciplinary knowledge. *Applied Linguistics, 20*(3), 341–367.
Hyland, K. (2002). Activity and evaluation: Reporting practices in academic writing. In J. Flowerdew (Ed.), *Academic discourse* (pp. 115–130). Harlow: Pearson Education Limited.
Hyland, K. (2004). *Disciplinary discourses: Social interactions in academic writing*. Ann Arbor: University of Michigan Press.
Kanoksilapatham, B. (2005). Rhetorical structure of biochemistry research articles. *English for Specific Purposes, 24*(3), 269–292.
Kanoksilapatham, B. (2012). Research article structure of research article introductions in three engineering subdisciplines. *IEEE Transactions on Professional Communication, 55*(4), 294–309.
Kwan, B. S. C. (2005). *A genre analysis of literature reviews in doctoral theses*. Unpublished doctoral dissertation, City University of Hong Kong.
Kwan, B. S. C. (2006). The schematic structure of literature reviews in doctoral theses of applied linguistics. *English for Specific Purposes, 25,* 30–55.
Kwan, B. S. C., Chan, H., & Lam, C. (2012). Evaluating prior scholarship in literature reviews of research articles: A comparative study of practices in two research paradigms. *English for Specific Purposes, 31,* 188–201.
Lee, S. (2001). *A contrastive rhetoric study of Korean and English research paper introductions*. Unpublished doctoral dissertation, University of Hawaii.
Ozturk, I. (2007). The textual organization of research article introductions in applied linguistics: Variability within a single discipline. *English for Specific Purposes, 26*(1), 25–38.
Posteguillo, S. (1999). The schematic structure of computer science research articles. *English for Specific Purposes, 18*(2), 139–160.
Ridley, D. (2012). *The literature review: A step-by step guide for students* (2nd ed.). London: Sage.
Rudestam, K., & Newton, R. (2007). *Surviving your dissertation: A comprehensive guide to content and process* (3rd ed.). Los Angeles: Sage.
Samraj, B. (2002). Introductions in research articles: Variations across disciplines. *English for Specific Purposes, 21*(1), 1–17.
Samraj, B. (2005). An exploration of a genre set: Research article abstracts and introductions in two disciplines. *English for Specific Purposes, 24*(2), 141–156.
Swales, J. M. (1990). *Genre analysis: English in academic and research settings*. Cambridge; New York: Cambridge University Press.
Swales, J. M. (2004). *Research genres: Explorations and applications*. Cambridge; New York: Cambridge University Press.
Tessuto, G. (2015). Generic structure and rhetorical moves in English-language empirical law research articles: Sites of interdisciplinary and interdiscursive cross-over. *English for Specific Purposes, 37*(1), 13–26.
Wen, Q. F. (2001). *Applied linguistics: Research methods and thesis writing*. Beijing: Foreign Languages Teaching Research Press.

Chapter 7
Citation Use in the Introductory Part

7.1 Introduction

This chapter presents the findings of the investigation into the use of citations in the two major rhetorical sections (viz., the Introduction and LR) of the introductory phase of ERAs in AL and CE. Cross-disciplinary and cross-generic variations in citation density (Sect. 7.2), the use of different types of citation forms (Sect. 7.3.1) and RVs (Sect. 7.4), and the rhetorical functions of citations (Sect. 7.3.2) are the focus of this study. The comparative analysis of citation use on such dimensions in Introduction and LR is significant and interesting since both of them are the potential locations for reviewing previous literature in the ERA, thereby providing possible contexts for the (intense) use of citations and RVs. A summary of the major findings yielded from the comparison concludes this chapter.

7.2 Citation Density

The different quantities of citations distributed in Introductions and LRs in AL and CE, as shown in Table 7.1, indicate the different degree of importance referencing previous works is to these two functionally distinct rhetorical sections in these two contrasting disciplines. From this table, it can be found that in both AL and CE,

Table 7.1 Citation distribution in Introductions and LRs in AL and CE

Disciplines	Genre parts	Total citations	Av. per text	Per 1000 words
AL	I	240	8	14
	LR	1032	34	16
CE	I	176	6	10
	LR	508	17	17

(Kathy). L. Lin, *Perspectives on the Introductory Phase of Empirical Research Articles*, Corpora and Intercultural Studies 5, https://doi.org/10.1007/978-981-32-9204-8_7

writers prefer using more citations in the LR section than in the Introduction, and this difference is much clearer in the field of CE in terms of the number of citations used per 1,000 words. While previous studies have identified the Introduction and Discussion (or the coalesced "Results and Discussion" section) as the preferred locations for citation use in RAs (e.g., Mansourizadeh & Ahmad, 2011) and no studies have hitherto compared specifically the distribution of citations in these two related neighboring sections (viz., Introductions and LRs), the finding here may suggest the different communicative functional foci of these two part-genres. As our genre analysis in Chap. 6 reveals that a considerable number of introductions are the Two-move Orientation type with the review of individual previous studies shifting to the subsequent LR sections, which may partly account for the less use of citations in Introductions when the introductory phase is structured in the "I+LR"[1] pattern.

For our interviewees who favor using Introductions and LRs as two separate sections in the ERA, many of them hold the view that the introductions used before the lengthy LR section aim to identify the problem/issue in a concise way and then to present the present work. This indicates that unlike the traditional CARS-like introductions, the review of previous literature may be no longer an obligatory element in introductions followed by an LR section. As CE1 maintained:

> I would usually tend to write a short and punchy introduction, which says this is the problem, and this is the area we are looking at, and then generally I would have a longer review, which looks at what other people have done in relation to that. I mean, the first one, the sort of the introductory, it may refer to some statistics or background figures which illustrates (sic) the nature of the problem. It would give an idea of the trends…and then the review would look at more specifically how people have addressed that issue.

When the detailed review of previous literature is shifted to and becomes an integral part of the LR section, it is not surprising that the denser use of citation is found in it than in the Introduction. However, as we also noted from Table 7.1, the quantities of citations used in Introductions and LRs are quite similar in AL ERAs when they were standardized per 1,000 words. Therefore, the extent to which writers would differ in relying on referring to the work of others in these two sections may require more future research conducted in other disciplines using a larger-size data.

While the numbers of citations per 1,000 words in the LR section in the two disciplines are quite similar, that in the Introduction section in AL is clearly higher than that in the Introduction in CE. The average number of citations per introductory phase (consisting of both Introduction and LR sections) in AL is also far larger than that in CE (with the two figures being respectively 21 and 11.5). The findings generally lend support to Hyland's (1999) conclusion about disciplinary variations in the density of citations in published RAs: a generally richer intertexuality could be observed in research writing of softer disciplines (e.g., sociology, marketing, philosophy and applied linguistics) than in that of hard disciplines (e.g., mechanical engineering and physics).

[1]"I+LR" represents an under-researched yet frequently-used structural format for the introductory phase of the RA that contains two independent sections: an Introduction section and a subsequent Literature Review section.

7.3 Citation Types

7.3.1 Citation Forms

In addition to the contrasting density of citations, variations in citation practices of research writers from the two disciplines in Introductions and LRs can also be perceived from their strategic deployment of different types of citations based on the formal and functional criteria. Table 7.2 presents the results from the analysis of citation form with related cross-disciplinary and cross-generic variations noted. With respect to the use of integral versus parenthetical citations, as might be expected, the latter is far more preferred in Introductions in both disciplines than the former while the reverse is true of the LR section in CE. In AL, although still more non-integral citations are employed in the LR section than integral ones, there is indeed a prominent increase in the use of the latter when writers proceed from the opening Introduction section to the subsequent elaborate LR.

Further, the distribution of citations across each file in the four sub-corpora also reveals a similar tendency: In CALI (the sub-corpus for the Introduction section of ERAs from AL) and CCEI (the sub-corpus for the Introduction section of ERAs from CE), the use of non-integral citations is quasi-obligatory (93.3% and 96.7% respectively) whereas 14 out of the 30 article introductions in AL and 18 out of 30 in CE do not have integral citations at all. Among the remaining 16 introductions in AL, 11 only use less than three integral citations, and this also applies to 50% of the CE introductions with the use of integral citations. In contrast, in CALL (the sub-corpus for the Literature Review section of ERAs from AL), integral citations occur in all files, and in CCEL (the sub-corpus for the Literature Review section of ERAs from CE), only CCEL1 does not contain integral citations. As many as eighteen out of the 30 article LRs in AL and nearly 50% of LRs in CE have more than ten integral citations. In contrast, the use of non-integral citations is comparatively sparse, e.g., in CCEL, there are 12 LRs with less than three occurrences of non-integral citations.

While previous research has suggested factors influencing writers' choices between the binary citation forms such as different citing systems (Swales, 1990), "the editing process and size restrictions of academic journals" (Ädel & Garretson, 2006: 278), and the length of the genre exemplars (Charles, 2006), the findings presented above could be more possibly attributed to the close link and interaction

Table 7.2 Citation forms in Introductions and LRs in AL and CE

	AL		CE	
	I	LR	I	LR
Non-integral	183 (76.3%)	588 (57%)	118 (67%)	196 (38.6%)
Integral	57 (23.8%)	444 (43%)	58 (33%)	312 (61.4%)
Integral-verb controlling	28 (11.7%)	281 (27.2%)	35 (19.9%)	240 (47.2%)
Integral-naming	28(11.7%)	133 (12.9%)	22 (12.5%)	71 (14.0%)

between the rhetorical functions of different citation forms and the respective communicative purposes of the two subgenres (viz., Introductions and LRs). As pointed out by many researchers (e.g., Clugston, 2008; Hyland, 1999; Swales, 1990, 2014; Samraj, 2013; Thompson, 2001), integral citations grant prominence to individual researchers, thereby being considered as a more convenient means to refer to and critique the specific research items, in particular those most relevant and important to the present work. The intense use of integral citations in the LR section thus comes as no surprise as this part-genre is more characterized by detailing and elaborating on individual research studies to create essential research space for the study. This is an important finding derived from my move and step analysis of this part-genre (see Chap. 6), which generally conforms to what our specialist interviewees contributed. By contrast, in many of the introductions used before the usually lengthy LR section, even though writers may still refer to prior scholarship in order to provide context for the study, usually a markedly high percentage of parenthetical citations are employed for "generalizing" the background and providing an overview of the research area (Samraj, 2008). Non-integral citations, which would not interrupt the information flow, seem more suitable to be used, considering the communicative and rhetorical needs of this section (Swales, 2014).

In terms of disciplinary variations, many previous studies (e.g., Clugston, 2008; Hyland, 1999; Mansourizadeh & Ahmad, 2011; Thompson, 2000, 2001; Thompson & Tribble, 2001) have confirmed that non-integral citations were generally more favored by scholars in hard disciplines as research writing in such disciplines is characterized by an impersonal ethos. However, this is not borne out by the present study in that applied linguists were observed to prefer using non-integral citations in both rhetorical sections and yet CE scholars much more favor using integral citations in the LR section. A plausible reason for CE professionals' contrasting use of the two citation forms in the two part-genre may be that, as CE 3 remarked, "In the LR section, the focus would be more on the individual studies, in which case you would refer to the authors explicitly whereas in the Introduction, you don't want to foreground the authors, you want to foreground the results, especially the more generalized findings in this area, or the more theoretical or the actual topic rather than the authors." However, to many applied linguists we interviewed, their choices of citation forms depend on the circumstance and the best way to make sure their own voices that could be heard (rather than the cited authors' words) is to use non-integral citations. In most of the cases, "the point people have made is more important than people who have made them. The research is more important than the researchers" (AL3). Nevertheless, they tend to use integral citations where they think the identity of the individual is important or if they regularly refer to the person's work, or if they think that they need to add variety to the reading experience. In spite of the interesting findings obtained in this study, to what extent writers' selections of citation forms may respectively reflect disciplinary influences and sub-genre discourse requirements is a question worthy of further inquiry.

As mentioned in Chap. 3, since there are only very few integral non-citations (Thompson, 2001; Thompson & Tribble, 2001)[2] identified, all integral citations were further classified based on whether they are verb-controlling or naming (Mansourizadeh & Ahmad, 2011). Table 7.2 shows that there is a much greater use of the integral verb-controlling sub-type in the LR section in both disciplines while the disparity in the quantities of verb-controlling versus naming citations in the Introduction in CE is much smaller and the number of the integral verb-controlling sub-type even equals to that of the integral naming sub-type in the Introduction in AL. This is partly in agreement with the findings of previous studies (e.g., Jalilifar, 2012; Samraj, 2013; Shooshtari & Jalilifar, 2010) that among the sub-categories preferred within integral citations, verb controlling is the most common citation, with the naming type as the second most frequent one and non-citations being very low in frequency. While Mansourizadeh and Ahmad (2011) have demonstrated that expert writers employ almost equal quantities of verb controlling and naming citations and novices use five times more verb-controlling citations than the naming type, indicating nominalization as less skilfully mastered by the emerging writers, the differences in writers' preferences over these two major sub-categories of integral citations in the part-genres of ERAs have hardly been addressed in the literature. However, the much larger number of integral verb-controlling citations employed (that usually thematize and point to the agentiveness of the cited authors) in the LR section than in the Introduction in both disciplines appears to correspond to the much denser use of RVs (Sect. 7.4) and a larger presence of authors in the LR. As for the naming type, which does not control the verb, concordance lines containing it were all examined to identify their regular patterns used in the two associated part-genres by writers of the two contrasting disciplines (see Table 7.3).

Table 7.3 indicates distinctive naming citation patterns that are more specific to the particular discipline or to the part-genre. For example, the pattern "X's (Year) hypotheses/notions/views/arguments…" is predominantly used in both rhetorical sections by applied linguists for referring to the conceptual models or key terms of others or to others' statements or research actions. In contrast, this pattern is absent in CE introductions and only occurs once in its LR section, as in:

(1) CEIS integration level constitutes the focal point of this research, and **Bhatt's (1995) definition** of enterprise system (ES) integration is utilized for CEIS integration. (CCEL30)

In CE introductions, the most frequently used pattern is "Organization name (Year)/the design guideline of Organization (Year)", referring to the profession-specific design guideline issued by some authentic organizations. Such design guidelines are commonly used in engineering fields and thus often cited in engineering research papers. Here are two examples of this pattern:

---

[2]As stated in Chaps. 2 and 3, non-citations are citations where references are made to researchers without the publication year or page. In this study, while a number of citations are identified as "extensive citations" (Swales, 1986), very few integral non-citations were found: 30 non-citations were identified in CALL and only one non-citation in the remaining three sub-corpora (viz., CALI, CCEL, and CCEI).

Table 7.3 Frequently used integral naming citation patterns in Introductions and LRs in the two disciplines

		Naming citation no.	Naming citation patterns	%
AL	I	28	**X's (Year)** hypotheses/framework/notion/proposal/admonition...	60.7
			described/reported **in X (Year)**	14.3
			including X (Year)	10.7
	LR	133	**X's (Year)** recommendation/views/argument... **X's (Year)** terms/theory/model/hypothesis/taxonomy... **X's (Year)** findings/comparison/analysis/study/work...	47.4
			proposed/reported/conducted **by X (Year)** studies/experiment/work/research **by X (Year)**	17.3
CE	I	22	**organization name (Year)/the design guideline of organization (Year)**	27.3
			work/explorations **of X (Year)**	22.7
			work/experiments **by X (Year)**	18.2
			found/documented **in X (Year)**	13.6
			including X (Year)	13.6
	LR	71	performed **by X (Year)**; evaluation/observations/analysis **by X (Year)**	36.6
			provided/found/tabulated **in X (Year)**	19.7

(2) Ten median treatments were identified across these eight states on the basis of **the AASHTO guidelines (2006)**. (CCEI24)

(3) Although design guidelines such as **ISIS (2001) and ACI 440.1R-06 (2006)** for the applications of FRP in reinforced concrete are well established, a design guideline addressing the applications of FRP in the design of reinforced masonry elements is not available in the literature. (CCEI7)

The other common patterns are those with the prepositions "of" and "by" in CE introductions, by means of which CE writers make reference to the research activities of other researchers. This is supported by the examples given in Table 7.3. The finding generally accords with what has been revealed in Thompson (2001: 121) about disciplinary preferences over the use of naming citation patterns: different from Agricultural Economics theses where the pattern "in X (Year)" is clearly much more favoured for referring to a book, in Agricultural Botany (the same as CE being a hard discipline) theses, "of X (Year)" and "by X (Year)" are more often used to indicate the research techniques, procedures or activities of other scientists. Therefore, it is not surprising that, in this study, "in X (Year)" which also refers to a book or an RA occurs second in the rank of the most frequent naming citation patterns in AL introductions. There is also a clear disposition towards this pattern in both sections of CE ERAs. As such, significant disciplinary variations in the use of this pattern are not revealed in the present study.

Despite much consistency in writers' preferences over the use of naming citation patterns in these two neighbouring sections at the outset of the ERA (e.g., the pattern "X's (Year) hypotheses/arguments…" favoured in both CALI and CALL and the pattern "by X (Year)" and "in X (Year)" preferred by CE writers in both part-genres), the pattern "by X (Year)" is far more frequently used in the LR section than in the Introduction section in both disciplines. In this pattern "by X (Year)", "the overall focus is on the work of particular researchers" (Jalilifar, 2012: 34). Thus, writers' preferential use of this pattern in the LR section might also suggest to some extent that more substantial, detailed reviews of individual studies are often shifted to LRs (see Chap. 6). Other naming citation patterns used with much lower frequency in Introductions and LRs are also identified in this study, e.g., "According to X (Year)", "Following X (Year)", "For X (Year)", and the free-standing noun phrase "X (Year)".

7.3.2 Citation Functions

This sub-section presents and discusses the findings about the quantitative and qualitative similarities and differences in writers' use of rhetorical functions of citations and their patterns in the Introduction and LR sections of AL and CE ERAs.

Table 7.4 shows the frequency and the proportional use of each citation function in the two part-genres. As can be seen from the table, in all 191, 578, 301 and 1312 citation functions were identified in the four sub-corpora (viz., CCEI, CCEL, CALI and CALL) respectively. In terms of the use of different types of citation functions, in both Introduction and LR sections in the two disciplines, a considerable number of citations are employed for the basic attribution purpose and thus retelling and presenting the existing framework of the knowledge of the field (Mansourizadeh & Ahmad, 2011; Petrić, 2007). This finding is not surprising as *attribution* has been documented in the literature as the "unmarked, most common and rhetorically the simplest" function (Petrić, 2007: 247) and matches with some common communicative purposes of the two part-genres (e.g., provide research background for the study to be advanced and display the knowledge of the field).

However, the cross-generic differences in functional use of citations mainly lie in the fact that, in the LR section, expert writers refer to the work of others for a greater variety of complex non-attribution rhetorical purposes (most typically *exemplification*, *support*, and *comparison and contrast between/among sources*) to a larger extent, in contrast to their apparently more frequent use of citations for the functions of *example* and *generalization from multiple sources* in its preceding Introduction section. Specifically, the data show that the LR sections in CE papers feature five times more citations with the function of *exemplification* (46.2% as compared with 8.9% in CE introductions) and those in AL ERAs also use a higher percentage of this rhetorical function (13.9% as compared with 3.7% in AL introductions). In stark contrast, CE introductions use two times higher percentage of Example citations (34% as compared with 12.8% in CE LRs) and AL introductions show a much higher proportion of citations used for the function of *example* as well (32.2% as compared

Table 7.4 Citation functions in Introductions and Literature Reviews in CE and AL

	Cit. functions	CCEI	CCEL	CALI	CALL
Rhetorically simpler cit. functions	Attribution	63 33.0%	125 21.6%	55 18.3%	312 23.8%
	Further reference	3 1.6%	7 1.2%	25 8.3%	61 4.6%
	Example	65 34%	74 12.8%	97 32.2%	247 18.8%
	Origin	0 0%	7 1.2%	20 6.6%	73 5.6%
	Identification	3 1.6%	7 1.2%	11 3.7%	15 1.1%
Rhetorically complex cit. functions	Exemplification	17 8.9%	267 46.2%	11 3.7%	182 13.9%
	Support	7 3.7%	32 5.5%	32 10.6%	216 16.5%
	Generalization from multiple sources	29 15.2%	30 5.2%	27 9.0%	47 3.6%
	Comparison and contrast between/among sources	1 0.5%	24 4.2%	10 3.3%	115 8.8%
	Statement of use	2 1.0%	1 0.2%	6 2.0%	22 1.7%
	Application	0 0%	0 0%	0 0%	2 0.2%
	Evaluation	0 0%	1 0.2%	4 1.3%	17 1.3%
	Comparison of one's study with other sources	1 0.5%	1 0.2%	2 0.7%	0 0%
	Total	191	578	301	1312

with 18.8% in AL LRs). The pair of citation functions, *Example* and *Exemplification*, as illustrated in Chap. 3, differ on the one hand in that they are respectively manifested in non-integral citations (for space-saving and being conciseness) and integral citations (for further elaboration and providing illustrative or evidential support) for most of the cases. This shows to some extent the interaction between the forms of citations and their functions. On the other hand, a closer examination of the data reveals that they differ in their use combined with other rhetorical functions forming distinctive patterns of functional use of citations in the two part-genres, which fit for the communicative purposes or functional foci of Introductions and LRs respectively.

Two distinctive citation functional patterns associated with this pair of rhetorical functions (i.e., "Example" and "Exemplification") frequently used in the Introduction and LR section respectively are listed below with illustrations by two authentic extracts in CE. It is commonly seen in the LR section in both disciplines, when reviewing the literature of the field, a statement generalized from multiple sources encapsulated in parentheses is firstly put forward, followed by elaborate reviews of the most relevant and important individual studies as evidential support or verification by using a number of RVs (see Extract 4). However, in the Introduction section, the background statement is often constructed with a non-reporting non-integral citing style (Extract 5). There seems to be a process proceeding from generality to specificity in the "I+LR" introductory phase with the citation style shifting from "parenthetical plonking" to "intertextual storytelling" (Swales, 2014).[3] As shown in Extract (4), the first sentence is a theme statement of the paragraph with a multi-reference non-integral citation used where a number of examples of studies (the *example* function) are listed to which the theme statement could be attributed to (the function *generalization from multiple sources*). Then, more details are provided about individual studies (the function *exemplification*) that might have been listed as the example studies in the Generalization citation in the foregoing theme statement, e.g., Sposito and Johnston (1998) in Extract (4). In exemplifying and justifying the theme statement (the function *support*), comparison of the findings of individual studies (the function *comparison and contrast between/among sources*) is possibly made to establish links between or among them, as marked by the adverb "similarly" in this extract.

In LR:

"Generalization" (with *example*) + "Exemplification" (often with *support* + *compare and contrast between/among sources*)

(4) The installation and maintenance of cable barriers has been shown to be less expensive than a similar installation of concrete barriers or w-beam median barriers **(Sposito and Johnston 1998; Sheikh et al. 2008; Albin et al. 2001; Outcalt 2004; Chandler 2007; Marzougui et al. 2007)**. **McClanahan et al. (2004) indicated** that when considering the cost of each available median barrier per foot, w-beam is about twice, precast concrete is about three times, single sloped concrete barriers are about five times, and castin-place concrete is about 10 times more expensive than cable barriers. **Similarly, Sposito and Johnston (1998),** when considering a 30-year life span of concrete and cable barriers, **concluded** that unless cable barriers exceeded approximately $3,900/km in maintenance costs per year, cable barriers are far more cost-effective…. (CCEL24)

In contrast, in the Introduction preceding the LR section (or called the prologue-style opening section), a frequently used citation functional pattern is "Generalization" + "Example" for providing an overview of the research area without the details of individual studies mentioned, as shown in Extract (5) below. This is consistent with our interviewees' accounts and the findings of the genre study of the two sections

[3] According to Swales (2014: 135), "parenthetical plonking" refers to the non-reporting non-integral citing style, where the attributed references are encapsulated within the parentheses and no reporting verbs are used. Swales found that this citation patterning was prevalently used when student writers accounted for the background related to the main arguments. This is in contrast to "intertextual storytelling", another distinct citing style with however much more frequent use of various RVs and integral citations to detail and critique specific studies in the field.

(see Chap. 6) that a main purpose of the Introduction with a subsequent LR section is to provide a setting or general context for the study rather than reviewing specifically the most important individual studies as in the LR section. Therefore, the frequent use of the two featured contrasting citation functional patterns in the two sections conforms to their respective communicative purposes or functional foci.

In Introduction:
"Generalization"+"Example"

(5) **In general**, construction-site defects result in rework costs of up to 6-12% of construction costs (**Josephson and Hammarlund 1999; Patterson and Ledbetter 1989**). (CCEI1)

Another point worth mentioning is that, among Support citations, those for justifying the significance of the research topic is more often used in the Introduction section (usually in the non-integral citation form, as shown in Example (17) in Chap. 3) whereas others for justifying or providing pillars for the findings or claims or methods of previous studies (see Example (18) in Chap. 3) are usually employed in the LR section. Very few Support citations for justifying the findings or claims of the present study were found in the present data, perhaps because such citations are more common in the Results and Discussion section where the significance of the findings of the study should be discussed in light of the existing literature (Mansourizadeh & Ahmad, 2011). This also explains writers' limited use of citations for *comparison of one's study with other sources* in both sections of the opening phase of the ERA (see Table 7.4). As such, distinguishing different types of Support citations according to in which part of the ERA they are most commonly used is helpful to academic writing by novice scholars.

In addition to Support citations for justifying the findings/arguments/methods of previous studies, Comparison and Contrast citations for explicating similarities or differences in the findings or claims of previous research are also far more common in the LR section. This reflects the greater importance of establishing various specific links or relationship between/among sources in the LR section than in the preceding Introduction section that places more emphasis on a general mapping out of the area and the presentation of the study to be undertaken.

In all, the more common use of Generalization citations and Example citations in the Introduction section for packing sources into a general statement in contrast to that of Exemplification citations, Comparison and Contrast citations, and Support citations in the LR section for expounding on previous individual studies and unfolding their interrelationship may indicate the greater information density and content specificity and complexity of the latter part-genre. A final noteworthy point concerning cross-generic variations is that far more multi-functional citations are distributed in the LR section than in the Introduction, which also suggests that citations are used in rhetorically and functionally more complex ways in the LR section. All the findings presented above on the distinct functional use of citations and citation patterns in these two neighbouring sections traditionally regarded as containing the element of reviewing literature render readers a better understanding of their communicative functions, especially those of the LR section, an underexplored part-genre of the RA.

With respect to cross-disciplinary variations in the functional use of citations in the two sections, applied linguists favour using citations for the functions of *further reference, origin, support* and *evaluation* than their CE colleagues. While the reason for AL scholars' preference for the use of Further Reference citations as compared to their CE colleagues is unclear, their more frequent employment of Origin citations, Support citations and Evaluation citations in both Introduction and LR sections may embody the more discursive nature and the particular ethos of their discipline. As shown in the following extracts, Origin citations either in the integral naming form (Thompson, 2001; Thompson & Tribble, 2001) or the non-integral form that are used in AL introductory parts are usually associated with the indication of the originator of theoretical constructs or concepts in the field of (second) language teaching and research. By contrast, Origin citations used in CE introductory parts more often suggest the creator of an engineering technique or research equation, as illustrated in Extract (14) in Chap. 3. In this sense, the different use of Origin citations in the two disciplines manifests the disparate disciplinary nature, objects of study and research content.

(6) ...which is based on **Engestrom's (1987) expanded activity system**... (CALI14)

(7) ...personal agency beliefs, which in educational psychology are embodied in two constructs: **self-efficacy beliefs (Bandura 1986)** and **self-concept (Shavelson et al. 1976)**... (CALL11)

(8) In the field of L2 motivation, the best known parallel of personal agency beliefs is **the L2 'Motivational Self System Theory'** proposed by **Dornyei (2005)**... (CALL11)

Twenty-one instances of occurrence of Evaluation citations in AL introductory phases in contrast to the only single instance of it in CE introductory part, together with the much more frequent employment of Support citations for providing various justifications in both sections of AL than in those of CE seem to corroborate the inferences of previous researchers (e.g., Hyland, 1999, 2002; Thompson, 2001, 2005): more discursive social science disciplines such as AL are more reliant on argumentative support drawn from various sources whereas hard disciplines such as CE are dependent on factual support to a greater extent. The following excerpts illustrate a typical use of negative evaluation citations in AL introductory phases for critiquing previous works and creating research space for the present study (Swales, 1990). Despite that, the majority of Evaluation citations used in the present data in both disciplines are those expressing positive evaluative voices as illustrated in Extract (23) in Chap. 3. This is generally in line with our subject informants' view that they prefer taking positive or neutral stance towards the reported content to establish allegiance to the community and harmonious relationship with other members. Expressing negative citing voices towards others is a cautious yet rare choice in their perceptions and there are other choices for creating research space for the study. In addition, a number of interviewees emphasized that they are engaging with new research areas where there is indeed not much existing research to be critiqued.

(9) However, one **limitation** of the Hirsh and Nation study was that the texts used were novels written for teenagers and adolescents... (CALL18)

(10) However, these studies, in which native speakers made offline judgement concerning the gravity of learner errors, have been **criticized** for **being subjective** and producing **inconclusive** results (Ellis 1994: 67; Ellis and Barkhuizen 2005: 67). (CALL7)

In the present data, citations are rarely used for other rhetorical functions such as *statement of use, comparison of one's study with other sources* and *application*, and thus there is not much cross-generic and cross-disciplinary difference in using citations for such rhetorical purposes.

7.4 Reporting Verbs (RVs)

7.4.1 Distribution of RVs in Introductions and LRs in AL and CE

Another textual feature in citation use to be examined is the choice of RVs. Before closely studying published writers' use of different categories of RVs regarding their denotation and evaluation in the two contrasting yet related part-genres (viz., Introductions and LRs), we firstly compare their distribution (in them) in AL and CE ERAs.

For the present 131,243-word corpus comprising introductions and LRs from ERAs of two disciplines, altogether 1946 RV tokens and 301 RV types were found. This suggests that a wide variety of RVs is densely employed in the introductory part consisting of the two rhetorical sections, in view of the fact that over 400 different RVs were found in Hyland's (1999) 500,000-word corpus of published RAs from eight disciplines and over 700 different RVs in Ädel and Garretson's (2006) 600,000-word corpus of upper-level student papers.

Table 7.5 demonstrates the different quantities of RVs distributed in the four sub-corpora with the top ten most frequently used RVs along with their frequencies outlined. As displayed in this table, far more RVs are employed in the LR section than in its preceding Introduction in both disciplines. After the frequency of occurrences of RVs have been standardized per 1000 words, it is found that the quantity of RVs used in CE LRs is three times larger than that of RVs employed in CE introductions. Although the gap between the standardized number of RVs used in AL LRs and that of RVs in AL introductions is not that large, a denser use of RVs is still found in AL LRs.

Further analysis reveals that in a number of introductions, no RVs are used, whereas all LRs in both disciplines contain RVs. Specifically, around one third of the 30 CE introductions (CE1, 2, 8, 11, 12, 19, 20, 27, 29) do not have any RVs and the other six CE introductions (CE7, 13, 14, 16, 22, 28) only contain one RV. All these introductions except CE8 are either Orientation-type introductions without the functional element of "reviewing items of previous research" as suggested in the traditional CARS model (Swales, 1990) or the PS introductions that mainly addresses a problem in the real world rather than a niche in the existing research. Therefore, little

Table 7.5 Distribution of RVs in CALI, CALL, CCEI and CCEL

Sub-corpora	Frequency of RVs	Standardized frequency of RVs (per 1000 words)	No. of files with RV use	Top-ranking RVs (starting with most frequent)
CALI	176	10.6	27	suggest (8), argue (7), propose (7), find (7), use (7), show (7), describe (6), investigate (6), focus on (6), report (5)
CALL	984	14.8	30	suggest (56), find (52), show (50), use (38), argue (36), examine (32), propose (30), report (25), investigate (21), define (19)
CCEI	106	6.3	21	use (15), propose (7), find (5), identify (5), show (4), observe (4), suggest (4), investigate (3), indicate (3), document (3)
CCEL	680	22.2	30	use (89), find (56), suggest (25), conclude (23), propose (22), report (19), show (19), develop (18), test (17), investigate (14), estimate (14)

Note The figures within the brackets in the last column indicate the frequency of occurrences of each top-ranking RV.

review of previous studies can be found in these introductions with no essential need to use RVs. In AL, three out of the 11 Orientation introductions (AL9, 15, 24) and the only "Building on the Writers' Own Previous Research" introduction (AL14) do not contain any RVs and a few Orientation introductions only have one RV. As our genre-based structural analysis in Chap. 6 reveals, all the 60 introductions embody functional and structural variability when they are used with a subsequent elaborate LR section and many detailed reviews of previous literature have been shifted to the LR section where the denser use of RVs is found. This is also confirmed by our interviewees who generally considered the respective major communicative purposes of Introductions and LRs as providing an overview of the area or the problem, and contextualizing and positioning the present study by selectively and critically reviewing the existing research of the field.

Also, the applied nature of the two disciplines can affect the quantities of RVs used by writers. According to the website of the International Association for Applied Linguistics (AILA), AL is "an interdisciplinary field of research and practice dealing with practical problems of language and communication". CE as a long-established professional engineering discipline dealing with the design, construction and maintenance of buildings, dams, bridges, tunnels, highways and other structures is also clearly of an applied nature (Wood, 2012). Therefore, among the 60 introductions, a considerable number of them (most typically the PS introductions in CE) highlight a practical problem to be solved by providing the real-world background and possibly briefly outlining how the problem will be examined rather than creating research space for the study through a critical review of the research literature. This partly explains the smaller number of RVs used in the introductions compared to the LR section that is commonly an integrated and substantial review of previous studies.

Table 7.5 also lists the most commonly used RVs in the Introduction and LR sections of AL and CE ERAs. In contrast to writers' distinctive choices of RVs across the hard-soft discipline divide as suggested by previous research (e.g., Hyland, 1999, 2002), the present study found that six out of the ten most common RVs are shared by AL and CE writers when they construct the introductory phase of ERAs. The six verbs include: two RVs implying previously established knowledge (*show* and *find*), another two discourse verbs of tentativity indicating inferences or conclusions cautiously raised by the cited author(s) but without signaling writers' evaluative stance (*suggest* and *propose*), and the other two Research Acts RVs reporting objectively general research actions of AL and CE scholars (*use* and *investigate*). This suggests that there may exist a large set of RVs that can be ascribed to general academic writing rather than being discipline-bound. Identifying RV items of this nature is important to the common EAP writing classrooms where the instruction modules are usually oriented to postgraduate students with varied disciplinary background.

On the other hand, the use of some particular RVs is also worth noting as it either embodies the contrasting nature of the two disciplines or is specially associated with some typical functional moves of the rhetorical section. For example, *argue* is commonly used in both rhetorical sections in AL; however, it falls outside the "top ten" in both sections of CE ERAs. This generally accords with findings from previous RV studies that have examined similar disciplines: Ädel and Garretson (2006) noted that *argue* as a "soft" verb is important in sociology, philosophy and linguistics; likewise, Hyland (1999, 2002) observed that it is one of the most frequently used RVs in social science RAs (including AL ones) but not in RAs from science and engineering disciplines such as biology, electronic engineering, mechanical engineering and physics. While *use* is identified as a common RV in all the four sub-corpora in this study, it is especially prevalent in both sections of CE ERAs. As many as 89 (nearly 60% of) *use* are employed in CE LRs in relation to equations, functions and other measurement techniques, which may be a stylistic feature of the engineering discourse, as in:

> (11) Zhang and Wu (2006) **used** data from the Mississippi NTPEP test deck to estimate the service life of durable tapes, 3-year waterborne paints, preformed thermoplastic, and thermoplastic pavement markings. Autoregressive integrated moving average (ARIMA) and spline fitting approaches were **used** to predict PMR as a function of time (age in months). **Using** the first 18 months of retroreflectivity data, the models were **used** to forecast the retroreflectivity at 21 and 24 months. … Additionally, the data **used** in the analysis were from transverse pavement markings **applied** at a test deck location… (CCEL22)

What is also interesting is that the top ten most frequently used RVs in the four sub-corpora are mostly Research Acts RVs and Discourse Acts RVs and only *focus on* and *estimate* are two Mental Acts RVs respectively identified in CALI and CCEL. While *focus on* is generally used by applied linguists to indicate their research targets, *estimate* is often used in connection with simulations, models and equations in CE discourse. This is shown in the following examples:

(12) Both Slaouti and Warschauer **focus on** the earlier version of the web, which they view as "an enormous database, a world-wide library" (Slaouti, 2002, p. 112), characterised by a content-based, one-way interaction with the user. (CALI20)

(13) Kopf (2004) collected PMR data using a mobile retroreflectometer along roadways with longitudinal markings in Washington State. Separate models of PMR were **estimated** for different regions of the state to control for environmental effects. Models based on different pavement marking colors (yellow or white) and traffic volume levels were also **estimated**. (CCEL22)

7.4.2 Different Types of RVs Used in the Two Part-Genres in AL and CE

This section outlines cross-disciplinary and cross-generic variations in the use of different categories of RVs in terms of their denotation and evaluative potential. Table 7.6 presents the results from the comparison of proportional use of four types of RVs according to their denotative meaning. As can be seen, there were substantial variations between the two disciplines in writers' of choices of RVs in both sections. Research Acts RVs are uniformly predominantly used in both Introductions and LRs in CE; however, while Discourse Acts RVs is observed as the most frequently used category in AL introductions, a slightly higher percentage of Research Acts RVs (as opposed to Discourse Acts RVs) are employed in AL LR sections. The results partly confirm those of Hyland (1999, 2000, 2002) and Thompson (2001) who reported writers' clear preferential use of Discourse Acts RVs in soft disciplines (including AL), in contrast to that of Research Acts RVs in hard disciplines (e.g., physics and electronic engineering). Hyland (1999, 2002) attributed this relatively clear division of denotative categories (that largely corresponds to the traditional division of disciplines into the soft and hard disciplines) to different epistemologies, values, and knowledge structure of the disciplines. As he further explicated, more rhetorical efforts are entailed in the more discursive soft disciplines where knowledge development does not proceed along a linear line but a "more reiterative and recursive"

Table 7.6 Classification of RVs in the four sub-corpora according to their denotative meaning

Sub-corpora	Research Acts	Discourse Acts	Cognition Acts	Stative
CALI	60 (34.1%)	80 (45.5%)	31 (17.6%)	5 (2.8%)
CALL	485 (49.3%)	413 (42%)	80 (8.1%)	6 (0.6%)
CCEI	68 (64.2%)	31 (29.2%)	7 (6.6%)	0 (0%)
CCEL	448 (65.9%)	169 (24.9%)	60 (8.8%)	3 (0.4%)

route (Hyland, 1999: 353). Consequently, in making knowledge claims or in highlighting significance or value of the study, a greater interpretation of the literature and a greater extent of contextualization are often needed for such disciplines. In contrast, in hard disciplines where there is a tradition of linear progression of knowledge, research proceeds along a well-defined path and more shared assumptions allow researchers to rely to a smaller extent on inter-textual warrants and interpretive arguments. As such, Discourse Acts RVs are presumably used more often in academic discourse of soft disciplines rather than that of hard disciplines. Thompson reached similar conclusions from his comparative analysis of RV use in 16 Ph.D. theses in an applied science (Agricultural Botany) and a social science (Agricultural and Food Economics): a more discursive discipline dealing mainly with interpretations will use Discourse Acts RVs predominantly, whereas a discipline grounding its research programme in experimental research in an empiricist paradigm will use more Research Acts RVs.

However, as noted above, similarly focusing on RAs, the present study and Hyland (1999, 2000, 2002) have yielded somewhat different findings about applied linguists' preferences over denotative categories of RVs in their writing. This may be explained by taking into consideration the different nature of the RAs compiled. Whereas Hyland's (1999, 2000, 2002) corpus comprised both theoretical and applied RAs, the RA Introductions and LRs under analysis in the current study were all drawn from ERAs. Consequently, applied linguists were found to use Research Acts RVs and Discourse Acts RVs to a similar extent (especially in the LR section) in this study.

In terms of cross-generic variations, a closer analysis reveals that in the Introduction section, Research Acts RVs used are more of indicating general research actions such as *investigate*, *study*, *research*, and *examine,* while in the LR section, a greater number of Research Acts RVs denoting specific research procedures or activities are employed, such as *calculate, measure, appraise, synthesize, theorize, compile,* and *recalibrate*. This implies that more details of relevant individual studies are reviewed in the LR section rather than in the Introduction.

The expert informants in our study generally subscribed to the position that writers' preferential use of denotative categories of RVs is closely related to the nature of the disciplines they belong to and what kind of research work they need to conduct to fit the needs of the study (e.g., "hypothesizing" that entails considerable guesswork and thus the use of Cognition Acts RVs). However, they all admitted that they would use only a few Cognition Acts RVs in the introductory phase of ERAs because: firstly, both AL and CE are more empirical fields, which attach greater importance to empirical evidence, actions and observations rather than personal views or conjectures; further, it is more likely that they would use Cognition Acts RVs in the Discussion (rather than in the introductory phase of ERAs) that more often involves reasoning for argumentation: "I perhaps use more Mental RVs in where I am discussing my findings and then say, 'Hunston considers this…'. They reflect on something more there…", as remarked by one of our interviewees (AL1). This is also confirmed by the result of our textual analysis, as illustrated in Table 7.5, that much lower incidences[4] of occurrence of Cognition Acts RVs were found in both sections in both disciplines compared to the two dominant denotative categories used (i.e., Research Acts RVs and Discourse Acts RVs). However, a noticeable feature in the use of Cognition Acts RVs in the Introduction preceding the LR section is that without detailing individual studies, research writers often employ Cognition Acts RVs such as *see, recognize* and *consider* together with the multiple-reference non-integral citations to report the consensus views of the entire disciplinary discourse community or of at least a group of researchers in the field, as in:

> (14) Transportation planners **have begun to recognize** carsharing as a potentially important component of a diversified and sustainable transport system (Enoch and Taylor 2006; Goldman and Gorham 2006; Parent 2006; Wright and Curtis 2004). (CCEI28)
>
> (15)…In contrast, other accounts **see** no necessary grammatical deficit for adult learners and argue that morphological realization problems are due to various other factors, such as default inflection (Bruhn de Garavito & White, 2002; White, 2003b; White et al., 2004) or difficulties in mapping grammatical features to Phonetic Form (Lardiere, 2000) or (re)assembling features in the L2 (Lardiere 2007, 2008). (CALI25)

Finally, the new category proposed in this study "Stative RVs" are also in a minority. As mentioned earlier, previous studies (e.g., Hyland, 1999, 2002; Lang, 2004; Mur-Dueñas, 2009; Thomas & Hawes, 1994; Thompson, 2001; Thompson & Ye, 1991) focus on RVs denoting dynamic research activities of various nature (i.e., mental, discourse and research) and yet have hardly addressed RVs reporting the state (existence, development, etc.) of phenomena, theories or other issues. Therefore, to give readers a greater sense of this largely overlooked category, two instances found in the sub-corpora are offered below:

> (16) Bardovi-Harlig and Dornyei's (1998) study **involved** the following samples: 370 Hungarian EFL learners in Hungary, 173 ESL learners in the United States, 25 Hungarian teachers of English, 28 American teachers of English, and 112 Italian elementary school teachers enrolled in an English training program. (CALL1)
>
> (17) The relatively few studies that **do exist** (e.g., Cooper, 1999; Liontas, 2002) seem to confirm that it is especially the more semantically opaque idioms that pose interpretability problems for L2 readers, and, as these more core idioms are relatively rare (Grant & Nation, 2006), Nation (2006) could be right in attenuating their significance in reading comprehension. (CALL18)

One last point worth mentioning here is that, as observed from the present data, this category (viz., Stative RVs) often implies both the citing writers' non-factive evaluative stance and the source authors' neutral attitude towards the reported information. However, in Example (17), the emphatic "do" together with the Stative RV "exist" indeed imply writers' strong commitment to the cited proposition (i.e., the existence of the relatively few studies such as Cooper (1999) and Liontas (2002) confirming

---

[4]Despite 17% of RVs in the sub-corpus CALI identified as Cognition Acts RVs, a much higher percentage than those found in the other three sub-corpora, the quantity of Cognition Acts RVs used is still quite small compared to Research Acts RVs and Discourse Acts RVs in the four sub-corpora.

that especially the more semantically opaque idioms pose interpretability problems for L2 readers).

Table 7.7 displays a clear dispersion of different categories of RVs respectively from writers' and authors' evaluative perspectives in the four sub-corpora. As might be expected, in both disciplines, writers prefer not showing directly their evaluative stance by using extensively Writer Non-factive RVs. This featured use of RVs is also revealed in a considerable number of existing studies (e.g., Hyland, 1999, 2000, 2002; Mur-Dueñas, 2009; Swales, 2014) focusing on quite varied disciplines. Swales (2014: 125) interpreted it as evidence that writers may not perceive findings from the literature "as necessarily valid but subject them to different intratextual reassessment". While realizing that there is a need to create research space for their studies, our expert informants insisted on the view that the niche creation is not completely embedded within the choices of RVs and there are many other choices, e.g., the first person pronoun, which can be an alternative strong marker of creating the niche (AL1). Instead, they often tend to ascribe an attitude to authors.

In addition to the overwhelming use of nonfactives, Table 7.7 also shows that writers tend to use more RVs that are factive rather than counter-factive. Generally, it may indicate that writers prefer referencing others' works by using RVs that are neutral and factive to create the context for the study, highlight the significance of this field, and establish solidarity with other members within the disciplinary community.

(18) Fly ash **has been shown** to effectively stabilize soft inorganic soils (Ferguson 1993; Acosta et al. 2003; Prabakar et al. 2004; Bin-Shafique et al. 2004; Trzebiatowski et al. 2005)… (CCEI14)

(19) In the field of language-learning motivation, Noels (2001) also **identified** intrinsic language-learning goals… (CALL11)

(20) Bacha (2001) **examined** timed essays written primarily by native Arabic speakers and **found** that, out of five different categories… (CALL13)

(21) Chapuis (2004) **demonstrated** that Eq. (6) provides better estimates of hydraulic conductivity for natural sands and glass beads… (CCEL15)

In stark contrast, only few Writer Counter-factive RVs were used, as indicated in Table 7.7. Hyland (1999: 361) underscored the "detached and impartial reporting

Table 7.7 Classification of RVs in the four sub-corpora according to their evaluative functions

Sub-corpora	Writer Factive	Writer Non-factive	Writer Counter-factive	Author Positive	Author Neutral	Author Tentative	Author Critical
CALI	28 (15.9%)	146 (83%)	2 (1.1%)	56 (31.8%)	91 (51.7%)	25 (14.2%)	4 (2.3%)
CALL	198 (20.1%)	776 (78.9%)	10 (1%)	309 (31.4%)	538 (54.7%)	126 (12.8%)	11 (1.1%)
CCEI	15 (14.2%)	90 (84.9%)	1 (0.9%)	25 (23.6%)	64 (60.4%)	16 (15.1%)	1 (0.9%)
CCEL	99 (14.6%)	580 (85.3%)	1 (0.1%)	160 (23.5%)	430 (63.2%)	90 (13.2%)	0 (0%)

style" of scientific and engineering academic discourse in relation to this. Nevertheless, in the present study, both our CE and AL informants conveyed their reluctance to use RVs to indicate negative critiques for not threatening others' face in public:

> Some people really get hurt if you criticize them in the public, although you say you make academic inquiry… (AL7)
>
> It's a good way of making academic enemies writing that kind of stuff, you know, saying something negative in the public. (AL4)

From authors' perspectives, there is also little cross-disciplinary and cross-generic difference in the proportional use of different categories of RVs (Table 7.7), though CE scholars hardly used any Author Critical RVs and yet their AL counterparts employed a few (e.g., *criticize, overlook, refute, lament,* and *question*). The only instance of Author Critical RVs used in the Introduction section of CE ERAs is provided below:

> (22) Casas (2007) applies the concept of accessibility to the case of individuals with disabilities in the Buffalo-Niagara region. Her research identifies…but she is cognizant that her method **ignores** time-budget and space-time constraints, issues to be addressed in this paper. (CCEI25)

Another finding is that AL writers used around 8% more RVs to indicate authors' positive evaluation of the reported proposition in both Introduction and LR sections than CE writers whereas CE scholars employed around 8% more RVs to suggest authors' neutral attitude in both sections than their AL counterparts. However, they make use of RVs to suggest authors' tentative evaluative forces to a very similar extent. Compared with CE, where researchers may assume relatively more common ground with less rhetorical need to demonstrate the reliability and relevance of previous studies using RVs, AL is a social science discipline that perhaps involves more discursive and interpretive arguments to convince readers the value of the study and of this field in general (Hyland, 1999, 2002). In other words, generally speaking, the "personality" of academics seems to play a marginal role in choosing RVs to express (explicitly or implicitly) appropriate evaluative stances towards the referenced works; instead, they would consider more what is accepted and valued by their own disciplinary discourse communities and the rhetorical need that matches with or is imposed to some degree by the communicative purposes of the particular genres or part-genres that are under construction. This is generally endorsed by our interviewees, who discussed substantially disciplinary identity and value (Hyland, 2012) and conformity to discourse community rather than individuality.

7.5 Summary

In this chapter, citation use in the introductory phase consisting of both the Introduction and the LR section from AL and CE ERAs has been examined. The cross-disciplinary and cross-generic comparison of citation density, the use of different types of citation regarding the functional and formal criteria, and the use of RVs concerning their denotative meaning and evaluative forces has yielded the following major findings:

1. In terms of citation density, while the numbers of citations used per 1,000 words in the LR section in AL and CE are quite similar, that in the Introduction of AL ERAs is clearly larger than that in the Introduction section of CE ERAs. The density of citations in the entire introductory phase in AL is also much higher than that in CE. These findings generally indicate applied linguists' greater reliance on referencing others' works to contextualize and justify the study at the outset of the paper than their CE counterparts.

Regarding cross-generic variations, a higher level of citation density was found in the LR section than in the Introduction in both disciplines and the difference is clearly larger in CE. This is not surprising as there is greater information density and content specificity with much use of citations in the LR section. The role of reviewing literature by using references is downplayed in the Introduction when it is followed by a substantial LR section. This suggests the possible shift of some communicative functions/purposes between the two part-genres. Therefore, most prominently, the element of "reviewing items of previous research" (Swales, 1990), once being obligatory to the conventional CARS-type introductions, is often shifted to its subsequent elaborate LR section, as also confirmed by our genre-based analysis of the two sections in Chap. 6. While a portion of the content element in the Introduction has been moved to the following LR section, communicative functional foci of this section may be changed: it mainly aims to identify a research issue/problem in a concise manner with perhaps a general context outlined, and then present the study, an insightful view shared by our expert informants in both disciplines.

2. The types of citations used do differ in the two rhetorical sections. In the Introduction section in both disciplines, non-integral citations are overwhelmingly employed. In contrast, in the LR section in CE, integral citations are much more favored; while a little higher percentage of non-integral citations (as opposed to integral ones) are used in AL LRs, there is a marked increase in the use of integral citations when AL writers proceed from the opening Introduction to the subsequent LR section. The findings may be attributed to the close link between the rhetorical functions of the binary citation forms and the respective communicative functions (or functional foci) of the two part-genres (viz., Introductions and LRs).

With respect to cross-disciplinary variations, parenthetical citations are preferred in both sections of AL ERAs, whereas integral citations are more favored in CE LRs, in contrast to non-integral ones preferred in CE introductions. Among the subcategories preferred within integral citations, verb controlling is the most common citation in CALL, CCEI and CCEL, even though the same percentages of the verb-controlling sub-type and the naming sub-type are employed in CALI. Regarding the naming sub-type, regular patterns are identified in the four sub-corpora. A comparison of the use of these patterns reveals the contrasting nature of the two disciplines and the featured content and functional elements involved in the particular part-genre.

3. Cross-generic and cross-disciplinary variations in the functional use of citations are also identified and discussed. Cross-generic variations mainly lie in the fact that in the LR section, expert writers refer to the work of others for a greater variety of complex non-attribution rhetorical purposes (most typically *exemplification*, *support*, and *comparison and contrast between/among sources*) to a larger extent, in contrast to their apparently more frequent use of citations for the functions of *example* and *generalization from multiple sources* in its preceding Introduction section. Two prominent citation functional patterns associated with the contrasting pair of functions (viz., *example* vs. *exemplification*) have been identified for the Introduction and LR section respectively. Concerning cross-disciplinary variations in the functional use of citations in these two part-genres, applied linguists favour using citations for the functions of *further reference, origin, support* and *evaluation* than their CE colleagues. Cross-generic and cross-disciplinary variations in the functional use of citations are accounted for mainly in the light of the communicative functions of the two partly analogous part-genres and the contrasting disciplinary nature, value, culture, history and tradition.
4. Considerable differences are also found in the density and the use of different types of RVs in the Introduction and LR sections of CE and AL ERAs. A much greater number of RVs are used in the LR section than in Introduction in both disciplines. This could be explained by the applied nature of the two disciplines (where the PS introductions have been identified in CE with little review of the research literature provided) and by the influence the use of an elaborate LR section may bring to its preceding Introduction section. Six out of the ten top-ranking RVs identified are shared in the four sub-corpora, which suggests that a considerable number of RVs may not be discipline-bound and part-genre-bound, and can characterize research writing in general sense. The use of some other particular RVs reflects disciplinary nature, e.g., *argue* as a common RV in both rhetorical sections of AL ERAs and *use* predominantly employed in CE discourse.

A relatively complex picture is revealed for the use of denotative categories of RVs. In CCEI and CCEL, Research Acts RVs are uniformly identified as the most frequently used category. However, in AL, while a little higher percentage of Discourse Acts RVs are employed in its Introduction section than Research Acts RVs, the latter turns out to be the most frequently used category in its LR section. In addition to disciplinary influence, the findings can be accounted for by the fact that the introductions and LRs analyzed in this study were all drawn from ERAs (entailing more use of Research Acts RVs in AL LRs). Concerning cross-generic variations, in the Introduction section, Research Acts RVs used are mostly those indicating general research actions (e.g., *investigate*, *study, research*, and *examine*), while in the LR section, a greater number of Research Acts RVs denoting specific research procedures or activities are employed, such as *calculate, measure, appraise, synthesize, theorize, compile,* and *recalibrate*. This is additional empirical evidence presented by this study for the point that more details of relevant individual studies are reviewed in the LR section rather than in the Introduction (Chap. 6).

A cross-disciplinary and cross-generic comparison of the use of RVs regarding their evaluative potential is also made. From writers' perspectives, the predominant use of nonfactives is consistently observed in the four sub-corpora. As for RVs that are factive or counter-factive, factives are more often used than counter-factives by both AL and CE writers in these two rhetorical sections. These are consistent with the perception and views of our expert informants that they prefer using RVs that express neutral or positive evaluation for establishing the context for the study. Using RVs to indicate negative critiques is rarely adopted as they are reluctant to attack others or threaten others' face in public but more willing to establish solidarity with other members within the disciplinary discourse community. From authors' perspectives, Author Neutral RVs appear as the most frequently used RV, followed by Author Positive and Author Tentative RVs. Author Critical RVs are occasionally used in both sections of AL ERAs but hardly employed in those of CE ERAs.

In contrast to the findings of the present study about cross-disciplinary and cross-generic variations in the use of multiple citation features mentioned above, most of the existing EAP writing textbooks mainly stress correct forms and formats of citations with some being over-reliant on referencing systems detailed in APA and MLA style guides (e.g., Dees, 2000; Rigby, 2001; Roth, 1999), while functions/motivations of using different sorts of citations have rarely been addressed (e.g., Day, 2007; Michaelson, 1990; Silyn-Roberts, 2013). In some popular research writing guides (e.g., Pyrczak & Bruce, 2007), only advice on how to prepare reference lists is offered without any instructions on in-text citations, indicating that the importance of referencing has not been fully addressed in the published advice. In most of the other EAP writing guides and reference manuals, there are often inexplicit general accounts of referencing in EAP writing course books for novice writers from a wide range of cultural and disciplinary background (Thompson & Tribble, 2001), whereas discipline-specific, genre-specific and part-genre-specific features in citation use have largely been overlooked (e.g., Buffa, 1997; Silyn-Roberts, 2013).

References

Ädel, A., & Garretson, G. (2006). Citation practices across the disciplines: The case of proficient student writing. In C. Perez-Llantada, R. Plo, & C.-P. Neumann (Eds.), *Academic and professional communication in the 21st century: Genres and rhetoric in the construction of disciplinary knowledge* (pp. 271–280). Zaragoza: Prensas Universitarias.

Buffa, L. (1997). *Research paper smart: Where to find it, how to write it, how to cite it*. New York, NY: Random House.

Charles, M. (2006). Phraseological patterns in reporting clauses used in citation: A corpus-based study of theses in two disciplines. *English for Specific Purposes, 25*(3), 310–331.

Clugston, M. (2008). An analysis of citation forms in health science journals. *Journal of Academic Language & Learning, 2*(1), 11–22.

Day, A. (2007). *How to get research published in journals* (2nd ed.). Aldershot: Gower.

Dees, R. (2000). *Writing the modern research paper* (3rd ed.). Boston: Allyn and Bacon.

Hyland, K. (1999). Academic attribution: Citation and the construction of disciplinary knowledge. *Applied Linguistics, 20*(3), 341–367.
Hyland, K. (2000). *Disciplinary discourses: Social interaction in academic writing*. London: Longman Pearson Education.
Hyland, K. (2002). Activity and evaluation: Reporting practices in academic writing. In J. Flowerdew (Ed.), *Academic discourse* (pp. 115–130). Harlow: Pearson Education Limited.
Hyland, K. (2012). *Disciplinary identities: Individuality and community in academic writing*. Cambridge: Cambridge Applied Linguistics.
Jalilifar, A. (2012). Academic attribution: Citation analysis in master's theses and research articles in applied linguistics. *International Journal of Applied Linguistics, 22*(1), 24–41.
Lang, H. L. (2004). *The use of reporting verbs in literature reviews of Taiwanese postgraduate business students*. Unpublished doctoral dissertation, The University of Manchester.
Mansourizadeh, K., & Ahmad, U. (2011). Citation practices among non-native expert and novice scientific writers. *Journal of English for Academic Purposes, 10*(3), 152–161.
Michaelson, H. B. (1990). *How to write & publish engineering papers and reports*. Phoenix, AZ: Oryx Press.
Mur-Dueñas, P. (2009). Citation in business management research articles: A contrastive (English-Spanish) corpus-based analysis. In E. Suomela-Salmi & F. Dervin (Eds.), *Cross-cultural and cross-linguistic perspectives on academic discourse* (pp. 49–60). Amsterdam: John Benjamins.
Petrić, B. (2007). Rhetorical functions of citations in high- and low-rated master's theses. *Journal of English for Academic Purposes, 6*(3), 238–253.
Pyrczak, F., & Bruce, R. R. (2007). *Writing empirical research reports: A basic guide for students of the social and behavioral sciences* (6th ed.). Glendale, CA: Pyrczak Pub.
Rigby, D. W. (2001). *Writer's handbook for engineering technicians and technologists*. Upper Saddle River, NJ: Prentice Hall.
Roth, A. J. (1999). *The research paper: Process, form, and content* (8th ed.). Belmont, CA.: Wadsworth Pub.
Samraj, B. (2008). A discourse analysis of master's theses across disciplines with a focus on introductions. *Journal of English for Academic Purposes, 7*, 55–67.
Samraj, B. (2013). Form and function of citations in discussion sections of master's theses and research articles. *Journal of English for Academic Purposes, 12*, 299–310.
Shooshtari, Z. G., & Jalilifar, A. (2010). Citation and the construction of disciplinary knowledge. *Journal of Teaching Language Skills, 2*(1), 45–66.
Silyn-Roberts, H. (2013). *Writing for science and engineering: Papers, presentations and reports* (2nd ed.). Amsterdam: Elsevier.
Swales, J. M. (1986). Citation analysis and discourse analysis. *Applied Linguistics, 7*, 39–56.
Swales, J. M. (1990). *Genre analysis: English in academic and research settings*. Cambridge; New York: Cambridge University Press.
Swales, J. M. (2014). Variation in citational practice in a corpus of student biology papers: From parenthetical plonking to intertextual storytelling. *Written Communication, 31*(1), 118–141.
Thomas, S., & Hawes, T. P. (1994). Reporting verbs in medical journal articles. *English for Specific Purposes, 13*(2), 129–148.
Thompson, G. (2000). *Reporting*. Beijing: Foreign Languages Publishing House.
Thompson, P. (2001). *A pedagogically-motivated corpus-based examination of PhD theses: Macrostructure, citation practices and uses of modal verbs*. Unpublished doctoral dissertation, The University of Reading.
Thompson, P. (2005). Points of focus and position: Intertextual reference in Ph.D. theses. *Journal of English for Academic Purposes, 4*(4), 307–323.
Thompson, P., & Tribble, C. (2001). Looking at citations: Using corpora in English for academic purposes. *Language Learning and Technology, 5*(3), 91–105.
Thompson, G., & Ye, Y. (1991). Evaluation in the reporting verbs used in academic papers. *Applied Linguistics, 12*(4), 365–382.
Wood, D. M. (2012). *Civil engineering: A very short introduction*. Oxford: Oxford University Press.

Chapter 8
Conclusion

8.1 Introduction

This final chapter begins with a restatement of the research questions (Sect. 8.2.1). I will then summarize the main findings of the study (Sects. 8.2.2–8.2.6), in terms of how they relate to the research questions. Following this, the contributions of the study and the implications of its findings for EAP theory, research and pedagogy are discussed (Sect. 8.3). After the study as a whole is evaluated and limitations of the study are indicated (Sect. 8.4), the book is brought a conclusion with recommendations for future research (Sect. 8.5).

8.2 Summary and Discussion of Findings

8.2.1 Research Questions

As stated in Chap. 1, the frequent appearance of the LR section in the introductory phase of the ERA, as observed by a number of genre scholars (e.g., Kwan et al., 2012; Yang & Allison, 2004) and student writers in the EAP classroom, is in stark contrast to the preoccupation with the "canonical" IMRD framework in EAP research and teaching. This inspired the present study on the macro-structure of the ERA for verifying the important status of the LR section and on the micro-structure of and citation use in the introductory phase structured in the "I+LR" pattern in the two contrasting disciplines (viz., CE and AL). Disciplinary insiders' accounts of their own and disciplinary structural and citation practices in these two rhetorical sections are also integrated to illuminate the findings from the textual analysis.

The study sought to answer the following research questions (as stated in Chap. 3):

1. What are the dominant macro-structures and the major sections of ERAs, and particularly, what is the status of the LR section?

(Kathy). L. Lin, *Perspectives on the Introductory Phase of Empirical Research Articles*, Corpora and Intercultural Studies 5, https://doi.org/10.1007/978-981-32-9204-8_8

2. What is the macro-structural development of ERAs in Applied Linguistics (AL) and Civil Engineering (CE), and particularly, is the LR section a new development?
3. What are the rhetorical structure of and citation use in the introductory phase structured in the "I+LR" pattern in AL and CE?
4. What are disciplinary academics' views and experience on structuring the introductory phase of the ERA and on using citations in it in AL and CE?

To address these questions, the present study uses a combination of research methods (viz., ESP genre-based structural analysis, corpus-based language study, and semi-structured interviews). A multi-perspective approach (viz., the cross-disciplinary, cross-generic, emic, and published advice vs. actual expert practices perspectives) is adopted to obtain clear and pluralistic views of the research issues. In the following sections, the results of the interviews and the findings as regards the macro-organization of the ERA, the macro-structural evolution of the ERA in AL and CE, and the rhetorical structure of and citation use in the Introduction and LR sections are summarized and discussed, in relation to the research questions.

8.2.2 The Macro-structure and Major Sections of ERAs (Question 1)

In the EAP literature, far fewer studies have been devoted to the overall structure of ERAs than those to the rhetorical structure of their individual sections (Kuteeva & McGrath, in press). This together with the long-standing preoccupation with the IMRD pattern lead to the fact that the status of the sections not fully accounted for in the IMRD model, such as the LR section, have tended to be overlooked by researchers, EAP practitioners and apprentice writers altogether.

Against this background, the first lead-in study entailed an ESP genre-based analysis of the macro-structure of ERAs based on a corpus consisting of 780 RAs published in 2007 in 39 disciplines in the fields of engineering, applied sciences, social sciences and the humanities. The analysis reveals that the conventional IMRD model is only the fourth most frequently used structural pattern and there are many other predominant patterns, e.g., ILM[RD]C, IM[RD]C, IMRDC, ILMRDC and ILMRD. In addition to the macro-structural diversity, the importance of the sections not fully accounted for in the IMRD model (viz., the LR, C and [RD] sections) has been verified and highlighted. Deviations from IMRD generally occur in the two "moving" processes in the opening (general-specific) and closing (specific-general) phrases of ERAs.

Regarding the discrete LR section, it has been found in over half (50.6%) of the ERAs examined; in 25 of the 39 disciplines, more than 50% of their ERAs include an individual LR section and in disciplines such as management and marketing, industrial and systems engineering, accounting and finance, electronic and information engineering, and logistics, the LR section is used in more than 80% of the RAs.

Some possible reasons for including a functionally distinct LR section have been given, i.e., it is likely to be used when there is a substantial body of the literature to review, or when there are several contentious theories or issues in a particular research area, or the target journal is especially interested in theoretically oriented research (Yang & Allison, 2004). A noteworthy point is that the term "literature review" seems to be limited in that it could not capture wholly the scope, propositional content, and function of this section. Besides a traditional review of the literature in the research field, it may also cover a description of the contextual background and institutional setting or a methodologocial chronological account.

The present research is a first study on macrostructural variations in ERAs across such a wide range of disciplines. The major structural patterns identified for each discipline[1] provide useful pointers for disciplinary research writing instruction (Appendix A). The number of the major structural patterns identified in each discipline indicates to some extent the within-disciplinary variations. An important finding is that in terms of macrostructure use, frequency of use does not necessarily equate to breadth of use. For instance, while being the most frequently used structural pattern, ILM[RD]C is not the most widely used one. In contrast, IM[RD]C, IMRDC, ILMRDC and ILMRD seem to be more dispersed.

Findings on discipline-specific macro-organizational use and marked cross-disciplinary variations in ERA macro-structure are also reported. For example, in the field of textiles and clothing, as many as 14 out of the 18 ERAs are structured in the pattern of IM[RD]C. While the IMRD pattern is preferred in many applied science disciplines and two social science disciplines (viz., psychology and education), ILM[RD]C is favored in engineering and social science disciplines such as civil and structural engineering, industrial and systems engineering, and management and marketing. Among social science disciplines, ILMRDC is most commonly used in applied linguistics/ELT, whereas ILMRD tends to be used by researchers in applied social sciences, archeology, education and sociology. CE and AL, in this study, have been confirmed as two of the disciplines with the frequent use of patterns containing an independent LR section. Therefore, they are chosen as the two focused disciplines for the study of the rhetorical structure of and citation use in the introductory phase structured with the "I+LR" format.

8.2.3 The Macro-structural Development of ERAs in CE and AL (Question 2)

The second lead-in study examines the macro-structural development of ERAs in CE and AL in the past 30 years (1980–2010), with a particular focus on the changing structural shapes of the introductory phase. The study provides specific diachronic evidence for the increasing importance of the LR section and reveals both the evolving

[1] As noted in Appendix A, the "major" structural patterns, defined as those that are employed no less than three times for each discipline, could not be identified for all of the 39 disciplines.

and the inherent "stabilized-for-now or stabilized-enough" nature of the genre of ERAs (Schryer, 1994: 108). With respect to the IMRD pattern, it is found in only 12 out of the 191 ERAs in AL and in none of the ERAs in CE. AL ERAs published before the 1990s tend to be comparatively more frequently structured in this conventional four-part model than their contemporary counterparts.

Corresponding with the limited use of IMRD, ERAs in these two disciplines demonstrate macro-structural diversity. However, clear cross-time structural changes have been documented. For instance, a significant increase in the use of much more complex patterns with the LR section (e.g., ILMRDC and ILM[RD]C) has been observed in AL, which could be possibly attributed to the nature and development of this discipline. Nevertheless, this macro-structural development is not found in CE, which is a well-established discipline with a long history. Another typical example is that, in both disciplines, the IMRC pattern was generally favored by research writers in the earlier period. On the other hand, ERAs in both disciplines reflect relative genre stability, as many component units with their typical rhetorical functions are consistently used, such as the Introduction and M sections. Also, some structural patterns continue to be used across a long period of time, e.g., ILM[RD]C has been used in CE ERAs as a major structural pattern since 1985 and ILMRDC appears frequently in AL ERAs since 1990.

Among ERAs in CE, a distinct category (viz., empirical simulation articles) with their common pattern "IS[MRD]C" is identified. Empirical simulation articles are somewhat different from the traditional ERAs as they often involve a simulation model and the test of the model through empirical studies. However, they have a distinct empirical nature. In general, they are RAs featured by the use of a real experiment or a set of specific empirical case studies for testing and evaluating the formulated model in real sites; they report simulation studies that represent specific real-world situations or whose key parameters are set (and calibrated) based upon data from real situations. In "IS[MRD]C", "S" refers to a stand-alone section presenting details of the computer simulation model, while "[MRD]" represents a single section where the elements of method, results and discussions are coalesced (usually for a real experiment or a set of case studies in real sites to test the validity of the computer simulated model). "IS[MRD]C" has been observed as a frequently used pattern for ERAs in CE throughout the past thirty years. However, it should be noted that the practice of categorizing empirical simulation articles as a special type of ERAs in this study is a preliminary attempt. It is conducted for both the convenience of analysis and highlighting this valuable pattern predominantly used in CE. It may entail more future studies, as empirical simulation RAs have hardly been addressed in the EAP literature.

A final important finding is that the LR section is a recent development of ERAs in both disciplines. While there are a few minor fluctuations in writers' adoption of the independent LR section in ERAs of both disciplines, an overall increase in the use of the LR has been found. This also embodies the dynamic and evolving nature of the ERA and further justifies the focused study of the rhetorical structure of and citation use in the introductory phase with the format of "I+LR".

8.2.4 *The Rhetorical Structure of the Introduction and LR Sections (Question 3)*

Bhatia (2004: xv) views the real world of written discourse in two senses: "genres within specific disciplinary domains" and "genre relationships across disciplinary domains". For this project, after the important status of the LR section has been verified from both cross-sectional and diachronic perspectives, the rhetorical structure of and citation language resources used in the Introductions and LRs in the two particular disciplinary domains (viz., CE and AL) are studied and compared.

The study reveals two major types of introductions used before the LR section in the two disciplines: the "Two-move Orientation" type and the "Research-oriented Traditional Creating a Research Space (RT CARS)" type. While a significant portion of the introductions with a following LR function to create a research space for the study (viz., the RT CARS type), a considerable number of them (33.3% in CE and 36.7% in AL) mainly aim to identify the research issue and inform the readers of the research to be undertaken (viz., the Orientation type). An integrated CARS model (Fig. 3.3) and the Two-move Orientation approach (Fig. 3.2) are proposed respectively for the rhetorical structure of the RT CARS introduction and that of the Orientation introduction. The integrated CARS model combines moves and sub-moves of the CARS model (Swales, 1990, 2004), some elements from other previous introduction studies (e.g., Del Saz-Rubio, 2011; Samraj, 2002, 2005), and the newly identified elements (viz., Sub-move 2.6 "State Theoretical Frameworks/Positions" and Sub-move 3.3 "Indicate the Literature Review content"). The Orientation approach contains two moves with a featured element identified (viz., "Suggest value of the issue"). This element is usually represented by only one or two sentences briefly indicating the potential significance of the research issue, which is worth studying. It is often immediately followed by Sub-move 2.1 that announces research purposes, foci, RQs or hypotheses of the study. Different from the traditional CARS type, the Two-move Orientation type does not contain the detailed rhetorical work involved in creating the research space, or rather, the substantial "niche-establishment" move. In addition to the different communicative functions and functional elements used in the two predominant types of the introductions, they differ from each other in terms of their length and rhetorical movements. The Orientation introductions are much shorter and rather straightforwardly structured. In contrast, the RT CARS introductions are comparatively more complexly and recursively structured. In addition to the two major types of the introductions, there are also some minority types identified, viz., five "Practical-problem Solving (PS)" introduction in CE and the single case of "Building on the Writer's Own Previous Research" introduction in AL. This shows to some extent variability in the rhetorical structure of the introductions followed by a usually lengthy LR section.

In general, when there is a subsequent LR section, the introductions are fairly flexibly yet simply structured with no dense use of sub-moves. This group of introductions in both disciplines contain far less the elements of reviewing individual research items, which has become a major task of its subsequent LR section. Another interesting finding is that there are some intriguing links between the Introduction and the subsequent LR sections, as typically embodied in the use of the element "Indicate the LR content" in a number of the introductions.

Despite many commonalities in the introductions with a subsequent LR section in the two disciplines in terms of their rhetorical structure, there are some salient cross-disciplinary variations. For example, the element "Claim Centrality in Research World" is more frequently used in AL RT CARS introductions than the element "Claim Centrality in Real World" while the opposite is true for the CE RT CARS introductions. Nevertheless, primarily due to the applied nature of both disciplines, the elements for indicating importance in the real world and for suggesting real-world problems or need for the research are all prominent ones used in the two dominant types of introductions in them. Another example is that the newly proposed element "Indicate the LR content" has been used in both types of introductions in AL but not in any of the CE introductions. The generalizability of this cross-disciplinary variation, however, needs to be tested by future research. Also, the specific frequencies for using particular sub-moves/moves and some sub-move combination patterns used and their frequencies are understandably different across the two contrasting disciplines.

In terms of the LR section, the present study reveals its four possible, functionally distinct components, namely, Advanced Organizer/Overview, Theoretical Review, Contextual Background, and Conclusion. Among these four functional components, Theoretical Review is the only obligatory one and all the other three are occasionally used in the LR sections. This is quite different from what Kwan (2005, 2006) has observed in the LR chapters of research degree theses, where the introductory texts appear in around 90% of them and the concluding texts are present in around 50% of them. One plausible reason is space concern in writing ERAs, for which journals usually stipulate strict length requirements of their submissions. Contextual Background, a distinctive component found in this study for the LR section, is more likely to be used in ERAs where the studies reported are set in particular contexts and the value and implications of their findings should be interpreted and understood in this context.

As Theoretical Review is the only mandatory component of the LR section, a systematic, ESP genre-based study of its rhetorical structure has been conducted. The vast majority (73.3%) of AL Theoretical Reviews are multi-thematic sections containing different numbers of sub-sections on various themes, while two-thirds of the CE Theoretical Reviews are stand-alone sections with no sub-sections embedded. This indicates that AL Theoretical Reviews may be structurally more complex than those in CE.

A four-move structure is identified for Theoretical Reviews and the four prototypical moves are: Move 1 Demarcate the Research Territory, Move 2 Review Key Studies, Move 3 Position the Study, and Move 4 Outline the Present Study. While the first two moves are related to the background to the study, the latter two respectively establish the links between the background with the study and outline its various aspects. The four moves have a strong presence in the 60 Theoretical Reviews, with the former three being predominantly used in both disciplines. However, Move 4 is only used in 63.3% of Theoretical Reviews in CE, but in 93.3% of those in AL. This corresponds to applied linguists' and CE researchers' contrasting preferences: applied linguists favor drawing together the reviews of literature from different research strands together at the end of this part, but CE researchers eminently attach much more importance to the results/scientific discovery and related discussions/applications. This perhaps partly results in the much shorter length of CE Theoretical Reviews than their counterparts in AL.

The structure of most Theoretical Reviews shows a strong cyclicity at move level, one reason for which is that, a considerable number of them consist of multiple thematic (sub-)sections, and the four-move structure or some of the moves or pairings of moves recur across such theme-bound (sub-)sections. The number of move units integrating the patterns for Theoretical Reviews is often large, conforming to their frequently multi-thematic-sectional structure and extended length. The strong cyclical nature shown by the moves of Theoretical Reviews and the different number of move units integrating move configurations leads to the occurrences of a vast variety of move configurations, many of which appear "irregular". However, within these patterns, the comparatively stable, repeated use of some pairings of move units are regular and prominent, such as the parings of Moves 1 and 3 ("1-3"), the sequenced use of the first three moves ("1-2-3"), and the sequential combined use of Moves 2 and 3 ("2-3"). An overwhelming majority of Theoretical Reviews open with Move 1 and end with Move 4, with an embedded, cyclical use of such regular move pairings or individual moves. This is the most prominent structural feature of Theoretical Reviews at move level.

As Move 2 does not contain different constituent elements, the frequency and distribution of sub-moves and sub-move configurations were only examined for the other three moves. Many relevant cross-disciplinary similarities have been revealed, with some discipline-specific featured use in these aspects highlighted. For instance, the frequency distribution of the three sub-moves within Move 1 is analogous between the two disciplines. In both disciplines, Sub-move 1.2 is most frequently used, followed by Sub-move 1.1. Sub-move 1.3 is, however, only used in a few cases. The high occurrences of the first two sub-moves are in agreement with writers' preferential use of the single sub-move configurations containing either of them and the composite Move 1 containing both in various combinations. There are four instances of the single sub-move configuration "Sub-move 1.3" in Theoretical Reviews in CE but in none of those in AL.

Among all Move 3 constituents, the element of gap-indication/counter-claiming (Sub-move 3.1) stands out as the most frequently used sub-move, suggesting locating a niche (to be occupied by the study) as the most common strategy for positioning the study against the background. However, other strategies such as "theoretical framework-synthesizing" (Sub-move 3.5) and "relevance-claiming" (Sub-move 3.3) figure prominently in Theoretical Reviews in AL but not in CE. This reflects prevalent disciplinary influence: compared with CE, AL is a more discursive discipline, where research is more reliant on other researchers' theoretical models, constructs, arguments/positions, and hypotheses. Concerning Move 4, the elements of "announcing research purposes/aims/research questions/hypotheses" (Sub-move 4.1) and "stating research methods/designs" (Sub-move 4.3) have been registered as the two most frequently used sub-moves in Theoretical Reviews from both disciplines. Nevertheless, salient cross-disciplinary variations have also been found. For instance, Sub-move 4.2 (Announce Theoretical Positions/Frameworks) was found to be employed in around one third of the Theoretical Reviews in AL but is missing in all CE Theoretical Reviews. The elements of terminological interpretations (Sub-move 4.4) and value-claiming (Sub-move 4.5) are more often used in Theoretical Reviews in AL than in those in CE.

For both Moves 3 and 4, most frequently used sub-move configurations are those with only one sub-move. For example, in both CE and AL, those with Sub-move 3.1a only are the most common realizations of Move 3, followed by those with Sub-move 3.3 only. As for Move 4, the sub-move configurations with Sub-move 4.1 only and those with Sub-move 4.3 only are frequently used in both disciplines. Nonetheless, eminent cross-disciplinary variations are noted. For instance, a wider variety of sub-move configurations were revealed for these two moves in AL Theoretical Reviews than in those in CE. Some single sub-move patterns revealed appear to be discipline-specific, such as "Sub-move 3.5 only" (Theoretical Framework-synthesizing) is a frequently used configuration in AL but not in CE. While the configuration "Sub-move 3.6 (Inconsistency-indication) only" is only frequently used in CE, there is a much higher frequency of the Sub-move 3.3 configuration (Relevance-claiming) in Theoretical Reviews in AL.

Based on the above analytical findings, it can be inferred that within the introductory phase consisting of both Introduction and LR sections ("I+LR"), the two sections share some communicative purposes (e.g., "to contextualize the study") and thus a number of moves (e.g., "to present the present study") and sub-moves (e.g., "centrality-claiming"). Nevertheless, they play their distinctive roles with distinguishable communicative functional foci fulfilled, structured in different forms. Although several recent studies (Kwan et al., 2012; Tessuto, 2015) have suggested that the CARS model may be applicable to the analysis of the LR section in RAs, the present study reveals a more complex picture of its structure and communicative functions than is generally assumed. The LR section in ERAs may contain four functional components as discussed above and its structure could not simply be described by the CARS model, which is traditionally used to describe the Introduction section.

Even for the predominant component of the LR section (i.e., Theoretical Review), its major communicative purposes go beyond establishing the niche for the study as indicated by the CARS model. Specifically, it mainly functions to provide substantial background for further contextualizing the study (after this has been partly accomplished in the Introduction) and position the study against the background by establishing various links between the two, one of which is locating the gap to be filled by the study. Other links that are more characteristic of the LR section include "claiming the relevance of the surveyed claims to one's own research", "asserting the irrelevance of the surveyed claims to one's own research for specifying its research scope", and "abstracting, synthesizing, or making inferences from previous knowledge claims to establish a theoretical position or framework". Such links are not (directly) related to the niche-establishment, but instead provide insights from the previous theoretical and empirical literature to the present study in a broader sense and sometimes to help clarify the scope of the study. However, all these links, together with others mainly for the niche-establishment (e.g., gap-indication), are for situating and locating the study against the background.

In terms of the organizational form, the introductions preceding the LR section are generally more simply structured than most of the Theoretical Reviews, as the latter often have multi-thematic-sectional structure and an extended length, and involve a high degree of cyclicity of move units. In contrast, many of the introductions used before the LR follow a liner structural pattern with no dense use of moves and sub-moves; they are generally straightforwardly structured and some of them only contain a single move. Notwithstanding a number of the RT CARS introductions involving cyclicity in their move structure, the numbers of move units integrating their entire structure are far smaller than those for Theoretical Reviews. This also explains the contrasting length between them.

Some structural and functional differences between Theoretical Reviews and the Introduction can be perceived through a comparison of the two frameworks (viz., the four-move structure formulated in this study for Theoretical Reviews and the CARS model for article introductions). The comparison shows that a number of functional elements are uniquely used in the Introduction, e.g., those of "Outline Article Structure" and "Announce Principal Outcomes", while some others are exclusively used in the LR section, e.g., "Irrelevance-claiming" (Sub-move 3.4), "Suggest the Subsequent Theme to be Reviewed" (Sub-move 4.6), "Relevance-assertion" (Sub-move 3.3), and "Theoretical Framework-synthesizing" (Sub-move 3.5). Another major difference is that, according to the CARS model, "Reviewing Items of Previous Research" is only a step embedded within the first move for establishing the territory for the study in introductions, whereas a similar element ("Survey Key Studies") is a distinguishable and prototypical move of Theoretical Reviews. The Two-move Orientation approach even does not contain the element of "Reviewing Items of Previous Research". This suggests that, when there is an independent LR section used after the Introduction, the use of this element frequently shifts to the LR. Identifying "Survey Key Studies" as an independent move of Theoretical Reviews helps to highlight this functional shift between the two sections and to further reveal their differences and connections.

The present study reveals that the Introduction and LR sections partly resemble each other functionally and structurally. However, they are two distinct part-genres with their own rhetorical organization and communicative functions/functional foci. They are closely connected to each other in that the Introduction acts as a kind of "set-up" mainly for scene-setting and identifying the problem/issue, whilst its subsequent LR section further develops the arguments or rationales briefly mentioned in the Introduction, functioning as a "build-up" (AL1).

8.2.5 Citation Use in the Introduction and LR Sections (Question 3)

As citation use is a language feature very likely to be shared in the Introduction and LR sections due to their partly overlapping communicative purpose (i.e., "reviewing previous studies"), the present study compares the use of multiple citation features (e.g., citation forms and functions and RVs) in these two sections. The study shows both cross-disciplinary and cross-generic similarities and differences in citation practices in the two part-genres.

With regard to citation density, the number of citations used per 1000 words in AL Introductions is much larger than that in CE Introductions, suggesting applied linguists' greater reliance on referencing others' works to contextualize and justify the study at the outset of the ERA than their CE counterparts. However, there is a similarly dense use of citations in the LR section in both disciplines. While in both AL and CE, more citations are used in the LR section than in the Introduction, the difference is more salient in CE. This is largely due to the functional shift between the two sections (i.e., the element for reviewing individual studies is absent in a considerable number of the introductions and is shifted to the subsequent LR section) and the greater information density and content specificity of the LR section. As Kwan and Chan (2014: 31) maintained, the previous move studies suggest that "citations are shaped by specific moves and steps in the sections".

The types of citations used do differ in these two sections across the two disciplines. In the Introduction in both disciplines, there is an overwhelming use of non-integral citations. In contrast, in the LR section in CE, integral citations are preferred. While a slightly higher percentage of non-integral citations (as opposed to integral ones) are used in AL LRs, there is a marked increase in the use of integral citations when AL writers proceed from the opening Introduction to the subsequent LR section. This is not surprising, as integral citations grant prominence to individual authors and are thereby a more convenient means to review and evaluate the specific items of previous research, in particular those most pertinent to the study reported. As suggested in the genre analysis (Chap. 6), the element for reviewing individual studies is absent in some introductions and is shifted to the LR section. In consequence, there is a marked increase in the use of integral citations in the LR section compared to the preceding Introduction in both disciplines. In contrast, in many Introductions, while the functional element for reviewing specific research is missing, a markedly high percentage of parenthetical citations are used for "generalizing" the research background and providing an overview of the research area (Samraj, 2008). Therefore, there seems to be a link between the use of different types of citations and the rhetorical needs and communicative functions of the sections. Among the subcategories preferred within integral citations, verb controlling is the most common citation in the LR of both disciplines and in CE Introductions, even though the same percentages of the verb-controlling sub-type and the naming sub-type are employed in AL Introductions. The fact that far more integral verb-controlling citations are used in the LR section in both disciplines (than in the Introduction) (commonly to thematize and point to the agentiveness of the cited authors) seems to be in line with a denser use of RVs and a larger presence of authors in the LR.

Regarding the naming sub-type, regular patterns are identified in both sections across the two disciplines. A comparison of the use of these patterns reveals the contrasting nature of the two disciplines and the featured content and functional elements involved in the particular part-genre. For example, the pattern "X's (Year) hypotheses/notions/views/arguments…" is predominantly used in both sections of AL to refer to the conceptual models or key terms of others or to others' statements or research actions, suggesting the more discursive nature of this soft discipline. In contrast, this pattern is absent in CE introductions and only occurs once in its LR section. In CE introductions, the most frequently used pattern is "Organization name (Year)/the design guideline of Organization (Year)", which refers to the profession-specific design guideline issued by some authentic organizations. Such design guidelines are commonly used in engineering fields and thus often cited in engineering ERAs. Another typical example is that the use of the pattern "by X (Year)" is favoured in the LR section than in the Introduction section in both disciplines. In this pattern "by X (Year)", "the overall focus is on the work of particular researchers" (Jalilifar, 2012: 34). Thus, writers' preferential use of this pattern in the LR section might also indicate to some extent that more substantial, detailed reviews of individual studies are often shifted to LRs (see Chap. 6).

Revealing findings on the functional use of citations in the two rhetorical sections across the two disciplines are also generated. In both sections of CE and AL, a significant number of citations are used for the basic attribution purpose, as *attribution* is "unmarked, most common and rhetorically the simplest" function (Petrić, 2007: 247). However, in terms of non-attribution citations, far more citations with rhetorically complex functions (most typically *exemplification*, *support*, and *comparison and contrast between/among sources*) are used in the LR section. By contrast, in the preceding Introduction section, a larger number of citations with rhetorically simpler functions (e.g., *example* and *generalization from multiple sources*) are employed. Two prominent citation functional patterns associated with the contrasting pair of functions (viz., *example* vs. *exemplification*) have been identified for the Introduction (viz., "Generalization" + "Example") and LR sections (viz., "Generalization" (with *example*) + "Exemplification" (often with *support* + *compare and contrast between/among sources*) respectively. The frequent adoption of these two featured citation functional patterns in the two sections basically conforms to the communicative purpose or functional foci of them. Subtle functional differences in the use of the same category of citations are also found across the two sections. For instance, among Support citations, those for justifying the significance of the research topic are more often used in the Introduction, whereas those for justifying or providing pillars for the findings or claims or methods of previous studies are commonly employed in the LR section. Another important finding is that far more multi-functional citations are distributed in the LR section than in the Introduction, which again confirms that citations are used in rhetorically and functionally more complex ways in the LR section.

As regards cross-disciplinary variations in the functional use of citations in these two part-genres, applied linguists prefer using citations for the functions of *further reference, origin, support* and *evaluation* than their CE colleagues. Cross-generic and cross-disciplinary variations in the functional use of citations are accounted for mainly in the light of the communicative functions of the two partly analogous part-genres and the contrasting disciplinary nature, culture, value, history and tradition.

Considerable differences are also found in the density and the use of different denotative and evaluative categories of RVs in the Introduction and LR sections of CE and AL ERAs. A greater number of RVs are used in the LR than in the Introduction in both disciplines and the gap is clearly much larger in CE. An important reason is that a considerable number of introductions with a following LR (e.g., many Orientation introductions and the PS introductions) do not contain the element of "reviewing previous research" and thus do not have the essential need to employ RVs, while all LRs in the present study use some RVs. With both disciplines being of an applied nature, in some introductions, the study is only contextualized and justified by a general statement of the real-world background plus the outlining of the real-world problems, which explains partly the smaller number of the RVs used in the Introduction preceding the LR in this study.

Six out of the ten top-ranking RVs identified are shared in the four sub-corpora: *show, find, suggest, propose, use, investigate*. This implies that a large set of RVs may not be discipline-bound and part-genre-bound, and can characterize general research writing. On the other hand, the use of some other particular RVs reflects the contrasting nature of the disciplines, e.g., *argue* as a common RV in both rhetorical sections of AL ERAs and *use* predominantly employed in CE discourse.

In the analysis of RVs in terms of their denotative meaning, a new category "Stative RVs", which reports the state (existence, development, etc.) of phenomena, theories or other issues, is identified and proposed. This is a category overlooked in the bulk of the previous RV research (e.g., Hyland, 1999, 2002; Lang, 2004; Mur-Dueñas, 2009; Thomas & Hawes, 1994; Thompson, 2001; Thompson & Ye, 1991), which focus on RVs denoting dynamic research activities of various nature (i.e., mental, discourse and research). Among the denotative categories of RVs, two predominant ones are Research Acts RVs and Discourse Acts RVs, while Cognition Acts RVs and Stative RVs are in the minority across the four sub-corpora. Substantial variations exist in the use of RVs in terms of their denotative meaning in the two sections across the two disciplines. There is a consistently overwhelming use of Research Acts RVs in both sections of CE ERAs; however, while Discourse Acts RVs is the most frequently used category in AL introductions, a slightly higher percentage of Research Acts RVs (as opposed to Discourse Acts RVs) are used in AL LR sections. In addition to the disciplinary influence, the findings can be accounted for by the fact that the introductions and LRs analyzed in this study were all drawn from ERAs (entailing more use of Research Acts RVs in AL LRs).

As for cross-generic variations, in the Introduction section, Research Acts RVs used are mostly those indicating general research actions (e.g., *investigate, study, research*, and *examine*), whereas in the LR section, more Research Acts RVs denoting specific research procedures or activities are employed (e.g., *calculate, measure, appraise, synthesize, theorize, compile*, and *recalibrate*). This is additional empirical evidence verifying that more details of related individual studies are reviewed in the LR section rather than in the Introduction (Chap. 6).

The use of RVs in terms of their evaluative stance is also investigated in the two sections across the two contrasting disciplines. The data show that, in both CE and AL, writers prefer ascribing an attitude towards the cited content to authors rather than showing their own evaluation directly by using predominantly Writer Non-factive RVs. This is consonant with many existing studies (e.g., Hyland, 1999, 2000, 2002; Mur-Dueñas, 2009; Swales, 2014) focusing on various disciplines. As for RVs that are factive or counter-factive, factives are more often used than counter-factives by both AL and CE writers in these two rhetorical sections mainly because of the principle of academic politeness they adhere to.

From authors' perspectives, there is also little cross-disciplinary and cross-generic difference in the proportional use of different categories of RVs, though CE scholars hardly used any Author Critical RVs and yet their AL counterparts employed a few (e.g., *criticize, overlook, refute, lament*, and *question*). Author Neutral RVs remain the most frequently used RV in the four sub-corpora, followed by Author Positive and Author Tentative RVs. The findings suggest that, in both disciplines, the "personality" of the research writers seems to play a marginal role in selecting RVs to express (explicitly or implicitly) appropriate evaluative stances towards the cited works; instead, they would consider more what is generally accepted and valued by the whole disciplinary discourse community and the rhetorical need that matches with or is imposed to some extent by the communicative function of the particular genre or part-genre under construction.

8.2.6 The Interviews (Question 4)

To complement textual findings, expert insider views were elicited to further understand disciplinary structural practices and citation practices and the relevant disciplinary culture and traditions. The overall impression from the interviews is that the expert informants from the two disciplines generally regard structuring an ERA as a complex issue, as there is not a fixed template and they may consider more their actual needs and the principle of "article content, form, and function matching" (AL2). As experienced writers, many of them noted that there are different ways for structuring RAs; they would be much more likely to write in their own ways while ensuring that the structure of the RA would not diverge too far from the corresponding requirements, if any, stipulated in contributors' pages. Even for the interviewees who recommended the IMRD as the "standard" structure for writing ERAs, they acknowledge that "there is a certain amount of creativity and flexibility allowed" (CE3) and competent writers do not necessarily follow this conventional format (AL7). Their views resonate what has been perceived from the present study (i.e., the macro-structural diversity revealed in contemporary ERAs).

They also commented on an array of factors that may influence the structural decisions. The most prominent factor is the type and nature of research conducted. For instance, a case study report may be structured quite differently from an experimental test paper (AL2). Other factors such as the writers' understanding of the communicative function or purpose of the rhetorical section, journal policy, editors and reviewers' suggestions, and co-authors' re-structural decisions all possibly affect the final shape of the articles. In their views, the blended Results and Discussion section can make papers "condensed and concise" (CE3) in that it can help to reduce unnecessary, repeated statements of the findings. With regards to the C section, they stressed its particular "promotional" function, i.e., to foreground the most important findings and contribution of the study; on the other hand, they noted the partly analogous functional elements between the traditional D section and the C section.

In terms of whether to use an independent LR section or to embed the element of "reviewing previous research" into the conventional Introduction, the interviewees contributed many thought-provoking insights. When they use both Introduction and LR sections in the introductory phase of the ERA, they consider the Introduction as a kind of "set-up" (AL1) mainly for scene-setting and identifying the problem/research issue, and the LR section as a "build-up" for further developing arguments and rationales based upon a focused, critical review of the literature, and possibly developing the theoretical or conceptual or methodological basis. The idea that the Introduction followed by an LR serves as a "general overview" (AL4) seems to be consistent with the finding from the genre-based analysis (Chap. 6) that a considerable number of the introductions with a subsequent LR have been identified as the Two-move Orientation introduction. This type of introduction, which is commonly short and persuasive, seeks to "sell" the paper by "explaining what and why" briefly to the readers without "boring them with the extremely theoretical and technical details" (AL7). When deciding whether they would use an independent LR section, they would firstly put the distinctive functions of the sections and reader experience as major concerns. Further, it depends on whether the study reported is data-driven or theory-driven (AL2). If it is a data-driven paper where much data need to be presented in the paper, then the writers presumably do not have adequate space to review the literature. Nonetheless, if it is a theory-driven article and especially when there is a vast body of the literature to review, research writers usually use a lengthy LR section to review the models and literature in order to provide the background for the study and build their own arguments and frameworks. Another noteworthy point is that, the LR is not "a ritual or a perfunctory step" (AL4); instead, it is a purpose-oriented section and "everything reviewed should be related to research questions explicitly or implicitly" (AL7). Therefore, how to strategically review and represent the literature selectively should a key issue concerning all research writers.

The interviewees' many perceptions of their disciplinary citation practices in the introductory phase of the ERA are also congruent with what we have perceived from the textual data. For example, regarding the use of citation forms, most of the expert informants maintained that, as in the LR section, the focus would be more on the review of individual studies, entailing the intensive use of integral citations (especially the verb-controlling ones for an indication of evaluative stances as well). By contrast, in the preceding Introduction, an orientation of the readers from the broader context towards the area generally includes an overview of the entire field, where the more generalized findings in the area (rather than the individual authors) should be foregrounded. This accounts for the dominant use of multi-reference parenthetical citations in the Introduction. However, some of the applied linguists interviewed choose citation forms based on the circumstance; in some circumstances, for example, one of their main concerns is to make sure that their own voices could be heard (rather than the cited authors' words), and they think the best way is to use the non-integral citations. Their other concerns are that, for example, sometimes they need to add variety to the reading experience by using different citation forms, and that, they may prefer using integral citations, if they think the identity of the individual is important or they regularly refer to the person's work.

The interviewees also by and large agreed with my assumptions (and observations based on the genre study of the Introduction and LR sections in Chap. 6) that, more citations are used in the LR section because they would have a substantial review of the literature in this section rather than in the Introduction. Therefore, there are some connections between the communicative functions and rhetorical structure of the two part-genres and citation use in them. In terms of RV use, the expert writers emphasized that they prefer taking positive or neutral attitude towards the cited work to establish allegiance to the community and the harmonious relationship with others. They think that sometimes it may cause unnecessary troubles or "puts them into kind of danger" (AL2) by using RVs to indicate strongly negative voices towards the cited work. In their opinions, this is neither the only nor an indispensable means to create a research space for the study. There are some other choices, e.g., using the first person pronoun for niche-creation (AL1). In addition, a number of the interviewees conveyed the point that they are engaging with new research areas where there is indeed not much research to be critiqued. Regarding cross-disciplinary variations in the use of different denotative categories of RVs, the interviewees from both disciplines endorsed the view that, their preferential choices are highly relevant to the nature of the disciplines they belong to, the research paradigms they follow, and what kind of research work they need to conduct to fit the needs of the study.

8.3 Contributions and Implications

This study contributes to EAP theory, research and pedagogy in a number of ways. The first lead-in study provides solid empirical evidence for the diversity of the macro-structure of contemporary ERAs and for the importance of the LR, C and [RD] sections, which are not represented in the canonical IMRD model. It highlights the limitations of the current EAP research that focuses intensively on the Introduction but barely on the discrete LR section in the introductory phase of ERAs. It also highlights the significant shortcoming of a great many EAP writing manuals and reference books that proffer advice merely based on the simplest "Introduction-Body-

Conclusion" ("IBC") model (e.g., Dees, 2000; Soles, 2010) or the canonical IMRD framework (e.g., Körner, 2008; Lester & Lester, 2006). On the pedagogical front, the study highlights the need for EAP course designers and teachers to raise research students' awareness of the range of possibilities available to them when writing for publication in their disciplines. The simplified knowledge of the IMRD framework for structuring ERAs, if it is instilled into postgraduate students disregarding their disciplinary background and the research paradigms they follow, may be of little avail in the long run (Becher, 1994; Becher & Trowler, 2001). Therefore, frontline EAP teachers need to translate the findings from the latest research (such as those presented in this study) to various instructional activities or lead their students to explore actively specialized corpora consisting of discipline-specific texts for useful structural patterns [see "the data-driven learning approach" in Anthony and Bowen (2013: 22)]. For disciplines where research writers prefer using the sections not represented in the IMRD model (e.g., the LR, C and [RD] sections), which are hardly accounted for in various instructional materials, particular attention should be paid to the possible communicative functions, structural flows and content elements of these sections.

The second study particularly confirms the increasing importance of the LR section in CE and AL ERAs from a diachronic perspective and contributes to our understanding of both cross-time structural changes and cross-disciplinary variations in this regard. In this study, "empirical simulation articles" in CE is identified for the first time in the EAP field, with their structural pattern "IS[MRD]C" noted. This new discovery facilitates discipline-specific research writing teaching and learning and inspires future research for further demystifying its micro-structure and language use. Also, our knowledge about the genre of ERAs is enriched as this diachronic textual analysis has revealed both its evolving and inherent "stabilized-enough" nature (Schryer, 1994: 108). In all, the two lead-in studies are valuable in that they not only open up many possibilities for future research, but have significant practical implications for EAP teaching, course design, and materials writing and development.

While knowledge about the information structure of the sections not represented in the IMRD model largely remains tacit and nebulous, the focused study presents pedagogically valuable structural models for the LR section and the preceding Introduction and demonstrates cross-generic and cross-disciplinary variations in citation use in the two sections across two contrasting disciplines (i.e., CE and AL). It contributes significantly to both genre research and citation research, considering what it has achieved as follows: the rhetorical structure of the introductory phase structured in the "I+LR" format has been for the first time systematically analyzed; the different types of introductions are identified (e.g., the "Two-move Orientation" introduction, the PS introduction, and the "Building on the Writer's Own Previous Research" introduction); the general organization of the LR section in ERAs has been revealed; the structural models are proposed for the two major types of introductions (i.e., the Orientation introductions and the RT CARS introductions) and the major component of the LR section (i.e., Theoretical Reviews); the similarities, differences and interrelationship between the Introduction and LR sections have been clarified; the frameworks suggested for the pre-LR introductions and Theoretical Reviews have been compared with the classic CARS model to highlight the theoretical contributions of this study; a new denotative RV category "Stative RV" is discovered; and a new typology of citation functions for classifying all categories into two large groups (viz., the group of rhetorically simpler citation functions and the other of rhetorically complex citation functions) has been put forward and successfully applied to the analysis of citation use in the two part-genres under investigation.

Unlike a multitude of previous RA studies (e.g., Sollaci & Pereira, 2004; Yang & Allison, 2003, 2004), the present study provides insights from disciplinary insiders into their actual structural and citation practices. The principle that they would not write to the formula but consider more their actual needs and the issue of "article content, form, and function matching together" are useful for current research writing instruction, as in fact diverse structural choices are available rather than the single conventional IMRD model. Their practical concerns for making structural decisions including those about when to use a separate LR section and when to embed the review of previous literature into the Introduction section without a subsequent LR section are of direct help to novices, as there is a noticeable dearth of published advice on the under-researched part-genres like the LR section.

In terms of citation practices, their many plausible accounts are beneficial to the novices' understanding and acquisition of the patterned use of citations and citation elements in these two partly analogous adjoining sections, e.g., their commonly more frequent use of non-integral citations in the Introduction (than in the LR section) as they intend to state generalized findings and point out the research trend in the very opening section whilst leaving specific items of research to be reviewed in the LR section, where a marked increase of integral citations occur. Clearly, the subject informants' accounts indicate that referencing others' works is a purposeful and strategic rhetorical activity, which concerns various aspects, e.g., the readership, the communicative purposes or functional foci of a particular part-genre or genre where citations locate, and private intentions. The disciplinary expert writers' experience sharing, particularly their explanations about the disciplinary citation and structural practices, are helpful to the apprentice writers' academic enculturation in these regards. This suggests the importance of "situated learning" (see e.g., Berkenkotter & Huckin, 1995) in both forms of "guided participation" (Rogoff, 1990, 1995) and "legitimate peripheral participation" (Lave & Wenger, 1991). The mixed mode of situated learning can facilitate student writers' both conscious and incidental learning of patterned structural and citation use. While some of the experienced writers interviewed mentioned that they had never received any "special" training like attending academic writing workshops when they were postgraduates, they emphasized the role of extensive reading and writing of RAs in the process of acquisition and learning of knowledge of their rhetorical patterns and language use. Therefore, we recommend different forms of situated learning to the student writers who strive for an entry to their particular disciplinary discourse communities.

8.4 Limitations of the Present Study

The present study has given a full account of the status of the LR section and of the rhetorical structure of and citation use in the type of the introductory phase formatted in “I+LR”. It has contributed to a clearer understanding of the variations that is possible within the two part-genres (viz., the Introduction and LR sections) in the two disciplinary domains regarding their structural and citation use. While it has yielded many helpful pedagogical insights, there are a number of limitations to the study.

Although the first lead-in study, which is a large-scale cross-section study of RA macro-structure, has covered an unusually wide range of disciplines, it has included only a modest number of RAs from each of the disciplines in the corpus and not all of these are empirical. This limits to a certain extent the generalizability and representativeness of the findings related to disciplinary variation, and thus future cross-disciplinary studies of macro-structures should ideally be based on larger samples of exclusively ERAs from a much smaller pool of disciplines.

Another limitation is that while this study has approached the rhetorical structural and citation aspects of the Introduction and LR sections respectively, the interaction between them has not been conducted. As Kwan and Chan (2014: 31) point out, “the move studies, in particular, suggest that citations are shaped by specific moves and steps in the sections”. It is also assumed in this study that many differences in the use of multi-layered citation features in both functional and formal terms relate to the communicative functions or functional foci of these two sections (Chap. 7). However, this assumption awaits a more detailed move-specific citation analysis for corroboration.

Compared with other genre-based analyses, the size of the data for the focused study (viz., 60 introductions and LRs) is moderate. However, when attempting to analyze the different types of introductions with the genre-based approach, it was found that the number of the Two-move Orientation introduction in each discipline is limited (i.e., only ten in CE and 11 in AL), which just suffice for an exploratory study of its rhetorical structure. As for the other minority types (five PS introductions in CE and only one “Building on the Writer’s Own Previous Research” introduction in AL), they only can be considered as peculiar cases and are not suitable for a systematic genre-based analysis. Therefore, the generalizability of some findings of this study may be limited due to the moderate size of the data selected. It is hoped that further research will extend, test and refine the insights and understandings that have been achieved in this study. The same also applies to the analysis of the rhetorical structure of the LR sections. The four-move structure formulated for Theoretical Reviews based on the analysis of the present data is a useful preliminary finding from this exploratory study. While ESP genre-based approach is critiqued by some for being somewhat subjective and intuition-based (Kanoksilapatham, 2005; Swales, 2004), the possible structure developed based on the 60 Theoretical Reviews in this study requires further close examinations from both the research and teaching circles.

From one point of view, it could be argued that the sample of disciplinary insiders is small. While the present study design does not set up ways to establish contrastive views across the two groups of disciplinary insiders (CE and AL) and the emic perspective is only supplemental to the entire study, interviews with a larger number of experienced writers in the two disciplines may produce a more extensive set of insights into the research issues. More importantly, when the interview data is not sufficiently large, the study may possibly induce doubts among readers (especially the ones who are more critical) that the interview data might point to individual preferences and not so much to degrees of compliance with rhetorical organization conventions.

8.5 Recommendations for Further Research

In view of the findings generated from the present research, many possibilities of great value are available for further studies. As argued before, the first two lead-in studies have presented empirical evidence for the prominence and importance of many rhetorical sections that are not represented in the "conventional" IMRD framework (e.g., the LR, [RD] and C section). However, theorizing and research into these sections to date is still underdeveloped. For this reason, the characteristic structure and language use of these sections and the relationship or interaction between them and their neighboring/the other sections with partly analogous communicative purposes or propositional content (such as the Introduction and LR sections studied in the present case, and the independent R, D, C sections, and the blended Results and Discussion sections) are worthy of closer scrutiny.

The present study has provided possible structures for the introductions (which are used before the LR) and the LRs, which however need to be validated by future research conducted in other disciplines. As the research literature on the comparison of structure and citation use between the Introduction and LR sections is still sparse, an extension of the present study should be made, using the same frameworks, to determine whether there are other variations in the other disciplinary areas. It may also be worthwhile to apply the modified classification frameworks of RVs, citation forms and citation functions adopted in this study to the analysis of citation use in other ERA sections such as the Discussion or the coalesced Results and Discussion section.

It is hoped that this project will engender further research along similar lines, e.g., the comparison of rhetorical structure, function and citation use in the thesis Introduction and LR chapters. It would be interesting to see how the relationship between this pair of part-genres differ from or resemble to that in the RA.

Like many other genre studies, this study aims to generate useful pedagogical insights, and thus attaches much importance to the shared and standardized (idealized) discursive and social conventions. However, the role of other aspects associated with the complex and dynamic world of academic discourse such as personal psychological reality to accomplish private intentions (Bhatia, 1993, 2001, 2012) and the relationship between individuality and discourse community (Hyland, 2012) have been largely neglected. Especially for the proficient student writers, with their knowledge about disciplinary discursive and socially accepted norms in mind, how to negotiate the relationship between the cultural norms of the academy and individual variation in text construction and comprehension to establish their individual scholarly identity whilst maintaining community membership is a particular facet they are particularly concerned about. However, this aspect has been insufficiently attended to in both EAP pedagogy and research and thus there is a need for more future research undertaken in this regard. Also, as remarked by Bhatia (2001: 87), "the nature of discourse structure is essentially socio-cognitive". While in genre research, disciplinary community consensus on discursive norms has been given foremost importance, other factors such as individual cognitive complexities that are most likely to bring in variations and contribute to allowable dynamic flexibility of the genre/part-genre also merit more scholarly attention (Bhatia, 2012).

References

Anthony, L., & Bowen, M. (2013). The language of mathematics: A corpus-based analysis of research article writing in a neglected field. *Asian ESP Journal, 9*(2), 5–25.

Becher, T. (1994). The significance of disciplinary differences. *Studies in Higher Education, 19*(2), 151–161.

Becher, T., & Trowler, P. R. (2001). *Academic tribes and territories: Intellectual inquiry and the culture of disciplines* (2nd ed.). Buckingham: Open University Press.

Berkenkotter, C., & Huckin, T. (1995). *Genre knowledge in disciplinary communication: Cognition, culture, power*. Hilldale: Lawrence Erlbaum Associates.

Bhatia, V. K. (1993). *Analyzing genre: Language use in professional settings*. New York: Longman.

Bhatia, V. K. (2001). Analyzing genre: Some conceptual issues. In M. Hewing (Ed.), *Academic writing in context: Implications and applications: Papers in honour of Tony Dudley-Evans* (pp. 79–92). Birmingham: University of Birmingham Press.

Bhatia, V. K. (2004). *Worlds of written discourse: A genre-based view*. London: Continuum.

Bhatia, V. K. (2012). *Critical reflections on genre analysis. Ibérica, 24,* 17–28.

Dees, R. (2000). *Writing the modern research paper* (3rd ed.). Boston: Allyn and Bacon.

Del Saz-Rubio, M. M. (2011). A pragmatic approach to the macro-structure and metadiscoursal features of research article introductions in the field of agricultural sciences. *English for Specific Purposes, 30*(4), 258–271.

Hyland, K. (1999). Academic attribution: Citation and the construction of disciplinary knowledge. *Applied Linguistics, 20*(3), 341–367.

Hyland, K. (2000). *Disciplinary discourses: Social interaction in academic writing*. London: Longman Pearson Education.

Hyland, K. (2002). Activity and evaluation: Reporting practices in academic writing. In J. Flowerdew (Ed.), *Academic discourse* (pp. 115–130). Harlow: Pearson Education Limited.

Hyland, K. (2012). *Disciplinary identities: Individuality and community in academic writing*. Cambridge: Cambridge Applied Linguistics.

Jalilifar, A. (2012). Academic attribution: Citation analysis in master's theses and research articles in applied linguistics. *International Journal of Applied Linguistics, 22*(1), 24–41.

Kanoksilapatham, B. (2005). Rhetorical structure of biochemistry research articles. *English for Specific Purposes, 24*(3), 269–292.

Körner, A. M. (2008). *Guide to publishing a scientific paper*. Abingdon: Routledge.

Kuteeva, M., & McGrath, L. (in press). The theoretical research article as a reflection of disciplinary practices: The case of pure mathematics. *Applied Linguistics*.

Kwan, B. S. C. (2005). *A genre analysis of literature reviews in doctoral theses*. Unpublished doctoral dissertation, City University of Hong Kong.

Kwan, B. S. C. (2006). The schematic structure of literature reviews in doctoral theses of applied linguistics. *English for Specific Purposes, 25,* 30–55.

Kwan, B. S. C., & Chan, H. (2014). An investigation of source use in the results and the closing sections of empirical articles in information systems: In search of a functional-semantic citation typology for pedagogical purposes. *Journal of English for Academic Purposes, 14,* 29–47.

Kwan, B. S. C., Chan, H., & Lam, C. (2012). Evaluating prior scholarship in literature reviews of research articles: A comparative study of practices in two research paradigms. *English for Specific Purposes, 31,* 188–201.

Lang, H. L. (2004). *The use of reporting verbs in literature reviews of Taiwanese postgraduate business students*. Unpublished doctoral dissertation, The University of Manchester.

Lave, J., & Wenger, E. (1991). *Situated learning: Legitimate peripheral participation*. New York: Cambridge University Press.

Lester, J. D., & Lester, J. D. (2006). *Writing research papers in the social sciences*. New York: Pearson/Longman.

Mur-Dueñas, P. (2009). Citation in business management research articles: A contrastive (English-Spanish) corpus-based analysis. In E. Suomela-Salmi & F. Dervin (Eds.), *Cross-cultural and cross-linguistic perspectives on academic discourse* (pp. 49–60). Amsterdam: John Benjamins.

Petrić, B. (2007). Rhetorical functions of citations in high- and low-rated master's theses. *Journal of English for Academic Purposes, 6*(3), 238–253.

Rogoff, B. (1990). *Apprenticeship in thinking*. New York: Oxford University Press.

Rogoff, B. (1995). Observing sociocultural activity on three planes: Participatory appropriation, guided participation, and apprenticeship. In J. V. Wertch, A. del Rio, & A. Pablo (Eds.), *Socio-cultural studies of mind* (pp. 139–164). Cambridge: Cambridge University Press.

Samraj, B. (2002). Introductions in research articles: Variations across disciplines. *English for Specific Purposes, 21*(1), 1–17.

Samraj, B. (2005). An exploration of a genre set: Research article abstracts and introductions in two disciplines. *English for Specific Purposes, 24*(2), 141–156.

Samraj, B. (2008). A discourse analysis of master's theses across disciplines with a focus on introductions. *Journal of English for Academic Purposes, 7,* 55–67.

Schryer, C. F. (1994). The lab vs. the clinic: Sites of competing genres. In A. Freedman & P. Medway (Eds.), *Genre and* the *new rhetoric* (pp. 105–124). London: Taylor and Francis.

Soles, D. (2010). *The essentials of academic writing* (2nd ed.). Boston, MA: Wadsworth.

Sollaci, L. B., & Pereira, M. G. (2004). The introduction, methods, results and discussion (IMRAD) structure: A fifty-year survey. *Journal of the Medical Library Association, 92*(3), 364–367.

Swales, J. M. (1990). *Genre analysis: English in academic and research settings*. Cambridge; New York: Cambridge University Press.

Swales, J. M. (2004). *Research genres: Explorations and applications*. Cambridge; New York: Cambridge University Press.

Swales, J. M. (2014). Variation in citational practice in a corpus of student biology papers: From parenthetical plonking to intertextual storytelling. *Written Communication, 31*(1), 118–141.

Tessuto, G. (2015). Generic structure and rhetorical moves in English-language empirical law research articles: Sites of interdisciplinary and interdiscursive cross-over. *English for Specific Purposes, 37*(1), 13–26.

Thomas, S., & Hawes, T. P. (1994). Reporting verbs in medical journal articles. *English for Specific Purposes, 13*(2), 129–148.

Thompson, P. (2001). *A pedagogically-motivated corpus-based examination of Ph.D. theses: Macrostructure, citation practices and uses of modal verbs*. Unpublished doctoral dissertation, The University of Reading.

Thompson, G., & Ye, Y. (1991). Evaluation in the reporting verbs used in academic papers. *Applied Linguistics, 12*(4), 365–382.

Yang, R. Y., & Allison, D. (2003). Research articles in applied linguistics: Moving from results to conclusions. *English for Specific Purposes, 22*(4), 365–385.

Yang, R. Y., & Allison, D. (2004). Research articles in applied linguistics: Structures from a functional perspective. *English for Specific Purposes, 23*(3), 264–279.

Appendix A
Distribution of ERAs and Major Structural Patterns in the 39 Disciplines

As the study was designed to underpin courses and materials on RA writing for research students across the University, the disciplines selected in the first stage of the study essentially corresponded to the institution's 24 departments. In some cases, these departments comprise more than one discipline (e.g., Applied Biology and Chemical Technology, Management and Marketing). This explains the "departmental" nature of some of the disciplines below. The second stage of the study involved collecting RAs from 15 disciplines (mainly in the social sciences and humanities) not taught at the University and generally under-researched in ESP. These are recognizable single disciplines (but each no doubt comprising various distinct areas or streams of research). Given that there are 20 RAs chosen for each of the 39 disciplines and not all of them are empirical, I report those structural patterns that are employed no less than three times as "major" structural patterns.

Disciplines	No. of ERAs (no. of structural patterns)	Major structural patterns (frequency)	Disciplines	No. of ERAs (no. of structural patterns)	Major structural patterns (frequency)
Applied biology and chemical technology	19 (8)	IMRD (5) IMRDC (5) IRDCM (3)	Accounting and finance	12 (5)	ILM[RD]C (5)
Building services engineering	19 (7)	ILM[RD]C (6) IM[RD]C (6)	Electronic and information engineering	12 (7)	IL[MRD]C (3) ILM[RD]C (3)
Applied linguistics/ELT	19 (12)	ILMRDC (5)	Electrical engineering	11 (6)	ILM[RD]C (4)

(continued)

(Kathy). L. Lin, *Perspectives on the Introductory Phase of Empirical Research Articles*, Corpora and Intercultural Studies 5, https://doi.org/10.1007/978-981-32-9204-8

(continued)

Disciplines	No. of ERAs (no. of structural patterns)	Major structural patterns (frequency)	Disciplines	No. of ERAs (no. of structural patterns)	Major structural patterns (frequency)
Optometry	18 (8)	IMRD (3) IMRDC (3)	Applied social science	10 (5)	ILMRD (3) IM[RD]C (3)
Textiles and clothing	18 (5)	IM[RD]C (14)	Applied physics	10 (5)	IM[RD]C (5)
Health technology and informatics	18 (5)	IMRD (9) IMRDC (4)	Anthropology	9 (7)	None
Education	16 (6)	IMRD (5) ILM[RD]C (4) ILMRD (3)	Economics	9 (5)	ILM[RD]C (3) IM[RD]C (3)
Management and marketing	16 (9)	ILM[RD]C (6) ILMRDC (3)	Design	8 (8)	None
Psychology	16 (8)	IMRD (7)	Logistics	8 (7)	None
Archaeology	15 (10)	IL[MRD]C (4) ILMRD (3)	Geography	7 (4)	ILM[RD]C (4)
Civil and structural engineering	15 (7)	ILM[RD]C (7)	Sociology	7 (4)	ILMRD (3)
Industrial and systems engineering	15 (10)	ILM[RD]C (6)	Music	6 (4)	IMRD (3)
Theoretical linguistics	15 (9)	IMRD (3) ILMRDC (3)	Applied mathematics	4 (3)	None
Building and real estate	14 (7)	ILM[RD]C (5) IM[RD]C (4)	Law	3 (3)	None
Computing	14 (8)	ILM[RD]C (5)	Political science	3 (3)	None
Hotel and tourism	14 (10)	None	History	1 (1)	None
Land surveying and geoinformatics	14 (7)	ILM[RD]C (4) IM[RD]C (4)	Literature	1 (1)	None

(continued)

(continued)

Disciplines	No. of ERAs (no. of structural patterns)	Major structural patterns (frequency)	Disciplines	No. of ERAs (no. of structural patterns)	Major structural patterns (frequency)
Nursing	14 (9)	IMRDC (4)	Philosophy	1 (1)	None
Rehabilitation sciences	14 (7)	IMRD (5) IMRDC (4)	History of art	0 (0)	None
Mechanical engineering	13 (5)	IM[RD]C (4) ILM[RD]C (4) ILMRDC (3)			

Appendix B
A List of Source ERAs

1. 30 ERAs with Their Introductory Phases Structured in "I+LR" from Five Journals in CE

(1) ***Transportation***

Farber, S., Paez, A., Mercado, R. G., Roorda, M., & Morency, C. (2011). A time-use investigation of shopping participation in three Canadian cities: Is there evidence of social exclusion? *Transportation, 38*(1), 17–44.

Kang, H., & Scott, D. M. (2011). Impact of different criteria for identifying intra-household interactions: A case study of household time allocation. *Transportation, 38*(1), 81–99.

Akar, G., Clifton, K. J., & Doherty, S. T. (2011). Discretionary activity location choice: In-home or out-of-home? *Transportation, 38*(1), 101–122.

Duncan, M. (2011). The cost saving potential of carsharing in a US context. *Transportation, 38*(2), 363–382.

Currie, G., Ahern, A., & Delbosc, A. (2011). Exploring the drivers of light rail ridership: An empirical route level analysis of selected Australian, North American and European systems. *Transportation, 38*(3), 545–560.

Alizadeh, A. H., & Talley, W. K. (2011). Microeconomic determinants of dry bulk shipping freight rates and contract times. *Transportation, 38*(3), 561–579.

(2) ***Journal of Computing in Civil Engineering***

Tang, P., Huber, D., & Akinci, B. (2011). Characterization of laser scanners and algorithms for detecting flatness defects on concrete surfaces. *Journal of Computing in Civil Engineering, 25*(1), 31–42.

De Gouveia, L. T., Costa, L. d. F., Senger, L. J., Albertini, M. K., & de Mello, R. F. (2011). Entropy-based approach to analyze and classify mineral aggregates. *Journal of Computing in Civil Engineering, 25*(1), 75–84.

Park, J., Kim, B., Kim, C., & Kim, H. (2011). 3D/4D CAD applicability for life-cycle facility management. *Journal of Computing in Civil Engineering, 25*(2), 129–138.

(Kathy). L. Lin, *Perspectives on the Introductory Phase of Empirical Research Articles*, Corpora and Intercultural Studies 5, https://doi.org/10.1007/978-981-32-9204-8

Chou, J., Chiu, C., Farfoura, M., & Al-Taharwa, I. (2011). Optimizing the prediction accuracy of concrete compressive strength based on a comparison of data-mining techniques. *Journal of Computing in Civil Engineering, 25*(3), 242–253.

Tatari, O., & Skibniewski, M. J. (2011). Empirical analysis of construction enterprise information systems: Assessing system integration, critical factors, and benefits. *Journal of Computing in Civil Engineering, 25*(5), 347–356.

Joshua, L., & Varghese, K. (2011). Accelerometer-based activity recognition in construction. *Journal of Computing in Civil Engineering, 25*(5), 370–379.

(3) ***Journal of Geotechnical and Geoenvironmental Engineering***

Cox, B. R., & Beekman, A. N. (2011). Intramethod variability in ReMi dispersion measurements and V_s estimates at shallow bedrock sites. *Journal of Geotechnical and Geoenvironmental Engineering, 137*(4), 354–362.

Tastan, E. O., Edil, T. B., Benson, C. H., & Aydilek, A. H. (2011). Stabilization of organic soils with fly ash. *Journal of Geotechnical and Geoenvironmental Engineering, 137*(9), 819–833.

Cote, J., Fillion, M., & Konrad, J. (2011). Estimating hydraulic and thermal conductivities of crushed granite using porosity and equivalent particle size. *Journal of Geotechnical and Geoenvironmental Engineering, 137*(9), 834–842.

Chittoori, B., & Puppala, A. J. (2011). Quantitative estimation of clay mineralogy in fine-grained soils. *Journal of Geotechnical and Geoenvironmental Engineering, 137*(11), 997–1008.

Rowe, R. K., Bostwick, L. E., & Take, W. A. (2011). Effect of GCL properties on shrinkage when subjected to wet-dry cycles. *Journal of Geotechnical and Geoenvironmental Engineering, 137*(11), 1019–1027.

Doherty, P., & Gavin, K. (2011). Shaft capacity of open-ended piles in clay. *Journal of Geotechnical and Geoenvironmental Engineering, 137*(11), 1090–1102.

(4) ***Journal of Transportation Engineering***

Gonzalez, A., Cubrinovski, M., Pidwerbesky, B., & Alabaster, D. (2011). Strength and deformational characteristics of foamed bitumen mixes under suboptimal conditions. *Journal of Transportation Engineering, 137*(1), 1–10.

Vadlamani, S., Chen, E., Ahn, S., & Washington, S. (2011). Identifying large truck hot spots using crash counts and PDOEs. *Journal of Transportation Engineering, 137*(1), 11–21.

Li, X., Lord, D., & Zhang, Y. (2011). Development of accident modification factors for rural frontage road segments in Texas using generalized additive models. *Journal of Transportation Engineering, 137*(1), 74–83.

Karwa, V., & Donnell, E. T. (2011). Predicting pavement marking retroreflectivity using artificial neural networks: Exploratory analysis. *Journal of Transportation Engineering, 137*(2), 91–103.

Khurshid, M. B., Irfan, M., & Labi, S. (2011). Optimal performance threshold determination for highway asset interventions: Analytical framework and application. *Journal of Transportation Engineering, 137*(2), 128–139.

Villwock, N. M., Blond, N., & Tarko, A. P. (2011). Cable barriers and traffic safety on rural interstates. *Journal of Transportation Engineering, 137*(4), 248–259.

(5) ***Journal of Composites for Construction***

Galal, K., & Enginsal, M. A. (2011). Flexural behavior of GFRP-reinforced concrete masonry beams. *Journal of Composites for Construction, 15*(1), 21–31.

Alves, J., El-Ragaby, A., & El-Salakawy, E. (2011). Durability of GFRP bars' bond to concrete under different loading and environmental conditions. *Journal of Composites for Construction, 15*(3), 249–262.

Shahi, A., West, J. S., & Pandey, M. D. (2011). Strengthening of Gulfport 230 kV wooden transmission structures with glass-fiber-reinforced polymer wrap. *Journal of Composites for Construction, 15*(3), 364–373.

Razaqpur, A. G., Shedid, M., & Petrina, D. (2011). Behavior of beams strengthened with novel self-anchored near-surface-mounted CFRP bars. *Journal of Composites for Construction, 15*(4), 625–634.

El-Mogy, M., El-Ragaby, A., & El-Salakawy, E. (2011). Effect of transverse reinforcement on the flexural behavior of continuous concrete beams reinforced with FRP. *Journal of Composites for Construction, 15*(5), 672–681.

Kirby, J. E., & Orton, S. L. (2011). Residual strength of impact-damaged CFRP used to strengthen concrete structures. *Journal of Composites for Construction, 15*(5), 782–789.

2. 30 ERAs with Their Introductory Phases Structured in "I+LR" from Five Journals in AL

(1) ***Applied Linguistics***

Millar, N. (2011). The processing of malformed formulaic language. *Applied Linguistics, 32*(2), 129–148.

Tin, T. B. (2011). Language creativity and co-emergence of form and meaning in creative writing tasks. *Applied Linguistics, 32*(2), 215–235.

Szczepaniak, R., & Lew, R. (2011). The role of imagery in dictionaries of idioms. *Applied Linguistics, 32*(3), 323–347.

Littlemore, J., Chen, P. T., Koester, A., & Barnden, J. (2011). Difficulties in metaphor comprehension faced by international students whose first language is not English. *Applied Linguistics, 32*(4), 408–429.

Kormos, J., Kiddle, T., & Csizér, K. (2011). Systems of goals, attitudes, and self-related beliefs in second-language-learning motivation. *Applied Linguistics, 32*(5), 495–516.

Luzón, M. J. (2011). 'Interesting post, but I disagree': Social presence and antisocial behaviour in academic weblogs. *Applied Linguistics, 32*(5), 517–540.

(2) ***Studies in Second Language Acquisition***

Charkova, K. D., & Halliday, L. J. (2011). Second- and foreign- language variation in tense backshifting in indirect reported speech. *Studies in Second Language Acquisition, 33*(1), 1–32.

Lee-Ellis, S. (2011). The elicited production of Korean relative clauses by heritage speakers. *Studies in Second Language Acquisition, 33*(1), 57–89.

Tremblay, A. (2011). Proficiency assessment standards in second language acquisition research: "Closing" the gap. *Studies in Second Language Acquisition, 33*(3), 339–372.

Fitzpatrick, T., & Izura, C. (2011). Word association in L1 and L2: An exploratory study of response types, response times, and interlingual mediation. *Studies in Second Language Acquisition, 33*(3), 373–398.

Spinner, P. (2011). Second language assessment and morphosyntactic development. *Studies in Second Language Acquisition, 33*(4), 529–561.

Omaki, A., & Schulz, B. (2011). Filler-gap dependencies and island constraints in second-language sentence processing. *Studies in Second Language Acquisition, 33*(4), 563–588.

(3) ***Language Learning***

Sagarra, N., & Herschensohn, J. (2011). Proficiency and animacy effects on L2 gender agreement processes during comprehension. *Language Learning, 61*(1), 80–116.

Serrano, R. (2011). The time factor in EFL classroom practice. *Language Learning, 61*(1), 117–145.

Park, E. S. (2011). Learner-generated noticing of written L2 input: What do learners notice and why? *Language Learning, 61*(1), 146–186.

Vidal, K. (2011). A comparison of the effects of reading and listening on incidental vocabulary acquisition. *Language Learning, 61*(1), 219–258.

Trude, A. M., & Tokowicz, N. (2011). Negative transfer from Spanish and English to Portuguese pronunciation: The roles of inhibition and working memory. *Language Learning, 61*(1), 259–280.

Wu, S. (2011). Learning to express motion events in an L2: The case of Chinese directional complements. *Language Learning, 61*(2), 414–454.

(4) ***TESOL Quarterly***

Ruegg, R., Fritz, E. & Holland, J. (2011). Rater sensitivity to qualities of lexis in writing. *TESOL Quarterly*, *45*(1), 63–80.

Sasaki, M. (2011). Effects of varying lengths of study-abroad experiences on Japanese EFL students' L2 writing ability and motivation: A longitudinal study. *TESOL Quarterly*, *45*(1), 81–105.

Collins, L. & White, J. (2011). An intensive look at intensity and language learning. *TESOL Quarterly*, *45*(1), 106–133.

Ferris, D., Brown, J., Liu, H. S., & Stine, M. E. A. (2011). Responding to L2 students in college writing classes: Teacher perspectives. *TESOL Quarterly*, *45*(2), 207–234.

Alptekin, C. & Ercetin, G. (2011). Effects of working memory capacity and content familiarity on literal and inferential comprehension in L2 reading. *TESOL Quarterly*, *45*(2), 235–266.

Martinez, R. & Murphy, V. A. (2011). Effects of frequency and idiomaticity on second language reading comprehension. *TESOL Quarterly*, *45*(2), 267–290.

(5) ***English for Specific Purposes***

Gray, B., & Cortes, V. (2011). Perception vs. evidence: An analysis of *this* and *these* in academic prose. *English for Specific Purposes, 30*(1), 31–43.

Maria, K. (2011). Wikis and academic writing: Changing the writer–reader relationship. *English for Specific Purposes, 30*(1), 44–57.

Koyalan, A., & Mumford, S. (2011). Changes to English as an additional language writers' research articles: From spoken to written register. *English for Specific Purposes, 30*(2), 113–123.

Stephen, P. (2011). Asserting or deflecting expertise? Exploring the rhetorical practices of master's theses in the philosophy of education. *English for Specific Purposes, 30*(3), 176–185.

Maria R., D. (2011). Exploring perception and use of everyday language and medical terminology among international medical graduates in a medical ESP course in Australia. *English for Specific Purposes, 30*(3), 186–197.

Wenhua, H. (2011). The vocabulary thresholds of business textbooks and business research articles for EFL learners. *English for Specific Purposes, 30*(4), 247–257.

Appendix C
CCEI28 as an Example of the Analysis of Two-Move Orientation Introductions in CE

After the move and sub-move analysis, the text is no longer paragraphed as its original version. It has been rearranged into segments representing different sub-moves. Additionally, some sub-moves are signaled explicitly as shown in the emboldened words below.

1.1 Carsharing is a membership-based service that provides short term access to automobiles (TCRP, 2005). Members can reserve one of a fleet of vehicles parked at various locations across a city. Payment for this service usually involves a small membership fee and a usage rate based on time and distance traveled, although the specifics of payment will vary with each carsharing organization. Unlike traditional car rentals or taxi service, carsharing can provide a relatively inexpensive alternative to auto ownership for those with occasional need of an automobile.

1.2 Transportation planners have begun to recognize carsharing as **a potentially important** component of a diversified and sustainable transport system (Enoch and Taylor, 2006; Goldman and Gorham, 2006; Parent,2006; Wright and Curtis, 2004).

1.1 It can compliment public transit, biking, and walking by serving certain trips that these non-auto modes cannot effectively cover (Huwer, 2004; Barth et al., 2004). Even in the most transit and pedestrian friendly locations, the flexibility, speed, and convenience of a private auto can significantly enhance a household's travel options. Carsharing can provide a measure of automobility without needing to incur the full expense and inconveniences of owning a vehicle (or a second or third vehicle as the case may be).

(Kathy). L. Lin, *Perspectives on the Introductory Phase of Empirical Research Articles*, Corpora and Intercultural Studies 5, https://doi.org/10.1007/978-981-32-9204-8

1.2 Carsharing forms a very small part of our current transport system **but has grown rapidly in recent years.** It **has been successful** in various European cities since the 1980s, came to Canada in the early 1990s, and then the US in the late 1990s (Shaheen et al., 2006, 1998). In the past decade, it **has gained some traction** and **expanded into** several dozen North American cities. Carsharing membership **has grown exponentially** to nearly 280,000 people in the US and an additional 40,000 members in Canada (Shaheen et al., 2009). For carsharing to generate significant aggregate benefits and truly improve sustainability, it must **obviously continue to expand.**

1.1 A few hundred thousand carsharing members make up only a tiny fraction of North American drivers.

1.3 **One key aspect** in the potential growth of carsharing is simply whether it can save people money (Schuster et al., 2005).

2.1 This paper seeks to address this issue by empirically examining the economic viability of carsharing from the perspective of potential customers in the San Francisco Bay Area. More specifically, this research estimates the share of Bay Area vehicles for which carsharing can provide a cost effective substitute.

Appendix D
CALI9 as an Example of the Analysis of Two-Move Orientation Introductions in AL

To show clearly how the move and sub-move analysis is conducted, the text is not paragraphed as its original version but rearranged according to different sub-move units. To facilitate readers' understanding, some sub-moves are signaled as shown in the emboldened words below.

1.1 Idiomatic expressions, with their colourful literal meaning, seem to lend themselves perfectly to a graphical presentation.

1.2 Popular ELT books (Watcyn-Jones, 1990; Hancock, 1992; Milton and Evans, 1998; Wright, 2002) have capitalized on this characteristic **for a long time** now, and a few idioms dictionaries (OID2, CID2) **follow suit**. **More interestingly**, the new editions of idioms dictionaries (CCID2, CID2, OID2) supply some of their entries with brief etymological notes.

1.1 Both methods——pictures and etymology——evoke mental imagery (as defined in Lakoff 1987), and can be treated as an application, or a reflection, of the cognitive linguistic (henceforth CL) views on idiomaticity.

2.1 **In this article, we investigate** 'imagery' in the sense of verbal and non-verbal elements (here, in the form of etymological information and pictures) that may stimulate the formation of conventional images (Lakoff 1987: 446-447) associated with the literal readings of idioms.

(Kathy). L. Lin, *Perspectives on the Introductory Phase of Empirical Research Articles*, Corpora and Intercultural Studies 5, https://doi.org/10.1007/978-981-32-9204-8

2.6 In order to assess the merits of placing illustrations and etymological notes next to traditional explanations of idioms, one needs to consider the findings in at least three fields: (i) idiom semantics from the CL perspective; (ii) the effect of motivating information on idiom acquisition; (iii) the role of visuals and etymology in pedagogical lexicography. Additional useful insights can be gained from research into picture perception and memory models. These issues will structure the selective overview of the literature in the first part of the article; the empirical part reports on the results of an experiment, which is an attempt to answer questions addressing the role of imagery in dictionaries of idioms.

Appendix E
CALL20 as an Example LR Text Containing Both "Theoretical Review" and "Contextual Background" Components

1. Wikis and Academic Writing
A wiki has been defined as a "freely expandable collection of interlinked web pages, a hypertext system for storing and modifying information-a database, where each page is easily edited by any user with a forms-capable Web browser client" (Leuf & Cunningham, 2001, p. 14). Its basic features include creating and editing texts, linking different pages through hyperlinks, inserting images and links to other sites, tracking changes and comparing different versions of the text. Most wiki engines are open source (e.g. Wikispaces, PmWiki, TWiki,TikiWiki, and the Wikipedia engine, MediaWiki). In the context of EAP, this software can be used for collectively producing, organising and sustaining textual, visual, and auditory resources, thus creating an environment that relies on learner interdependence. From the sociocultural point of view, the wiki holds the potential for advancing and realizing a collective zone of proximal development (Vygotsky, 1978, as discussed by Lund, 2008).

Thus, a wiki provides a platform for collaborative writing. Wikipedia, the largest wiki project, is often frowned upon in academic circles, largely due to its alleged bias and lack of credibility, reminiscent of the earlier perception of the web (Slaouti, 2002). Nevertheless, the scale of the project makes it unique, and, whether we as teachers like it or not, many students use it in their studies. As Dalby (2007, p. 6) it: "Wikipedia contains nonsense alongside the sense; it contains propaganda and error alongside the facts. It's fiercely up to date, except when it isn't. Wikipedia is an encyclopedia for the world as it is". Thanks to the success of the Wikipedia project, an overwhelming majority of people in academic life are familiar with the wiki software, including its major functions and the layout of a typical wiki page (article, discussion, edit, and history), which is different from traditional html websites. In fact, the Wikipedia article can be considered one of the new academic genres (Myers, 2010), but this question will remain outside the scope of our discussion. What is of interest for our purposes is the democratic nature of the Wikipedia and the collaborative philosophy behind it. If any reader can become a writer of the same text, does writing become more reader-oriented? In other words, does a wiki provide a more natural environment for reader-oriented writing?

(Kathy). L. Lin, *Perspectives on the Introductory Phase of Empirical Research Articles*, Corpora and Intercultural Studies 5, https://doi.org/10.1007/978-981-32-9204-8

In EAP, writing has been seen as a social activity dependent on the relationship between writer, reader and the social context (e.g. Hyland, 2000; Thompson, 2001). Hyland (2002) refers to reader-oriented approaches to teaching and researching writing, including writing as social interaction, writing as social construction, and writing as power and ideology. The first two perspectives are particularly relevant here, since they lay emphasis on the writer-reader relationship and the notion of the writer as a member of a given discourse community. Although Hyland describes the interactionists and the constructivists as opposing schools, the former working from individuals to groups and the latter proceeding from social groups to individuals, in practice, these two approaches seem to be complementary. This way, we can perceive writing as a cyclical process in which writers simultaneously shape their discourse to involve the reader and are influenced by the reader's expectations resulting from community practices; it is this view of writing that inspired the study presented in this paper.

Related to reader-oriented writing is the concept of metadiscourse, "the cover term for the self-reflective expressions used to negotiate interactional [emphasis added] meanings in a text, assisting the writer (or speaker) to express a viewpoint and engage with readers [emphasis added] as members of a particular community" (Hyland, 2005, pp. 37–38); one of its key principles is to express writer-reader interaction. Metadiscursal devices can be viewed as resources indicating the writer's position towards the content or the reader of the text. There are several taxonomies of metadiscourse (e.g. Crismore, Markkanen, & Steffensen, 1993; Hyland & Tse, 2004; Thompson, 2001; Adel, 2010), but "no taxonomy can do more than partially represent a fuzzy reality" (Hyland & Tse, 2004, p. 175), which is why there is no general agreement among metadiscourse researchers. As my main focus is on collaborative writing on the wiki, the distinction between 'interactive' and 'interactional' resources is particularly relevant: "interactive resources help to guide the reader through the text, while interactional resources involve the reader collaboratively in the development of the text" (Thompson, 2001, p. 58). The former concern organisational features of the text such as transitions, frame markers and text patterns (e.g. problem-solution), whereas the latter are meant to involve the reader in the argument of the text by commenting on and evaluating the content through modality and evaluation, and by assigning speech roles to the writer and the reader. Examples of such interactional resources include rhetorical questions (Widdowson, 1984), commands (Swales et al., 1998), statements from the reader to be contradicted, as well as different forms of modalisation (Thompson, 2001, pp. 65–66). Hyland and Tse (2004) offer a more comprehensive classification of interactional resources under five categories: hedges, engagement markers, boosters, attitude markers and self-mentions. These functional categories can have exponents of very varied formal types; for example, phrases with I can be attitude markers or self-mentions, depending on the context and collocation. Hyland and Tse's taxonomy, together with elements of Thompson's (2001), will form a basis for the ensuing analysis of interactional resources in the texts published by students on the wiki (further described in Sect. 4).

A convergence of the reader with the reader-in-the-text creates involvement which is perceived as "a crucial step in most types of argumentative, persuasive text, including academic papers and assignments; and collaboration is central form of involvement" (Thompson, 2001, p. 62). This idea ties in with the philosophy behind collaborative writing on the course wiki, echoing Bakhtin's (1986) views on the dialogic nature of language use and sociocultural and constructivist approaches in education which rely on learner collaboration and dialogue (Vygotsky, 1978). In other words, this paper draws links between two theoretical approaches; while collaborative learning theorists argue that learning arises out of interaction, metadiscourse can be used to measure how this interaction is manifested in writing.

2. Background to the Study

Effective Communication in English is a one-semester 10 ECTS-credit course at Stockholm University. Its overarching aim is to improve the students' ability to employ English for academic and professional purposes, covering a range of written and spoken genres (formal correspondence, argumentative texts, academic and professional reports, abstracts and summaries and oral presentations). The course is also designed to improve the students' overall language proficiency (both accuracy and fluency); a strong emphasis is also placed on the acquisition of general academic vocabulary and the development of formal writing skills. Throughout the course, each student is required to submit four written assignments, including a formal letter, an argumentative text, a summary/abstract of a formal report, and a special genre project based on each student's choice and needs. Some of these written assignments involved publishing on the course wiki.

Thus, the core elements of the Effective Communication course focus on various aspects of formal English use, leaving some leeway for each student to adapt the major tasks and assignments to his/her specific needs. This flexibility is important because in terms of linguistic, cultural, social, and educational backgrounds, the course participants comprise a very diverse group, including local and exchange students from different subject fields, as well as working or graduate students who need to improve their English for professional reasons. In the autumn semester of 2008, the Effective Communication group under investigation included fourteen students (eight females and six males), whose mother tongues included Bengali (1), Chinese (1), Czech (1), Finnish (1), French (1), German (1), Russian (1), Spanish (2) and Swedish (5). Their ages ranged from 20 to 54 (four students aged 18–25, six students 25–34, three students 35–49, and one student 50–64). Heterogeneous groups have long been a reality in higher education, but more with regard to language proficiency. In the case of Effective Communication, heterogeneity extends to students' subject fields and cultural backgrounds, thereby diversifying the learners' characteristics as L2 writers, i.e. their learning experiences, sense of audience and writer, ways of organising text, and so forth (Silva, 1993 in Hyland, 2003, p. 25). On the other hand, this kind of student diversity presents opportunities for opening a dialogue between different cultures and discourse communities and can be taken into consideration in the development of writing tasks.

A combination of two main approaches, genre and process orientation, was used to teach writing (Hyland, 2003). This arrangement allowed students to learn about the main genres of academic and professional writing, and, at the same time, fostered peer collaboration through brain-storming, drafting and peer review. Many students of Effective Communication had problems writing paragraphs and structuring texts in English, so they undoubtedly benefited from some more formal instruction in this regard. On the other hand, whenever possible the writing process involved peer revision and feedback, both in class and with the support of the course wiki. All written assignments were evaluated in terms of structure, content and accuracy. Good academic and professional writing in English is often measured by how reader-oriented a given text is, so the course participants were encouraged to write for other fellow students and, whenever relevant, for the members of their respective discourse communities, rather than for the teacher alone.

The course wiki (powered by MediaWiki, the Wikipedia engine, see Fig. 1) provided a platform for carrying out writing tasks and assignments focusing on three major topics: paragraph structure, coherence, and argumentation. The structure of the wiki was defined by the course instructor, but students participated in the choice of topics. The texts posted by the students on an individual basis were also analysed and discussed in class and afterwards revised online, thus fostering and extending peer review and collaboration.

The wiki task focusing on paragraph structure and coherence was designed around eight major topics: four related to academic life ('Internationalisation in Higher Education', 'Research and the industry', 'The Bologna process' and 'Education and ICT') and the other four to professional contexts ('Communication in a multinational company', 'Globalisation and the EU', 'Recent trends in financial reporting' and 'Humour in advertising'). Separate wiki pages were created for these eight topics, and students were divided into groupsaccordingly. Each student in a group had to come up with a topic sentence on one of the aspects of the major topic. These topic sentences were read and coordinated in class to avoid any overlap. Then, each student was required to write a paragraph around his/her topic sentence and post it on the appropriate wiki page so as to create a coherent text together with other students working on the same topic. It was up to each student to decide where to place the paragraph, what kind of linking expressions to use, and how to adapt the paragraph to the rest of the text. In this task, students were advised to employ 'interactive' resources (Thompson, 2001) such as transitions and frame markers. The discussion page of the wiki could be used for coordinating the content and structure of a given text. These collaboratively created texts were written over a period of up to 3 weeks and varied in terms of coherence and overall organisation. They were read and analysed in class by students not belonging to the same group, who then suggested further improvement and revision on the wiki. In this assignment, the wiki was used for collaborative writing and editing of texts on general topics. Thanks to the history tool, it was possible to see the stages in the creation of the texts and to trace each student's contribution.

The other major task to be carried out on the wiki concerned the writing of an argumentative essay. This type of text was chosen as one of the compulsory assignments because argumentation represents an essential part of academic writing, since all academic discourse is essentially persuasive (Hunston, 1994). Besides, Connor (1987) argues that there is a universal argumentation style that transcends cultural boundaries, which diminishes any potential problems in such a culturally diverse group. For this task, a separate wiki page was created for each student in the group.

After posting their contributions on the wiki pages, the students were required to read and discuss each other's texts in class, following the guidelines for peer review (Bjork & Raisanen, 2003) and to write comments concerning the structure, content and, if possible, correctness on the discussion page associated with each topic. In this case, each article page was meant to serve as a platform for individual, process-oriented writing and editing, whereas peer comments and feedback were posted on the discussion pages. The MediaWiki platform proved to be very suitable for this task, since it offers instant access to the text and tracks any changes.

In both tasks, using the wiki contributed to extending the readership of the students' texts and to encouraging peer feedback and collaboration, providing the course participants with a sense of a wider audience. Thanks to the history function, it was possible to trace each student's contribution and the number of revisions, including different versions of the text and stages in its creation. The discussion pages provided space for comments, feedback and exchange of ideas on a given topic, which was particularly useful for working students. However, it would be wrong to assume that the course wiki was received with the same degree of enthusiasm by all students. The ensuing sections are dedicated to an empirical study focussing on the students' self-reported experiences of writing on the wiki and on the analysis of interactional metadiscourse resources in their argumentative essays. More specifically, the following questions are addressed:

- Does writing on the wiki make students' texts more reader-oriented?
- Does writing on the wiki make students pay attention to structural organisation and grammatical correctness?
- What kind of interactional metadiscourse resources are used in argumentative texts published by students on the wiki?

Appendix F
CCEL_TR3 as an Example of the Analysis of Theoretical Reviews in CE

To show explicitly how the move and sub-move analysis is conducted, the text is not paragraphed as its original version but rearranged according to different sub-move units. To facilitate readers' understanding, some sub-moves are signaled as shown in the emboldened words below.

3.1a **Disadvantages of the previous research efforts can be summarized as follows.** First, **to the best knowledge of the writers**, 3D/4D CAD application areas through the entire project life cycle **have not yet been fully enumerated**. **Only** one of the design, construction, or operation phases is typically chosen, and the CAD model is developed **only** for that phase. In particular, **very little attention** has been given to the planning or operation and maintenance phases. Second, practitioners, such as construction field engineers, have played **limited** roles by confirming the discoveries of the researchers who are the main directors of these studies. More active roles by practitioners are desirable. Third, previous efforts to verify research results have generally relied on a **limited** number of case studies. **Few studies** have been devoted to discovering statistically meaningful results for understanding those projects for which 3D/4DCAD technology can be used effectively to improve existing construction processes.

4.1 **The main objective** of this research was to identify the areas in which 3D/4D CAD can significantly improve traditional construction processes. **The specific objectives** included:

--A survey result that included a large number of construction experts was produced, such that statistically valid conclusions could be derived.

--In the survey, the complete cycle of the construction projects--planning, design, construction, and operation and maintenance--was considered to understand the integrated effects of 3D/4D CAD in the construction industry.

--Construction practitioners' opinions were actively reflected in designing and conducting the survey to provide the industry perspective on 3D/4D CAD.

Mo\

(Kathy). L. Lin, *Perspectives on the Introductory Phase of Empirical Research Articles*, Corpora and Intercultural Studies 5, https://doi.org/10.1007/978-981-32-9204-8

and for improving construction simulation **(Behzadan and Kamat, 2007). Manrique et al., (2007)** combined an optimization model, 3D CAD, and animation to avoid potentially costly on-site errors. **Jongeling et al., (2008)** showed a novel way to extract different types of quantitative information from 4D CAD models for time-space analyses of construction operations. **Russell et al., (2009)** presented a dynamic visualization environment that combined 3D CAD and linear scheduling for shortening project duration, assessing their workability, and judging schedule quality. **Young et al., (2009)** surveyed thousands of A/E/C participants in North America to understand how many values were generated with the use of building information modeling.

1.2 The previous studies have significantly advanced the use of 3D/4D CAD in construction applications. These pioneering efforts have awakened industry practitioners to the possibility of process innovation by better visualizing, communicating, and integrating construction operations.

3.1b However, according to Young et al.,(2009), engineers believe that the functionality of 3D/4D models, or Building Information Modeling, **"does not apply well enough to what they do."** This finding indicates **the strong need** to identify existing and new construction applications for 3D/4D CAD, **from the perspective of practitioners**, to reach its full potential.

Appendix G
CALL19 as an LR Example with Its Theme-Bound Subsections Having Different Nature, Propositional Content and Functional Contribution to It

2. Literature Review

2.1. Demonstratives, Cohesion, and the Problem with Prescriptivisms

Cohesion is classically defined as "where the interpretation of some element in the discourse is dependent on that of another" (emphasis in original, Halliday & Hasan, 1976, p. 4), and it is because of the demonstratives' referential function that the structures carry so much cohesive weight. The debate as to whether or not cohesion is achieved when demonstratives are used as pronouns rather than determiners is a question of clarity. As Quirk, Greenbaum, Leech, and Svartvik (1985) point out, demonstratives may refer to a simple noun phrase, a clause, a sentence, or even a sequence of sentences. When a demonstrative is followed by a noun, that noun is actually the true reference item, and the noun provides lexical cohesion.

While the prescriptive rule provided by style manuals suggests that any problems of cohesion or clarity can be resolved by using a demonstrative determiner + noun phrase rather than a pronoun, this claim is not supported by literature on demonstratives. Demonstrative pronouns, such as this or these, often refer back to the entire sense of the preceding sentence or clause. Because of this ability to refer anaphorically to extended units of meaning, Finn (1995) and Halliday and Hasan (1976) remind us that it is not always possible to try and portray that meaning with a single noun or even a noun with structural modification. For example, consider the following excerpt, which comes from the second corpus being investigated in this study, a corpus of research articles in Materials and Civil Engineering (MCE).

(1) *For the clogging procedure, 63.5 g of clogging material is poured uniformly over the top of the specimen. Water is then showered over the specimen. This allows the clogging material to slowly penetrate into the specimen with minimal disturbance to the unbound aggregates. (MCE)*

In this example, a suitable noun would need to refer back to the ideas represented in the two sentences preceding the pronoun this, and finding such a noun is not always as simple as the style manual's instructions might suggest.

Halliday and Hasan (1976), while stating that cohesion is achieved regardless of whether a demonstrative is used as a determiner or a pronoun, claim that when used

(Kathy). L. Lin, *Perspectives on the Introductory Phase of Empirical Research Articles*, Corpora and Intercultural Studies 5, https://doi.org/10.1007/978-981-32-9204-8

as a determiner, the meaning of the structure is always the same as the antecedent, even if the authors or speakers do not use exactly the same word. When this is used as a pronoun, they claim that the "reference may still be identical; but it may be broader, referring to the general class denoted by the noun" (pp. 63–64).

A further distinction between demonstratives as determiners or pronouns is that pronominal use is an instance of ellipsis. Halliday and Hasan (1976) and Quirk et al. (1985) both concur that when a demonstrative is used as a pronoun and a noun could be easily added, then ellipsis occurs. Ellipsis, too, achieves cohesion, and is often a result of the quest for economy. Thus, the prescriptive debate concerning demonstratives comes down to balancing clarity with economy. This idea is supported by many researchers who investigate the use of demonstratives, such as Finn (1995), who argues that using a noun after a demonstrative may achieve clarity through redundancy, and that redundancy has advantages in that readers can clearly understand what the demonstrative structure refers to and disadvantages in that "using more symbols to convey the same amount of information slows down the flow of new information" (p. 244).

2.2. Previous Investigations into Demonstratives as Pronouns Versus Determiners

Few studies have focused specifically on the use of demonstratives in anaphoric reference and in relation to text cohesion. The studies that do exist primarily focus on the pronominal use, which may be a consequence of the prescriptive rules that exist. For example, Moskovit (1983) seeks to determine when pronominal this constitutes 'broad reference'–when the demonstrative refers back to something more than a nominal. Moskovit attempts to determine when broad reference is unclear by examining 28 examples of pronominal this, offering his own judgments of whether or not each example is clear or unclear. Steinberg et al. (1984) and Geisler et al. (1985) question Moskovit's interpretations and conclusions, but they are unambiguous in stating that their goal is to identify what is clear, not what is actually used, and to develop prescriptive rules to help student writers evaluate whether or not to use pronominal *this*.

Although these early studies offer a starting point, they focus on establishing prescriptivism, a practice which has in some circles fallen out of fashion. In addition, the research methodologies are problematic in that the examples being used are not justifiably representative of any specific register of language use. Furthermore, these studies focus primarily on the use of pronominal this, and little (if any) attention is paid to demonstrative determiners as a way of validating the prescriptive rules that have arisen. Although prescriptive rules call for the use of a demonstrative plus noun in order to eliminate referential ambiguity, attention is paid only in passing to whether or not having a noun following the demonstrative makes the message any clearer.

One exception to this focus on pronominal uses is Tyma's (1981) article that examines seven examples of demonstrative determiners in anaphoric reference from two Engineering textbooks. Tyma concludes that such anaphoric structures are utilized to give implicit classifications or definitions of the antecedent, and serve to overcome barriers to textual cohesion caused by "the problem of describing a nonlinear concept with the necessarily linear surface grammar of expository English" (p. 73). Again, this study looks at a very limited set of data–seven examples from two textbooks.

Swales (2005) is a second exception to the limitations mentioned above. Using a corpus of research articles from 10 disciplines, he compares 'attended' and 'unattended' *this*, finding that anywhere from 25 to 56% of sentence-initial this are pronominal uses within each discipline. Swales also looks at the five most frequent nouns which occur after attended this. Swales determines that these most frequent nouns can be classified as metadiscoursal (*this study, this article*), method-related (*method, process*), and result-related (*result, finding*).

In other studies, the focus of inquiry is a linguistic feature that often co-occurs with demonstratives, and thus demonstratives are also discussed. For example, Aktas and Cortes (2008) focus on 'shell' nouns (Hunston & Francis, 2000; Schmid, 2000), which can act as cohesive devices through the encapsulation of meanings expressed in prior discourse. Aktas and Cortes find that the pattern demonstrative determiner + shell noun is used by both student and professional writers, and that the novice writers particularly used this pattern in order to create inter-sentential cohesion. Charles (2003) also investigates shell nouns (although she calls these nouns 'retrospective labels' following Francis, 1994), focusing on nouns used after sentence-initial this that express the writer's epistemic or attitudinal stance. However, Charles concentrates on the encapsulation and stance-expressing functions of the nouns rather than the use of the demonstrative. In both Aktas and Cortes (2008) and Charles (2003), demonstratives are only a small part of an analysis focusing on another linguistic feature. Interestingly, as the results of the present study will show, it turns out that these shell nouns play important roles in the overall patterning of demonstrative determiners as well.

Our study investigates differences in the use of this/these as determiners and pronouns because prescriptivism claims that problems of clarity can be solved by simply using demonstratives as determiners rather than pronouns. Biber, Johansson, Leech, Conrad, and Finegan (1999) point out that using demonstratives as determiners allows for more noun phrase modification, which can either efficiently give readers more information or further clarify what the coreferent is. Additionally, Biber et al. (p. 237) report that noun phrases with demonstrative determiners are generally rare except in academic prose, where 20% of all anaphoric reference involves a demonstrative determiner and repeated noun or synonym. This difference in use across registers could be an indication that demonstrative determiners fulfill a significant function in academic writing.

Appendix H
The Working Guide for RV Classification and Analysis

I. The main categories of RVs in terms of denotation are the following.

Discourse (verbs refer to the verbal expression):*state, argue, claim and etc.*
Mental (verbs indicate the cognitive activity): *believe, regard, value, and etc.*
Research (verbs are related to the activity in the cited researcher's work): *calculate, measure, analyze, examine, and etc.*
Stative (verbs indicate the state of some phenomena, theories or other things in citations): *appear, become, exist, remain, retain, occur, and etc.*

II. The main categories of RVs in terms of evaluation are the following.

Writer Perspectives
Writer Factive (verbs express writers' acceptance and present the reported information as true): *find, acknowledge, reveal, point out and etc.*
Writer Counter-Factive (verbs express writers' disagreement and present the reported information as false): *fail, misuse, ignore, overlook and etc.*
Writer Non-factive (verbs does not indicate writers' attitudes towards the reported information but ascribe a view to the source author): *assume, predict, report, refer to and etc.*
Authors' perspectives (Writer Non-Factive)
Author Positive (verbs report the author of the cited work as positive): *assert, highlight, argue, recommend and etc.*
Author Neutral (verbs that does not indicate the attitude of the author): *quote, investigate, assess, conduct, examine and etc.*
Author Tentative (verbs that report the author as tentative): *suggest, indicate, posit, hypothesize and etc.*
Author Critical (verbs that report the author as critical): *disown, oppose, refute, condemn, object and etc.*

(Kathy). L. Lin, *Perspectives on the Introductory Phase of Empirical Research Articles*, Corpora and Intercultural Studies 5, https://doi.org/10.1007/978-981-32-9204-8

Appendix H
The Working Guide for RV Classification and Analysis

Appendix I
Interview Guide

Part I Structural Practices

1. Have you ever received any formal training on research writing? Any teaching or other working experience on writing for international publication?
2. Is there a strong convention in your field for structuring empirical RAs?
3. What are the major sections you usually use in your empirical RAs?
4. Do journals in your field have some recommendations or requirements in terms of structuring empirical RAs?
5. What are the sections you use before the Method? Why?
6. Can you compare the two approaches for structuring the opening phase of empirical RAs: using only an independent Introduction before the Method, and using both an Introduction and an LR section before the Method?
7. What are the functions of the Introduction and LR sections?
8. What is the relationship between the Introduction and LR sections?

Part II Citation Practices

1. Invite the interviewees to comment on my findings from the corpus-based analysis of citation distribution, citation formal and functional use, and RV use in Introductions and LRs (refer to an example text or more from my data whenever necessary).
2. Invite the interviewees to explain some interesting or potentially significant points found in their citation use and RV use in Introductions and LRs, no matter the findings here are similar to or different from those derived from my data.

(Kathy). L. Lin, *Perspectives on the Introductory Phase of Empirical Research Articles*, Corpora and Intercultural Studies 5, https://doi.org/10.1007/978-981-32-9204-8

Appendix J
CCEI2 as an Example of Practical-Problem Solving Introductions that Follow Feak and Swales's (2011) Structural Model for "Problem-Focused" Introductions

Mineral aggregates (rock fragments) are the main components of several materials used on construction, including portland cement concrete, asphalt concrete, road foundations, railroad ballast, drains, and filtering systems. Therefore, millions of tons of mineral aggregates are annually produced and consumed by the construction industry (Chandan et al., 2004; Macedo 1998; Murtagh et al., 2005).

Aggregates shall meet the quality requirements of the target application, based on technical specifications. Those requirements are directly related to appropriate properties of such materials. Physical properties such as compression and abrasion resistance, virtually necessary for all purposes of construction, are mainly determined by the original rock characteristics. However, the production process (in quarries) can significantly affect the quality of aggregates by removing weak layers altered, commonly observed in the middle layers of rocks (Kim et al., 2004; Roberts et al., 1996; Wettimuny and Penumadu, 2004).

Several issues such as construction failures and premature defects are attributed to the presence of weathered aggregates (Pinard and Jackalas, 1987; Tagnit-Hamou et al., 2005). Therefore, stone-quarries engineers and builders are strongly interested in the detection of weathered materials and, thus, to ensure quality and to avoid construction problems.

The weathering process begins when rocks are exposed to environmental conditions different from those existing at the time of their formation, due to the contact with new physical and chemical processes. Different weathering processes usually act simultaneously on the rock surface and the consequences may only be visible on surfaces (Baer and Snethlage, 1996). The weathering process usually changes the aggregate color appearance, causing discoloration, browning, and rust marks. In other words, weathered aggregates present superficial coloring different from the ones which present an original mineralogical condition (Gifkins et al., 2005).

There are many tests to evaluate weathered aggregates, among which is the petrographic analysis and mechanical tests. Mechanical tests are used to detect the decrease of aggregate mechanical strength caused by the weathering process (Bartley et al., 2007). Most tests employed to assess aggregates require appropriate laboratories and specialized technicians. Therefore, those tests make difficult the fast detection

(Kathy). L. Lin, *Perspectives on the Introductory Phase of Empirical Research Articles*, Corpora and Intercultural Studies 5, https://doi.org/10.1007/978-981-32-9204-8

of weathered aggregates, which is necessary on production environments such as in stone quarries, where extraction, transportation, breaking, and stocking up occur simultaneously. Any delay in the detection of altered aggregates may increase the production costs of the quarries. This happens mainly due to the time involved in extracting the rock, transporting, breaking, and stocking it up as well as the cost in terms of equipments and people to interrupt the production to remove altered material from stockpiles.

This paper presents an automatic method to detect weathered aggregates by assessing changes in colors and textures. This qualitative classification method is a particularly simple and fast way to detect the weathering process. The method extracts aggregate features from images and automatically classifies them based on surface characteristics. Results confirm that the method supports the detection of weathered aggregates.

Appendix K
CCEI7 as an Example of Practical-Problem Solving Introductions Involving Both the "Comparison" Move and the "Research-Gap Indication" Element

Masonry is one of the ancient construction methods and has been used by number of civilizations for centuries. Beams in masonry construction are mostly used as bond beams or lintel beams. They are located at the roof level or at floor levels and may have multiple functions such as tying the structure around its perimeter, transferring the diaphragm action of the roof to the shear walls, and spanning over the openings in the walls supporting the gravity loads coming from above.

Current limit states design (LSD) codes for reinforced masonry structures, such as the Canadian Standards Association CSA S304.1-04 (2004a), enforce the use of reinforced masonry beams even for short spans. Although reinforced masonry flexural members exhibit similar behavior compared to reinforced concrete members, design difficulties may be encountered with conventional steel bars due to the limited width of the masonry units. Considering the underreinforced design principle of the steel-reinforced masonry, design of beams with deep cross sections is inevitable for most of the cases, giving rise to higher material and labor costs, as well as an increase of the floor height. In addition to that, conventional steel reinforcement is prone to degradation due to corrosion which is a well-known phenomenon.

Concrete elements reinforced with fiber-reinforced polymer (FRP) rods have been extensively examined by researchers in the past decade and has been identified as an alternate construction material for reinforcing and strengthening concrete primarily due to its promising strength and durability characteristics. FRP comes with several significant advantages over steel, such as high durability, noncorrosiveness, high strength-to-weight ratio, and resistance against fatigue. On the other hand, unlike conventional steel reinforcement, FRP uses overreinforced design approach in that there will not be any upper limit for reinforcement ratio as long as the deflections are within the allowable limits set by, for example, the design guidelines of ISIS (2001) and ACI 440.1R-06 (2006). In this sense, it is suitable to say that one could explore the benefits of the overreinforced design concept of FRP-reinforced concrete-based elements, beside other advantageous characteristics of FRP rebars compared to steel ones, toward an efficient and durable structural element.

To the writers' knowledge, applications of FRP as an internal reinforcement for reinforced masonry beams have not yet been investigated. Although design guide-

(Kathy). L. Lin, *Perspectives on the Introductory Phase of Empirical Research Articles*, Corpora and Intercultural Studies 5, https://doi.org/10.1007/978-981-32-9204-8

lines such as ISIS (2001) and ACI 440.1R-06 (2006) for the applications of FRP in reinforced concrete are well established, a design guideline addressing the applications of FRP in the design of reinforced masonry elements is not available in the literature.

Appendix L
CALL_TR24 as an Example of the Analysis of Theoretical Reviews Containing Multi-thematic Sub-Sections in AL

To show explicitly how the move and sub-move analysis is conducted, the text is not paragraphed as its original version but rearranged according to different sub-move units. To facilitate readers' understanding, some sub-moves are signaled as shown in the emboldened words below.

2. Literature Review

2.1. Lexical Coverage

1.1 Vocabulary may be a **good** predictor of reading comprehension (Hu & Nation, 2000; Qian, 2002). A rich vocabulary makes a reading task easier to perform and limited vocabulary may be a **major** source of difficulty in reading an English text. Concerning the relationship between vocabulary and reading comprehension, **much research** has been conducted on lexical thresholds in terms of how large a vocabulary is needed for reasonable comprehension (Hirsh & Nation, 1992; Laufer, 1989, 1992; Nation, 2001, 2006). In the literature review, the lexical threshold has **often** been approached from the perspective of lexical coverage and then the vocabulary size needed for understanding a text.

(Kathy). L. Lin, *Perspectives on the Introductory Phase of Empirical Research Articles*, Corpora and Intercultural Studies 5, https://doi.org/10.1007/978-981-32-9204-8

1.2

Lexical coverage refers to "the percentage of running words in the text known by the reader" (Nation, 2006, p. 61). It is calculated by counting the number of the known words in a text, multiplying them by 100 and then dividing the result by the total number of running words in the text. For instance, if learners have reached 95% or 98% lexical coverage, this means that they may understand 95% or 98% of the running words of the text. Ninety-five percent and 98% lexical coverage are not equal to 95% and 98% comprehension. Instead, as Laufer (1989) has pointed out, the two coverage points suggest probabilistic thresholds over which learners have a chance of gaining a certain level of comprehension. The idea of using lexical coverage to determine the optimal percentage of known words in a text is based on the assumption that there is a lexical knowledge threshold which marks the boundary between having and not having sufficient vocabulary knowledge for adequate reading comprehension. A lexical threshold is contingent upon the lexical coverage predetermined because certain coverage points may indicate the vocabulary size necessary to understand the text.

Past studies have differed in the amount of lexical coverage that is needed for adequate comprehension to occur.

Move 2

Laufer (1989) suggested that 95% coverage is necessary for reasonable comprehension of a text. Namely, one unknown word in every twenty words, roughly in every two lines of a text, is regarded as the necessary level beneath which readers are not expected to read an authentic text successfully. **Hirsh and Nation (1992)** recommended that 98% coverage is needed for learners to read for pleasure. Other estimates for the same coverage figure are 98% for adequate unassisted reading comprehension **(Hu & Nation, 2000)** and 98% for ideal coverage of written text **(Nation, 2006)**. **Hu and Nation (2000)** found that nobody could read adequately at 80% coverage but a minority of learners could at 90% and 95%. At 100% lexical coverage, most learners were able to understand the text.

Move 2

In revisiting the issues of lexical coverage by using more updated research instruments, **Laufer and Ravenhorst-Kalovski (2010)** suggested two lexical thresholds: (1) an optimal comprehension, which involves the knowledge of 8000 word families yielding 98% lexical coverage including proper nouns, and (2) a minimal comprehension (where minimally acceptable comprehension can occur), which is 4000–5000 word families reaching 95% coverage, inclusive of proper nouns. This also echoes earlier studies, such as that of **Liu and Nation (1985)**, concerning guessing from context for successful comprehension. **Liu and Nation (1985)** suggested that 95% coverage is necessary for learners to guess words from the context in written texts and **Nation (2001)** suggested that 98% coverage is ideal for guessing words from the context when reading.

3.5 **Taken together,** 95% may represent reasonable comprehension (Laufer, 1989; Laufer & Ravenhorst-Kalovski, 2010) and 98% ideal comprehension of written text (Nation, 2001, 2006). These two putative coverage points signal the possible lower and upper boundaries associated with a lexical threshold.

2.2. Vocabulary Levels and Vocabulary Size

1.2 The vocabulary size necessary for comprehension varies with the type of text and the degree of comprehension required.

Nation (2006) examined the vocabulary size needed for the reading and listening comprehension of a variety of texts by trialing fourteen 1000 wordfamily lists made from the British National Corpus, and checked what coverage they provided of a variety of written and spoken texts. **According to Nation (2006)**, if 95% coverage is required, a vocabulary size of the most frequent 4000 word families may be necessary for comprehension of novels and newspapers. If 98% coverage is needed for unassisted comprehension, then an 8000 word-family vocabulary may be necessary to understand newspapers, and knowing 9000 word families would be necessary for understanding a novel, and a vocabulary of 6000-7000 word families for spoken text. Once the lexical coverage (the percentage of known words necessary for a certain degree of comprehension) is decided, we need a tool to calculate the vocabulary size needed to reach the predetermined lexical coverage. **Nation and Heatley (2002)** created the RANGE program, which incorporated fourteen British National Corpus (BNC) 1000 word lists plus a proper noun list and marginal words. As per **Nation's (2004) investigation** into the most frequent word families in the BNC, the BNC consists of 100 million
Move 2 running words (tokens) of English with 10% of the total running words drawn from spoken sources and 90% from written sources. Out of the 90% written language, 70% is formal, informative text plus 6% lectures, speeches and commentaries from the 10% spoken language. The fourteen 1000 word lists derived from the BNC for use with RANGE provide an estimate of the vocabulary level of a text. They were ranked based on English words' occurring range, dispersion and frequency in the BNC. One key concept for understanding vocabulary levels is rank. In the BNC scale, the second 1000 words are more frequent than the third 1000 words and less frequent than the first 1000 words. By analogy, the 4000-word level refers to the vocabulary of a text reaching a level that embraces the first, second, third and fourth 1000 most frequent words of English. In **Nation's (2006) research** concerning the coverage of the BNC's high-frequency word lists across several types of discourse (i.e., graded readers, movies, conversation, newspapers and novels), the data results show that the first BNC 1000 most frequent word families provided a coverage of 78-81%, the second thousand an additional 8–9%, the third thousand 3–5%, the fourth and fifth thousand together 3%, the sixth to ninth thousand collectively 2%, and the tenth to fourteenth thousand, less than 1%. Proper nouns and marginal words
Move 2 (such as oh, uh, mmm and ah) may cover 2–4% of written texts, while words not found in any word lists above may account for 1-3% of the texts.

3.3 The BNC lists cover a very large amount of vocabulary and can thus give more detailed estimates of the vocabulary load of texts, **which was fit for the purpose of this research**.

This study sought to answer the following three pairs of questions concerning the vocabulary thresholds for business postgraduates:
1. How many words do EFL learners need to know to understand a business research article? Is there a difference between the vocabulary size of research papers of different business subject areas?
2. How many words do EFL learners need to know to understand a business
4.1 textbook? Is there a difference between the vocabulary size of textbooks in different business subject areas?
3. What is the difference between the vocabulary size necessary to reach 95% and 98% lexical coverage of a business text-book and a business research article? Among 12 business subject areas, what is the individual difference between the vocabulary load of textbooks and the corresponding research articles in the same subject matter?

Bibliography

Anderson, D. (1985). *Truth and interpretation*. Oxford: Clarendon Press.
Banfield, A. (1973). Narrative style and the grammar of direct and indirect speech. *Foundations of Language, 10*, 1–39.
Banfield, A. (1982). *Unspeakable sentences: Narration and representation in the language of fiction*. Boston: Routledge and Kegan Paul.
Björkman, B. (2011). English as a lingua franca in higher education: Implications for EAP. *Ibérica, 22,* 79–100.
Burton, J. (2011). Book review: Literature reviewing. *Journal of English for Academic Purposes, 10*(1), 61–64.
Chen, M. F. (2006). *Reporting in literature reviews of English dissertations*. Unpublished doctoral dissertation, Xiamen University.
Clark, H. H., & Gerrig, R. J. (1990). Quotations as demonstrations. *Language*, *66*, 764–805.
Collins, D. E. (2001). *Reanimated voices: Speech reporting in a historical-pragmatic perspective*. Amsterdam: John Benjamins Publishing Company.
Coulmas, F. (1985). Direct and indirect speech: General problems and problems of Japanese. *Journal of Pragmatics, 9,* 41–63.
Davidson, D. (2001). *Inquires into truth and interpretation*. Oxford: Oxford University Press.
De Oliveira, J. M., & Pagano, A. S. (2006). The research article and the science popularization article: A probabilistic functional grammar perspective on direct discourse representation. *Discourse Studies, 8*(5), 627–646.
Dixon, R. M. W. (1991). *A new approach to English grammar: On semantic principles*. Oxford: Clarendon Press.
Ehrlich, S. (1990). *Point of view: A linguistic analysis of literary style*. London and New York: Routledge.
Fairclough, N. (1992). *Discourse and social change*. Cambridge: Polity Press.
Geach, P. T. (1972). Quotation and quantification. In P. T. Geach (Ed.), *Logic matters* (pp. 205–209). Oxford: Blackwell Publishers.
Gong, P. M. (2002). *A functional approach to language reports in English*. Unpublished master's thesis, Qu Fu Normal University.
Harwood, N. (2005). What do we want EAP teaching materials for? *Journal of English for Academic Purposes, 4*(2): 149–161.
Harwood, N. (2010) Issues in materials development and design. In N. Harwood (Ed.), *English language teaching materials: Theory and practice*. Cambridge: Cambridge University Press.
Henry, A., & Roseberry, R. L. (1997). An investigation of the functions, strategies and linguistic features of the introductions and conclusions of essays. *System, 25*(4), 479–495.
Hu, J. (2010). The schematic structure of Literature Review in research articles of applied linguistics. *Chinese Journal of Applied Linguistics, 33*(5), 15–27.

(Kathy). L. Lin, *Perspectives on the Introductory Phase of Empirical Research Articles*, Corpora and Intercultural Studies 5, https://doi.org/10.1007/978-981-32-9204-8

Huckin, T. N. and Olsen, L. A. (1991). *Technical writing and professional communication for non-native speakers of English* (international edition) (2nd ed.). New York: McGraw-Hill.
Janssen, Theo A.J.M., & Wurff, Wim van der (Eds.). (1996). *Reported speech: Forms and functions of the verb*. Amsterdam: John Benjamins Publishing Company.
Jespersen, O. (1924). *The philosophy of grammar*. London: Allen & Unwin.
Jordan, R. (1992). *Academic writing course*. London: Nelson.
Leech, G. N., & Short, M. (1981). *Style in fiction*. London: Longman.
Lucy, J. A. (1993). *Reflexive language: Reported speech and metapragmatics*. Cambridge: Cambridge University Press.
Lyons, J. (1968). *Introduction to theoretical linguistics*. Cambridge: Cambridge University Press.
Miller, C. (1994). Rhetoric community: The cultural basis of genre. In P. Medway & A. Freedman (Eds.), *Genre and the new rhetoric* (pp. 67–78). London: Taylor & Francis.
Myers, G. (1989). The pragmatics of politeness in scientific articles. *Applied linguistics, 10*, 1–35.
Nwogu, K. N. (1991). Structure of science popularizations: A genre-analysis approach to the schema of popularized medical texts. *English for Specific Purposes, 10*(2), 111–123.
Page, N. (1973). Forms of speech in fiction. In N. Page (Ed.), *The language of literature* (pp. 83–97). London: Macmillan Press.
Partee, B. H. (1973). The syntax and semantics of quotation. In P. Kiparsky & S. Anderson (Eds.), *A festschrift for Morris Halle* (pp. 410–418). New York: Holt.
Peng, J. W. (2003). *A cognitive study of language reports*. Unpublished doctoral dissertation, Fudan University.
Quine, W. V. (1940). *Mathematical logic*. Cambridge, MA: Harvard University Press.
Quine, W. V. (1951). Semantics and abstract objects. *Proceedings of the American Academy of Arts and Sciences, 80*(1), 90–96.
Quirk, R., Greenbaum, S., Leech, G., & Svartvik, J. (1985). *A comprehensive grammar of the English language*. London: Longman.
Reichenbach, H. (1947). *Elements of symbolic logic*. New York: Macmillan.
Rimmon-Kenan, S. (1983). *Narrative fiction: Contemporary poetics*. London: Methuen.
Salager-Meyer, F. (1999). Referencing behavior in scientific writing: A diachronic study (1980–1995), *English for Specific Purposes, 18*, 279–305.
Scott, M. (2008). *WordSmith tools version 5*. Liverpool: Lexical Analysis Software.
Short, M., Semino, E., & Culpeper, J. (1996). Using a corpus for stylistic research: Speech and thought presentation. In J. Thomas & M. Short (Eds.), *Using corpora for language research* (pp. 110–131). London: Longman.
Sperber, D., & Wilson, D. (1986). *Relevance: Communication and cognition*. Oxford: Blackwell Publishers.
Swales, J. M., & Feak, C. B. (1994). *Academic writing for graduate students*. Ann Arbor: University of Michigan Press.
Tannen, D. (1989). *Talking voices: Repetition, dialogue, and imagery in conversational discourse*. Cambridge: Cambridge University Press.
Tardy, C. (2006). Researching first and second language genre learning: A comparative review and a look ahead. *Journal of Second Language Writing, 15*, 79–101.
Tarski, A. (1956). The concept of truth in formalized languages. In J. Woodger (Ed.), *Logic, semantics, and metamathematics* (pp. 152–278). Oxford: OUP.
Thompson, G. (1996). Voices in the text: Discourse perspectives on language reports. *Applied Linguistics, 17*(4), 501–530.
Triki, M., & Bahloul, M. (2001). The reported speech revisited: A question of self and expressions. *Academic Research, 2*, 1–35. Sfax, Tunisia: Faculty of Letters and Humanities.
Volosinov, V. N. (1929/1973/1986). *Marxism and the philosophy of language*. (L. Matejka & I. R. Titunik, Trans.). Cambridge, MA: Harvard University Press.
Wierzbicka, A. (1974). The semantics of direct and indirect discourse. *Papers in Linguistics, 7*, 267–307.

Wood, A. S. (1982). An examination of the rhetorical structures of authentic chemistry texts. *Applied Linguistics, 3*(2), 121–143.

Yagisawa, T. (1997). A somewhat Russellian theory of intensional contexts. In J. E. Tomberlin (Ed.), *Mind, causation, and world* (pp. 43–82). Oxford, UK: Blackwell.

Zhou, Y. (2004). *A cognitive-pragmatic analysis of language reports in written discourse*. Unpublished master's thesis, Hunan University.

The manufacturer's authorised representative in the EU is Springer Nature Customer Service Centre GmbH, Europaplatz 3, 69115 Heidelberg, Germany. If you have any concerns regarding our products, please contact ProductSafety@springernature.com

Printed and bound by CPI Group (UK) Ltd, Croydon, CR0 4YY
25/09/2026
02222898-0011